Treasures of the Silk Road

Treasures of the Silk Road

Other titles by the same author

The Armenian Kingdom in Cilicia During the Crusades:
The integration of Cilician Armenians with the Latins 1080-1393
ISBN 0-7007-1418-9

The Mediterranean Legacy in Early Celtic Christianity:
A journey from Armenia to Ireland
ISBN 1-898948-70-4

Turkey: The heritage of the land
ISBN 978-07552-1172-2

Treasures of the Silk Road

The Religions that Transformed China

Jacob G. Ghazarian

New Generation Publishing
London

Treasures of the Silk Road

Published by New Generation Publishing in 2014

Copyright © Jacob G. Ghazarian 2014

First Edition

The author asserts the moral right under the Copyright, Designs and Patents Act 1988 to be identified as the author of this work.

All Rights reserved. No part of this publication may be reproduced, stored in a retrieval system or transmitted, in any form or by any means without the prior consent of the author, nor be otherwise circulated in any form of binding or cover other than that which it is published and without a similar condition being imposed on the subsequent purchaser.

www.newgeneration-publishing.com

ISBN: 978-1-910053-43-0

 New Generation **Publishing**

A Dedication

Saint Francis Xavier, SJ (1506-1552)

Born Francisco de Jaso y Azpilicueta of Navarre. His mission to China was interrupted by his premature death from a fever on the island of Shangchuan near Guangzhou, Guangdong Province.

MAY WE RECEIVE HIS GRACE AND WISDOM

Contents

A Dedication	v
A Note on names	xi
A further note to the reader	xii
List of Plates	xiii
List of Maps	xvi
List of Tables	xvii
List of Figures	xviii
Acknowledgments	xix
Preface	**1**
Introduction	**7**
The Middle Kingdom	8

CHAPTER ONE
Historical Perspectives-Ancient China	**15**
Chinese Social Hierarchy	16
Shang Period (c 1600-1027 BC)	17
Xi Period (Western Zhou/Chou) (1027-771 BC)	19
Chinese Concept of Heaven	20
Spring and Autumn Period (772-481 BC)	21
Warring States Period (475-221 BC)	22

CHAPTER TWO
Historical Perspectives-Imperial China	**37**
Qin/Ch'in Period (221-206 BC)-The First Empire	37
Han Period (206 BC-AD 220)	39
Intervening Years (AD 221-265)	42
Western Jin Period (AD 265-316)	43
Dynastic Proliferations (AD 316-581)	43
Sui Period (AD 581-618)	45
Tang Period (AD 618- 907)-The Second Empire	45
Song/Sung Period (AD 960-1279)-The Third Empire	52
Yuan Period (AD 1279-1368)	53
Ming Period (AD 1368-1644)	55
Qing/Ch'ing Period (Manchu) (AD 1644-1912)	56

CHAPTER THREE
Ancient Central Asia	**67**
Sogdiana	70

Bactria	72
Gandhara	74
Ferghana	75
Indeginous People of Central Asia	77
Arab Conquest of Iran 637 AD	80

CHAPTER FOUR
Shaanxi, Gansu and Xinjiang — 85

Demographic History of Shaanxi Province	85
Where it all began; the City of Chang'an (Xi'an)	87
Demographic History of Gansu Province	88
Demographic History of Xinjiang Province	91

CHAPTER FIVE
Settlements of the Silk Road in Gansu Province — 105

Lanzhou - the Frontier	108
Destination Zhangye	111
Yumen and Anxi	114
Mingsha Shan	116
Splendour of Dunhuang Legacy	117

CHAPTER SIX
Settlements of the Northern Silk Road in Xinjiang Province — 143

Destination Hami	143
Turfan	149
Korla	152
Kuqa	154
Aksu	157
Kashgar	159

CHATER SEVEN
Settlements of the Southern Silk Road in Xinjiang Province — 179

Destination Loulan	179
Miran	181
Chakilik	183
The Alternate Route from Chakilik through Qinghai	184
Cherchen	186
Niya	188
Khotan	192
Yarkand	198

CHAPTER EIGHT
Coming of the Maritime Routes to China   201
South China Sea Routes   207
East China Sea Routes   211

CHAPTER NINE
Buddhism in China   215
Buddhism   217
The Hellenic Contacts   219
Advances into the Tarim Basin   221
Faxian   225
Song Yun   227
Xuanzang   228
Disciples for Xuanzang   231
Yi Jing   232
Hui Chao   233

CHAPTER TEN
Christianity in China   237
Early Church Dogmas   237
The Nestorian Church in Mesopotamia   240
Nestorians in Central Asia   244
Nestorians in China   246
Nestorian Monument of Xi'an   248
The Olopun Documents   257
Later Christian Missions to China   262

CHAPTER ELEVEN
Islam in China   271
Distribution   272
Emergence of Islam   274
The People of Uyghuristan   280
The Mughals   283
Later Islamic History of Xinjiang Province   289
The Khojas   294

CHAPTER TWELVE
Gnostic Religions in China   317
Manichaeism   318
Expansion to the East   320
Transmission of Manichaeism by the Uyghurs   323
Manichaean Literary and Artistic Legacy   325

Zoroastrianism in China   326

EPILOGUE   **331**

BIBLIOGRAPHY
General Reading   339

APPENDIX
Selected Glossary   341
Detailed dynasties of ancient and imperial China   345
Dynastic emperors of imperial China   347
Alphabetical list of the Thirty-Six Kingdoms   357
List of the officially recognized 56 ethnic groups in China
and their relative numbers   358
List of Mongol khans   359
Chronology of the Popes: 4th – 20th centuries   360
Chronological history of the Silk Road   366

A note on names

Effort has been made to associate dynastic, personal and place names in modern or common usage with their corresponding older names appearing in their histories, when applicable. However the reader should be aware that this has often been very difficult to achieve given the variety of ways Chinese names are used, or which have fallen out of use over time. Therefore, in most cases, the text is confined to the use of the most familiar or official names. It is hoped that this practice will render the reading of the text more enjoyable and less cumbersome.

A further note to the reader

It should be noted the author has deemed it unnecessary to uniformly append a series of individual notes to specific events or quotations which appear throughout this book. Had this been done as a matter of procedure, inclusive of the comprehensive histories of China and Central Asia covered in this book, the notes as such would have provided only limited information in respect to the narratives in point. Furthermore, given the scope of the historical narratives discussed, such notes, should they had been inserted, would have made the present volume unnecessarily voluminous and expensive to print. Instead, following in the style of many narrative historical writings, it was decided that the citation of a limited number of appropriately chosen references, which address the key points and which also provide a broader field of information, was the better choice.

Also for the benefit of the reader, certain passages are regurgitated in part or in varied forms either as subtle reminders for helping the reader distinguish the relevance of the mentioned names, dates or places without confusion, or the passages are given as examples of points under discussion.

List of Plates

FIRST GROUP

1. Four-horse drawn bronze carriage of the First Emperor	29
2. A squad of the Terracotta Warriors	29
3. Tomb of Princess Yongtai	30
4. Wall painting from Yongtai's tomb depicting the princess	31
5. Wall painting from Yongtai's tomb depicting members of the royal court	32
6. Wall painting from Yongtai's tomb depicting a military procession	33
7. Tang dynasty walls of the city of Xi'an	34
8. Nanmen Gates of the Xi'an city walls	35

SECOND GROUP

9. The Yellow River near Lanzhou	125
10. Qing dynasty Xi Guan (West Gate) Mosque	125
11. Heping Peace Mosque	126
12. A stelae in the courtyard of the Heping Peace Mosque, Lanzhou	126
13. Hui congregation of Heping Peace Mosque	127
14. Genealogical stelae of Abdu al-Kadir al-Jeylani and teachings of Sufism in Linxia in Arabic script	127
15. Huancheng Xi Lu Mosque in Linxia	128
16. The main thoroughfare in the centre of Linxia	128
17. The western terminus of the main thoroughfare of Linxia	129
18. The mausoleum of Imam Hamuz Ali in Linxia	129
19. Praying at the shrine of Imam Hamuz Ali in Linxia	130
20. Traditional praying in a Sufi cemetery in Linxia	130
21. A tombstone in the Sufi cemetery	131
22. The main gate of Labrang Monastery in Xiahe	131
23. The huts of Labrang Monastery	132
24. The central shrine in Labrang Monastery in Xiahe	132
25. The author seated with the monks of the Yellow Hat sect in Xiahe	133
26. A Tibetan child in traditional winter clothing in Xiahe	133
27. The main shopping street in Xiahe	134
28. Typical modes of transport by the residents of Xiahe	134
29. The Hexi Corridor	135
30. The Bronze 'Flying Horse'	135

Treasures of the Silk Road

31. The wooden Pagoda Temple in Zangye	136
32. A reclining Buddha in the Giant Buddha Temple in Zangye	136
33. Remains of a Buddhist stupa at the ruins of the Maijishan Monastery	137
34. Northern Liang dynasty image of an Indian Bodhisattva	137
35. Northern Liang dynasty wall paintings of Bodhisattvas	138
36. The author seen at the vast cave complexes of Dunhuang	138
37. Tang dynasty clay figures in Dunhuang	139
38. Wei dynasty mural of a Flying Devi	139
39. Sui dynasty mural of Flying Devis	140
40. Wei dynasty mural of Flying Devis	140
41. Sui dynasty clay figures of Kasyapa and a Bodhisattva	141

THIRD GROUP

42. Double-humped camels painted on a brick from Wei and Jin dynasties	167
43. Tang dynasty figurine of an Arab lute player.	167
44. The mausoleum of Qais ibn Sa'ad Ansari in Hami	168
45. The tomb of Qais ibn Sa'ad Ansari in Hami	168
46. Path leading to the tomb of Abi Waqqas in Guangzhou	169
47. The tomb of Abi Waqqas in Guangzhou	169
48. Ancient Muslim holy grounds in Turfan	170
49. A venerated tomb with a prayer *mihrab* in the holy grounds in Turfan	170
50. A section of the original Silk Road near Korla	171
51. The Iron Gate allowing access to Korla	171
52. Kashgar's Old Town	172
53. The Id-Kah Mosque in Kashgar	172
54. The mausoleum of Abakh Khoja	173
55. The tombs of Abakh Khoja and of his father Yusuf Khoja	173
56. The mausoleum of the Uyghur poet Haji Yusuf Hajif in Kashgar	174
57. Official permit to travel on the Karakorum Highway	174
58. A traditional traveler on the Karakorum Highway	175
59. On the way to Khunjerap Pass in Pakistan	175
60. The Karakorum Highway	176
61. Tea break in a Kyrgyz hut in Gez	176
62. The author with a Kyrgyz family outside their hut in Gez	177
63. The Stone Fort in Tashkorgan	177
64. Tajik woman in Tashkorgan	178
65. The author at China-Pakistan border	178

FOURTH GROUP

66. A typical residential street in Cherchen	305
67. Uyghur woman in Cherchen	305
68. The mosque adjacent to the shrine of Sayyid Makhdum-i-Azam near Khotan	306
69. The shrine of Sayyid Makhdum-i-Azam near Khotan	307
70. Town centre of Yarkand	307
71. A group of Uyghur men at the entrance of Altunluk Mosque in Yarkand	308
72. The mausoleum of Sultan Sa'id Khan in Yarkand	308
73. The tomb of Sultan Sa'id Khan in Yarkand	309
74. The tomb of Queen Ammanisahan in Yarkand	309
75. Epitaph of Queen Ammanisahan in Arabic script	310
76. Huai Sheng Mosque in present-day Guangzhou	310
77. Yuan dynasty Islamic tombstone recovered in Guangzhou	311
78. The Xin Shi District Islamic cemetery in Guangzhou	311
79. Old tombstones in the Xin Shi District Islamic cemetery in Guangzhou	312
80. Stelae of the Nestorian Christians	313
81. Eastern Han dynasty gilded bronze Christian cross	314
82. Church of Our Saviour in present-day Guangzhou	315
83. Chinese mother and her child at the Zion Christian Church in present-day Guangzhou	315

List of Maps

Central Asia & the Fertile Crescent	xxi
The Middle Kingdom	13
Chinese Dynasties	25
Chinese Dynasties	26
Chinese Dynasties	60
The Settlements of the Silk Roads	122
Land & Sea Routes for Silk & Spice Trade	123
Indo-European Migrations Circa 2500 BC	191

List of Tables

Table 1	Dynasties of ancient and imperial China	10
Table 2.	The early ruling powers of the Iranian plateau	68
Table 3.	Population densities in the settlements of the Northern branch of the Silk Road	164
Table 4.	Distribution of the early Nestorian churches	243

List of Figures

Figure 1.	The ceramic art of China	62
Figure 2.	The ceramic art of China	63
Figure 3.	The early Christian Church in Mesopatamia	242
Figure 4.	The lineage of Genghis Khan	285
Figure 5.	Chagatai Khanate after 1346 AD	288
Figure 6.	The lineage of Yunus Khan	293
Figure 7.	The lineage of Sayyid Kamal-ud-Din	299
Figure 8.	The lineage of Khoja Ishaq Wali	299
Figure 9.	The last of the Chagataid khans	300
Figure 10.	The lineage of Khoja Ishan-i-Kalan	301

Acknowledgments

My first thanks most certainly go to my wife Qin Jing for her graceful understanding of my predicaments throughout the writing of this book. With the patience of a saint she silently shared my endless angst awaiting the end of my many years of relentlessly self-absorbing and often obsessive writing. I am also most grateful for the expert and informed assistance I received from Waheed Karakhan. A native of Xinjiang's Uyghur community, Waheed's expertise in guiding me to some of the remotest sites described in this book made my travels most exhilarating, and especially noteworthy was the memorable time we spent with the Kyrgyz family in Gez. His intuitive knowledge of the history of the Uyghur people was an invaluable asset to my search for the details of the Muslim history of the khans of the Tarim Basin. My thanks also go to Chen Jian Wu who assisted me in my conversations with the sedentary peoples of the provinces of Gansu and Xinjiang throughout my seven-week mid-winter journeys in those frozen wastelands. Above all, but not least, I am grateful for the assistance given to me by Dr. Dashdondong Bayarsaikhan, Professor in the Department of History at the National University of Mongolia in Ulaanbaatar. I had had the pleasure of making her acquaintance in 2005 when she was pursuing a D. Phil. at the University of Oxford as a member of Wolfson College. Her broad academic achievements in oriental studies were quite impressive. Her directions in finding some of the literature regarding Christianity amongst the Mongolian Altaic Turks paved the way for elaborating in this book the extent of Christian involvement in Mongolia. Last but not least I acknowledge my many friends and colleagues who on so many occasions read various sections of my manuscript and to my chagrin often chastised much of what was on offer with their destructive criticisms whilst cleverly instructing me for a constructive finale - my sincere thanks to all of them for their unmitigated courage.

CENTRAL ASIA

CENTRAL ASIA AND THE FERTILE CRESENT

Preface

The ancient trade routes, known as the Silk Road, linked the opposite ends of the known world during the second half of the first Christian millennium – Europe in the west and the empire of China (the Middle Kingdom, Zhong-gua, or Zhong-hua) in the east.[1] These routes stretched from their eastern terminus at Chang'an, the ancient capital of China, to their western terminus at Constantinople, the New Rome of the Roman Empire. The Roman historian Florus, who lived in the time of emperors Trajan (98-117 AD) and Hadrian (117-138 AD) has described the visits of numerous embassies to the first Roman emperor, Augustus (BC 27-14 AD) as follows:

> Even the rest of the nations of the world which were not subject to the imperial sway were sensible of its grandeur, and looked with reverence to the Roman people, the great conqueror of nations. Thus even Scythians and Sarmatians sent envoys to seek the friendship of Rome. Nay, the Seres (*the Chinese*) [italics by the author] came likewise, and the Indians who dwelt beneath the vertical sun, bringing presents of precious stones and pearls and elephants, but thinking all of less moment than the vastness of the journey which they had undertaken, and which they said had occupied four years. In truth it needed but to look at their complexion to see that they were people of another world than ours.

Indeed, the silk trade with Rome became such a lucrative enterprise for the Chinese and a gold drain from the coffers of the Roman republic that the Roman Senate issued several edicts to prohibit the wearing of silk and disguised its reasons on moralistic grounds.[2-4] The Roman statesman Seneca the Younger (3 BC-AD 65) wrote in his chronicles:

> I can see clothes of silk, if materials that do not hide the body, or even one's decency, can be called clothes. Wretched flocks of maids labour so that the adulteress may be visible through her thin dress, so that her husband has no more acquaintance than any outsider or foreigner

with his wife's body.[5]

We shall see later, a similar situation in reverse nearly nineteen centuries later unfolded in China regarding the Chinese ban on the import of British-traded opium which eventually precipitated the first of the Opium Wars in 1842 AD.

As is true for most forms of transport, there were branch routes from the main thoroughfares of the Silk Road which led to important destinations, such as India in the south and Tashkent and Samarkand in the north. But, it should be borne in mind that numerous trading posts, oasis towns and open markets scattered all across Central Asia that linked varied countries and communities with China, were part and parcel of what we know today as the Silk Road. These parts collectively formed an extensive interconnected network of strategic facilities that literally allowed goods to be exchanged throughout the known world during the first millennium of the Christian era just as it is done in our present time albeit at a much faster tempo. The routes that the camel caravans followed and the emporia they visited were the highway complexes of their times and were in use when pre-modern China was most receptive to outside influences. Although we lack the experience of the traders treading the brutal desert sands, we nonetheless can follow in their footsteps and appreciate the extent of their ordeals by the power of our imagination. Yet also our exotic images of camel caravans treading the endless sandy seas of the Central Asian deserts surrounded by snow-capped mountains circling the far horizons instantly bring into focus an aspect of human history that raises our awareness of the common denominator which has been fundamental to virtually all human interactions from very early times. This common denominator is commerce. But commerce has never been viewed as a medium for the exclusive exchange of goods and services. With commerce came opportunities for art and artists, music and musicians, architecture and architects, diplomacy and diplomats and, finally, religion and monks, to permeate the social fabric of all the trading communities throughout. Their activities brought luxury, beauty and strength of convictions into the forefront of daily human endeavours everywhere.

The routes of the Silk Road across the Central Asian deserts were immensely perilous but the courage of those who followed them was reinforced by the presence of fertile oasis towns. These, like a string of Buddhist prayer beads, were lined up along the main routes of the Silk

Preface

Road and provided safety and sustenance to the enterprising travellers. It was not until the tenth century AD that population densities in these oasis towns began to decline and eventually extinguished. Undoubtedly, political, demographic, climatic and economic shifts contributed to this decline, but perhaps the most significant was the geographic settings in which these oasis towns were founded. The towns were surrounded and isolated by large expanses of unforgiving and all-prevailing deserts. Arid lands and high mountain-passes were constant threats to survival for man and beast alike. Serious considerations were given to the security of the cargo caravans and to their safe arrival to an oasis where, after a long day's journey, water, nourishment and rest could be procured. Their existence was precarious at best of times.

Although the origins of the Silk Road can be traced to the second century BC, as we shall see later, the first great era of the road's potential as a commercial conduit only began to be extensively utilized from the second century AD onward. The dynamics of the trade along the Silk Road encouraged a wider regional participation that expanded with time. Eventually two major alternate routes, one the Southern route[6] and the other the Northern route,[7] became the main trails that connected the wider regional trading destinations.

The second great era of the Silk Road began after the use of the Southern and the Northern routes had reached their nadir in the sixth century AD. Early in the following century the Tang dynasty inherited China from its predecessors the Sui dynasty which during their short-lived reign had actually succeeded in unifying the Chinese nation. China by then had become a major trading centre in which all manners of goods, music, fashion and ideas had found a receptive audience. The Tang dynasty became a watershed for the cultural renaissance of the Middle Kingdom and the Silk Road played a significant role in perpetuating this age of renaissance that continued to thrive until the end of the eleventh century.

The gradual decline in the entrepreneurial use of the Silk Road reached a crescendo in the early thirteenth century with the devastation of China by the Mongol hordes who were spearheaded by Genghis Khan. The oasis towns that supported the Silk Road were irretrievably laid to waste and hence were abandoned. What remained of them still standing was eventually engulfed by the surrounding deserts and became ghost towns amidst a sea of constantly shifting sands.

Treasures of the Silk Road

The decline in the commercial use of the Silk Road had actually begun, for all intended purposes, in the early twelfth century with the destabilization of the Northern Song dynasty in 1115 AD brought about by the invasions of the Jurchen of the Manchurian Tungut tribe whose Northern Jin dynasty was later destroyed by Genghis Khan. The founding of the Southern Song dynasty in Hangzhou subsequent to the Jurchen invasions and the sacking of Kaifeng, forced the Middle Kingdom to rely on maritime routes in its quest to reach the lucrative foreign trading markets. These routes began operating from the coastal towns of China first from Guangzhou on the South China Sea and later from Quanzhou and Xiamen on the coasts of East China Sea.

Finally, we should noted that a general concept of the trade routes between China and the lands west of its frontiers is not sufficient for us to thoroughly grasp the significance of their physical aspects unless the precise geographical histories that formed the backbone of these trade routes are clearly understood. It is only then that we can fully comprehend the historical relevance of this monumental human endeavour. Ironically, very few authors of the Silk Road have adequately addressed the origins of this road. How and where did the road(s) begin and end? Was trade the original and only purpose of the road? Who were its principal architects? Once these fundamental questions are comprehensively answered we can then proceed to dissect facts from fiction, myth from reality and attempt to understand the politics of a world envisioned by the road's greatest enthusiasts. Their impact continues to be seen and experienced in twenty-first century China. Throughout the width and breath of this vast land, from its most populated cities to the unimaginably dusty communities of its remotest parts, we witness in present-day China a diverse population participating in the creation of a nation with religious roots first seeded by the early travellers of the Silk Road. They brought with them the beliefs of Christianity followed by those of Islam and added them to the Buddhist traditions that had first entered China along the same ancient routes in the beginning of the first half of the first century AD. Ultimately the goal of the present work is to follow in the footsteps of those who brought the faiths of Buddhism, Christianity and Islam into China and assess the historical impacts of their legacies.

Jacob G. Ghazarian
Oxford, 2013

Preface

References

1. Elisseeff, V., *The Silk Roads: Highways of Culture and Commerce*. Berghahn Books Ltd., Oxford (2000).
2. Ball, W., *Rome in the East: The Transformation of an Empire*. Routledge, London (2000).
3. Sinor, D., *Inner Asia and its Contacts with Medieval Europe*. Variorum, London (1997).
4. Young, G. K., *Rome's Eastern Trade: International Commerce and Imperial Policy 31 BC-AD 305*. Routledge, London (2001).
5. Seneca the Younger, *Phaedra*. Cornell University Press, New York (1986).
6. Baumer, C., *Southern Silk Road: In the Footsteps of Sir Aurel Stein and Sven Hedin*. Orchid Press, Bangkok (2000).
7. Baumer, C. *Traces in the Desert: Journeys of Discovery Across Central Asia*. I. B. Tauris, London (2008).

Treasures of the Silk Road

Introduction

The Chinese often refer to themselves as the descendents of a number of deified legendary emperors but most notably of Emperors Yan and Huang.[1] Emperor Huang, or the Yellow Emperor, (Huangdi) is believed to have reigned from 2,697 to 2,598 BC. According to the received tradition, Huangling County in Shanxi province is where the emperor is said to have found his last resting place. There are no extant records in support of any of this. However, the title 'Huangdi', meaning emperor, was certainly a later creation. A further discussion of this is presented below in the section concerning the history of the Qin dynasty. The created title resonated with considerable religious implications at the level of deities. For example, the traditional two-millenium old annual Tomb Sweeping Day Festival (also known as the Qingming Festival) honouring deceased ancestors often include ritualised sacrificial ceremonies in remembrance of the legendary apotheosised fathers of the Chinese people, particularly of Emperor Huangdi.

The earliest ruling Chinese dynasty on the other hand mentioned in traditional Chinese sources is the Xia dynasty (c 2205-1766 BC) said to have been founded by Emperor Fu Xi (Fu Hsi), son of Yu the Great, but as is the case with emperors Yan and Huang, the existence of emperors Yu and his son Fu Xi also appear to have a mythological provenance.[2,3] But regardless of Xia's historical authenticity, it is abundantly clear that there were many settled communities in China scattered from west to east along the Wei and Yellow rivers reaching all the way into the Shandong peninsula in the Bohai Bay. These communities in the central plains constituted the historical heartland of ancient China and have traditionally been known collectively as the "Middle Kingdom", the land under Heaven (*tianxia*) with its central core inhabited by northern Chinese. It was characterized with single superior hegemonic civilization achieved by virtue of the values, morals and teachings of its venerated sages.[4-9] Thus, imperial China of the Middle Kingdom was embraced by its people as a Sino-focused civilization surrounded by many disorderly nomadic tribal barbarians of varied origins.

The Middle Kingdom

The term Zhong-gua, or Zhong-hua, is a construct of the words *zhong* (middle or central) and *gua* (nation, state or kingdom) thus 'Middle Kingdom.' Its first use appears in the Chinese Classic Histories, a compilation of documentary records devoted to events in the ancient histories of the Xia, Shang and Zhou dynasties. The text of the records consists of 58 chapters of which 33 are generally considered authentic works from the Warring States period or earlier. Throughout the centuries and until the advent of its extensive contacts with Europe in the nineteenth century (as a consequence of China's humiliating defeats at the hands of the British and Japanese navies), China believed, with great arrogance and self-confidence, that it was the centre of the world. It was the 'Land under Heaven' (*tianxia*) by virtue of the sheer brilliance of its civilization hence the 'Centre of Civilization.' To distinguish itself from states beyond its borders, the Middle Kingdom represented itself graphically as a series of concentric circles or rectangles, with Beijing at the epicentre. The core of such imagery was considered to represent the northern Chinese. Moving outwards from the core centre, the successive circles represented the outer regions inhabited by other Chinese, barbarians, tributary states and finally those deemed incapable of being civilized. Within this social construct China considered itself in every respect a single self-contained superior civilization surrounded by those who are measured by their cultural proximity to the core. In this context, an interesting anecdote concerns China's attitude towards its foreign diplomatic and trade relations. The British East India Company was very much anxious to open up the massive Chinese market to manufactured British and colonial goods but was frustrated by China's constant indifference towards the company's overtures. And when the Court of King George III of England sent Lord George Macartney to China in 1792 in behalf of the East India Company to ask Emperor Qianlong for installing British diplomatic and trade representatives in Peking (Beijing), the Emperor was not impressed and his response sent to King George was that China was not interested in increasing its foreign trade because it required nothing from Britain.[10,11] The response read further:

> We have never valued ingenious articles, nor do we have the slightest need of your country's manufactures. Therefore, O King, as regards your request to send someone to remain at the capital, while it is not in

Introduction

harmony with the regulations of the Celestial Empire we also feel very much that it is of no advantage to your country.

The recorded history of China can be conveniently divided into three segments which are defined in the present work as Ancient, Imperial and Modern. Nevertheless, a cursory examination of the chronological periods of China's history given in Table 1 should leave little doubt regarding the complexity of the historical periods associated with the development of Chinese civilization and its unyielding tradition-based culture.

For a further study of the complexity of the components of the Chinese civilization, a detailed breakdown of the dynasties and the kingdoms that reigned in China over four millennia can be found at the end of this book. The dynastic subscripts in the table indicate the initial accession of the dynasties to power and their subsequent return to power after an interim absence.

Given the title of the present work it is understood that its focus will be devoted primarily to the Chinese historical periods within the years of the Christian calendar (AD, Anno Domini). However, the Chinese history periods in the years Before Christ (BC) will also be presented, brief though they may be, only for the purposes of clarity and completeness. The history of modern China beginning in the year 1911 to the present is deliberately excluded from this work as its relevance in the promulgation of the various faiths in present day China is outside the scope of the present subject. It is hoped that this approach will assist the reader to be more familiar with the chronology of events that ultimately gave impetus to the evolution of modern China. For the reader whose interest in China may go beyond the contents of the present work, the reader is referred to many excellent published treatises on the subject. The following titles are recommended: *The Legacy of China*, edited by R. Dawson, Oxford University Press, 1964 and *The Cambridge Illustrated History of China* by P. Ebrey, Cambridge University Press, 2006. For a more condensed reference to the history of China, the reader is referred to the beautifully illustrated *The Dragon Throne* by J. Fenby, Quercus Publishing plc, 2008.

Treasures of the Silk Road

Table 1. Dynasties of ancient and imperial China

PERIOD	SUB-PERIOD	TIME SCALE
Ancient		
Xia		c 2205 -1766 BC
Shang		c 1600 -1027
Zhou	Western	1027 - 771
	Eastern	770 - 256
	Spring-Autumn	772 - 481
	Warring States	475 - 221
Imperial		
Qin		221 - 206
Han	Western (Former) Han	BC 206 - 8 AD
Wang Meng userpurs		9 - 24
Han	Eastern (Later) Han	25 - 220
Three Kingdoms	Wei	220 - 265
	Shu	221 - 263
	Wu	222 - 280
Western Jin		265 - 316
Eastern Jin		317 - 420
Southern kingdoms	Song	420 - 479
	Qi	479 - 502
	Liang	502 - 557
	Chen	557 - 589
Northern kingdoms	Northern Wei	386 - 534
	Eastern Wei	534 - 550
	Northern Qi	550 - 577

Introduction

	Western Wei	535 - 556
	Northern Zhou	557 - 581
Sui		581 - 618
Tang		618 - 907
Five Dynasties	Later Liang	907 - 923
	Later Tang	923 - 936
	Later Jin	936 - 947
	Later Han	947 - 950
	Later Zhou	951 - 960
Song	Northern	960 -1127
	Southern	1127 -1279
Jin (Jurchen)		1115 -1234
Yuan (Mongol)		1279 -1368
Ming		1368 -1644
Qing (Manchu)		1644 -1911
Modern		
Republic of China		1911 -1949
People's Republic of China		1949– Present

Treasures of the Silk Road

Introduction

THE MIDDLE KINGDOM

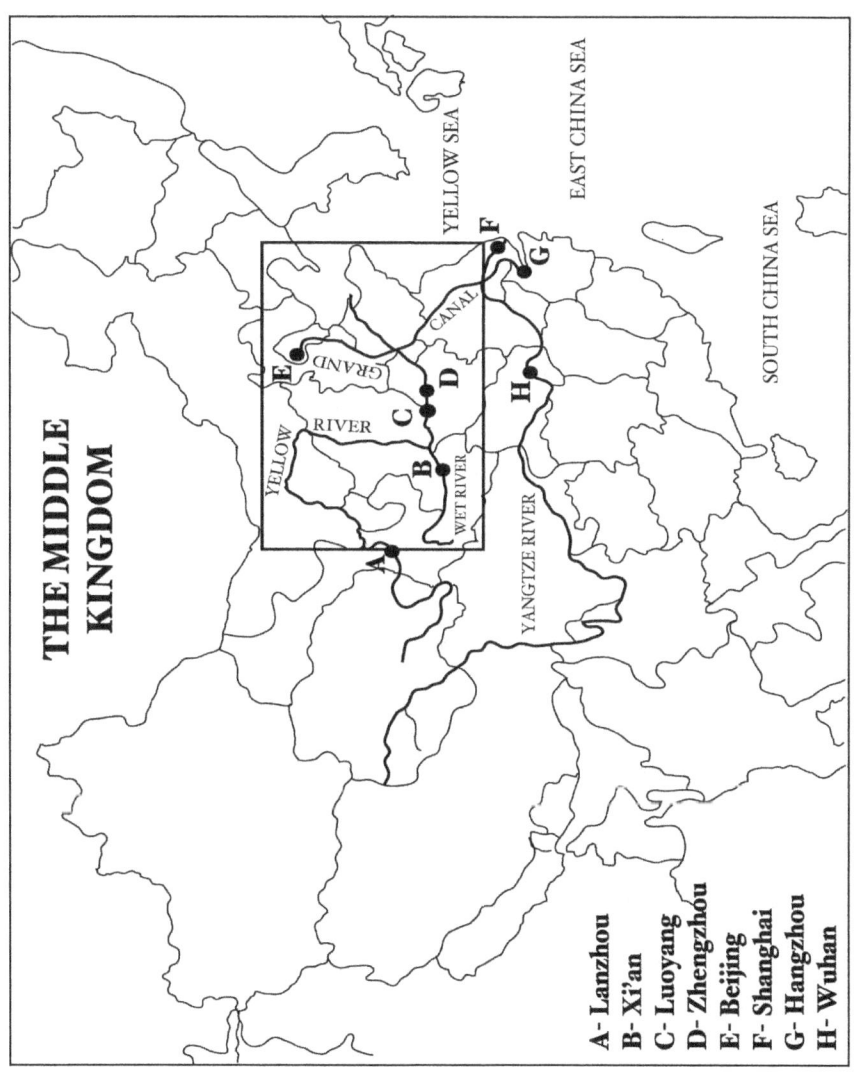

References

1. Sautman, B., Myths of Descent, Racial Nationalism and Ethnic Minorities in the People's Republic of China. In F. Dikötter (ed.), *The Construction of Racial Identities in China and Japan: Historical and Contemporary Perspectives*. Hurst and Co., London (1997).
2. Birrell, A., *Chinese Mythology: An Introduction*. John Hopkins University Press, Baltimore (1993).
3. Sanders, T. T. L., *Dragons, Gods and Spirits from Chinese Mythology*. Schocken Books, New York (1983).
4. Rossabi, M. (ed.), *China among Equals: The Middle Kingdom and its Neighbors, 10th-14th Centuries*. University of California Press, Berkeley (1983).
5. Williams, S. W., *The Middle Kingdom: A Survey of the Geography, Government, Literature, Social Life, Arts, and History of the Chinese Empire and its Inhabitants*. Scribner, New York (1883).
6. Wilson, J. H., *China: Travels and Investigations in the "Middle Kingdom." A Study of its Civilization and Possibilities; With a Glance at Japan*. Appleton, New York, (1887).
7. Zhang, Y. J., *China in the International System, 1918-20: The Middle Kingdom at the Periphery*. St. Martin's Press, New York (1991).
8. Geil, W.E., *A Yankee on the Yangtze: Being a Narrative of a Journey from Shanghai Through the Central Kingdom*. Hodder and Stoughton, London (1904).
9. Wang, A., *Cosmology and Political Culture in Early China*. Cambridge University Press, Cambridge (2000).
10. Carter, M. and Harlow, B., *Archives of Empire: From the East India Company to the Suez Canal*. Duke University Press, Durham, North Carolina (2004).
11. Seaman, L. C. B., *Victorian England: Aspects of English and Imperial History*. Routledge, London (1973).

Chapter One

Historical Perspectives – Ancient China

Before we embark upon the task of describing the history of the ancient Chinese dynasties, a few introductory remarks may ease the challenges of understanding this immensely complex subject. Chinese history is normally described and compartmentalized according to the dynasties that ruled the land. Major historical developments therefore are discussed in relation to the dynastic periods in which they took place, and since two or more dynasties co-existed and each simultaneously ruled by successive emperors in different parts of China, it is often difficult to bring the discussion of the relevance of a specific historical event to a satisfactory and a meaningful end point; the history of the construction of the Grand Canal is such an example. The basic characteristic of Chinese rule, much the same as anywhere else in world history, was that there was only one primary leader enthroned as the head of a dynasty that was succeeded by his bloodline descendants until an opposing individual took over. However, unlike most ancient histories where only one leader ruled a land at any one time, Chinese history is replete with co-dynasties that frequently ruled concurrently in various parts of the vast Chinese land. This inevitably raises the question of genealogy in connection with issues of rightful succession to the throne of the Chinese realm. One case in point worthy of mention is the story of Empress Wu Zetian who usurped the throne of her dead husband Emperor Taizong of the Tang dynasty by murdering her own offspring and proclaimed herself the first empress of China. We, therefore, should consider at this point a few aspects of traditional Chinese lineage principles.*

---

* Parts of the following principles were taken from David K Jordan's online revision of Staunton, George Thomas (tr.), *Ta Tsing leu lee, being the fundamental laws,* and a selection from the supplementary statutes of the penal code of China. T. Cadell & W. Davies, London, 1810.

Chinese Social Hierarchy

Traditional Chinese social hierarchy draws clear boundaries between descent, lineage and clan. A *Patrilineal* descent is a term that means a descent is calculated through men, that is, a male offspring inherits his family membership from his father. Ancient China was extreme in that a woman's membership was quite explicitly deleted from the family of her birth.

Thus, the term *Patrilineage* in China rigidly identifies descendancy from a single, specific male ancestor. The ancestor is referred to as an 'apical' ancestor because he is at the 'apex' of the genealogy by which the lineage membership is determined for his descendants whose descent-links to him are known. A woman is a member of her father's lineage at birth, but at marriage she is transferred to her husband's lineage. Because different descent lines from the apical ancestor might have fared differently economically with the passing of generations, the richer members tended to provide 'lineage' resources to be used by the less fortunate members thus recycling wealth and reducing the social class differences within the kins.

Reverence of ancestors by the living men in a family means the worship of their male ancestors and their wives. For a living unmarried woman it means the worship of her immediate male ancestors and their wives but upon marriage her reverence is shifted to her husband's male ancestors and their wives. In traditional popular belief, deceased ancestors depend upon their living male heirs, their wives and offsprings for becoming the object of perpetual reverence (expressed at the grave site of the deceased by making offerings of sacrificial foods and the burning of mock paper money, clothing, etc.), and therefore the failure to produce a male offspring was/is considered a misfortune.

The Chinese family was, and to a large extent still is, *Patriarchal*, a term meaning the family is hierarchically organized with the prime institutionalized authority vested in the most senior male. No two members of a Chinese family are equal in authority. Senior generations are superior to junior generations, older people are superior to younger ones, and men are superior to women.

In contrast to the kinship-dependent identities in *patrilineal* descent, a clan is only a property-holding group made up of members who claim descent from an apical ancestor, who may or may not have actually existed. Thus clans are often created on the basis of common surnames but all are bound by the common obligation of protecting and ensuring

Historical Perspectives – Ancient China

the survival of the clan and of its holdings. Buddhist monasteries, on the other hand, were perhaps a slightly modified version of a clan. Individuals might take vows that removed them from their original families (if any) and affiliated them in perpetuity with other members of a Buddhist monastery who are united only by a common purpose. Their vows include the life-long practice of 'ancestral' reverence to a line of earlier members. Unlike the clan, members of a Buddhist monastery owned nothing but, like the members of a clan, the individual Buddhist monk is bound by his loyalty to the welfare of his monastery.

Finally, we should also note it was a common Chinese practice to make reference to dates according to the extant reigning emperor's years in power, and because the names of the emperors of the many dynasties were frequently similar, the dates also cited the dynasty during which a personality or an event was considered. For example, dating the beginning of the use of a specific royal pottery pattern might be indicated as 'the fifth year of the Kang Xi Emperor of the Qing dynasty.' Although this might seem cumbersome to the itinerant reader, this system of dating however allows placing the subject in an unequivocal point in time. It is therefore inevitable that dynasty-based discussions of Chinese histories are the logical approach in dissecting the details such histories impart.

Shang Period (c 1600-1027 BC)

The Shang dynasty came into prominence in the lands that now constitute the provinces of Henan, Hebei and Shandong along the floodplains of the Yellow river with its capital at Anyang.[1] Archaeological finds unearthed in Xiaotun village in the province of Henan in 1899 have included a large collection of tortoise shells inscribed with jiaguwen, the precursor of modern Chinese characters, that have allowed archaeologists to develop a picture of Shang dynasty as a culture often engaged in war utilizing horse-drawn chariots and weapons made of bronze.

Wu Ding is the first historically verifiable ruler from the ancient dynasties that ruled China and the contemporary accounts of his reign were recorded in the form of oracular script as found on the inscribed tortoise shells mentioned above.[2] These were used by diviners to explore whether their patron's proposed activities would be favoured by the gods, and also to foretell the outcome of personal issues. Wu Ding ruled from 1250-1192 BC from his capital Yinxu who was described by the ancient Chinese historian Sima Qian as the twenty-second Shang king succeeding his father Xiao Yi. Sima Qian (ca.145-86 BC), who lived during the Western Han dynasty, is renowned for his careful and accurate historical recording, especially of his major work the *Shiji*.[3]

Wu Ding's most successful policy for subduing aggression against his kingdom by the many nomadic neighbouring tribes was to establish alliances with them by marrying one woman from each of the tribes. His most accomplished and favoured wife Fu Hao entered the royal household through such a marriage and by virtue of her strength of character and intelligence advanced through the ranks to become a major personality in Wu Ding's court. This form of establishing alliances through marriages or importing concubines into the royal harems was a practice that survived well into the sixteenth century China as we shall see later.

The oracular records have presented a fascinating insight into the remote history of China as do into the ruling affairs of Wu Ding including his purported visions that had led him to many military victories. We learn from these records, for example, the first king of the Shang dynasty was King Tang in whose honour ceremonial rituals were conducted by Wu Ding at the Royal Temple during the twenty-ninth year of his reign. In the third year of his reign, Wu Ding ordered the compilation of rules of governance, and in the twelfth, he gave Shang Jia Wei a military command to exercise control over the neighbouring Qi tribe. We also learn that in the twenty-fifth year of Wu Ding's reign his son Zu Ji had died in exile. The inscriptions continue with informative accounts of many military campaigns led by Wu Ding from his thirty-second to fiftieth years of reign and of his victories over the Yi and the Qiang tribes.

The Shang period was a semi-matriarchal slave society which allowed high ranking women to hold their own fiefdoms. One such woman was Queen Fu Hao who is believed to have served also as a military general and a high priestess of the royal court.[4,5] Her tomb was unearthed in 1976 at the ruins of the Shang capital Yin and was discovered to contain a collection of jade articles many thousands of years old belonging to the Liangzhu culture, and also many military weapons and battle axes. The Liangzhu was a Neolithic jade culture which was

Historical Perspectives – Ancient China

centred around the Yangtze River delta and in parts of northern Zhejiang province in eastern China from 3400-2250 BC.[6] Their jade and ivory-based culture describes the Shang as a highly socially stratified society with the poorer sector relegated to the ownership of only simple pottery and earthenware utensils.

In her capacity as a military general and with the assistance of her subordinate generals Zhi and Hou Gao, Fu Hao led many successful campaigns against the neighbouring feudal tribes of Tu Fang (Tu tribe), Qiang, Yi and the Ba (eastern Sichuan area). The Tu, Qiang and Yi semi-nomadic tribes are related descendants of the ancient Tibetan Tangut tribe. They are believed to have migrated from the south-eastern regions of the Tibetan plateau and settled mostly in the western regions of Yunnan, Gansu, Sichuan and Ningxia provinces.

It is perhaps necessary at this point to note that the Yellow river's basin may conveniently be considered the cradle of the Chinese civilization. The river flows a distance of around 2,000 kilometres through nine provinces of China (Qinghai, Sichuan, Gansu, Ningxia, Inner Mongolia, Shaanxi, Shanxi, Henan and Shandong) before emptying into the Bohai Bay of Shandong province in north-east China. It originates in the Bayan Har Mountains in Qinghai then flowing through the city of Lanzhou in Gansu, it first loops northwest then northeast into Inner Mongolia before turning sharply south and forming the boundary between Shaanxi and Shanxi provinces. The river then ends its course by flowing through Shandong province in a north-easterly direction towards the bay. Most of the history of northern Chinese civilization, perhaps justly until the close of the imperial history at the beginning of the twentieth century AD, took place in the river's valleys and in the cities of its floodplains (Lanzhou in Gansu, Chang'an (modern Xi'an) in Shaanxi and Luoyang and Kaifeng in Henan).

Xi Period (Western Zhou/Chou) (1027-771 BC)

The concept of 'Mandate of Heaven' was a belief system during the Shang dynasty that had its roots in the ancient practice of 'Ancestral Worship'.[7] It perpetuated the belief that political power stemmed from spiritual power through the intercession of deceased ancestors with the heavenly deities on behalf of the living king. It should be noted here that this type of ruling and wielding political power over the masses were not unknown in the West and in fact were commonly practiced by the kings of France and England as their 'Divine Right' to rule as late as the seventeenth century. In the Chinese version, victories for the king and prosperity for his subjects were the physical manifestations of an appeased heaven as opposed to defeats and failures that gave rebellion legitimacy. Thus, a former vassal of the Shang, the house of Zhou, disenchanted with the Shang's failures usurped power from their masters and began to nurture the development of a feudal system based on fiefs granted to the king's kinsmen and to the members of his inner circle of supporters. Their power-base was in the Wei river valley west of the Shang domain.[8] The Wei River is the largest tributary of the Yellow river and its source is in Weiyuan County in Gansu province. The Yellow and the Wei rivers meet in the vicinity of Chang'an, a city which historically was the site of eleven Chinese dynastic capitals spanning over a thousand years of northern Chinese civilization including the Qin, Han and the Tang periods. Truly the two rivers represent the cradle of Chinese civilization. The Zhou dynasty at first established its capital in Chang'an but during the reign of King Ping, it abandoned the city in 770 BC and moved the capital to the east in Luoyang as a result of attacks from the west by the nomadic barbarian Quanrong tribe thus marking the beginning of the Eastern Zhou dynasty.[9] The two Zhou dynasties became the longest ruling house in Chinese history spanning nearly eight centuries.

Chinese Concept of Heaven

The familiar Christian concept of the genesis of our world is a much later invention than the classical Chinese concept of 'Heaven'. Heaven was seen by the Chinese as superior to all aspects of our metaphysical world without reference to a creative role for a heavenly creator. In contrast to the Western application of kings' rule by Divine Right, which required bloodline continuity, the Chinese concept of rule by Mandate of Heaven applied a more practical approach. It required the cultivation and the establishment of moral and virtuous standards for holding power, a concept deeply rooted in Confucian philosophy. This requirement permitted the ruled masses to assess the suitability of their rulers to rule. To the Chinese masses, bad harvests, chronic endemic poverty, natural calamities, draughts or floods signaled the displeasure of heaven with their extant ruler and brought into question the legitimacy of his rule. Hence, this heavenly displeasure gave the masses the right to rebellion believing that the Mandate of Heaven had been withdrawn from their ruler.[10]

Historical Perspectives – Ancient China

Spring and Autumn Period (772-481 BC)

Zhou's dynastic sovereignty over their vassals eventually began to wane as the nobles of many of their constituent states began to seek their own power-bases thus gradually confining the authority of the house of Zhou to its territories immediately in the vicinity of Luoyang.[11] The Spring and Autumn period represents roughly the history of the first half of the Eastern Zhou rule, namely, 772-481 BC. The name for this period is derived from the *Spring and Autumn Annals* of the state of Lu. The annals were a record of the history of the state of Lu but also chronicled the chronological history of the inclusive years of the Eastern Zhou period. There was a good reason for this. Situated in the central and south-western regions of Shandong province, Lu was a vassal state of the Western Zhou dynasty but came into prominence during the Eastern Zhou period and became one of the smaller of the warring states. It was ruled by nobles who used Ji as their family name.

The founder of the Lu state, Ji Bonqin, was the son of Ji Dan, a member of the court of the Eastern Zhou dynasty. The state is believed to have been the home of the scholar and social philosopher Kong Fuzi (Confucius) whose commentaries on the Chinese literary classics and personal morality in politics (*The Analects*) developed into a pragmatic philosophy for successful governance as well as for the practice of an ethical personal lifestyle.[12] The *Analects* defined ideas on discipline, social morality, good conduct, respect and good personal behaviour. Furthermore, while the *Analects* offered guidelines for the proper performance of rites, of prayers, mourning, dressing, eating, praise, the conduct of celebrations and the observance of anniversaries, it also emphasized the importance of accepting responsibility, acting benevolently and showing compassion towards others. In short, Confucianism has been the cornerstone of Chinese civilization throughout the ages. It describes a state ideology which by far incorporated the most sophisticated ethical doctrines in a bureaucratic system of governance. The precepts of Confucianism still to this day define the roots of governance in Chinese, Japanese, Korean and Vietnamese, and in many other regional East Asian societies. In the main, Confucianism advocated two institutions: one was government and the other the family.[13] The elements of the former advocated that the exclusion of the people from governmental decision-making processes was a positive virtue allowing the government officials to function in their capacity in keeping with the ethics and ideals with which they had been inculcated. Hence, the state has consistently been seen as the apogee of the Chinese social order enjoying sovereignty over its decisions as opposed to the European societies in which historically the power of governments has always been subject to competing sources of authority, such as the Church, the capitalists and special interest groups.

The Confucian concept of state supremacy over all else has its foundation in the second Confucian advocacy: filial piety within the family. This is the duty of the offspring to respect the authority of the nuclear father who, in return, is required to take care and protect the members of his family. The nuclear father is the role model for the state, which in dynastic times meant the emperor. Continuity in the enactment of this fundamental Confucian precept is inherently seen in the common practice of the ritual of ancestral worship which emphasizes the reverence, veneration and subordination of the living member(s) of the family to the dominance and the permanency of its ancestral spirits.[14] It is important to note here that myths inform rituals and rituals are the enactments of the myths. The practice of rituals in China therefore, by analogy, informs the general Chinese populace of their mythologic emperors and of the virtues inherint in the show of obedience to the state institutions on the model of filial piety. The state is immortal and dependant upon for the protection of the origins of the ancient Chinese civilization.

Warring States Period (475-221 BC)

The Warring States period represents the history of the second half of the Eastern Zhou period and, as the name implies, it was a period of political struggle and escalating disorder.[15] Somewhat similar to the history of the first half of the Eastern Zhou period, the name of the second half, the Warring States period, is derived from the *Record of the Warring States*, a historical chronicle compiled early in the Han dynasty.

The breakdown of centralized authority established during the Zhou period led to endemic wars between the separate constituent states. The larger relatively powerful vassal states annexed or claimed suzerainty over the smaller states. By the end of the sixth century BC most of the smaller weaker states had disappeared and the larger southern states, such as the Chu and the Wu, consolidated their rule and began to claim independence from the Zhou. Eventually the Zhou lost all real influence over their vassal states which led to the collapse of Zhou's

Historical Perspectives – Ancient China

feudal system, though the Zhou kings continued to rule, albeit in name only, under the concept of Mandate of Heaven. From the ashes of this turmoil rose into prominence the Seven Warring States, which were the Qi, Chu, Yan, Han, Zhao, Wei and Qin.

Despite these unsettling events disrupting the authority of the house of Zhou, the idea of widespread trade seems to have first developed during this period bringing into practice entrepreneurial ventures for profit and the creation of wealth by independent merchants. This may have been a natural outcome of the political strife of this period as each powerful state began to seek its own wealth and fortunes through trade, taxation and tribute collection. They were eager to maintain independent aristocratic privileges as opposed to the traditional feudal ideology of supporting a confederation of states. Thus trade began to define social status and gave rise to class distinctions – the most esteemed were the scholars (*shi*) and then, in a descending order, came the farmers (*nong*), labourers (*gong*) and finally, the least respected, the merchants (*shang*). It was inevitable therefore that philosophical thought and scholarly interests would germinate and flourish during this period of unrest in an effort to stem the tide of social and political disintegration. A major proponent of such ideals was Confucius (551-479 BC) whose philosophical doctrines on personal benevolence and submission to moral standards as the cornerstones of leadership came to be known as Confucianism.[16] Although, as would be expected, his teachings did not find much favour with the feudal warlords of his time, his doctrines nevertheless continued to gain prominence and to this day continue to define the behaviour of Asiatic societies. Confucius was perceived as an obsessive person, one who refused to talk at meals, but when he did talk, he is purported to have said of himself: 'I set my heart on the Way, base myself on virtue, lean upon benevolence for support and take my recreation in the arts.' He had defined the good man, or the good ruler, as one with moral force, in other words, 'the virtuous.' The relationship between master and disciple, or ruler and advisor, he had said, should be based on the mutual cultivation of virtue which allows the development of the capacity to listen and therefore understand. Benevolence he stressed was an aspect of virtue that permits one to be considerate of others. His most famous pronouncement regarding stability in society was: 'Let the ruler be a ruler, the subject a subject, the father a father and the son a son.'

During the Warring States period, the farming lands were cultivated by farmers to whom the farms were assigned by local rulers much the same way as practiced by the noble houses of the fiefdoms of medieval Europe a millennium later. The farmers worked the land with iron tools and ox-drawn ploughs. The spiritual aspects of their lives contained the practice of rituals associated with the various annual agrarian cycles, such as the seasons for sowing, planting and harvesting. These were fixed calendar events regulated by the land-owning rulers and were required to be followed by the farming communities.

By way of military innovations, unlike the preceding period, the Warring States period saw the combined infantry and cavalry units come into use in battles as a tactical advantage that gradually made the use of battle chariots obsolete. Military armaments began to be produced *en mass* made of iron rather than bronze, notably the eighteen-foot long dagger-axes popularized by the Qin. This was the period that heralded the birth of imperial China.

Historical Perspectives – Ancient China

Regional maps of the earliest documented imperial Chinese dynasties

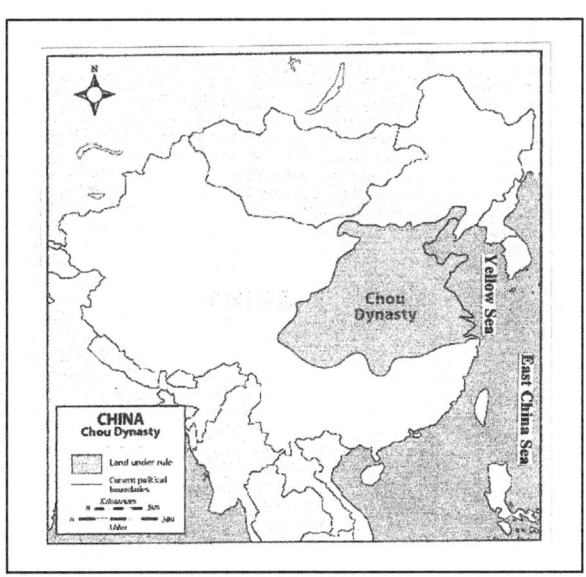

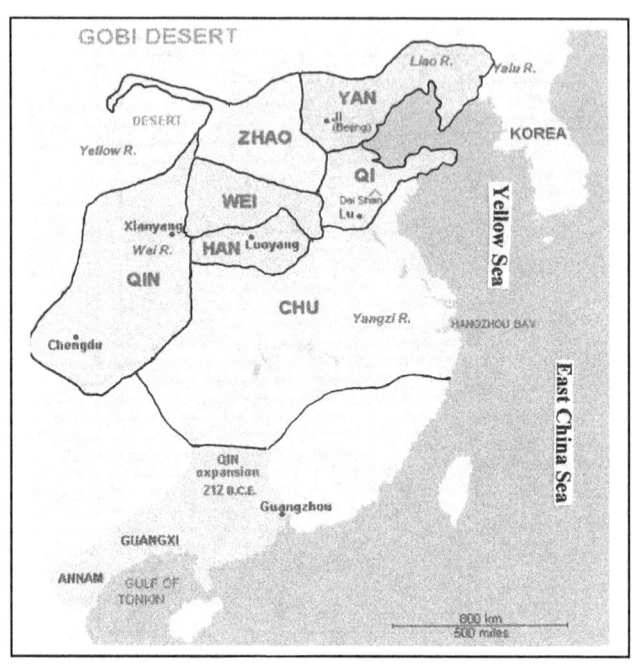

References

1. Keightley, D., The Shang: China's First Historical Dynasty. In *The Cambridge History of Ancient China: From the Origins of Civilization to 221 BC*. M. Loewe and E. L. Shaughnessy (eds.), Cambridge University Press, Cambridge (1999).
2. Hessler, P., Oracle Bones: *A Journey Through Time in China*. Harper Perennial, New York (2006).
3. Sima Qian, *The Records of the Grand Historian: Han Dynasty II*, revised edition, B. Watson (trans.), Columbia University Press, New York (1993).
4. Ebrey, P. *The Cambridge Illustrated History of China*. Cambridge University Press, Cambridge (2006).
5. Ebrey, P., *Shang Tomb of Fu Hao*: *A Visual Sourcebook of Chinese Civilization*. University of Washington, St. Louis (2007).
6. Zhou, Y., *The Dawn of the Oriental Civilization: Liangzhu site and Liangzhu culture*. China Intercontinental Press, Beijing (2007)
7. Fairbank, J. K. and Goldman, M., *China: A New History*. Harvard University Press, Cambridge (2006).
8. Shaughnessy, E., Western Zhou History. In *The Cambridge History of Ancient China: From the Origins of Civilization to 221 BC*. M. Loewe and E. L. Shaughnessy (eds.), Cambridge University Press, Cambridge (1999).
9. Li, X., *Eastern Zhou and Qin Civilizations*. K. C. Chang (trans.), Yale University Press, New Haven (1985). Li, X., *Eastern Zhou and Qin Civilizations*. K. C. Chang (trans.), Yale University Press, New Haven (1985).
10. Pye, L. W., *The Spirit of Chinese Politics*. Harvard University Press, Cambridge Massachusetts (1992).
11. Hsu, C. Y., The Spring and Autumn Period. In *The Cambridge History of Ancient China: From the Origins of Civilization to 221 BC*. M. Loewe and E. L. Shaughnessy (eds.), Cambridge University Press, Cambridge (1999).
12. Dawson, R., *Confucius*. Oxford University Press, Oxford (1982).
13. Fingarette, H. *Confucius : The Secular as Sacred*. Waveland Press, Long Grove, Illinois (1998).
14. Creel, H. G., *Chinese Thought from Confucius to Mao Tse-tung*. University of Chicago Press, Chicago (1953).
15. Lewis, M. E., Warring States Political History. In *The Cambridge History of Ancient China: From the Origins of Civilization to 221 BC*. M. Loewe and E. L. Shaughnessy (eds.), Cambridge University Press, Cambridge (1999).

16. Creel, H. G., *Confucius and the Chinese Way*. Harper-Collins Publishers, New York (1949).

Historical Perspectives – Ancient China

Group 1

1. Four-horse drawn bronze carriage (chariot) of the First Emperor Qin Shihuangdi excavated from a pit near the emperor's tomb mound at Mount Li 22 miles north-east of Xi'an in Lintong County, Shaanxi province. Some 130 chariots were unearthed all dated circa the third century BC.

2. A squad of Terracotta warriors of some 8,000 individually distinct warriors unearthed one mile east of the emperor's tomb mound in Lintong County north-east of Xi'an. The life-size clay figures after kiln firing were completed with painted details and arranged in full attention guarding the emperor's tomb.

3. The underground tomb of Princess Yongtai. The multi-chambered tomb lies about 10 metres below ground and is accessed through long and gated inclining corridor. The black granite sarcophogus is profusely inscribed with various epitaphs and is protected by metal railing. Most of the walls are decorated with paintings of courtly scenes typical of the Tang dynasty period.

Historical Perspectives – Ancient China

4. A wall painting from Princess Yongtai's tomb depicting the princess, first from left, identified by the marking (hanfu) at the parting of her hair just above the forehead which was popularized by the royalty during the Tang dynasty. She is accompanied by her entourage of maidens carrying a bowl, a lit candle and a lantern where a gratuity is apparently being offered for delicacies (note maiden's hand in her purse).

5. A wall painting from Princess Yongtai's tomb depicting various members of the royal court dressed in official judicial garments and engaged in consultation.

Historical Perspectives – Ancient China

6. A wall painting from Princess Yongtai's tomb depicting what appears to be a Tang dynasty military procession within the walls of the city of Xi'an, perhaps an honour guard to the Princess.

7. The ancient Tang dynasty walls of the city of Xi'an enclosing the entire central city. It is 12 metres high, 14 metres wide at the top and 16 metres wide at its base.

Historical Perspectives – Ancient China

8. The triple Nanmen Gates in the southern wall of the city of Xi'an.

Treasures of the Silk Road

Chapter Two

Historical Perspectives – Imperial China

Qin/Ch'in Period (221-206 BC) – The First Empire

The decline in the power of the Zhou dynasty accelerated the struggle for supremacy amongst the many warring states warlords. The most powerful of them came to be known as the 'Seven Overlords' of whom only the overlords of the western state of Qin ultimately triumphed.[1] They ruled large expanses of territories that included lands as far west as present-day Sichuan province.[2] Their king, Ying Zheng crushed the remnants of the weaker separatist states and in 221 BC successfully organized the unification of the Chinese empire from the Liaodong Peninsula in the north-east to Hainan Island in the south under one centralized bureaucratic system that abolished the old feudal fiefdoms. Abolishing the feudal system allowed Zheng to divide the Qin territories into thirty-six provinces with each given a governor, an army commander and an inspector. This division of bureaucratic governance limited the possibilities of regional insurrections and rebellion. Yet his shrewd authoritarian mentality drove him to institute further laws for the prevention of rebellions. For instance, he required that all weapons be brought to the capital to be melted for making bronze bells. He insisted that his realm's nobility move to the capital where they could be kept under a watchful eye. But most importantly, the new king in 214 BC directed massive demographic relocations to the north and south in his bid to subdue and colonize border areas. This was an extension of his 219 BC directive that had sent freely willing families to occupy and farm the under-populated areas in the south-eastern provinces of his empire.

China in 221 BC was primarily an agrarian society that focused on the production of rice, wheat and soybeans. Pigs and chickens were raised on commune farmlands where ownership and duties were shared.[3,4] Whilst horses and oxen were used for ploughing the fields, sheep were kept mainly for the production of wool. In contrast to this agrarian environment that typified the Middle Kingdom, the peoples of the grasslands beyond the borders to the north and north-west of the Qin heartlands were primarily nomadic dwellers of open pastures "the barbarians' who frequently raided adjacent lands in China.

Ying Zheng had given himself the elevated title of Shihuangdi (Qin ShiHuang-di). The title stood for 'First Emperor' and gave Ying Zheng supreme royal authority. 'ShiHuang' was his adopted royal name and Qin identified his state. The suffix 'di' meaning 'first.' formed the compound name 'ShiHuang-di' which reflected a considerable religious and political significance. The 'Huang' part of the emperor's name means 'august, or majestic' and it was compounded with 'di' to 'Huangdi' to create the new and the self-elevating term 'First Emperor.' The selection of 'di' in this context had a much deeper symbolic connotation. More than a thousand years earlier, the Shang dynastic rulers had worshipped 'di' as their supreme deity and, later, they used the term to deify their legendary sages and rulers of antiquity by simply attaching 'di' to the names.[5] Such titles survived the vicissitudes of Chinese historical disunities and were successfully retained by Chinese rulers throughout the centuries until the demise of the Qing dynasty in 1911.

As the First Emperor of China, Ying Zheng had proclaimed with great self-praising modesty: 'Insignificant as I am, I have raised troops to punish the rebellious princes; and thanks to the sacred power of our ancestors all six kings have been chastised as they deserved, so that at last the empire is pacified.'[6] He was born the son of a royal concubine in the first month of the year 259 BC and was given the name Zheng signifying uprightness and correctness. Upon the death of his father in 247 BC, Zheng took over the reigns of the empire at the age of thirteen and over the following two and a half decades he is reputed to have established himself as a tyrannical and a ruthless king whose fall is traditionally regarded as a result of internal corruption. He died in 210 BC. In 1975, the discovery of a cache of documents in the tomb of a Qin dynasty official who had died in 217 BC and interred at the place of the Sleeping Tiger northwest of Wuhan in Hubei province, shed new light on the life and reign of the First Emperor.[7] These documents included sections of the Qin legal code and an explanation of the code's legal terms used by officials. The texts were written on 1,200 long, narrow strips of bamboo, which was a common practice in China long before the use of paper became widespread.

Historical Perspectives – Imperial China

The importance of the discovery of the Qin legal code rests in the revelation that the First Emperor, contrary to the historical consensus painting him as being a cruel and an arbitrary despot, used laws and punishments that were clearly set out and carefully arranged according to circumstances. Two hundred and one of the bamboo strips dealt with official tasks ranging from agricultural supervision to feeding and clothing those on labour service. There were strips that dealt with regulations relating to accounting and unifying the system of measurements. A series of strips were concerned with military affairs in legal terms while others were a collection of laws on specific public offences and crimes.

Within a period of fifteen centuries since the rule of the Shang dynasty, we witness the progression of Chinese political infrastructure from a feudal system based on fiefdoms and warloards to a bureaucratic system of government instituted under the Qin dynasty that was to endure for the next 2,000 years. Zheng's enduring legacy includes his mausoleum guarded by the Terracotta Army – an army of an estimated 8,000 life-size clay warriors with chariots and horses unearthed in 1974 - that had laid buried for more than two millennia in Xiyang village, Lintong County, Shaanxi province. They stand erect and appear mobilized and ready for action in defence of their supreme monarch.

The empire of the First Emperor at its zenith stretched from just north of present-day Beijing down to the southern borders of Guangdong province in the south including the territories of Sichuan province in the west, and from the vicinity of Lanzhou, where the Yellow River makes its sharp turn north along the borders of Gansu and Shaanxi provinces, to the eastern seaboard of the Middle Kingdom. This was a massive territorial empire for its time and remained so before further extensions were made into Gansu and Xinjiang provinces by the succeeding Han dynasty.

Han Period (206 BC-AD 220)

Upon ShiHuangdi's death a rebel army led by Liu Bang, a former local official, took control of power. He named his dynasty Han, which is the reason the Chinese people today call themselves Han-ren (Han people). However this terminology adopted by modern Chinese to define their race, in reality is an invention as there has never been such a race.[8] It is nothing more than a cultural construct introduced in the late nineteenth century by the nationalist writer Zhang Taiyan that came to a widespread acceptance because it was during this period that China began a long and agonizing search for a clear sense of identity. The term's hidden intent was distinctly racial, a means of inclusion and exclusion – us versus them. It was first used to separate the native Chinese of the Middle Kingdom from the Manchu who had founded the progressively objectionable Qing dynasty in 1644. But later this usage also came into practice against the Europeans who had colonized the seaboards of China and were seen as undermining the basic fabric of Chinese traditions and destroying the foundations of their ancient civilization. A number of events coincide with these historical developments in China. The long-lasting Taiping Uprising (1850-64) staged against the Qing dynasty is an example. With the imperial power badly shaken by its humiliating defeats at the hands of the British in the Opium Wars, and by the famine that followed, the stage was set for the beginnings of the uprising in southern China before moving north and west to the doorsteps of Peking (Beijing). Another example is the Boxer Uprising of 1900. It was the culmination of the growing anti-Western sentiments, which had its origins in the eastern province of Shandong that precipitated the widespread attacks on foreign missionaries. It is to be noted here that the popularly shared Sino-centric sentiments of the Chinese people continue to shape and inform their nationalism to the present day.

Another aspect of Chinese nationalism emanating from the term 'Han' was the emergence of the racial term 'Yellow.'[9] The Chinese began to describe themselves as yellow rather than white to distinguish themselves from all other races, but especially from Europeans, as the Chinese began to resist the growing European threat to their civilization. The term 'Yellow' impressed upon the Chinese a strong sense of association with the Yellow River and the Yellow Emperor thus, again, turning the attention of the Chinese masses to their origins in the mythical Yellow Emperor[10] and to the cradle of their cultural civilization which was defined and nourished by the Yellow River.

One of the first major reforms instituted by Liu Bang was a result of his recognition that it was not politically prudent to rule a vast empire strictly on legalistic basis. He thus relaxed the supreme authority of the emperor and began to restore Confucian ideology in his system of government. Ministers and civil servants were recruited based on personal merits and on their knowledge of the Confucian classics, which gave the public a modicum of social mobility. The dynasty is referred to as the Western (Former) Han because it settled its capital in

Historical Perspectives – Imperial China

Chang'an (Xi'an).[11] During the reign of its sixth emperor, Emperor Wudi (141-87 BC), a limited centralized authority was restored in his bid to avert the possibility of rebellions by influential nobles. In this he was very successful to the extent that he relied upon the nobles of his court to lead expeditions into Central Asia beyond the western borders of the empire seeking alliances and new trading markets. For example, in 139 BC Zhang Qian was sent seeking alliances against the Xiongnu nomadic horsemen who were a source of security concerns with their marauding attacks along the empire's northern and north-western frontiers.[12] The Xiongnu (a Mongolic confederation of nomadic tribes of Central Asia) had a long history of harassing the empire as evidenced by their incursions into Shanxi province and by their nearly total annihilation of the large Chinese army at Datong which was composed mostly of infantrymen dispatched by Emperor Gaodi in 201 BC. Similar attacks by the Xiongnu had taken place in 182 and 177 BC and again during the reign of Emperor Wendi (Wen Ti) in 169 BC.

Zhang Qian's mission to establish a vast array of alliances with the nomadic tribal units bordering the empire in its northern and north-western frontiers was the earliest shoots of a process that ultimately gave rise to the major thoroughfares of the Silk Road. They facilitated the export and distribution of Chinese silk but more importantly the import of religious influences in the first century AD.[13] The roads thus traveled by Zhang represent the earliest trade and social networking systems that in time came to be known to us as the Silk Road (*si chóu zhi lu*). However all this was to come much later than Zhang Qian's forays for he was captured by the Xiongnu and only managed to escape after several years of imprisonment and found refuge further west in Ferghana and Bactria (in parts of present-day Kazakhstan, Tajikistan and northern Afghanistan). The people of Bactria, called the Yuezhi, were a confederation of five Indo-European tribes – same as or closely related to the Tocharians[14,15] - who had originally settled along China's western frontiers in the arid wastelands of eastern Tarim basin (what is today eastern Xinjiang and western Gansu) but who had been displaced by the Xiongnu nomads and forced to migrate westward. However, within two centuries the Yuezhi consolidated their power, conquered Bactria and moved south into Gandhara - in parts of present-day Pakistan - and finally established their own Tocharian Yuezhi/Kushan Empire in the plains of northern India, later to be known as the Mughals. The Han dynasty in the meantime had defeated the Xiongnu and had secured the empire's borders by establishing military garrisons along the north-eastern edges of the Taklamakan Desert as well as along the southern edges of the Gobi Desert. These military installations secured the flow of trade and tribute missions in and out of the Middle Kingdom. The tactical planning of these installations was made possible only through the geographical information Zhang Qian had provided the Han dynasty upon his return to China in 126 BC. The independent tribal settlements along Zhang's journeys gradually evolved to become the core way-stations of the Silk Road that supplied the Chinese with a variety of goods, chemicals, dyes, medicinal vegetables and the most basic military machine, the horse.[16] The horse became an instrument of Chinese lore and legend that evolved into the idea of the Heavenly Horse (the celestial horse). It not only later adorned the tombs of the Tang dynasty emperors Taizong and Wu Zetian but also one presumably with spiritual attributes was given as a celestial gift by Emperor Zhangdi (75-88 AD) to his paternal uncle.

Intervening Years (AD 221-265)

For a brief period of fifteen years (9-24 AD) the Western Han dynasty's rule was interrupted by a usurper named Wang Meng. He was the nephew of the wife of Emperor Chengdi (33-7 BC) and had emerged as a dominant figure in the royal court. After the early death of Chengdi's successor, Emperor Aidi (7-1 BC), Wang Meng served as regent to the next two infant emperors Pingdi and Ruzi. In 9 AD he had the Han dynasty declared defunct and made himself emperor. Although he shrewdly continued some of the fundamental policies of the Han dynasty to conduct his governance, his reign nonetheless was short and ended as a result of major flooding, social unrest and famine in the Shandong region. These events brought into question the legitimacy of his rule under the Mandate of Heaven. The all-certain ensuing rebellions succeeded in dethroning him and bringing his brief rule to an abrupt end. Upon the installation of the house of Liu Xuan to rule, a descendant of the former Hans, the Han dynasty during this second period of their reign moved the capital to Luoyang. Thus from the beginning of the restoration to the end of the Han dynasty this period came to be known as the Eastern (Later) Han period, perhaps rightly considered by many as China's 'Golden Age.'[17] The country continued to expand rapidly achieving its furthest extent in the period 141-87 BC when the Chinese armies penetrated into southern Manchuria and the Korean Peninsula in the north-east, and into the south and south-west as far as northern Vietnam.[18] However despite this accolade bestowed upon the Eastern Han for their social and political achievements,[19] the authority of the house of Liu deteriorated and power was gradually

Historical Perspectives – Imperial China

exercised by a general named Cao Cao whose son forced the abdication of the emperor in 221 AD and founded the Wei dynasty (220-265 AD). In opposition to the house of Wei, two rival clans established their own separate kingdoms, the Shu Han Kingdom in the southwest (221-263 AD) and the Wu Han Kingdom in the east (222-280 AD) thus creating the 'Three Kingdoms.'

Western Jin Period (AD 265-316)

It was unlikely that the three kingdoms would promote unification of the fragmented empire. With their constant endemic internal struggles, and their conflicts with other small petty regional lords, they in fact facilitated the deterioration and the further fragmentation of the empire. Eventually only the Wei clan emerged with a meaningfully intact political structure and power but it in turn was overcome by yet another clan, the Jin, thus founding the Western Jin dynasty that lasted from 265 to 316 AD with its capital in Luoyang.[20] Yet again, as in the other periods of Chinese history, the Jin dynasty struggled to contain the constant incursions by the northern nomadic peoples thus it resorted to shifting the seat of the capital from Luoyang. The dynasty with its capital relocated in Jiankang near present-day Nanjing came to be known as the Eastern Jin dynasty (317-420 AD). But these were troubling times. Only a year later in 316 AD the marauding nomadic tribes along China's northern frontiers became successful in establishing footholds within China which accelerated and expanded further encroachments by many other nomadic tribes along China's northern frontiers.

Dynastic Proliferations (AD 316-581)

The encroachments by the nomadic tribes into China proper prompted a period that saw the rise of many small regional kingdoms in the north. They set claims to realms within their own spheres of influence not unusual for the political trends of the time. These kingdoms included those established by the nomadic Mongolic Xianbei and the Tangut tribes. It was during this period that the Xianbei Tuoba tribe[21,22] unified the many Central Asian steppe tribes in the north and established the Northern Wei dynasty under its emperor Xiao Wendi. A cursory review of Table I will demonstrate the scope and breath of the dynasties that were established during these disruptive years which literally confined the remnants of the former Chinese empire to the eastern portions of the Yangtze river basin.

The Xianbei were nomadic people residing in today's Inner Mongolia and in the north-eastern parts of China called Manchuria. They were a federation of tribes of which the most important was the Tuoba tribe. After the demise of the Han dynasty, the descendants of the Xianbei formed a number of mini-empires which were ruled by many dynasties that included the Yan, Western Qin and the Northern Wei dynasties, as mentioned above. The Tangut, on the other hand, were nomadic people regarded mostly to be related to the Qiang tribe with bloodline links to the ruling classes of the Xianbei. They eventually occupied lands and settled in the regions of present-day Ningxia, Gansu and Shaanxi provinces. The ancestral Qiangs were peoples who lived along the mountainous fringes of the northern and eastern Tibetan plateau.

Many of the nomadic tribes that formed the core of the regional dynasties during the period of dynastic proliferation, in the main, were unfamiliar with bureaucratic administrative system of governance and lacked agrarian skills. Yet in time they learned to adopt the local Chinese methods and administrative infrastructure to an extent that within two centuries they successfully produced a multiculturally ethnically mixed functional society. And in 581 AD General Yang Jian seized authority over the northern and southern dynasties and consolidated China again under one dynasty that came to be known as the Sui dynasty.

Historically, the west-east course of the Yangtze River often defined the political boundaries between the vacillating Chinese northern and southern dynasties. During the Spring and Autumn period of Imperial China the homeland of the Shu Han tribe lay along the western part of the river covering the areas of modern Sichuan and western Hubei while the Chu occupied areas around the central portion of the river's course corresponding to eastern Hubei, Hunan, Jiangxi and southern Anhui. Along the eastern portion of the river's course were the homelands of the Wu and the Yue of what are today Shanghai and the provinces of Jiangsu and Zhejiang.

During the Han period, Yangtze's course became increasingly important for China's agricultural economy as irrigation canal systems were expanded to meet the increased demand for agricultural produce and for their transport. Canal expansions included the most famous irrigation canal called the Dujiangyan system built during the Warring States period in 256 BC near the ancient city of Chengdu in Sichuan province. It is not difficult, therefore, to describe the Yangtze River basin along with the other two basins of the rivers Yellow and the Wei, as being the core areas within which the history of China was unfolded. The thirteenth century famous traveller Marco Polo of Venice, then Europe's greatest seaport, described the Yangtze as follows:

> I assure you that this river runs for such a distance and through so many regions and there are so many cities on its banks that truth to tell, in the amount of shipping it carries and the total volume and value of its traffic, it exceeds all the rivers of the Christians put together and their seas into the bargain.[23]

Sui Period (AD 581-618)

The short-lived Sui dynasty produced China's most glorious period of cultural and economic sophistication, and its legacy had held China in high esteem for a considerable length of time amongst its neighbouring nations. The Sui in effect set the foundations for the coming of the renowned Tang dynasty that was to last for three centuries. Yang Jian mentioned above, though a member of a simple northern tribal clan of mixed Chinese heritage, was a far-sighted man of vision thus focused his efforts on consolidating China into one unified nation. He put an end to four centuries of disunity, and enforced a structured administrative government that was later to serve the Tang dynasty throughout their period of reign. His successor Yangdi, who assumed power in 604 AD, utilized Yang Jian's administrative infrastructure already in place to implement his agenda on economic growth. This included the connection of minor often derelict networking canals into one major waterway that extended from Beijing to Hangzhou. It came to be known as the 'Grand Canal.' It linked all the economic power-houses in the north with those in the south and integrated the transportation of goods and services. Cultural exchange between the north and the south was also facilitated by means of the canal, which greatly aided the promotion of art and literature. Unfortunately, however, Yangdi's political interests turned far beyond the borders of China. He led disastrous military campaigns in Korea which ultimately bankrupted his court and led to his demise.

Tang Period (AD 618-907) – The Second Empire

The period of Tang dynasty's rule was a time when China's cultural sophistication and economic prosperity reached new heights.[24] Its emperors actively pursued and expanded foreign trade opportunities, promoted education and literature and allowed foreign religions to flourish in China. Most notable of its poets included the distinguished Li Bo, Wang Wei, Du Fu and Po Chu Yi. The latter is remembered for his most famous poem 'Song of Everlasting Sorrow,' which immortalized the fateful love affair between Emperor Xuanzong (712-756 AD) and his concubine Yang Guifei. The poem, included below, is not only a eulogy on the emperor's sorrowful love affair, but is also the poet's magnificent rendition of Tang history that reflects upon the dynasty's courtly life, cultural practices and of its submission to the ravages of war:

> China's Emperor yearning, for beauty that shakes a kingdom
> Reigned for many years, searching but not finding,
> Until a child of the Yang, hardly yet grown,
> Raised in the inner chamber, unseen by anybody,
> But with heavenly graces that could not be hidden
>
> Was chosen one day for the Imperial household.
> If she turned her head and smiled she cast a deep spell,
> Beauties of Six Palaces vanished into nothing.
> Hair's cloud, pale skin, shimmer of gold moving,
> Flowered curtains protected on cool spring evenings
> Those nights were too short. That sun too quick in rising.
>
> The emperor neglected the world from that moment,
> Lavished his time on her in endless enjoyment.
> She was his springtime mistress, and his midnight tyrant.
> Though there were three thousand ladies all of great beauty,
> All his gifts were devoted to one person.
>
> Li Palace rose high in the clouds.
> The winds carried soft magic notes,
> Songs and graceful dances, string and pipe music.
> He could never stop himself from gazing at her.
>
> But the Earth reels. War drums fill East Pass,
> Drown out 'The Feathered Coat and Rainbow Skirt.'
> Great Swallow Pagoda and Hall of Light,
> Are bathed in dust – the army fleeing Southwards.
> Out there Imperial banners, wavering, pausing
> Until by the river forty miles from West Gate,

Historical Perspectives – Imperial China

The army stopped. No one would go forward,
Until horses' hooves trampled willow eyebrows.
Flower on a hairpin. No one to save it.
Gold and jade phoenix. No one retrieved it.
Covering his face the Emperor rode on.
Turned to look back at that place of tears,
Hidden by a yellow dust whirled by a cold wind.

As Shu waters flow green, Shu mountains show blue,
His majesty's love remained, deeper than the new.
White moon of loneliness, cold moon of exile.
Bell-chimes in evening rain were bronze-edged heartbeats.
So when the dragon-car turned again northwards
The Emperor clung to Ma-Wei's dust, never desiring
To leave that place of memories and heartbreak.
Where is the white jade in heaven and earth's turning?

Lakes and gardens are still as they have been,
T'ai-yi's hibiscus, Wei-yang's willows.
A flower-petal was her face, a willow-leaf her eyebrow,
How could it not be grief just to see them?

Plum and pear blossoms blown on spring winds
Maple trees ruined in rains of autumn.
Palaces neglected, filled with weeds and grasses,
Mounds of red leaves spilled on un-swept stairways.

Burning the midnight light he could not sleep,
Bells and drums tolled the dark hours,
The Ocean of Heaven bright before dawn,
The porcelain mandarin birds frosted white,
The chill covers of kingfisher blue,
Colder and emptier, year by year.
And the loved spirit never returning.

A Taoist priest of Ling-chun rode the paths of Heaven
He with his powerful mind knew how to reach the Spirits.
The Courtiers troubled by the Emperor's grieving,
Asked the Taoist priest if he might find her.
He opened the sky-routes, swept the air like lightning,
Looked everywhere, on earth and in heaven,
Scoured the Great Void, and the Yellow Fountains,

Treasures of the Silk Road

But failed in either to find the one he searched for.
Then he heard tales of a magic island
In the Eastern Seas, enchanted, eternal,
High towers and houses in air of five colours,
Perfect Immortals walking between them,
Among them one, they called The Ever Faithful,
With her face, of flowers and of snow.

She left her dreams, rose from her pillow,
Opened mica blind and crystal screen,
Hastening, unfastened, clouded hair hanging,
Her light cap unpinned, ran along the pavement.
A breeze in her gauze, flowing with her movement,
As if she danced 'Feathered Coat and Rainbow Skirt.'
So delicate her jade face, drowned with tears of sadness,
Like a spray of pear flowers, veiled with springtime rain.

She asked him to thank her love, her eyes gleaming,
He whose form and voice she lost at parting.
Her joy had ended in Courts of the Bright Sun,
Moons and dawns were long in Faerie Palace.
When she turned her face to look back earthwards
And see Ch'ang-an - only mist and dust-clouds.
So she found the messenger her lover's gifts
With deep feeling gave him lacquer box, gold hairpin,

Keeping one half of the box, one part of the hairpin,
Breaking the lacquer, splitting the gold.

'Our spirits belong together, like these precious fragments,
Sometime, in earth or heaven, we shall meet again.'
And she sent these words, by the Taoist, to remind him
Of their midnight vow, secret between them.
'On that Seventh night, of the Herd-boy and the Weaver,[*]
In the silent Palace we declared our dream was
To fly together in the sky, two birds on the same wing,
To grow together on the earth, two branches of one tree.'

Earth fades, Heaven fades, at the end of days.
But Everlasting Sorrow endures always.

****

* The Herd-boy and the Weaver Girl are the stars in the constellation Eagle, and Vega in the constellation Lyra. They are lovers separated by the Milky Way. She is allowed to visit him once a year on the seventh night of the seventh month, the first month of autumn, when she passes across the heaven as a meteor.

During the reign of the second Tang emperor, Taizong (627-649 AD), the network of China's economic base extended from India and Central Asia in the West to Korea and Japan in the east.[25] His capital Chang'an (Xi'an) became China's gateway to unprecedented wealth and a magnet for foreign merchants, monks and students but more importantly for the embassies of many nations, in particular, of the rival Persian and Byzantine empires.[26] This cosmopolitan atmosphere of the capital encouraged the exchange of information and knowledge to an extent that the Tang legal code and the characters of the Chinese language (pictographs) became China's most important exports to Korea and Japan. Moreover, with the influx of many foreign nationals, who enjoyed the prevailing openness and the relaxed attitudes in the capital, came the indtroduction of several eclectic religions such as Nestorianism, Manichaeism and Zoroastrianism. Yet there was room for the import of Judaism by Jewish merchants and Islam by Muslim Arab missionaries and merchants. Moreover, although some elements of Buddhist beliefs were brought to China in 148 AD, the faith only began to be established in China on a firmer footing beginning in the fourth century AD. But during the Tang dynasty Buddhism found its golden age and enjoyed royal patronage from successive emperors. Briefly, by way of introduction, Nestorianism was considered a heretical Christian sect named after Nestorius, a Syrian ecclesiastic of the fifth century who was the patriarch of Constantinople. He denied the validity of the One Nature person of Christ and held that Christ possessed two natures, one Human and the other Divine. Manichaeism, which thrived between the third and seventh centuries, was propagated by the prophet Mani (AD 210-276) whose teachings were a mixture of Mediterranean and Semitic belief systems that defined the universe as a struggle between a good spiritual world of light and an evil material world of darkness in which light will eventually triumph. Zoroastrianism (synonymous with Mazdaism) was a religion that reflected the ancient Iranian religious background of the prophet Zarathustra (Zoroaster) who exalted the Parthian deity Ahura Mazda as the supreme divine authority. As a monotheistic religion, Zoroastrianism shared formative links with both Western and Eastern religious traditions. Buddhism, on the other hand, with its origins in north-eastern India around the fifth century BC, is a system of beliefs and practices based on the teachings of Siddhartha Sakyamuni Gautama (also known as the Buddha 'the awakened one'), which instructs the path to liberation from the life's cycle of suffering, death and rebirth until Nirvana - a state of eternal bliss - is achieved. It is imbued with a psycho-philosophical approach to the conditioning of the mind in order that a transcendent state of harmonious and a contented mode of existence are realized until Nirvana is achieved.

Following the death of Emperor Taizong in 649 AD, his royal court eventually fell into the hands of his talented and most capable concubine; Wu Zetian. She entered the court of Taizong at the age of thirteen and quickly became the favourite concubine of the emperor. But upon Taizong's death she first became the concubine then the wife of Taizong's son and successor, Emperor Gaozong, and gave birth to four sons, Li Zhong, Li Xi'an, Zhongzong (or Zhanghuai) and Ruizong. She is reputed to have killed her eldest son Li Zhong to frame Gaozong's empress Wang for the evil deed. Also, she had forced the exile of her second eldest son Li Xi'an to facilitate her claim to the throne. After the death of Gaozong in 683 AD, Wu Zetian ruled from behind the scenes first in the name of Zhongzong, who was later compelled to commit suicide, then later in the name of her youngest son Ruizong. She ultimately usurped the throne from Ruizong in 690 AD by first deposing him and then forcing him to commit suicide. She proclaimed herself 'Shengshen', the first woman ever to use the title of empress, and named her ruling period 'the Zhou dynasty' in honour of her father's small fief. Wu Zetian occupied the throne as China's sole empress from 690-705 AD. Fearing her grandson Prince Yide (Li Chongrun), Zhongzong's eldest son, and her granddaughter, Princess Yongtai, that one day they might pose a challenge to her throne, it is believed she took the decision to put them to death.

Wu Zetian shares the tomb of her emperor husband Gaozong in a mausoleum situated on the summit of Liangshan in an area known as Qianling some 80 kilometres north-west of Xi'an. Two columns mark the southern entrance to the mausoleum where mythical winged horses are the first of the animal sculptures that line the approach to the tomb. A stone staele on the site carries an inscription attributed to Wu Zetian that describes the achievements of her husband Gaozong. A second satele with carved dragons remains curiously without inscriptions (the Blank Tablet) and is believed was erected by Wu Zetian for future generations to record her assessed deeds and achievements.

Not far from the mausoleum there are numerous underground tombs and the most important of which are those of the nineteen-year old Prince Yide and the seventeen-year old Princess Yongtai. Their chambers are richly decorated with colourful murals depicting scenes from Tang life. Princess Yongtai, named Li Xian Hui – who called herself Nong Hui - was the seventh daughter of Emperor Zhongzong. In 700 AD Yongtai at the age of sixteen was married to Wu Yanji whose father was Wu Zetian's nephew, and only a year after her marriage she was cruelly put to death by her formidable grandmother, the empress. The walls of her resting chamber are adorned with fine paintings which depict scenes of her courtly life accompanied by elegantly dressed young maidens of honour. The chamber of her underground tomb is 87.5 metres in length, 3.9 meters in width and 3.7 metres in height with its ceiling 13 metres below the surrounding external surface level.

The Tang dynasty reached its zenith of success under its emperor Xuanzong (712-756 AD), who was called 'Ming-Huang' (Brilliant Emperor). Just before his last year of reign in 755 AD he suffered a rebellion led by An Lushan, an ethnic military commander from Sogdiana (in parts of present-day Uzbekistan and north-eastern Turkmenistan), who was the adopted son of the emperor's favourite concubine, Yang Guifei. It was finally suppressed after a decade of struggle that required the military aid received from Uyghur (Uygur/Uighur) tribes – Turkic-speaking people with roots in Mongolia and Central Asia whose descendants now live mostly in Xinjiang province.[27] But the Uyghur extracted a heavy toll from the emperor by demanding vast payments and rewards as compensation for their help. The cost of suppressing the rebellion thus had been so great that it had discouraged the emperor from resuming his role as a ruler, and being infatuated with Yang Guifei he had increasingly sought solace in her embraces. Eventually the emperor abdicated in favour of his son, Suzong who ruled until 762 AD. Yang Guifei, as the culprit for these misfortunes in her role as the mother of An Lushan, was killed by one of the emperor's body guards. Subsequently, mournful Xuangzong fell into a deep depression and died in 762 AD in Chengdu in Sichuan province where he had retreated.

The significance of the An Lushan rebellion had far greater implications for the Tang dynasty than just the abdication of its emperor. China as early as the Han period had committed significant military presence in the Tarim basin in present-day Xinjiang province to protect its Silk Road trading interests. But the rebellion of An Lushan had forced the dynasty to withdraw its troops from the many western outposts in order to bolster the defence of the interior regions. The vacuum left at the outposts by this withdrawal was quickly filled by Tibetan forces which eventually took control of the whole basin by 791 AD. The Tibetans were eventually driven out from the Tarim basin by the Uyghur in 851 AD and continue to live in the region to the present day. It was not until 1759 AD that China was able to reclaim this territory and hold it politically.

The Tang dynasty survived for a further century and a half but power gradually shifted into the hands of the regional military commanders who entertained separatist tendencies for their own independence thus once again setting into motion the fragmentation of the empire - a cyclic scenario which had plagued China throughout its history. China again entered a period of economic turbulence peppered with the constant fear of barbarian invasions from the north of its borders. This precipitated mass migrations of the sedentary Chinese populations away from the northern borders in their effort to seek safer havens further south. Consequently, China's economic centre shifted from the Yellow river basin in the north to the safer and temperate regions of the south. But the resentment of the common people and particulary the gievances of the farmers against the inability of the government to bring stability, exploded in the form of several rebellions. Many improvished farmers, tax-burdened landowners and merchants joined forces with regional officers and formed the bases for anti-government movements. One of the most notable leaders of these rebellions was Huang Chao who seriously weakened the mighty Tang dynasty. He died in 884 AD but within a few decades of these ribellions, the renowned and sophisticated Tang dynasty came to an end bringing upon the Chinese empire yet again a period of fragmentation and the beginning of the Five Dynasties period.

Song/Sung Period (AD 960-1279) – The Third Empire

In 960 AD, following the collapse of the Tang dynasty, Zhao Kuangyin, a former military officer, founded the Northern Song dynasty with its capital set in Kaifeng in Henan province. Later the capital was moved to Hangzhou in Zhejiang province and came to be known as the Southern Song dynasty. Under the Song dynasty, China was once again unified and was able to maintain stability for more than three centuries by curbing the power of regional officers who had contributed to the downfall of the Tang dynasty.[28] New fiscal policies were put in place by informed ministers, such as Fan Zhongyan and Wang Anshi, who regulated and controlled China's commodity-based economic growth. Paper money was printed for the first time to facilitate commercial trading and merchandizing, especially of porcelain products which had gained ascendancy in the export of durable goods markets. Conflicts with northern tribes were kept at bay mostly by appeasement and economic incentives which had formed the basis for the political stability realized earlier by the Northern Song dynasty. But this precarious peace was eventually broken in 1115 AD by the warring Jurchen from Manchuria. The Jurchen lived in parts of Mongolia but mostly in Manchuria. As a result of their attacks, the reigning emperor of the Song, Huizong (1100-1127 AD), abandoned his capital in Kaifeng and, as mentioned above, fled south to Hangzhou where he established the Southern Song dynasty. The Jurchen were thus able to establish their on empire in the north and came to be known as the Northern Jin dynasty. This dynasty later in 1234 AD was overrun and destroyed by a new wave of invaders who came from yet further north of Jurchen homelands. They were the Mongol under the command of Genghis Khan. Before Genghis Khan, the Mongols were ruled from 1175-1203 AD by the Nestorian Toghril Khan. Genghis Khan was a vassal of Toghril for over a decade, but as recorded by the Venetian Marco Polo, Genghis Khan usurped power when he was refused the hand of Toghril's daughter in marriage and killed Torghil in battle.

The Southern Song court managed to survive until 1276 AD but was finally liquidated by Genghis Khan's grandson Kublai Khan.

Yuan Period (AD 1279-1368)

The Yuan dynasty was officially established by Kublai Khan with Kanbalu (present-day Beijing) as its capital; and in effect it incorporated China into the Mongol Empire.[29] The dynasty ruled rather harshly with an iron fist making clear distinction between the four classes of its population (scholars, farmers, labourers and merchants).[30] This discriminatory application of authority was intended to prevent the assimilation of the minority Mongols into the majority native Chinese population. Though the Mongols adopted the Chinese bureaucratic system of governance, their discriminatory practices went as far as denying employment to the native Chinese in the Mongols' bureaucratic civil services. Nevertheless, with the help of the Chinese wide-ranging trading expertise the Mongols were able to establish extensive trade routes that linked the Near East and the Far East into a single political hegemony. This political strategy facilitated the interchange of aesthetic motifs in art and architecture. More importantly, however, new trading markets were opened in Europe and trading charters were issued to many Europeans, most notably to Venetian and Genoese merchants. Marco Polo was perhaps the first European trading intermediary who served in the court of Kublai Khan. This was a period that allowed opportunities for many to travel not least for artists and historians. Ibn Battuta, who was born in Tangiers and died in Fez (Iran), traveled throughout the length of Asia, mainly within the framework of the Islamic world. He sailed from Calicut - in the northern part of the state of Kerala in southern India - to China on a Chinese vessel, which he recorded was manned by more than 1,000 Chinese sailors; in other words a very large ship indeed. This observation by Ibn Battuta provides us with specific evidence that the Chinese themselves were indeed sailing to India in the mid fourteenth century. He reached China in 1346 AD and praised the Chinese porcelain ware and gave a detailed and fairly accurate description of how they were made. He recorded that the exquisite Chinese porcelain was carried to other countries surrounding China but also to India and the Yemen, and even to the Maghreb, the country of his birth. Under the Yuan dynasty the pottery shapes tended to be massive in scale, large dishes, bowls and tall vases quite different from the delicate and small scale wares of the preceding Song dynasty.

The Mongols were proselytized by the Nestorians when this heretical Christian sect reached China in the seventh century. Although Christianity never achieved a prominent position in the Mongol empire of the Yuan dynasty, the many great khans of this dynasty were raised and educated by Christian mothers and tutors.[31] A major Christian personality among the Mongol was Sokaktani-beki, Genghis Khan's daughter-in-law and mother of the great khans Mongke, Kublai, and Hulagu. Other noteworthy personalities were Tokuz Khatun, wife of Hulagu and the mother of his son Abaqa. Another personality was General Kerbogha who had earned his place in history by laying siege to the city of Antioch and capturing it after the city had fallen to the Crusaders led by the Norman Bohemond, son-in-law of King Philip I of France.

The Yuan dynasty survived intact until 1368 AD but none of the khans

Historical Perspectives – Imperial China

who followed Kublai had the charisma or the strength of authority as did their predecessor. Thus it was inevitable that social unrest and opposition to the foreign rule would entice the majority Chinese to rebellion. This led to the eventual overthrow of the Mongol dynasty in 1368 AD by a group of insurgents led by a peasant named Zhu Yuanzhang.

Ming Period (AD 1368-1644)

From its inception in AD 1368, the Ming dynasty was credited for re-conquering most of the Chinese northern territories periviously lost to the Mongols. They restored Chinese independence from the Mongols and laid the basis for a successful economic foundation by introducing a policy of major public works. Zhu Yuanzhang took the initial charge of governance and set up the dynasty's capital in Nanjing. His policies of national reconstruction were a major step forward for the dynasty's political influence which extended to Mongolia, Manchuria and Vietnam. Major artistic, commercial and diplomatic ventures underscored the grandeur of the Ming culture.[32] Zhu Yuanzhang's reign lasted until 1398 AD, and he is remembered posthumously by reference to his period of rule 'Hongwu' (Great Military Power). The Ming dynasty's third emperor, Cheng Tsu, undertook the additional security for the protection of China's northern frontiers by building the eastern sections of the Great Wall. This addition was a further measure for preventing the return of the 'barbarian' Mongol and the Manchu tribes. During Yongle's reign trading and maritime exploration reached new heights especially under Admiral Zheng He (AD 1371-1435) who commanded large Chinese fleets that reached the western shores of the Indian Ocean and the shores of Arabia and Africa.[33] The development of an urban trading economy reached new heights during this period especially in the regions around the Yangtze River basin. Cash crops, like cotton and tea, became the major agricultural commodities of the basin. However, the impoverishment of the peasants as a result of their economic loss in the face of competing large and efficient agricultural estates created significant discontent amongst this large sector of the Chinese population. Their discontent was reinforced by the urban population which was pressurized by increasing state regulations and taxations. These potentially troublesome social circumstances were exacerbated by the vision of West's trade opportunities in Asia. They pursued their European interests in Asia with vigour and with discrete self-serving agendas. At first in AD 1514 came the Portuguese to the shores of southern China (Canton, Guangzhou) followed by the more assertive Dutch and then the British in AD 1637. Although specific rules were instituted forbidding the Chinese merchants from conducting private trade with foreigners, the Europeans, nonetheless, were undeterred in their pursuit of the lucrative Chinese commercial prospects. The dynasty's concerns were that their coastal trading centres with un-controlled trading links with foreign lands might prove a conduit for generating opposition to the dynasty's stability hence by 1775 AD Canton (Guangzhou in this context) was the only southern port from which legal trade was allowed to be concluded. These social and political stresses imposed on the dynasty's authority collectively and gradually weakened the Ming imperial power. Confronted with the unrest of the populace, the last Ming emperor, Chuang Lieh, took his own life and set the stage for the collapse of his dynasty and the surrender of the state power to the Manchu, who in AD 1644 installed themselves in Beijing as China's new masters.

Qing/Ch'ing Period (Manchu) (AD 1644-1911)

The seventeenth century of the Christian era heralded the Qing rule in China. The princes of this Manchurian dynasty ruled the land for nearly three centuries but not so much as royal sovereigns but, to a large degree, as unwilling partners advancing the commercial ambitions of foreign nations. Amongst these nations with enterpenurial interests in China were Austria, Hungary, France, Germany, Italy, Japan, Russia, Britain, the Dutch and the United States of America. These nations saw China as a lucrative market for their manufactured products hence actively and forcibly entered into trade agreements favourable to their objectives with the passive approval of the ruling Manchu dynasty.

But, by the mid-nineteenth century the political fortunes of the Manchu dynasty looked bleak indeed and continued to deteriorate at an accelerated rate. The economic development of the traditional Chinese agrarian society had come to a halt as a consequence of the limitations of its own man-powered pre-industrial mode of production devoid of modern mechanization. Furthermore, the threat to China's development and industrialization became iminent as Japan's interests in expansionism across the East China Sea were taking form. Likewise, the Russians from the north saw their opportunity to take their lion's share from the lucrative Chinese markets at a time when the gun-powder diplomacy of the European naval forces was reaching new crescendos.

Historical Perspectives – Imperial China

The Qing dynasty's woes were further compounded by the vast and lucritave opium trade with China by the British East India Company. In the early decades of the nineteenth century this trade was causing severe deficits in China's foreign fiscal balance. Although the consumption of opium was banned by the emperor Yongzheng in 1792, by the 1830s China's economy and society were being seriously affected by the huge import of opium. Thus bold economic measures were imposed by China upon the recommendation of an official named Lin Zexu (Lin Tse-hsu) who had constantly opposed the opium imports arriving at the southern port city of Guangzhou in Guangdong province. His forceful opposition to the trade on moral and social grounds was intended to rescue China from certain economic collapse and bankcruptcy. Hence the importation of opium was once again officially banned and trade embargos were placed on European goods. These measures did nothing more than give the British the tacit excuse to retaliate by starting the First Opium War (1839-42 AD) which bombarded south China into submission. It was the outcome of British insistence over their alleged rights to trade Indian-grown opium with China in an open competitive market which had proved a highly profitable business both for Britain and its Indian colony. The British display of their overwhelming military advantages led the Chinese to accept the terms of the 1842 Treaty of Nanjing (Nanking) that dictated trading terms unfavourable to China and compelled it to cede Hong Kong Island to be declared a Crown colony under the jurisdiction of the British Empire. This treaty was the first of the so-called unequal treaties that imposed the creation of four treaty ports along China's eastern seaboard (Shanghai, Ningbo, Xiamen and Fuzhou) as independent and free trading centres declared immune to Chinese trade laws. However, the persistent Chinese sense of superiority and self-confidence against all things foreign, continued to hinder further foreign encroachments into the Chinese markets to the dissatisfaction of the West.[34,35] Frustrated with its efforts to extract further trade concessions unfavourable to the proud Chinese empire, the West in despiration launched the Second Opium War (1857-60 AD). The resulting 1858 Treaty of Tianjin added to the West's commercial advantages in China and established new free-trading ports exempt from Chinese laws. It also granted the West the right to place foreign military bases in mainland China, and freedom for missionaries to travel into China's interior. Moreover, under the terms of the 1860 Treaty of Peking signed on 24 October, Britain acquired Kowloon in mainland China directly across the bay from Hong Kong Island. Prince Gong represented the empire's delegation on behalf of the Qing emperor.

The opium wars fragmented the Chinese economy and left it in disarray. The eventual collapse of the economy sparked off a series of internal rebellions that became the nucleus for failed secessionist movements by the Hui Muslims in the provinces of Yunnan, Gansu and Xinjiang (1855-73 AD). By the late nineteenth century the orchestrated and organized abuse of the Chinese empire by the West for self-serving economic gains had not yet run its full course. Additional major political and territorial concessions continued to be extracted by the West from the outcomes of the two opium wars. In 1884 the French succeeded in defeating the Chinese navy in the South China Sea and ended Vietnam as a Chinese colony.[36] A decade later in the Sino-Japanese War of 1894 China suffered a humiliating defeat at the hands of the Japanese as they attacked and destroyed the much weakened Chinese naval fleet at Shandong's Weihai naval base giving Japan full control of the Bohai Bay. And by the terms of the ensuing Treaty of Shimonoseki China lost part of southern Manchuria and the island of Formosa (modern Taiwan) as war reparations[37] and Korea was ceded to Japan as a protectorate. The decisive turning point in the fortunes of the Qing dynasty came with the 1898 Convention for the Extension of Hong Kong Territory which added the 'New Territories' adjacent to Kowloon to the British possessions as a necessary measure for the defence and development of Hong Kong harbour.

European powers having witnessed a nation in tatters took further advantage of China's circumstances and divided China into zones of interests overseen and managed by Western legations placed in Peking (Beijing). The divisions included the annexation of the port city of Chiaochow (Qingdao) in Shandong province by Germany in 1897 followed a year later in 1898 with the annexation of Weihai (Shandong province) by the British, the port of Dalian (Liaoning province) by the Russians and the port city of Guangzhou in Guangdong province by the French.

The severity of the European exploitation of the Qing dynasty and its empire's resources left the Chinese masses progressively impoverished which ultimately gave rise to the rather sanguine Boxer Uprising (Rebellion). This was a movement aimed specifically against the imperialist foreign expansionists and the missionary evangelists in China. The core of the rebellion was directed by a village sect based in the eastern province of Shandong which saw in their practice of the martial arts and calisthenics (hence the Western term the Boxer) the remedy to their impoverished environment and deteriorating life styles.

They believed their training in the martial arts would ultimately bring forth spirit soldiers from the heavens to assist them in purifying China from the foreign devils. However, the rebellion was successfully quelled by forces of a European alliance despite the partial support it received from the imperial court. The failure of the rebellion forced the reigning empress Dowager Cixi (Tsu Hsi) in Peking to sue for peace. The Boxer Rebellion spelled the beginning of the end of the Manchu rule which came to a close a decade later in 1912.[38]

Treasures of the Silk Road

Regional maps of imperial Chinese dynasties

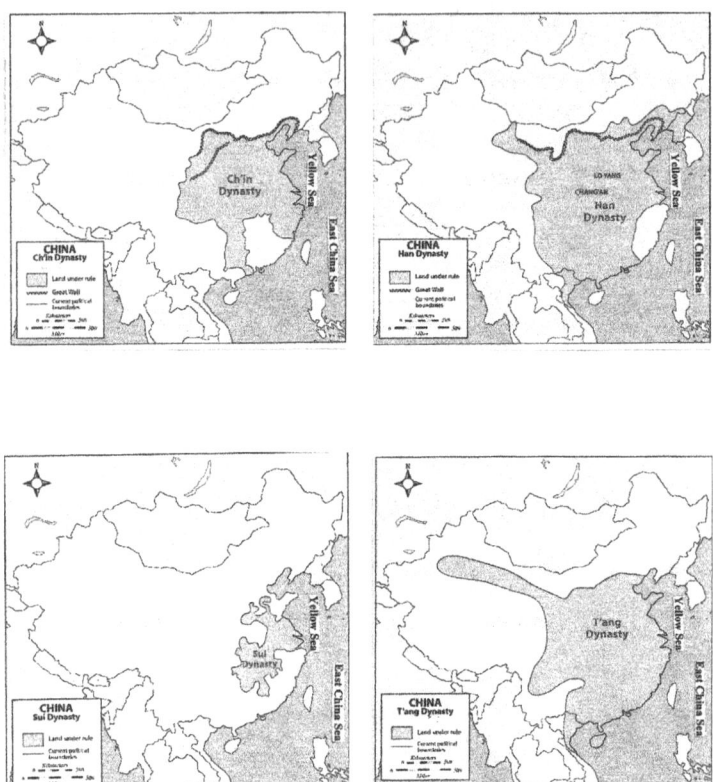

Historical Perspectives – Imperial China

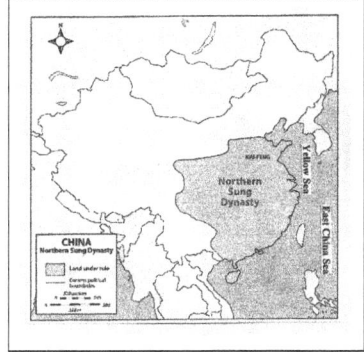

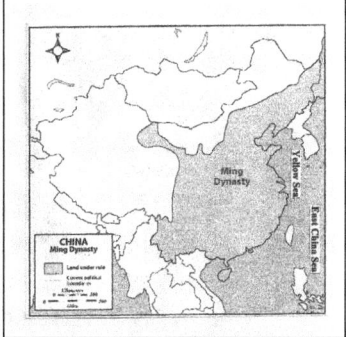

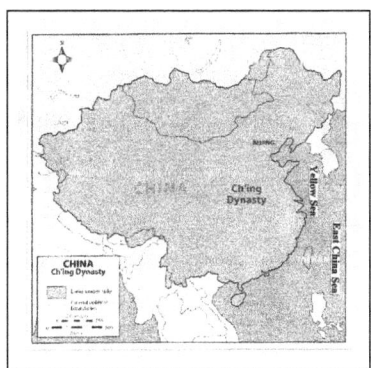

Treasures of the Silk Road

Figure 1. The ceramic art of China

Top row, left to right: Square vase, Ch'ing dynasty, Kang Xi period (1662-1722); Temple vase, Yuan dynasty (1279-1368); Vase of Tsun Form; Shang dynasty (16th-11th century BC).

Bottom row, left to right: Famille Rose vase, Ch'ing dynasty, Chen Lung period (1736-1795); Plum Blossom vase, Ch'ing dynasty, Kang Xi period (1662-1722); Bottle vase, Ming dynasty, Hsuan Te period (1426-1435).

Historical Perspectives – Imperial China

Figure 2. The ceramic art of China

Top row, left to right: Rouleau vase, Ch'ing dynasty, Kang Xi period (1682); Covered vase, Ch'ing dynasty, Tao Kuang period (1821-1850); Export porcelain vase, Ming dynasty, Portuguese period (1557).

Bottom row, left to right: Double Gourd vase, Ming dynasty (1522-1566); Mei-Ping vase, Song dynasty (960-1279); Vase with Handles, Han dynasty (202 BC - AD 220).

References

1. Li, X., *Eastern Zhou and Qin Civilizations*. K. C. Chang (trans.), Yale University Press, New Haven (1985).
2. Fairbank, J. K. and Goldman, M., *China: A New History*. Harvard University Press, Cambridge (2006).
3. Bray, F., Agriculture. In J. Needham (ed.), *Science and Civilization in China*. Cambridge University Press, Cambridge (1984).
4. Gernet, J., A History of Chinese Civilization. 2nd edition, Cambridge University Press, Cambridge (1997).
5. Bodde, D., The State and Empire of Ch'in. In *The Cambridge History of China. Vol. 1, The Ch'in and Han Empires: 221 BC-AD 220*. D. Twitchett and M. Loewe (eds.), Cambridge University Press, Cambridge (1986).
6. Li, Y., *The First Emperor of China: The Poilitics of Historiography*. International Arts and Sciences Press, White Plains, New York (1975).
7. Hansen, V., *The Open Empire: A History of China to 1600*. Norton Press, New York (2000).
8. Sautman, B., Myths of Descent, Racial Nationalism and Ethnic Minorities in the People's Republic of China. In F. Dikötter (ed.), *The Construction of Racial Identities in China and Japan: Historical and Contemporary Perspectives*. Hurst and Co., London (1997).
9. Jenner, W. J. F., *Race and History in China*. New Left Review, 11 September/October (2001).
10. Zhao, S., *A Nation-State by Construction: Dynamics of Modern Chinese Nationalism*. Stanford University Press, Stanford, California (2004).
11. Hulsewé, A. F. P. and Loewe, M. A. N., *China in Central Asia: The Early Stage 125 BC- AD 23: an annotated translation of chapters 61 and 96 of the History of the Former Han Dynasty*. E. Brill Publications, Leiden (1979).
12. Sima Qian, *The Records of the Grand Historian: Han Dynasty II*, revised edition, B. Watson (trans.), Columbia University Press, New York (1993).
13. Boulnois, L., *Silk Road: Monks, Warriors and Merchants on the Silk Road*. H. Loveday (trans.), Odyssey Books and Guides, Hong Kong (2004).
14. Sims-Williams, N., *Indo-Iranian Languages and Peoples*. Proceedings of the British Academy, 116. Oxford University Press, Oxford (2003).

15. Mallory, J. P. and Adams, D. Q., *The Oxford Introduction to Proto-Indo- European and the Proto-Indo-European World*. Oxford University Press, Oxford (2006).
16. Esin, E., *The Horse in Turkic Art*. Central Asian Journal ,10 (1965).
17. Hill, J. E., *Through the Jade Gate to Rome: A Study of the Silk Routes during The Later Han Dynasty; 1st to 2nd Centuries CE*. Book Surge, Charleston, South Carolina (2009).
18. Fairbank, J. K. and Goldman, M., *China: A New History*. Harvard University Press, Cambridge (2006).
19. Yu, Y. S., Han Foreign Relations. In *The Cambridge History of China*. Vol. I: *The Ch'in and Han Empires: 221 BC-AD 220*. D. Twitchett and M. Loewe (eds.), Cambridge University Press, Cambridge (1986).
20. Wang, Z., *History of Wei, Jin, Southern and Northern Dynasties*. China Press, Beijing (2007).
21. Chen, S. A., *Tuobas Cultural and Political Heritage*. Journal of Asian History (1996).
22. Liu, X., The History of Xianbei. Nantian Press, Taipei (1994).
23. Elvin, M., *The Pattern of the Chinese Past*. Eyre Methuen, London (1973).
24. Lovell, J., *The Great Wall: China Against the World 1000 BC-AD 2000*. Atlantic Books, London 920060.
25. Wang, Q., *Emperor Taizong of the Tang*. Chinese Social Sciences Press, Beijing (2008)
26. Maitra, K. M., *A Persian Embassy to China*. An extract from *Zubdatu't Tawarikh of Hafiz Abru*, K. M. Maitra (trans.), Lahore (1934).
27. Mackerras, C. (ed. and trans.), *The Uighur Empire According to the Tang Dynastic Histories: A Study in Sino-Uyghur Relations 744-840 AD*. University of South Carolina Press, Durham, South Carolina (1972).
28. Gernet, J., A History of Chinese Civilization. 2nd edition, Cambridge University Press, Cambridge (1997).
29. Jackson, P., *The Mongols and the West: 1221-1410*. Pearson Education Ltd., Edinburgh (2005).
30. Allsen, T. T., *Mongol Imperialism. The policies of the Grand Qan Möngke in China, Russia, and the Islamic Lands, 1251-1259*. University of California Press, Berkeley (1987).
31. Dawson, C. (ed.), *The Mongol Mission. Narratives and Letters of the Franciscan Missionaries in Mongolia and China in the Thirteenth and Fourteenth Centuries*. Sheed and Ward Publications, New York (1955).

32. Clunas, C., *Superfluous Things: Material Culture and Social Status in Early Modern China*. Polity Press, Cambridge (1991).
33. Dreyer, E. L., *Zheng He: China and the Oceans in the Early Ming Dynasty, 1405-1433*. Pearson Longman, New York (2007).
34. Wong, R. B., *China Transformed: Historical Change and the Limits of European Experience*. Cornell University Press, Ithaca (2000).
35. Pye, L. W., *The Spirit of Chinese Politics*. Harvard University Press, Cambridge Massachusetts (1992).
36. Chapuis, O., *A history of Vietnam: from Hong Bang to Tu Duc*. Greenwood Publishing Group, Westport, Connecticut (1995).
37. Hoare, J.E., *Japan's Treaty Ports and Foreign Settlements: The Uninvited Guests, 1858–1899*. Routledge, London (1995).
38. Crossley, P. K., Orphan *Warriors: Three Manchu Generations and the End of the Qin World*. Princeton University Press, Princeton, New Jersey (1991).

Chapter Three

Ancient Central Asia

In the following chapters there will be many occasions when the historic territories of Sogdiana, Bactria, Gandhara and Ferghana in ancient Central Asia will be discussed, especially in regards to their impact on the development of China's trade and religious past keeping in mind that the most basic diference between the peoples who lived in these parts of Asia was linguistic. There were speakers of Iranian dialects and those who used one of the many Turkic languages. This distinction persists to the presnt day between the Iranian-speaking Tajik and the Turkish-speaking Uzbek. In the seventh century, generally speaking, the Iranian speakers were the inhabitants of the towns and villages surrounding the cultivated lands and who were mostly engaged in trade and commerce as opposed to the Turkish speakers being the region's nomadic pasturalists. Therefore it is prudent early at this point to become relatively familiar with the histories of Sogdiana, Bactria, Gandhara and Ferghana, albeit briefly, in order that our comprehension of their relevance is more substantially enriched.

The sedentary populations of eastern Iran and Central Asia were fundamentally Iranian in culture long before the advent of Islam; therefore a cursery listing of the empires of Iran of antiquity that ruled in eastern Iran and Central Asia, collectively known as the Persian Empire, is quite appropriate at this point. The Persian Empire was a series of empires that ruled over the Iranian plateau, western Asia, Central Asia and the Caucasus. It began with the founding of the Achaemenid Empire in 550 BC by King Cyrus the Great after his conquest of Media (the mountainous land of the Medes extending from the plains of Mesopotamia to the central deserts of Iran with ancient Hamadan its capital). Table 2 lists the powers that constituted the Persian Empire.

Table 2. The early ruling powers of the Iranian plateau

Achaemenid Empire	550-330 BC
Seleucid Empire	330-150 BC
Partian Empire	247 BC-226 AD
Sasanid Empire	226-651 AD
Arab conquest of Iran	637-651 AD
Umayyad Caliphate rule	651-750 AD
Abbasid Caliphate rule	750-1258 AD
Samanid Empire (as vassals of the caliphate)	819-999 AD
Seljuk conquest of Iran	circa 1000 AD

The Parthian Empire, also known as the Arsacid Empire, originated in Parthia (western Khurasan; north-east Iran), which was a satrapy first of the Achaemenids and then of the Seleucids. Its founder Arsaces I was a leader of the Parni tribe which successfully recovered Parthia from the Seleucids in 247 BC and ruled it until his death in 211 BC. His son Arsaces II (211-191 BC) was unable to maintain independence and was overcome by Seleucid overlordship and made a vassal to Antiochus III but Priapatios (191-176 BC) son of Arsaces II, regained Parthian independence after Antiochus was defeated by the Romans in 189 BC. Parthia then began a slow expansion which later under the leadership of Mithradates I (171-138 BC) grandson of Priapatios, became a major power and created an empire that included Mesopotamia in the west and Central Asia in the east.

By way of an introduction to the four historic territories mentioned above we may repeat that Sogdiana was part of the eastern Iranian-Central Asian area of antiquity. The people of Sogdiana (Sogdians) were in the main traders and merchants whose colonies could be found in Mongolia, in the Western Regions of China and in the interior of the Middle Kingdom itself.[1] They were Iranian in origin and who had migrated and settled in the fertile lands between the rivers Jaxartes (Syr Darya) and Oxus (Amu Darya). Their borders to the east were confined by Ferghana and Bactria.

Ancient Central Asia

The dominant religion in Sogdiana in the seventh century was Mazdaism but Manichaeism, Nestorian Christianity and Buddhism were also practiced. Although Buddhist centres were flourishing in Sogdiana's neighbouring-state of Bactria, the Huns' invasion* of Bactria in the early third century AD soon to be followed by their conquest of Sogdiana prevented the full flowering of Buddhism in Sogdiana.² As we shall see later in the chapters to follow, the Chinese Buddhist pilgrim monks Faxian, Xuanzang and Yijing who passed through Bactria in the fourth, seventh and eighth centuries, respectively, witnessed there the practice of Buddhism by its Turkic rulers in well maintained and active Buddhist monasteries. Yet, essentially in all areas of ancient eastern Iran and Central Asia early Nestorian Christian and Buddhist iconography was not prevalent compared to the Manichaeins who had developed an advanced artistic heritage. Zorostrianism was entirely iconoclastic and there is little evidence that Mazdaism had developed any religious art. There will be further discussions on these subjects in later chapters.

According to Herodotus, the Greek chronicler of the fifth century BC, the Tocharians in the eighth century BC were displaced from their native homelands in Central Asia by their neighbours the Scythians who first migrated towards the Caucasus and settled in the Russian steppes before moving in waves into central Europe. In 331 BC Sogdiana and Bactria were made satrapies to the Greek empire of Alexander the Great. However, towards the end of the second century BC, the Tocharian tribes themselves began to move towards their neighbouring regions within Central Asia and brought with them the Turkic term 'Tocharian' to Bactria. Ferghana was situated directly north of Bactria and bounded by Sogdiana on its west.

---

*The Huns were a group of nomadic people who inhabited regions near the Caspian Sea in 91 AD. They began their migrations in several waves first towards the south-east into Central Asia around 150 AD and then westward towards Europe around 370 AD. as they conquered and ended the Greco-Bactrian kingdom. Consequently, Alexander's Mediterranean Hellenism in Bactria was replaced by the Tocharian shamanistic and partly Buddhist traditions. By the fifth century AD, Bactria's capital Balkh had become a great centre of Buddhist culture which during the succeeding three centuries greatly influenced the development of Buddhism in China.

Ferghana's old capital Chach was first conquered by the Mongols in 565 AD when the first Mongol empire founded in the region of the Altai Mountains expanded towards the west and south-west. It was then that the name of the capital was changed to Tashkent 'Stone City.' At the time of the Muslim conquests of Central Asia in the beginning of the eighth century, Ferghana's population was predominantly Turkic of Iranian cultural heritage.

The fourth territory relevant to our discussion of eastern Iran and Central Asia is Gandhara. It was situated directly south of Bactria and today corresponds to parts of northern Pakistan. Much of Gandharan cultural activities, trade and learning began in the second century AD, nearly four centuries after it had adopted Buddhism as its national religion. Under Buddhist Kushan kings in the fifth century AD, the Gandharans developed a unique form in the art of sculpture which typified what is known today as the Gandharan Art. But because of Gandhara's proximity to India, by the seventh century Buddhism in many of its major communities had lost much of their strength especially in the lowland fronteir regions in the east where resurgent Hinduism was replacing Buddhism. The Hinduism influences in Gandhara were strong enough to the extent that conquering Muslims in the eighth century had much difficulty with combating and containing the Hindu resistance.

Sogdiana سُغد

Ancient Sogdiana, which essentially occupied lands in modern Uzbekistan and Turkemistan, is first mentioned in the Zoroastrian sacred book Avesta and also appears in the records of the Achaemenid Persia as being a satrapy (vassal territory) of the Persian Empire during the reign of King Darius I (519 BC). The twilight of the Persian Empire however descended in 333 BC with the victory of Alexander the Great of Macedonia over the last Persian king, Darius III. They met at a pass near the village of Issus in Cilicia (present-day south-eastern Turkey) in a battle in which Alexander's forces prevailed against Darius's larger army. Darius, badly out-maneuvered by Alexander, retreated to fight another day. Alexander proceeded to take Egypt and Syria and crossed the Mesopotamian rivers, the Tigris and Euphrates. They met again in battle in 331 BC near Mosul (in present-day northern Iraq); this time however Alexander won a decisive victory and completely annihilated

Ancient Central Asia

the Persian army.³ This victory was the impulse that opened the way for Greek primacy in Asia. Sogdiana was soon taken by Alexander in 329 BC and his armies ultimately reached India in 326 BC. After the premature death of young Alexander at the age of 33 in 323 BC, Seleucus I Nicator (358-280 BC) took Asia Minor, Syria, Babylonia, Egypt, Persia, Sogdiana and Bactria as his share of the divided Hellenic empire.⁴

The history of Sogdiana is mostly a series of occupations by invading nomadic peoples who came after the Greeks and who occupied the land and then left in pursuit of new conquests.⁵ The first to supplant the Greeks from Sogdiana in the early decades of the second century BC were the Yuezhi people who had left their adopted lands in the Tarim basin, crossed the Tian Shan Mountains and had settled in the regions north of Bactria (in the southern parts of present-day Kazakhstan). They ultimately moved south and conquered Bactria in 124 BC before moving west and taking Sogdiana. During the ensuing centuries, especially in the second and the third centuries of the Christian era, Sogdiana emerged as a centre of commercial activities that fostered the growth of trade in Chinese silk and porcelain. The Sogdians soon became major traders and merchants of the Silk Road travelling and maintaining trade connections from Chang'an (Xi'an) in China to Greek Constantinople in the west. However in the regional struggle for conquests, Sogdiana became a repeat victim to invading tribes seeking new conquests. The successful trading activities of the Sogdian's were first disrupted when the Huns of Central Asia invaded Sogdiana in the third century AD. The Huns were followed by the Hephthalites (White Huns) in the fifth century, and eventually by the Mongolian Turks in the sixth century. In the ninth century, during a brief rule by the Uyghurs, the ancient Sogdian cities of Suyab and Talas renewed their reputation as two principal hubs in the worldwide commercial trade of silk. They dominated the trade on the Silk Road to near monopoly especially from the sixth to the ninth centuries.Thus they became the magnet that attracted to Sogdiana peoples from many cultures as diverse as Arabs, Armenians and Europeans. Understandably, this conglomurations of peoples with diverse cultures led Sogdiana into becoming a crucible of many faiths. Its original Persian Zoroastrian heritage was replaced partly by Manichaeism which had found a sympathetic ear in Sogdiana after the persecution of the Zoroastrians in Persia by the Sasanian dynasty (224–651 AD). By the end of the first millennium of the Christian era, Islam became the dominant faith in

Sogdiana brought there by the conquests of the Arabs in the seventh and the eighth centuries AD.

Bactria باختر

Bactria was the ancient Greek name for the region of Bactra with Balkh its capital. Bactria's lands in Central Asia occupied the region directly east of the north-south flowing river Amu Darya (Oxus River) and extended south to northern Afghanistan. This region today corresponds to lands in parts of northern Afghanistan, eastern Turkmenistan and most of Tajikistan. During the reign of King Cyrus the Great of Persia in the sixth century BC, Bactria was a satrapy (vassal state) of the Persian Empire. However, it was lost to the Greeks when Alexander the Great defeated Darius III in 331 BC.[6] In the decades that followed, Greek rulers in Central Asia founded and expanded a regional kingdom that came to be known as the Greco-Bactrian Kingdom. It minted its own Greco-Roman coins, especially during the reign of its kings Euthydemus (230-200 BC), Demetrius I (200-180 BC), Kanishka (151-128 BC) and Khuvishka (circa 128-124 BC).

King Euthydemus and his son Demetrius were the first of the Greco-Bactrian kings to begin a campaign of expansion. In this pursuit they crossed the Pamir Mountains and gradually conquered most of northern Afghanistan. They successfully ended Bactrian submission to the Persian Empire as the empire's satrapy. Successive Bactrian kings followed suit and by crossing the Hindu Kush and the Karakorum mountain ranges they extended the realms of the Bactrian kingdom to the northern reaches of the Indian sub-continent.

Greek reign in Central Asia flourished for three centuries and much of this was a result of the Greek's inherent ability to administer and profit from the regional trading activities, particularly from the overland trade which reached the Indian sub-continent and China via the Silk Road.

> As of Bactria, a part of it lies alongside Aria towards the north, though most of it lies above Aria and to the east of it. And much of it produces everything except oil. The Greeks who caused Bactria to revolt grew so powerful on account of the fertility of the country that they became masters, not only of Bactria and beyond, but also of India, as Apollodorous of Artemita says: and more tribes were

subdued by them than by Alexander.

However the over-expansion of Bactrian bureaucracy and its division into feuding factions many of them with independent civil and military prowesses brought the Greek power in Bactria to its lowest ebb. The possession of individualized state domains by the feuding officials and their greed for increasing the wealth of their personal estates contributed greatly to the weakening of the central power of the Greco-Bactrian kingdom.[7] The slowly deteriorating kingdom survived until it was overrun in 124 BC by the Yuezhi/Kushan people who had come from the Tarim basin across the Tian Shan Mountains and had settled in the regions north of Bactria, in the southern parts of present-day Kazakhstan.[8]

During the reign of Darius I, Parthia was a vassal state to Achaemenid Persia. Its territory spanned across the eastern halves of present-day Uzbekistan and Turkmenistan and also northern Afghanistan. One of its puppet governors named Phrataphernes had at one time fought against the armies of Alexander the Great. During his governance, Parthia had served as a buffer state between Bactria and the Yuezhi/Kushan tribes north and west of the Tian Shan Mountains. But in 124 BC, in their bid for conquests, the Yuezhi had secured a decisive victory in a battle against the Parthian king Artabanus I and thus had paved the way for the Yuezhi advance into Bactria.

It was at this point in history, after the Yuezhi conquest of the Greco-Bactrian kingdom that we begin to witness the events leading to the birth of the Silk Road. In the previous chapter the mission of Emperor Wudi's envoy to Central Asia headed by Zhang Qian was discussed. Now we can see how Zhang's experiences during his travels must have intermingled with the conglomeration of the commercial pursuits undertaken by the sedentary as well as the conquering tribes of Sogdiana and Bactria. This no doubt had enriched his vision of the trading potential China could achieve with its neighbours across China's western frontiers. The following is a quote from the *Hanshu:*

> The Son of Heaven on hearing all this reasoned thus: Ferghana (Dayuan) and the possessions of Bactria (Daxia) and Parthia (Anxi) are large countries, full of rare things, with a population living in fixed abodes and given to occupations somewhat identical with those of the Chinese people, but with weak armies, and placing great value on

the rich produce of China.

Gandhara گَند هاٗرآ

The ancient kingdom of Gandhara was situated in what is today northern Pakistan and southern Afghanistan. Very little is known of Gandhara's clouded ancient Bronze Age history apart from the fact that its early sedentary inhabitants were likely to have been a part of the Indo-European migrations that originated from the regions of the Caspian Sea. In India's folklore mythological tale of Mahabharata, Gandhara is sited as the place where Lord Rama's younger brother Bharata, his sons and their descendents had ruled. Their capital was Pushkalavati and their other principal cities with thriving populations were Takshashila (Taxila) and Purushapura (Peshawar).

The name Gandhara appears in the records of Achaemenid Persia as being a vassal territory (satrapy) of the Persian Empire during the reign of King Darius I (519 BC). But it was recorded as a part of the Persian Empire as early as during the reign of King Cyrus the Great (558-530 BC) whose empire had stretched from Greece to the limits of the entire valley of the Indus River. By the time Darius III came to rule the Persian empire in the fourth century BC, many small regional kingdoms in Gandhara had gradually usurped power from the Persians thus contributing to Alexander the Great's victory over Darius III in 331 BC. Pataliputra (modern Patna) was a vassal state to Alexander's successor Seleucus I Nicator (358-280 BC) whose share of the Hellenic Empire after the death of Alexander had included Asia Minor, Syria, Babylonia, Egypt, Persia and Bactria, as stated earlier. Pataliputra's ruler was Chandragupta, also known as Sandracottus, who later founded the Chandragupta Mauryaian Empire. The vassal state was situated at the confluence of the Ganges and Gandhaka rivers; and became the capital of the Mauryan emperors, Chandragupta Maurya and his grandson Ashoka the Great (Ashoka Bindusara Maurya). In 305 BC, Chandragupta won a battle against Greco-Bactrian armies and set the stage for his grandson Ashoka (273-232 BC) to extend the limits of the Mauryan Empire throughout the Indian sub-continent including all of Gandhara and eastern Afghanistan. Around 185 BC, however, the Greco-Bactrian king Demetrius I invaded and conquered northern India and restored all of the formerly lost satrapies in Gandhara. Gandhara was thus a part of the Greco-Bactrian kingdom before the latter was overrun by theYuezhi/Kushan in 124 BC.

Ancient Central Asia

Gandhara was a thriving cross-raods for the trade with India originating in Central Asia and flourished during the reign of the Greco-Bactrian king Kanishka (151-128 BC).[9] Kanishka was a zealous Buddhist who took an active part in religious ceremonies and built numerous Buddhist sanctuaries. The coinage he minted carried only images of deities from his heritage of Hellenic and Iranian cultures. Gandhara's major city, Taxila, became a great metropolis where Mahayana Buddhist texts were translated, studied and analyzed by local monks and pilgrims. These activities became the vehicle through which Buddhism reached China.

Ferghana فرغانه

> Dayuan lies south-west of the territory of the Xiongnu, some 10,000 *li* directly west of China. The people are also settled on the land, plowing the fields and growing rice and wheat. They also make wine out of grapes. The region has many fine horses which sweat blood; their forebears are supposed to have been foaled from heavenly horses. The people live in houses in fortified cities, there being some seventy or more cities of various sizes in the region. The population numbers several hundred thousand. The people fight with bows and spears and can shoot from horseback. Dayuan is bordered on the north by Kangju, on the west by the kingdom of the Great Yuezhi, on the south-west by Daxia, on the north-east by the land of the Wusun, and on the east by Yumi and Yutian.*

---

* The Wusun were a nomadic Central Asian people who lived in the region of Lake Issyk Köl north of the Tian Shan Mountains in eastern Kyrgyzstan. The Kangju, on the other hand, was most likely a reference to an ancient people who occupied areas in southern Kazakhstan. Kangju was described by Zhang Qian in the records of his travels in 139 BC. He wrote: Kangju is situated some 2,000 li north-west of Da Yuan. Its people are nomads and resemble the Yuezhi in their customes. They have 80,000 or 90,000 skilled archers. The country is small, and borders Da Yuan. It acknowledges sovereignty of the Yuezhi people in the south and the Xiongnu in the east.

The geographical description of the land of Dayuan in the above excerpt from the *Hanshu*, places Ferghana in an area to the north-east of the Pamir Mountains, bordered in the west by the Sogdiana and by Bactria in the south. The original source of this information comes from the reports of Zhang Qian's travels in 139 BC which correctly places Da Yuan at a time before the Yuezhi conquest of Bactria in 124 BC. Therefore, it seems probable that the Yuehzi tribes must have advanced westward from their settlements in the Tarim basin, crossed the Tian Shan Mountains and reached the lush pasturelands of Ferghana (present-day Kyrgyzstan).

They then moved further west and occupied Sogdiana and, still in pursuit of new conquests, appear to have turned their attention towards their south and conquered Bactria. Ferghana eventually became part of the Yuezhi/Kushan Empire which extended from Sogdiana to northern India. The apparent counter-clockwise advances of the Yuezhi from the Tarim basin to Ferghana, and then to Sogdiana, Bactria and northern India, respectively, describe a sequence of occupations that perhaps was a manifestation of pre-Buddhist Shamanistic and Animistic cultural practices characteristic of many ancient Central Asian and Siberian tribes. The spiritual significance of counter-clockwise circumambulation in practice always keeps the sacred corona of the sun in full view. This no doubt was also a part of the religious practices of the Yuezhi tribes in their native homelands in the southern reaches of the Gobi desert prior to their migration westward and eventual conversion to Islam.

By the end of the first century BC, one of the five tribes of the Yuezhi, the Guishuang (origin of the word Kushan), took control of the Yuezhi confederation, advanced to the north-western areas of the Indian sub-continent and founded the Kushan Empire. During the early centuries of the Christian era, the Kushan Empire consolidated its regional influences and placed itself at the center of the lucrative Central Asian commerce reaching China through the Silk Road. After their adoption of Islam in the early years of the eleventh century, the Yuehzi/Kushan came to be known as the Mughals of Northern India. In the early thirteenth century, the ancient city of Adijan was destroyed by Genghis Khan, but Kaidu Khan (1230-1301 AD) Genghis Khan's great grandson, the grandson of Ogotai Khan, rebuilt Adijan in the late thirteenth century and made it the capital of Ferghana.

Regarding the Yuezhi Guishaung tribe, the *Hanshu* describes the following:

More than a hundred years later, the *xihou* of Guishuang attacked and exterminated the four other *xihou*. He set himself up as king of a kingdom called Guishuang. He invaded Anxi and took Gandhara. Yan Gaozhen became king and defeated Tianzhu and installed a General to supervise and lead it. The Yuezhi then became extremely rich.

The general population of Ferghana no doubt included the descendants of the Macedonians who had come to Central Asia with the armies of Alexander the Great in the fourth century BC. Da Yuan can literally be translated to 'Great Ionians' in reference to the Greeks from Ionia. Although Buddhism was embraced by the inhabitants of Ferghana, including the Yuezhi, it was nonetheless not Ferghana's native religion. The historical religious practices in Ferghana seem to have been originally uniquely Zoroastrian which point to a population mostly of Iranian heritage. But, in view of the fact that Alexander the Great ended the Achaemenid Empire, and that all the former Persian satrapies in Central Asia were vanquished by the Greco-Bactrian kingdoms, the conclusion must be that the practice of Zoroastrian faith must have re-surfaced in Ferghana sometime in the first or the second century AD when Ferghana was made part of the Parthian Empire. As discussed earlier, the founder of the Parthian Empire was Arsaces I of Parthia, leader of the Parni tribe who rebelled against the Greek Seleucid Empire in eastern Iran and planted the seeds of a great empire that survived until 226 AD.

Indeginous People of Ancient Central Asia

It is clear from the preceding descriptions of the history of Sogdiana, Bactria, Gandhara and Ferghana that the peoples who inhabited these areas were a collage of people with various ethnic origins that included Persians, Greeks, Indians, Huns, Yuezhi and no doubt many others. Clearly, however, they do not represent the native sedentary stock people of antiquity who had inhabited these areas prior to their dilution by foreign invaders. The Persians, and particularly the Greeks, were natives of foreign lands and for the most part were conquerors who through their shear military might had succeeded in creating for themselves in Central Asia vassal kingdoms and governed them by appointing their own kinsman into positions of authority. It is therefore clear who the governors were. But this begs the question of who were the governed people? And who were the native sedentary indigenous inhabitants of Central Asia?

Comparative philology has demonstrated that Sanskrit, the ancient Indian classical language, is closely related to early European languages.[10] For instance, the word for 'king' in Sanskrit is *raj*, *rex* in Latin. The Latin word for 'sheep' is *pecus*; it is *pasu* in Sanskrit and *pekos* in Greek. Similarly, 'fire' is *agni* in Sanskrit and *ignis* in Latin. It is appropriate therefore that we should be concerned with whether there ever was a single language from which these related idioms were derived, whether a people that spoke it ever existed and where they might have lived. In the philologists' terminology these concerns are encompassed in the terms, Ur-Languages, Ur-people and the Ur-homeland, or collectively referred to as 'Indo-European Studies'. Such studies have demonstrated that no less than eleven basic Indo-European languages are related in the same way as are those listed above. Among them are: Tocharian, Hittite, Indo-Iranian, Armenian, Slavic, Baltic, Illyrian and Germanic. But if we have to identify a singular Ur-homeland - keeping in mind that the people who occupied it would have had to had access to the Urals and Western Siberia, the Balkans, the Baltic, the Hindu Kush, the Caucasus and Anatolia - in order for it to have been the original root of the common idiomatic usages in the languages acquired by the successive inhabitants of the areas mentioned above, the only region that fulfills this criteria is the plains of the Lower Volga river.[11]

Several Bronze Age cultures were flourishing in the mid-third millennium BC (circa 2500 BC) and one such culture was the Kurgan whose people lived in the region of the Lower Volga, Lake Aral and the Caspian Sea, the homeland of what we might call the Proto Indo-Europeans. The name of their culture is derived from Cyrillic meaning 'mound' in reference to the practice of burying its dead in a single grave in the shape of a mound in which the corpse was laid out with stretched-out legs and covered with ochre, a preferred dye with uncertain significance. The Proto Indo-Europeans were a 'patrilineal society' (belonging to the father's lineage), nomadic, relying on animal husbandry, notably of cattle and sheep. They also domesticated the horse. Their spoken language is presumed to have been the singular ancestral hypothetical language from which all of our presently characterized Indo-European languages are ultimately derived.

Amongst the ancient descendants of the Kurgan Proto-Indo-Europeans were the Scythians, considered by the Greeks as one of the great barbarian peoples. The earliest surviving archaeological evidence of their existence dates from around 700 BC, though they may have existed as early as 1800 BC. Herodotus, the Greek historian of the fifth century BC, describes the Scythians as follows:

> Each of them cuts off an enemy's head and takes it back home. He then skewers it on a long wooden stave and sets this up so that the head sticks up far above the house, often above the chimney. They maintain that the head is put there as guardian of the whole house...With the heads of their worst enemies they proceed as follows: once they have sawn off everything below the eyebrows, they carefully clean out the head. If the owner is poor he will merely stretch calf-leather round it and use it thus. But if he is rich, he will also line the inside with gold and use it as a drinking vessel...When guests arrive he will bring out these heads and say how they...attacked him, and how he defeated them.[12]

What is certain about the Scythians however is that around 700 BC they had begun a series of migrations in waves from the regions of the Caspian Sea moving in several directions that included towards the south-east to Central Asia and Northern India, the south to Iran, north-west across the Volga River to Northern Europe and west across the Black Sea to Eastern Europe. Their migrations had driven yet another indigenous group of Indo-Europeans to migrate in turn from their homelands north of the Black Sea and establish new settlements east of the Black Sea in the Caucasus. They were known as the Cimmerians and their language is regarded as being related to Iranian.

The Yuezhi people of the Tarim basin have often been described as Tocharians. Although we cannot be certain that Tocharians were the descendants of the Scythians, they were nevertheless the easternmost speakers of an Indo-European language called 'Tocharian'. The first Greek mention of the Tocharians appear in the chronicles of the first century BC Greek historian Strabo who described the Tocharians as Scythians fighting the wars against the Greeks during the conquest of the Greco-Bactrian kingdom in 124 BC.[13] The demise of this kingdom at the hands of the Yuezhi, discussed earlier, seems to parallel Strabo's description of the Tocharians and would equate the Yuezhi to the

Tocharians. The discovery of 2,000-year old mummies in the Tarim basin will be discussed in Chapter 7. They together with many Tocharian texts and paintings unearthed there may be taken as evidence in support of an Indo-European provenance for the Tocharians. Their arrival in the Tarim basis is also discussed in the same chapter.

There appears to have been two forms of spoken Tocharian; the East Tocharian, or Turfanian, and West Tocharian, or Kuqaian, both are in reference to the Tarim basin oasis towns of Turfan and Kuqa, respectively. As a result of centuries of conflicts and occupations of the Tarim basin by Turkic speaking peoples such as the Uyghur, the Göktürk and the Mongol, Tocharian gradually had gavin way to the various forms of the Turkic language which ultimately came to dominate the entire Central Asian plateau.

Arab Conquest of Iran 637 AD

The death of Yazdegird III in 651 AD, the last Sasanian ruler of Iran, was metaphorically similar to the end of the last Achaemenid king, Darius III. The detailed military accounts that led to the conquest of Iran by the Arabs in 637 AD are beyond the scope of our present objective but, briefly, the beginning of the end of the Sasanian Empire can be traced back to the time of the Arab conquest of Syria and their victories against the Byzantines in Palestine and Asia Minor in 635 AD. Caliph Umar ibn al-Khattab, committed to his Islamic task with great confidence and dedication, sent Sa'ad ibn abi Waqqas (further discussion of him is in Chapter 6) against the Persians with a greater number of troops than had been gathered at any of the previous raids against the Sasanian Empire.[14] It is reputed that Caliph Umar had urged Yazdegrid and the Persians to avoid bloodshed and adopt Islam peacefully but had failed to receive a favourable response. Henceforth, in 637 AD a battle took place at al-Qadisiyya to the west of the Arabian kingdom al-Hira in present-day southern Iraq, which in the seventh century was a vassal state to the Sasanian Empire. The Persian army broke ranks and and fled when their commander Rustam was killed during the battle. This significant defeat dealt to the Persian imperial army at al-Qadisiyya had left Persian Mesopotamia with no effective resources to reassemble future retaliatory forces. Hence in the absence of defensive Persian forces in southern Mesopotamia, the Arabs upon their victory at al-Qadisiyya were able to found two military bases first at Basra followed by a second at Kufa. These two bases were placed under the command of Sa'ad ibn abi Waqqas for the defense of southern and central Mesopotamia but they also permitted the Arabs during the years from 637 to 641 AD to slowly expand eastward into Persia proper. Then in 642 AD the Arabs won a second decisive victory against the Sasanians at the battle of Nihavand (near Hamadan) and henceforth the central authority of the Sasanian state was effectively destroyed.

After the victory at Nihavand the Arabs quickly occupied vast swaths of the Iranian Plateau and continued their advances towards the north, the south and the east. Azerbaijan in the north was taken in 643 AD followed in 649 by the Iranian province of Fars in the south where Yazdegird had taken refuge after his defeat at Nihavand. Upon the loss of the province of Fars, Yazdegird fled to his Sasanian army stronghold in Merv in Central Asia (in present-day Turkmenistan). From Merv, Yazdegird sent envoys to China's Tang dynasty pleading for direct military intervansion to counter the Arab advances. But the dynasty's assessment of the Arab threat to the Middle Kingdom did not warrant Chinese involvement. Faced with certain annihilation many Persian troops converted to Islam and chose to join the Arab armies. Their defection to the ranks of the Arabs and conversion to Islam were more likely to have been a matter of personal survival rather than of religious convictions. Nonetheless their decisions had made certain the capitulation of Merv.

The historical records of the last days of the Sasanian Empire do not reveal whether the Arabs were intent on killing Yazdegird but he was nonetheless murdered in Merv in 651 AD. The Christian bishop of the Nestorian Bishopric of Merv is reputed to have recovered the dead body of the last Sasanian ruler. Many members of Yazdegird's immediate family and a number of his court's nobility had fled with him to Merv and many had continued their flight and sought refuge in China. Amongst them was Yazdegird's son Peroz who was allowed to serve the Tang dynasty as the representative of the Sasanian royal court in exile. He died in China.

Although the Tang dynasty at the time was interested in the political events developing in Central Asia, there was little hope for any Chinese assistance reaching the Sasanians. The economic interests of the Chinese and the wealth-obsessed Tang dynasty perceived the Arabs as renowned traders and potential future trading partners. They posed little threat to the Middle Kingdom given the vast formidable distances separating them.

Merv was eliminated as the military stronghold of the Sasanian Empire's fronteirs in Central Asia. Hence, Merv in the fashion of Basra, which was a bastion for Arab conquests in southern Mesopotamia, became the power base for the Umayyad caliphate in their bid for the full occupation of Central Asia. Iran was no longer a military threat to Muslim rule throughout the vast territories from Mesopotamia to Merv.

It is arguable whether the Arab motives for their interests in Central Asia were driven primarily by economic considerations. Although Central Asia's potential as a vast source of economic wealth and revenues for the caliphate was significant, it cannot be construed that the caliphate's Islamic aspirations during their conquests were less important and secondary to their commercial objectives. The sedentary populations of the occupied territories had joined the ranks of Islam and had made the new faith's message their own dedicated mission. Sogdiana, Bactria, Gandhara and Ferghana with their age-old renowned cities of Bukhara, Samarkand, Balkh and Tashkent, collectively referred to as Transoxiana (or Transoxania), became important centres of Islamic theology and learning. The Arabs did not voluntarily withdraw from Central Asia because of diminished economic returns. Their demise was a product of the caliphate's inability to contain the regional tribal aspirations for identity with their national Turkic heritage.

References

1. Sims-Williams, W., The Sogdian Merchants in China and India. In *Cina e Iran Da Alessandro Magno alla dinastia Tang.* A. Cadonna and L. Lanciotti (eds.), Orientalia Veneziana, Florence (1996).
2. Grenet, F. and Zhang, G., *The Last Refuge of the Sogdian Religion: Dunhuang In the Ninth and Tenth Centuries.* Bulletin of the Asia Institute, n.s. 10 (Studies in Honour of Vladimir A. Livshits (1996).
3. Dupuy, R. E. and Dupuy, t. N., *The Harper Encyclopedia of Military History from 3500 BC to the Present.* Harper-Collins Publishers, New York (1993).
4. Bernard, P., Alexander and his Successors in Central Asia. In *History of Civilizations of Central Asia.* Vol. II. Motilal Banarsidass Publishers, New Delhi, (1994a).
5. Bernard, P., The Greek Kingdoms of Central Asia. In *History of Civilizations of Central Asia.* Vol. II: *The Development of Sedentary and Nomadic Civilizations 700 BC to AD 250.* J. Harmatta (ed.), UNESCO Publishing, Paris (1994).
6. Holt, F. L., *Into the Land of Bones: Alexander the Great in Afghanistan.* University of California Press, Berkeley (2005).
7. Holt, F. L., *Thundering Zeus: The Making of Hellenistic Bactria.* University of California Press, Berkeley (1999).
8. Benjamin, C., The Yuezhi: Origin, migration and the conquest of northern Bactria.Turnhout, Brepols (2007).
9. Cribb, J., The Early Kushan Kings: New Evidence for Chronology: Evidence from the Rabatak Inscription of Kanishka I. In *Coins, Art, and Chronology: Essays on the pre-Islamic History of the Indo-Iranian Borderlands.* M. Alram and D. E. Klimburg-Salter (eds.). Verlag Der Osterreichischen Akademic Der Wissenschaften, Wein (1999):
10. Beekes, R. S. P., *Comparative Indo-European Linguistics: An Introduction.* John Benjamins, Amsterdam (1995).
11. Ghazarian, J. G., *The Mediterranean Legacy in Early Celtic Christianity: A Journey from Armenia to Ireland.* Bennett and Bloom, London (2006)
12. De Selincourt, A. (trans.), Herodotous. Penguin Books, London (1954).
13. Strabo. *Geographica.* A. Meineke (ed.), Teubner, Leipzig (1877).
14. Frye, R. N., *The Golden Age of Persia: The Arabs in the East.* Weidenfeld, London (1993).

Treasures of the Silk Road

Chapter Four

Shaanxi, Gansu and Xinjiang

Demographic History of Shaanxi Province

Shaanxi province occupies a prominent position in the history of the Middle Kingdom. It is located in the heart of the Yellow river basin and boasts Chang'an (modern Xi'an) as its current capital, which historically had served as the seat of no less than eleven former dynasties over a period of 1,100 years.[1] The course of the Yellow river, after it turns sharply south in Inner Mongolia, forms nearly the entire eastern border of the province separating it from the neighbouring province of Shanxi. The Qinling Mountains cut across Shaanxi province in its southern part but the northern reaches of the province contain a large portion of the Loess Plateau (also known as the Huangtu Plateau). The plateau is an alluvial deposit of very fine compacted sand and silt which covers almost all of Ningxia, Gansu, Shaanxi and Shanxi provinces. It can be easily carved out into room-size openings that can serve as shelter from the searing heat of the summer months, and from the cold winds of winter that blow from the Gobi Desert. Such shelters, which are still commonly used by the local residents as permanent homes, are called *Yao-Dong*.

As the land of many former imperial dynasties that presided over the Middle Kingdom, (e.g. the Zhou, Qin, Han, Sui and the Tang), Shannxi's population has been consistently nearly all of Han stock with a very small fraction represented by the Hui who traverse the borders from the nearby province of Ningxia.

The Hui, or Huihui, population of Shaanxi province is generally recognized as a people with multicultural lineage.[2] The Hui of Shaanxi and Ningxia are mostly the mixed descendants of the various Islamic steppe tribes of Central Asia who had intermarried with Mongols and Han Chinese. Unlike the Uyghur and the Tajik, who have a particular non-Chinese national language associated with their stock, the Hui's primary spoken and written language is Mandarin Chinese though they retain a few Arabic and Persian words in their lexicon.

During the Yuan dynasty (1279-1368) and the Ming dynasty (1368-1644), the word Huihui was the common generic term for China's Muslims regardless of language or origin. It stemmed from the much earlier term Huihe, or Huihu, which was the Chinese reference to the First Uyghur Empire of the eighth and the ninth centuries. The widespread and rather generic use of the term Huihui, especially during the Ming dynasty, was noted by the Jesuit missionary Matteo Ricci in Beijing in 1598 to stand not only for Saracens (Muslims) but also for Jews and even for Christians. However, the term Hui in today's China is used specifically to denote non-Uyghur Mandarin-speaking Muslims.

Apart from the provinces of Shaanxi and Ningxia, the Hui also inhabit the south-eastern coastal provinces of present-day China. The south-eastern Hui have descended from the Arab and Persian traders who settled in China but retained their ancestral Islamic religion. They are totally socially and politically assimilated into the mainstream Chinese culture and are indistinguishable from the Hans albeit for their celebrations of the Islamic holidays. Historically their ancestors were late arrivals into China who came around the twelfth century during the Northern Song dynasty (960-1127 AD) when the maritime routes to China were commonly in use. Initially, the maritime routes were used mostly to avoid the periodic regional wars along the overland routes but by the twelfth century they had totally replaced the traditional overland Silk Road(s). Almost all of the traders who arrived by sea settled in Guangzhou (Guangdong Province), in Xiamen (also known in ancient times as Amoy, in Fujian Province), in Hangzhou (Zhejiang Province) and in Yangzhou (Jiangsu Province) where many of the mosques and the houses of worship erected during the Song dynasty are still standing today. In contrast, the north-western Hui in Gansu, Shaanxi and Ningxia, though also retained the Islamic faith of their ancestors, maintain and practice the full Islamic social and religious traditions throughout their daily lives. Their men wear white tunic tops over baggy white trousers and almost all wear long beards and cover their heads with embroidered white kippas. They represent a significant portion of the north-western population of present-day China as they did particularly during the Mongol-based Yuan dynasty of the thirteenth and the fourteenth centuries.

Shaanxi, Gansu and Xinjiang

Where it all began; the City of Chang'an (Xi'an)

Chang'an has been settled since Neolithic times but its glory days came when the Qin dynasty's First Emperor, Qin ShiHuangdi, chose nearby Xianyang for the seat of his imperial court. It was located on the northern bank of the river Wei and necessarily became the centre of political, economic and cultural life of the Qin Empire. Later, Liu Bang of the Han dynasty would establish his capital in Chang'an across from Xianyang on the southern banks of the Wei. Chang'an has China's best preserved city walls which were initially at the base 3.5 metres wide tapering upwards to a height of 8 metres with a top width of 2 metres. The walls were later expanded to 12-16 metres at the base and 12 metres high. Surrounding the wall, a moat was built with a width of 6.13 metres and a depth of 4.62 metres but as the wall was expanded so was the moat to a width of 8 metres. The moat was spanned by several stone bridges each 13.86 metres long. Twelve city-wall gates provided access into the city. These gates were installed three to each side of the square-patterned city. Each gate in the eastern and western walls led an access road to an imposing central avenue that was 45-metres wide. The avenue ran north from the main central gate in the south wall to the imperial palace built against the north wall facing south.[3]

It was during the Western Zhou dynastic rule in Xi'an (1027-771 BC) that the origins of native Chinese philosophical treatises were synthesized from within the capital's aristocratic corridors.[4] The great Chinese social philosophers who lived several centuries later drew upon Xi'ans ancient literary records to leave their own indelible marks on the Chinese neoclassical concepts of logic and social structure. They were Lao Tse (Latin: Lao Zi, sixth to fifth centuries BC), founder of Daoism (Taoism) (Daoist *ethics* emphasize compassion, moderation, and humility whilst Daoist *though*t focuses on the relationship between humanity and the cosmos, and between health and longevity), Kong Fuzi (Latin: Confucius, 551-479 BC), Mo Tzu (Latin: Mencius, 470-391 BC) who expanded Confucianism, Shang Yang (fourth century BC) and Han Fei Zi who together with Shang Yang expanded the ancient Chinese ideas on legalism.[5]

Chang'an was also the eastern terminus of the Silk Road with a large cosmopolitan urban community which in the Tang dynasty's census of the year 742 AD was estimated to have a metropolitan population approaching two million. As such, Chang'an was a hub for foreign traders who flocked to the city with their goods of gold, jewels and jewellery, jade, textiles, coral, musical instruments, all kinds artistic paraphernalia and, often, horses. In exchange, the Chinese offered furs, silk, carved jade, ceramics, medicinal herbs, weapons made of bronze, cinnamon bark and also many exotic spices highly relished in the West.[6]

Demographic History of Gansu Province

The province of Gansu lies directly west of its neighbouring province of Shaanxi and is bordered by the provinces of Qinghai and Xinjiang in its west, Sichuan in the south and Inner Mongolia in the north. It also shared a small stretch of international border with its neighbouring country of Outer Mongolia.

The history of human habitation in Gansu can be traced back to the Neolithic and Bronze Age periods with many distinct sedentary cultures thriving at various locations in the upper reaches of the Yellow and Wei rivers. It should be noted that our understanding of these cultures has attached a greater significance to the Hexi Corridor as a communication link between the various cultures many millennia before the founding of the Silk Road(s). The site of the Qijia culture (2400-1900 BC), for instance, was distributed around the upper Yellow river regions of western Gansu and eastern Qinghai provinces. It was first unearthed in the small village of Qijiaping in the early 1920s by the Swedish geologist Johan Gunnar Andersson. This Late Neolithic-Early Bronze Age culture exhibits northern Eurasian influences in the lifestyles of its members who may have shared links with various Indo-European groups who appear to have migrated into Xinjiang province from Central Asia. Archaeology in the 1940s unearthed further evidence of the Qijia culture in Qinghai and also in Ningxia north of the Hexi Corridor. Another pre-historic culture that flourished in Gansu is the Majiayao culture (3100-2700 BC). The Majiayao-type finds are mostly localized in the central and southern regions of Gansu, in the north-eastern parts of Qinghai and in southern Ningxia. These Bronze Age cultures have produced some of the earliest known bronze and copper objects in China.

Early Neolithic-period cultures had also flourished in Gansu. The Dadiwan culture (circa 6000-3000 BC), for instance, was discovered in Qin'an just north of the city of Tianshui. The Dadiwan culture site is located on a mountain slope south of the Qingshui River, a tributary of the Wei River. The artifacts of this culture are the oldest unearthed at

Shaanxi, Gansu and Xinjiang

the site though artifacts from younger layers (periods) have also been recovered belonging to the Yangshao culture (5000-3000 BC) and the Longshan culture (3000-2000 BC). The former was an extensive culture that flourished mostly in Henan province; it was discovered in 1921 by the Swedish archaeologist Johan Gunnar Andersson (1874-1960). The Longshan culture, discovered in 1928, flourished mainly in Shandong Province but its influences and social practices seem to have reached as far west as Gansu province.

During the zenith of the Silk Road's history, Tianshui became and important half-way stop between Lanzhou and the road's eastern terminus Chang'an. Nearby can be seen the impressive fourth century Maijishan Buddhist grottoes. But in a pre-historical context, however, Tianshui is said to have been the birthplace of Emperor Fu Xi (Fu Hsi) (circa 2200 BC), one of the three mythological founding fathers of the Chinese civilization. His legend relates that the land was swept by a great flood and only Fu Xi and his sister Nuwa (Nu-gua or Nu-Kunas) survived. They retreated to the Kunlun Mountains where they prayed for a sign from the Emperor of Heaven. The source of this legend is Li Rong, a Tang dynasty Taoist sage who lived sometime between 618 and 907 AD and gives the account in his commentaries on the Taoist book of Lao Zi as follows:

> There was a brother and a sister living on the Kunlun Mountain, and there were no ordinary people at that time. The sister's name was Nuwa. The brother and sister wished to become husband and wife, but felt shy and guilty about this desire. So the brother took his younger sister to the top of the Kunlun Mountain and prayed: If Heaven allows us to be man and wife, please let the smoke before us gather; if not, please let the smoke scatter. The smoke before them gathered together. So Nuwa came to live with her elder brother. She made a fan with grass to hide her face. Fu Xi then came to rule over his descendants. He lived for 197 years and died at a place called Chen.

Fu Xi was apotheosized and Li Rong's legacy survives today in the belief that the true home of the Qin dynasty (221-206 BC) and the foundations of the First Empire rest in Tianshui.

One additional prehistoric culture that merits mention is the Huoshaogou culture which was discovered in Qingquan near Yumen.

The Huoshaogou culture is the successor to Qijia thus belongs to the first half of the second millennium BC (1900-1500 BC). The site was identified from the artefacts recovered from the more than 300 excavated graves. The artefacts included axes, sickles, chisels, knives, daggers, spearheads, arrowheads, needles, braclets, hammers and mirrors, all made of cast tin or lead-amalgamated bronze. These items have suggested a non-stratified hunting, farming society capable of manufacturing tools and ornaments for use by its people.

Gansu province, presently, is home for many ethnic peoples who in the main still live in a rural environment beyond the city of Lanzhou. By far, the majority are Han (91%), but the minority includes the Muslim Hui (5%), Tibetans (2%) who are concentrated mostly in the south-western corner of the province. The Muslim Bonan and Dongxiang together make up 2% of Gansu's population and the remaining 1% is represented in fractional proportions by the Buddhist Tu (of Mongol descent), Manchu, Uyghur, Mongol, Salar and Kazakh.[7,8]

For imperial China, as was true for pre-historic China, Gansu was an important strategic outpost and communications link by virtue of its Hexi Corridor - a natural land passage stretching from Lanzhou in a north-westerly direction some 1,000 kilometres towards the Jade Gate Pass. This corridor was a major natural defensive bulwark for the Han dynasty (BC 206-23 AD), which used the corridor to its advantage by clearing and taxing the Silk Road trade destined for consumption in the Middle Kingdom   In view of the importance of the corridor, the dynasty extended China's Great Wall to the limits of the empire near Dunhuang and built there the forts of Yumenguan (Jade Gate Pass) and Yangguan to reinforce the wall and ensure the safety and the strength of its defenses. The Ming dynasty (1368-1644 AD) augmented this defensive strategy by building yet another defensive fort in the wall at Jiayuguan at the foot of the Qilian Mountains facing the great Gobi Desert.

Throughout history, Gansu province has undergone many name changes. In antiquity the region was first known as Lunsi in reference to its geographical position in the foothills of Longshan Mountains. During the Wei rule of the Three Kingdoms period (220-265 AD) the region was known as Suzhou and continued to be known as such as late as the Tang period (618-907 AD). The first official name of Gansu appears after the Tang dynasty in the records of the Northern Song dynasty (960-1127 AD) when the first military protectorate was established in Ganzhou (modern Zhangye) which developed into a major military garrison by the time of the Ming dynasty.

Demographic History of Xinjiang Province

Xinjiang province, a 640,000 square miles of mostly barren land containing at its centre the world's second largest desert, the Taklamakan, lies in the westernmost part of China and shares international boundaries with seven countries. From its south-west corner and moving clockwise, they are Pakistan, Afghanistan, Tajikistan, Kyrgyzstan, Kazakhstan, Russia and Outer Mongolia with the latter two sharing borders with the province at its north and north-east. Xinjiang has played a significant role in the history of the Silk Road as well as in the demographic history of China's western multicultural regions. The province occupies a pivotal position with regard to land access to China from the west as it is situated directly above the inaccessible Tibetan Plateau, which itself borders four additional countries along its southern frontier; namely India, Nepal, Bhutan and Myanmar.

The history of this region of China can be best understood if its present multicultural composition is first defined. Only then the impact of the region's history can be best appreciated.[9] By far the largest number of the inhabitants of Xinjiang is represented by the Uyghur (circa 45%) followed closely by the Han at circa 40%. The Kazakh make up nearly 7% of the population followed by the Hui at around 4.5%, the Mongols make up a little over 1% and the Kyrgyz at 0.9%. The remainder is composed at fractional proportions of Pamiris, Manchu, Uzbek, Tibetans and Russians.[10]

The demographic history of Xinjiang province goes back several millennia but over time it became mostly the home of the nomadic Yuezhi, Xianbei and Xiongnu tribes that harassed the Middle Kingdom with their constant raids along the frontiers of the kingdom. Although the origins of the ancient settlers of Xinjiang are shrouded by the mist of time, it is however clear that a number of Indo-European nomadic tribes from Central Asia had migrated east and south and settled in the Tarim basin in north-central Xinjiang. In general terms, Central Asia - often referred to as Turkistan - is a region of Asia bounded in the west by the Caspian Sea and by present-day China in the east. Southern Russia forms the northern boundary of this region and Afghanistan its southern reaches. A clearer description of this region may be said to consist of modern Kyrgyzstan, Kazakhstan, Uzbekistan, Tajikistan and Turkmenistan, and may also include Siberia, Mongolia, Afghanistan and northern Pakistan. During pre-Islamic and in early Islamic periods, Central Asia was under the Persian Sasanian sphere of influence, politically and culturally, and over time became home for many nomadic peoples both of Turkic and Mongolic stock who spoke ancient Iranian, Sogdian, Tocharian, Tibetan, Nestorian, Arabic and Chinese. Peoples of Iranian stock who inhabited these areas were the Scythians from the Caspian Sea area, the Tajik mainly from eastern Iran, the Pushtuns and the Pamiris and the Turkic peoples that included the Uzbeks, Kazakhs, Kyrgyz and the Uyghur.[11]

Many diverse Mongolic or Turkic nomadic tribes at one time or another had occupied parts of present-day Xinjiang province (e.g. Yenisei Yuezhi, Xiongnu, Xianbei, and Göktürk). The second century BC historian Sima Qian had recorded in his chronicles a description of the Yuezhi as follows:

> The Yuezhi originally lived in the area between the Qilian Mountains and Dunhuang, but after their defeat by the Xiongnu they moved far away to the west, beyond Dayuan (Farghana), where they attacked and conquered the people of Daxia (Bactria) and set up the court of their king on the northern bank of the Gui River. A small number of their people who were unable to make the journey west sought refuge among the Qiang barbarians in the Southern Mountains, where they are known as the Lesser Yuezhi.

The Gui is a river in south-central modern China. Although the mention of the Gui in the above excerpt in a modern setting is not consistent with the geography of Dayuan and Daxia, it perhaps was used by Sima Qian in reference to the Chu River, or to the Oxus River (Amu Darya), that satisfy its geographic relationship to Dayuan and Daxia.. We cannot be certain whether today's name of the river also applies to the ancient river Gui mentioned by Sima Qian. Often rivers flowing in different regions have similar names or may be given new names. Ancient river-beds are testimony to driep-up or truncated rivers that have shifted their course over time. The shifting courses of the now lost Lop Nor River in the north-central deserts of Xinjiang province is a case in point. We may, therefore, accept Sima's account of the Yenisei Yuezhi as a people who had lived in a region north of Gansu province bordering north-eastern Xinjiang but who had migrated west to the Chu

River valley and conquered Bactria and Ferghana. The excerpt also describes a small number of the Yuezhi who had migrated south of the Tian Shan Mountains and settled in the Tarim basin.

Ancient Chinese records refer to the Xinjiang area as Xiyu (Xi, west and yu, frontier/territory) hence, 'Western Regions'),[12] a term that was used to imply a collection of barbarian settlements along the fringes of the Middle Kingdom. The Roman historian Pliny the Elder has given us the curious description of the Seres people made by an embassy from Taprobane (Ceylon) to Emperor Tiberius Claudius (41-54 AD):

> They also informed us that the side of their island which lies opposite to India is ten thousand stadia in length, and runs in a south-easterly direction - that beyond the Emodian Mountains (Himalayas) they look towards the Serve (Seres), whose acquaintance they had also made in the pursuits of commerce; that the father of Rachias (the ambassador) had frequently visited their country, and that the Serae always came to meet them on their arrival. These people, they said, exceeded the ordinary human height, had flaxen hair, and blue eyes, and made an uncouth sort of noise by way of talking, having no language of their own for the purpose of communicating their thoughts.

Pliny's use of this description may have been intended to demonstrate the existence of ancient barbarian populations of non-Chinese stock who occupied lands west of the Middle Kingdom. The mention of their physical attributes point to their origins as being potentially Aryan (peoples composed of the proto-Indo-Europeans and their descendants).

It is important at this point to emphasize and underscore the complexity of the Western Regions' tribal history and to note how over the centuries the various parts of the region were ruled by many regional tribal powers which sought to control and dominate the lucrative trade routes of the Silk Road. Such powers included the Han and the Tang dynasties, the Göktürk, Tibetans, Uyghur and the Mongol - not necessarily in that order. The 'Western Regions' was finally annexed by the Qing dynasty in 1759 and given the current name Xinjiang, meaning 'The New Frontier.'

The struggle for the control of the Western Regions had begun earnestly during the Han dynasty.[13] As was alluded earlier in Chapter 2, the Xiongnu tribe of Mongolian stock, who lived along the northern frontiers of the Middle Kingdom, had defeated the dominant Yenisei Yuezhi in the second century BC and had established some modicum of supremacy over the Western Regions that included the Tarim basin. This had given the Xiongnu tribe the ability to prevent the expansion of Han dynasty's commercial interests into Central Asia.[14] Hence, Zhang Qian, a commander in the dynasty's armed forces, was dispatched in 139 BC by Emperor Wudi to establish military and commercial alliances with the Yuezhi further west in Ferghana and Bactria (in the areas of present-day southern Kazakhstan, Tajikistan northern Afghanistan). In this endeavour, Zhang Qian and a guide named Gan Fu while passing through enemy territory were captured and imprisoned by the Xiongnu and held captive for ten years. Zhang eventually had managed to escape and had made his way in a southerly direction passing through the oasis town of Loulan on the eastern edge of the Taklamakan desert. He then travelled west along the northern edges of the Altun and Kunlun Mountains taking refuge along his way in successive settlements that eventually led him to the fertile pasturelands in the kingdoms of Farghana and Bactria. In effect, these settlements visited by Zhang were to become the string of the oasis towns along the southern fringes of the Taklamakan desert that supported the germination and growth of what we now call the Southern branch of the ancient Silk Road. This journey had given Zhang the opportunity to document a large amount of information, both of geographic and demographic nature, of much commercial and military significance. This was delivered to his emperor upon his return to China in 126 BC. Sima Qian's chronicles note the following:

> The emperor learned of the Dayuan, Daxia, Anxi, and the others, all great states rich in unusual products whose people cultivated the land and made their living in much the same way as the Chinese. All these states, he was told, were militarily weak and prized Han goods and wealth.

Zhang Qian's records concerning the many places he was able to travel make a fascinating reading about ancient geographic locations and of the life-styles of the sedentary peoples who inhabited them.. For example he described Loulan as a fortified city near Lop Nor (Lop Nur) and that Dayuan (Ferghana) lay south-west of the territory of the Xiongnu some 10,000 *li* directly west of China, or that the Great Yuezhi live some 3,000 *li* west of Dayuan and north of the Gui River (Oxus) and that they have some 100,000 or 200,000 archer warriors. He reported that Daxia (Bactria) is situated over 2,000 *li* south-west of Dayuan and south of the Gui River. The land is ruled by petty chiefs with a population nearing 1,000,000 persons who are clever at commerce. Its capital is Lanshi where all kinds of goods are exchanged. It is not clear exactly how far Zhang Qian had actually travelled, but his reports also contain similar geographical and demographic commentaries on Kangju (north-eastern Sogdiana – southern Kazakhstan), Anxi (Parthia), Shendu (India) and on the Yancai (in the steppes of Central Asia), perhaps in reference to the Yuezhi.

Since some of the history of the Yuezhi was described in Chapters 2 and 3, additional information concerning the Yuezhi is now presented to further enrich the timeframe of the historical events discussed in this work that shaped the geo-political landscape of the western frontiers of China.

The earliest references to the Yuezhi can be found in seventh-century BC Chinese literature which describes the Yuezhi as peoples in the north-west of the Middle Kingdom who extracted Jade from the Yuzhi Mountains in Gansu and offered it to the Chinese royal courts. Also, the Han dynasty's chronicles in the Book of Han indicate that the Yuezhi were flourishing during the time of the First Emperor, (Qin Shihuangdi, 221-206 BC), and that they were regularly in conflict with the neighbouring tribe of Xiongnu to their north-east. Around 177 BC, the Xiongnu, led by Modu Shanyu, invaded the Yuezhi settlements north of Gansu and forced the mass assimilation of the Yuezhi into the Xiongnu's tribal social structure. Those who managed to escape the assimilation initially settled in areas immediately north of the Tian Shan Mountains but again were dislodged by the Xiongnu and forced to move west and south and settle along the banks of the Chu and Oxus rivers in the region of southern Kazakhstan where they began to consolidate their power and later founded their Yuezhi Empire further south.

In an effort to curtail the constant raiding incursions by the Xiongnu into Chinese frontier areas, China in 77 BC usurped the kingdom of Loulan lying at the north-eastern end of the Taklamakan desert. The kingdom included the walled city of Loulan near the mouth of Tarim River that flowed into the salty Lake Lop Nor (now lost). Thus, the kingdom came under the Chinese sphere of influence and was renamed the kingdom of Shanshan.[15] As such, Shanshan occupied a strategic position along the main routes from China to the west controlling the movement of goods along the roads that ultimately became the main thoroughfares and byways of the Silk Road. Although Shanshan remained under Chinese control until the period of the Tang dynasty in the seventh century AD, the military presence of China in Shanshan was sporadic. A military garrison was established at Loulan in 260 AD only to be abandoned seventy years later. An interesting aspect of the history of Shanshan rests in the observations of the Chinese pilgrim monk, Faxian, who in 399 AD remained in Loulan for a month after his seventeen-day journey from Dunhuang in Gansu province.[16,17] He noted that there were more than four thousand Buddhist monks in Loulan, all students of the Hinayana Buddhism. They studied the Indian language and read Indian texts, clearly indicative of Indian religious influences in the region during the fourth century AD.

The struggle between China and the Xiongnu was chronic and had remained problematic for the Middle Kingdom well into the second century AD. But with China's massive military resources, it was able to control Xiongnu's aggressions by establishing what was called the 'Protectorate of the Western Regions.' This was a policy based on a series of militarily fortified posts managed from a regional centre first placed in 60 BC at Wulei (in the vicinity of modern Luntai) that protected the entire region as far west as the Pamir Mountains. The centre was later re-organized in the first century AD during the Eastern Han dynasty and moved further west to Tagan, near modern Kuqa (Kucha). Over a period of seventy years from the time the policy was first put in place in 60 BC, a total of eighteen centres were established but this policy of a defensive strategy was abandoned during Emperor Wang Meng's period (9-24 AD). It was eventually re-instituted in 74 AD during the Eastern Han dynasty and placed first under the command of General Chen Mu and then of General Ban Chao, and continued to be the policy of the subsequent dynasties until the middle of the sixth century.[18]

Here, a brief remark is necessary to alert the itinerant reader regarding the potential confusion beteen the Xianbei and the Xiongnu tribes. As stated earlier in Chapter 2, the Mongolic Xianbei tibes were nomadic pasturalists residing in today's Inner Mongolia and in the north-eastern parts of China called Manchuria. They were a federation of non-Han peoples of which the most important was the Tuoba tribe. The Tuoba Xianbei controlled the pasturelands in Inner Mongolia and northern China. Other related Xianbei tribal groups were the Rouran, who ruled in Outer Mongolia; the Khitan in southern Manchuria and north of

Korea; and the Shiwei in areas further north from those ruled by the Khitan.

Several centuries after the Chinese containment and defeat of the Xiongnu, the struggle for supremacy in the Chinese frontier regions was soon to take centre stage again driven by the rise of the Göktürks in 555 AD, the Uyghurs in 745 AD and the Yenisei Kyrgyz in 840 AD.[19-21] The Göktürks, originating from the steppes of Central Asia, though racially not distinct from their employers, were the metal-working servants of the Xianbei Rouran tribe. The latter was known in medieval Chinese sources as the Tujue (Tūjué).

Beginning in the mid sixth century AD, the Göktürks, under the leadership of Bumin Khan and his sons, consolidated the nomadic Altaic Turkic tribes into an empire but the empire eventually collapsed in 745 AD due to internal dynastic rivalries.[22] Their name, Göktürk, is a combination of the Turkish word Gök, meaning 'blue', with reference to the colour of the sky, and the ethnic term 'türk' thus reverberating with overtones of 'Celestial Turks' mandated by Heaven to conquer and rule. At the zenith of their power, the empire stretched from the Aral Sea in the west to the shores of Lake Baikal in the east. In 583 AD they split into Eastern and Western khanates (dynasties or kingdoms) with parts of the Western Regions coming under the rule of the eastern khanate. The western khanate by virtue of its distant location from the Middle Kingdom was less likely to be in direct conflict with the Chinese ruling dynasties. However, the Tang emperor Taizong (626-649) after successfully subjugating the Eastern Göktürk khanate closer to home turned his attention to the Western Göktürk khanate. In 630 AD, the emperor's forces under the command of Hou Junji attacked and managed to secure Gaochang, the seat of the western khanate (in the vicinity of modern Turupan "Turfan"). Four years later, the surviving far western clans of the western Göktürk khanate and the Yanqi kingdom (known in Turkish as Karashahir, or Black(Great) City, an ancient Buddhist kingdom in the area of modern Aksu on the Northern branch of the Silk Road) joined forces and fought as allies against Emperor Taizong. But at the end, the Tang commander Guo Xiaoke prevailed. Ultimately in 648 AD the kingdoms of Yanqi and Kucha, or Kuqa, (the largest of the Buddhist kingdoms founded along the Northern branch of the Silk Road) were conquered by Tang's forces under the command of Ashina She'er who consolidated the entire Xinjiang region as far west as Kashgar (modern Kashi) including the settlements of Shule and Yutian. Beginning in the same year, the Tang dynasty undertook the installation of what was called the 'Four Garrisons of Anxi'[23] that required a decade for completion. This was a series of military posts fashioned in the manner of the Han dynasty's creation of the 'Protectorate of the Western Regions,' in 60 BC - the defensive strategy that was practiced seven centuries earlier to protect the north-western frontiers of the Middle Kingdom. The first of the Tang dynasty's garrisons was stationed in Kucha, then moving west in Aksu, Kashgar and Khotan (Hotan). This defensive posturing in effect allowed the dynasty to control the entire stretch of the territory along the Northern branch of the Silk Road. The installation of the garrisons was a monumental task but it offered the dynasty several decades of secure trading routes that were conflict-free from the capital Xi'an in the east to the foothills of the Pamir Mountains in the west.

In the late seventh century AD, after several decades of generally secure commerce traversing the northern edges of the Taklamakan desert, the main remainig adversary to the Middle Kingdom's Tang dynasty was the Tibetans who between 670 and 692 AD began to seize and control territories in China's north-western region. Yet during these years the Tibetan conquests were not absolute as they struggled in their confrontations with the Tang's defensive garrisons. Their struggle often involved capturing and re-capturing the same towns in the arid lands that typified China's north-western region. The Tibetan struggle continued relentlessly well into the eighth century and by the middle of that century they had succeeded in establishing more permanent occupations in the region and had extended their control along the entire length of the Hexi Corridor in Gansu province. Their gains included the cities of Liangzhou, Ganzhou, Suzhou, Guazhou, Yizhou and Shazhou, and in the final decade of the eighth century the 'Four Garrisons of Anxi' was also taken. The Tibetans thus had established a firm control over the entire north-western region of China (Xinjiang) as well as the north-western half of Gansu province. Moreover, they soon turned their attention south and occupied the lands of present-day provinces of Yunnan and Sichuan. However, the Tibetan apetite for conquests was not yet satisfied. By virtue of their determined occupation of the vast swaths of territories in the western frontiers of the Middle Kingdom, the Tibetan military confidence by the close of the eighth century had driven them to the very gates of the Tang dynasty's capital Chang'an (Xi'an).

It has been argued that the above-described territorial gains by the Tibetans during the period from 670 AD to the close of the eighth century were not the results of sheer efficient and effective military prowess excersised by the Tibetans. During the reign of Tang dynasty's emperor Xuanzong (712-756 AD), much of dynasty's defensive strength in the Western Regions had diminished due to the gradual deterioration in the organizational structure of the 'Four Garrisons of Anxi.' Emperor Xuangzong's neglect of his state responsibilities due to his fascination with his concubine Yang Guifei had ultimately brought about the An Lushan rebellion which sealed the demise of the emperor himself. Much of the Tibetan gains had coincided with the gradual weakening in the dynasty's defenses during Xuangzong's reign and with the eventual complete withdrawal of the reminents of the Chinese troops from the garrisons to reinforce the capital Xi'an against the rebellion. These events argues in favour of the conclusion that in the main the Tibetans had confronted much diminished Tang military resistance and thus were opportunistically and conveniently filling a power vacuum. In a historical sense, it was not until 1759 AD that the Ming dynasty was able to reclaim the lost lands in the western regions and retain them to the present.

The eighth century saw the height of the Tibetan hegemony which was ultimately destroyed by the rising power of the Uyghurs during the first half of the ninth century.[24,25] A discussion of this subject will be beyond the scope of the present work. But, whilst the Tibetans were pursuing their military engagements in far away Sichuan and Yunnan, the Uyghur tribes along the northern fringes of the Western Regions were systematically strengthening their power with dynastic tentacles extending east into Mongolia and west into Central Asia. This subject will be discussed in detail in later chapters. Presently however, suffice it to state that today's population in the Western Regions is ethnically predominantly Uyghur despite the concerted efforts made by China's central government over many decades to redress this issue. Historically, China has encouraged the settling of Hans in Xinjiang from other parts of the country as a measure of safety against the inherent dangers of separatist movements that constantly lurk in the province.

In 751 AD, a composite army of Uyghurs from Central Asia and Abbasid caliphate mercenaries driven by Islamic zeal defeated the Tang dynasty's forces at the battle of Talas (Talas River) and took control of the southern parts of Kazakhstan.[26] Moreover, the victory at Talas had given the Uyghur the impetus to re-engage their enemy the Göktürks in battle that culminated with a decisive victory for the Uyghurs. With this victory, the Uyghur Turks founded their First Uyghur Empire (Orkhun Uyghur Empire) in the mid eighth century with its capital in Ordunbaliq, in the original Uyghur homelands in north-central Mongolia, and exercised dominance over territories to their south that included Gaochang and the north-western parts of China's Western Regions. However, the fortunes of the new empire were short lived and it survived only until 840 AD. The glory days of its people were still six centuries in the future. They were to rise again to prominence as a second empire under the Islamic khanates of the Karakhojas and the Karakhanids with their centres of power in Kashgar and Turfan, as we shall see later in Chapter 11. However, in 840 AD the Yenisei Kyrgyz from the northern steppe plains invaded the Uyghur homelands in Mongolia and vanquished the first Uyghur Empire.

Chinese sources of the twelfth century describe the early Kyrgyz as red-haired people with white skin and blue eyes. Their two centuries of dominance over the lands formerly held by the Uyghur tribes was unremarkable and by the early twelfth century that dominance had declined precipitously and was giving way to the rising power of the Mongols under the leadership of Genghis Khan.[27] The Kyrgyz influence remained confined mostly to the immediate vicinity of the Tian Shan Mountains but was eventually brought to an end in1207 by Genghis Khan's son Jochi.

Upon the loss of their first empire, the Uyghur tribes scattered across Central Asia, primarily in areas of present-day Uzbekistan and Turkmenistan. But gradually they formed the nucleus for the founding in 940 AD the Karakhanid Uyghur Khanate which was a federation of a number of regional tribes including the Karluk, the Turgesh and the Basmyl - all related nomadic tribes residing in the regions of Kara-Irtysh (Great or Black Irtysh) River and the Altai Mountains in the Central Asian steppes. This federation functioned as an 'empire' under the sovereignty of the Karakhan clan whose leaders had converted to Islam in 934 AD and had maintained Kashgar as their capital. It ruled all of West Turkistan, western Xinjiang and much of Central Asia. The khanate was composed of four Il-khanates (subordinate khanates) with the centralized power maintained in Kashgar. The northern Il-khanate covered territories in Kyrgyzstan and Kazakhstan with its capital in Balasaghun. The smaller southern Il-khanate covered Khotan. The eastern Il-khanate presided over the sedentary Buddhist Uyghur tribal clans in the Tarim basin with its capital in Turfan and, finally, the western Il-khanate, which had its capital in Samarkand/Bukhara, ruled over Ferghana, Bactria and parts of northern Afghanistan in a joint alliance with the Samanids of Sasaninan Iran. Initially, the combined population of the Il-khanates was a composite of a large percentage of Muslims with lesser proportions of Buddhists, Shamanists, and possibly a few Christians, all subjects of a unified Il-khanates answerable to the central authority in Kashgar. Gradually, the segment of the population composed of Buddhist disintegrated either due to internal conflicts, conversions or departures thus giving the area a predominantly Muslim presence. The decline of the Karakhanid sovereignty began around 1040 AD and culminated with its submission to Jochi in 1212 AD.

As a closing addition to the present chapter, it should be noted that after Genghis Khan had unified the Mongolic tribes north of the Chinese frontiers early in the twelfth century, he advanced south towards the Western Regions and, more specifically, towards the Karakhanid federation. Although the Karakhanid khans judged it prudent in 1212 AD to offer their allegiance to the Mongols and avoid a certain destructive confrontation, their decision effectively ended the Karakhanid sovereignty. The allegiance required of the Uyghurs to pay tribute to the Mongols and provide troops when called upon to do so. Despite their submission to the Mongols, the Karakhanids prevailed and impacted upon the history of the region until the middle decades of the seventeenth century. Their former domains remain today ethnically characteristically Uyghur within present-day China and are referred to collectively as the Xinjiang Uyghur Autonomous Region.[28]

References

1. Cotterell, A., *The Imperial Capitals of China - An Inside View of the Celestial Empire*. Pimlico, London (2007).
2. Dillon, M., *China's Muslim Hui Community: Migration, Settlement and Sects*. Routledge, London (1999).
3. Steinhardt, N. S., *Chinese Imperial City Planning*. University of Hawaii Press, Honolulu (1999).
4. Waley, A. S., *The Re-making of China*. EP Dutton and Company, New York (1914).
5. Legge, J., *The Religions of China: Confucianism and Taoism Described and Compared with Christianity*. Hodder and Stoughton, Cambridge, Massachusetts (1880).
6. Bonavia, J., *The Silk Road From Xi'an to Kashgar*. Revised by Christoph Baumer. Odyssey Books and Guides, Hong Kong (2004).
7. *China's Population across the Century (Gansu)*. China Statistical Publishing House, Beijing (1994).
8. *Gansu Statistical Yearbook - 2001*. China Statistics Press, Beijing (2001).
9. Guo, P., Xinjiang: The Land and the People. New World Press, New York (1989).
10. *Major Figures on 2000 Population Census of China*. China Statistics Press, Beijing (2001).
11. Cavendish, M., *Peoples of Western Asia*. Marshall Cavendish Corp., Singapore (2006).
12. Yu, T., *A Comprehensive History of Western Regions*. China New Press, Beijing (2003).
13. Millward, J. A., *Eurasian Crossroads: A History of Xinjiang*. Columbia University Press, New York (2007).
14. Yap, J. P., *Wars with the Xiongnu - A Translation from Zizhi Tongjian - Chapters 4-17*. AuthorHouse, Milton Keynes (2009).
15. Brough, J., Supplementary Notes on Third-Century Shan-shan. *Bulletin of the School of Oriental and African Studies*. No. XXXIII, London (1970).
16. Brough, J., Comments on Third-Century Shan-shan and the history of Buddhism. *Bulletin of the School of Oriental and African Studies*. No. XXVIII, London (1965).
17. Giles, H. A. (trans.), *The Travels of Fa-hsien (399-414 AD): or Record of the Buddhistic Kingdoms*. Cambridge University Press, Cambridge (1923).
18. Yu, T., *A Study of the History of the Relationship between the Western and Eastern Han, Wei, Jin, Northern and Southern Dynasties*

and the Western Regions. Chinese Academy of Social Sciences, Beijing (1995).
19. Khazanov, A. M., *Nomads and the Outside World.* University of Wisconsin Press, Madison, Wisconsin (1984).
20. MacKerras, C., *The Uighur Empire According to the T'ang Dynasty Histories.* Australian National University Press, Canberra, Australia (1972)
21. Bartold, V. V., *The Kyrgyz: A Historical Essay.* Frunze (1927).
22. Sinor, D. (ed.), The Establishment and Dissolution of the Turk Empire. *The Cambridge History of Early Inner Asia.* Cambridge University Press, Cambridge (1990).
23. Chen, C., Anxi Sizhen (The Four Garrisons of Anxi). *In Encyclopedia of China: Chinese History.* Beijing (1978).
24. Beckwith, C. I., *The Tibetan Empire in Central Asia.* Princeton University Press, Princeton, New Jersey (1987).
25. Beckwith, C. I., *Empires of the Silk Road: A History of Central Eurasia from theBronze Age to the Present.* Princeton University Press, Princeton, New Jersey (2009).
26. Wang, X., *Political Relationships Between the Chinese, Tibetans and Arabs.* Peking University Press, Beijing (1992).
27. Grousset, R., *The Empire of the Steppes.* Rutgers University Press, New Brunswick, New Jersey (1970).
28. Mackerras, C., *China's Minority Cultures: Identities and Integration since 1912.* Longman Publishing, London (1995).

Treasures of the Silk Road

Chapter Five

The Settlements of the Silk Road in Gansu Province

The term Silk Road, in German *'Seidenstrasse,'* was coined in 1877 by the German explorer and geographer Baron Ferdinand von Richthofen. Despite this rather recent term describing a road that has served China well for many centuries, parts of it, at least, have been in use since the first millennium BC as demonstrated by finds of Chinese silk in Southern Siberia.

The Middle Kingdom's main access to lands west of its frontiers was by the Hexi Corridor (*Hexi Zoulang*) which ran west of Lanzhou in Gansu province leading directly to the oasis town of Anxi (Guazhou) in the far north-western corner of Gansu. Gansu's capital Lanzhou was the first major town within China lying west of Xi'an (Chang'an). The trade for Chinese silk going west began in Xi'an and ended there with foreign goods coming east. By the end of the first millennium BC China was importing jade through the Hexi Corridor arriving from the kingdom of Khotan (Hotan) nestled in a mountainous region in the south-western part of of the province of Xinjiang. It was this kingdom that the Chinese imperial envoy led by Zhang Qian first encountered when sent by the Han emperor Wudi in 139 BC to seek alliances against the Xiongnu nomads. When Zhang Qian returned to China in 126 BC he brought with him valuable ideas about trading possibilities with the many kingdoms he had visited. Goods of interest to the Chinese, for example, were horses from Ferghana and glass, silver and gold from Persia.

Most accounts of the Silk Road depict the walled-city of Xi'an as the starting point of the merchants with their goods-laden camels on their way west. However, the actual caravan trains were not allowed inside the city walls but were assembled some distance away from the western wall. Very few traders or merchants would actually travel the full length of the rather complex and demanding stretches of the Silk Roads. The majority of the traders were local residents of the towns, villages and the oasis settlements through which the trade routes meandered their way west. They would travel from their home markets to one in an adjacent market where they would exchange their goods and then return home within a few days. The traded goods would then be carried by other merchants further along the traditional Silk Road:

> A degree of civilization prevails amongst all the people of this country, in consequence of their frequent intercourse with the towns, which are numerous and but little distant from each other. To these the merchants continually resort, carrying their goods from one city to another, as the fairs are successively held at each.

The Sogdians, in particular, who lived essentially at the center of the network of the Silk Roads, enjoyed the luxury of being able to travel east to Xi'an or west to Constantinople. Nevertheless, there were a very small number of travelers who did indeed journey from one end of the Silk Roads to the other but they were in the main missionaries driven with the zeal to spread the elements of their faith.

Anxi was a branching point for the two major silk routes most frequently used by the camel caravans, commonly referred to as the Northern and Southern routes. From Anxi, the older Southern route, prominent from the second to the fourth centuries, proceeded south-westerly through the great Buddhist center in Dunhuang and reached Miran. Alternatively, from Dunhuang the road turned directly west to Loulan and then cut a southerly path to join the main track at Miran. From Miran the road turns directly west and progresses between the southern edges of the Taklamakan Deserts and the northern slopes of the Altun and Kunlun mountains to reach first Chakilik and then Cherchen, Niya, Keriya, the kingdom of Khotan, Yarkand and finally Kashgar,[1,2] respectively.

Beyond Gansu province, the less direct Northern route to Kashgar beginning at Anxi was longer but was also less perilous than its southern counterpart and became prominent later in the fourth century AD. From Anxi in a north-westerly direction the Northern route first reached Hami then Turfan (Turupan) and Korla. From Turfan a short section of the road led north to Urumqi. From Korla the main road follows a path between the northern edges of the Taklamakan Desert and the southern slopes of the Tian Shan Mountains heading west to reach first Kuqa then Aksu and, finally, joins the Southern route at

The Settlements of the Silk Road in Gansu Province

Kashgar. From Kashgar the trading caravans could continue their journey in three alternative directions. First in a westerly direction, they could traverse the Torugart Pass in the Tian Shan range and reach Tashkent and Uzbekistan's Samarkand and Bukhara. Alternatively, travelling south from Kashgar and passing through the town of Tashkorgan, the caravans could negotiate the high-altitude Khunjerap Pass in the Karakorums and reach Taxila. A passage across the Hindu Kush Mountains then led to Kabul. The Buddhist centres in Gandahara and the great sub-continent of India lay just beyond Taxila. And finally, the caravans could follow a third route running in a south-westerly direction from Kashgar and reach Balkh and Merv that lay beyond Erkashtam Pass in the Pamir Mountains.

There were also secondary routes to the north of the Northern route which were diversions from Turfan. The oasis town of Turfan was a staging point for roads leading directly north for trade with Mongolia, Russia and Siberia, or for roads leading west through Urumqi to Tashkent and to Samarkand and Bukhara. From Bukhara the roads skirted the northern shores of the Caspian Sea and reached the Black Sea that provided access to the port cities of Constantinople and Trabizond. A road from Bukhara also led to the Iranian stronghold of Merv and continued towards Tehran, Hamadan, Baghdad and Damascus and to ports on the Mediterranean Sea, respectively.

Other secondary roads criss-crossed Xinjiang's central deserts, the Taklamakan and the Lop, and divided the deserts into several segments. These roads mostly followed the banks of the rivers Khotan Darya and the Kuruk Darya; the former ran north from the southern kingdom of Khotan and, traversing the Tarim river basin, connected the kingdom with the oasis town of Kuqa (Kucha) on the main Northern route. A road known as the Middle Silk Road branching from Korla led to Loulan across the Lop Nor Desert. The oasis town of Loulan was located on the shores of brackish salty Lop Nor Lake into which the Tarim River emptied. The site is now completely submerged below the arid desert sands. Loulan was a key staging post for the trading caravans until the fourth century AD, especially for the caravans preparing for their perilous journey west. Few caravans, if any, ventured away from the secondary roads criss-crossings the central deserts because what lay away from them spelled a certain death in the endless sandy horizons devoid of water, vegetation or shelter.

Treasures of the Silk Road

Lanzhou - the Frontier

Surrounded by Gaolan Mountains to its south and White Pagoda Mountains in the north Lanzhou was, as early the sixth century BC, the Middle Kingdom's gateway to the Western Regions bringing the kingdom virtually face to face along its south-western frontiers with the troublesome Qiang tribes of Tibetan ancestry. Lanzhou is situated in the south-eastern corner of the province of Gansu some 350 kilometres east of the headwaters of the Huang He (Yellow River), which at a point just past Lanzhou begins its sharp turn to the north flowing towards Inner Mongolia. Trapped in the narrow valley of the two mountain ranges through which the Yellow river makes its course, Lanzhou could only expand horizontally along the southern and northern banks of the river thus creating its present dimensions of about 20 kilometres long (east/west) and 1-2 kilometres wide (north/south). By virtue of its location at the southern end of the Hexi Corridor and poised nearly as an extension of the corridor, Lanzhou during the Han dynasty was known as Jincheng (Golden City) and commanded the approaches to the Silk Road's eastern terminal city of Chang'an (Xi'an). After the fall of the Han Dynasty, Lanzhou served as the capital of a number of successive tribal states. For example, in the fourth century Lanzhou was briefly the capital of the independent state of the Former Liang (317-376 AD). Under the Sui Dynasty (581–618 AD) the city became the seat of Lanzhou prefecture and in the eighth century (763 AD) Lanzhou fell within the conquered territories of the Tibetan Empire until it was recovered by the Tang dynasty in 843 AD.[3] Lanzhou was relatively secure when the Western Xia dynasty (1032-1227 AD) ruled the Wei river valley but all was changed when the frontier areas were plundered by the Mongols under the command of Genghis Khan.

Lanzhou's present population represents a mix of different ethnic heritages. They include, but not exclusively, Han, Hui, Bonan, and Dongxiang as well as Tibetans, Uyghurs and Salar peoples. The Dongxiang and the Bonan are Chinese Muslims of Mongol descent mixed with various ethnic groups predominantly of Central Asian origins. Their Mongol origins stem from the Mongolian troops stationed in the Xunhua area of Qinghai province and Hezhou (old name of Linxia in Gansu) during the reign of Genghis Khan (1162-1227 AD) and later during the Yuan dynasty. They converted to Sun'ni Islam in the thirteenth century. The Bonan in particular were converted to Islam by the Hui Sufi master Hajji Ma Laichi (1681- 1766 AD).

The Settlements of the Silk Road in Gansu Province

The Salar on the other hand, are the descendants of the Salyr tribe, which belongs to the Oghuz tribe of the Seljuk Turks. The word *Salyr* means 'those who wave swords.' They entered the Chinese territories from Central Asia during the Tang Dynasty when trade along the Silk Road was at its nadir.

Lanzhou's rich Islamic heritage is reflected in the number of impressively built mosques that dominate the city's skyline. The earliest mosque, Xiuheyan, dates back to 1308 AD during the reign of Emperor Hong Wu (Wu Tsung). By the end of the seventeenth century there were fourteen mosques in Lanzhou that included the Xiguan, Nanguan and the Pagoda mosques. The architectural features of the mosques in general incorporate the Chinese iconic multi-storied central pagoda of carved wood decorated with Islamic features, such as pointed arches, and either gilded or painted green. A more traditional architecture of Middle Eastern Arabian origins is the use of the onion-domed central prayer hall constructed with four tall pencil minarets installed at each compass-point of the hall.

Following the Buddhist traditions at Dunhuang in the western reaches of the province, Lanzhou became the logical eastern extension of Buddhism in the fifth century AD as the new faith gradually penetrated the Middle Kingdom from the west.[4] By the eleventh century Lanzhou had become a thriving centre of Buddhism. The Bingling Thousand Buddha Caves, very much a prototype of Dunhuang's Mogao Caves discussed below, are located on the rocky Jishi Hill in Yongjing about 35 kilometers south-west of Lanzhou. Access to the caves is by boat from Yongjing across the Liujiaxia Reservoir. There the grottoes have one of the biggest surviving sculptured statues of the Buddha carved on sheer virtical rock faces dating from the Tang dynasty period (618-907 AD). The largest statue stands about twenty seven meters high. Stylistically, it is much similar to the monumental statue of the Buddha at Bamiyan in Afghanistan, which was carved about 250 years earlier but unfortunately destroyed recently by radical anti-Buddhist factions in Afghanistan during a surge in their iconoclastic movement. Nonetheless, these giant statues of the Buddha represented the classic blend of Gandharan art in the early Chinese artistry.

The earliest Buddhist cave paintings at Bingling were begun towards the end of the Western Jin dynasty around 420 AD and their numbers continued to increase unabated throughout the Wei, Sui, Tang, Song, Yuan, Ming and Qing dynasties.[5] The legacy of the Buddhism at

Bingling extended further east and are seen in the stylistically similar grottoes of Yungang near Datong and in Longmen near Luoyang. The number of Buddhist monasteries has steadily increased in modern China and one major monastery, the Labrang monastery (Labuleng Si) can be visited in the village of Xiahe about 180 kilometres south-west of Lanzhou. The village itself offers a glimpse into the semi-nomadic lifestyle of a small Tibetan community which lives mostly by herding. But many of the small traders in the village are Muslim whose ancestors had ventured beyond the Muslim town of Linxia and precariously settled amongst the Tibetans in these outer limits of Islam in Gansu. The Labrang monastery on the other hand is one of the most important Tibetan Gelugpa (Yellow Hat) schools of Tibetan Buddhism in China. It was founded by the first generation Living Buddha in 1709, Ngawang-tsondru (1648-1712 AD). The monastery thrived due to the continued benefaction it received from the Qing emperors who were much devoted to the Buddhist faith. Perhaps not surprisingly, the monastery is now home to the largest number of Buddhist monks outside the Tibetan Autonomous Region.

On the road to Xiahe from Lanzhou lies the small town of Linxia, the capital of the Hui Autonomous Prefecture. The Hui, as discussed in the previous chapter, are a product of the convergence and mixing of a large number of ethnic groups from Mongolia, Central Asia and the Middle East which retained the Islamic faith and became a dominant group in the north-west of China, particularly during the Mongol-based Yuan dynasty of the thirteenth and fourteenth centuries. Their Islamic faith originated from the Muslim Arab and Central Asian ancestors who came as merchants and traders along the ancient Silk Road. Their primary settlements were in Lanzhou where today's large number of mosques and the majority Muslin population continue to play an important role in their regional political landscape. From Lanzhou the faith trickled south to Linxia where solid foundations of Hui Muslim communities were established.[6] They thrive to the present day amongst their some twenty odd mosques despite the town's dusty remoteness and its parched environment. As a reminder of Linxia's Arab connections, a tablet erected in the grounds of the Dongguan Mosque gives a genealogy of its founding imams beginning in the eleventh century with Sheikh Abud al-Kadir al-Jeylani (Year of Hijra 470-561). Also the tomb of the region's first Arab missionary, Hamuzeli (Hamuz Ali) but known in Chinese as Han Zeling, stands on the summit of a local hill. It is believed he had come to Linxia sometime in the eighth or ninth century AH (Anno Hijra). His mausoleum on the hillside cemetery is a venerated holy site for pilgrimage and prayers.

There has been some Christian presence in Linxia since the early parts of the twentieth century. However, the Muslim Hui, Bonan and the Dongxiang have been reticent to proselytization hence the vast majority of people in Linxia today have not been exposed to the Christian Gospels.

Destination Zhangye

The Silk Road merchants in caravans usually of no less than sixty camels in tandem in the nadir of the road's trading activities would begin their journey west out of Lanzhou carrying goods of silk and spices destined for the markets beyond the western frontiers of the Middle Kingdom. This journey would take them through the relatively non-arduous Hexi Corridor and lead them to Zhangye, the first oasis town in the province of Gansu on the southern edges of the Gobi Desert. The corridor, as the name implies, is a narrow relatively flat fertile valley nestled between the northern periphery of the Qilian Mountains and the southern rim of the Longshou Mountains. It begins near Lanzhou and extends in a north-westerly direction and ends in the vicinity of Jiayuguan Gate where segments of the western limits of the Great Wall are still visible in the form of undulating crumbled earthen mounds dating back to the times of the Western (Former) Han dynasty.

Zhangye, formerly known as Ganzhou and referred to as Campichu by Marco Polo, lies in the center of the Hexi Corridor. Its surrounds was the frontier for much of the history of the Middle Kingdom and served as a natural defensive barrier and a forward base for military advances into the Western Regions. The city became the garrison headquarters for General Huo Qubing of the Western Han dynasty who, despite his premature death at the age of 24 in 117 BC, had established in his capacity as a military leader a firm control over the Hexi Corridor. As a result of Huo's successes, Zhangye, in 111 BC, was declared the administrative centre for the extended authority of the Middle Kingdom. It grew to prominence along with the expanding use of the Silk Road and virtually all caravans travelling east or west were required to stop at this oasis town for administrative processing. Zhangye's prominence continued to grow with time. It was considered important enough for the Sui dynasty (581-618 AD) to send Pei Ju as an official representative of the royal court to supervise the trading markets and enforce payment of tribute to the court. By the end of the Silk Road era, during the Ming dynasty (1364-1644 AD), the town had taken the form of a large military garrison with an imposing fortress to guard not only its strategic location but also the western limits of the Great Wall.

A Gulou (Drum Tower) of typical traditional Chinese architecture, built by the Ming dynasty in 1507 AD, characteristically houses a large bronze bell and marks the centre of present-day Zhangye. Drum towers are often referred to as bell towers and the four streets that radiate out from them identify the four compass points (*bei* for north, *nan* for south, *dong* for east and *xi* for west).

Zhangye's present sedentary population includes Han, Yugu, Tibetans, Hui, Mongat, Zhuang and Uyghur. The legacy of the Tibetan occupation of the Hexi Corridor which has endured the vicissitudes of centuries of regional conflicts is visible today in the Buddhist temples of Mati Si (the Horse's Hoof Temple) and Sunan Yugu, some 60 kilometres south of Zhangye. The latter consist of a large collection of Buddhist grottoes set in a vast area of hilly valleys from which Buddhist teachings were transmitted to the Middle Kingdom. These temple areas were the eastern tentacles of the immensely extensive and the more established grottoes at Dunhuang further west in Gansu near the province's boundary with Xinjiang. Today Zhangye enjoys a wide representation of a number of faiths within its own city limits including Daoism, Buddhism, Catholicism, Protestantism and Islam.

Zhangye's religious history is deeply engraved with Buddhism as a result of its geographic location along the Silk Road, which permitted continued Buddhist influences to permeate the royal courts of the Middle Kingdom. The city is the site of the Giant Buddha Temple which houses Asia's notably largest indoor reclining Buddha cast in wood and clay that measures some fifty feet in length. Marco Polo in the accounts of his travels gives quite an elaborate description of the temple. Furthermore, we have learned from a number of ancient chronicles that in the first year of the Yong An Period in the reign of Chong Zong of the Western Xia dynasty, corresponding to the first year of the Yuan Fu Period in the reign of Zhe Zong of the Northern Song dynasty (AD 1098), the emperor's Buddhist tutor, Wei Mie, had claimed that a chorus of heavenly music had led him to dig out from the ground an ancient statue of the Buddha in the Nirvana posture. The statue depicted the historical Buddha, Sakyamuni, in Shayana (Final

The Settlements of the Silk Road in Gansu Province

Nirvana) posture lying on his right side, his head resting on the palm of the upturned hand of his right arm and his left arm stretched out flat along his left side. Thus a foundation was laid there in the ground upon which the Temple of the Reclining Buddha was later built. For the sake of clarity, it should be noted that the Western Xia dynasty existed from AD 1038 to 1227 in areas what are now the south-western parts of Inner Mongolia bordering Outer Mongolia and the provinces of Xinjiang, Ningxia, Gansu and Shaanxi. The dynasty was decimated by the Mongols who founded the Yuan dynasty (1279–1368 AD).

The Reclining Buddha Temple abounds with mythological anecdotes. For example, it is said that after the Southern Song dynasty was vanquished by the Mongols, the dynasty's deposed emperor Bing Di converted to Buddhism and moved to live in the temple where he became Master He Zun. It is also claimed that the Yuan dynasty's second emperor, Kublai Khan was born in this temple.

During the Ming dynasty in the ninth year of the Cheng Tsu Period (AD 1411), the Reclining Buddha Temple was restored and expanded to include twenty buildings and was commissioned under a provincial jurisdiction to administer the new office of Regional Buddhist Religious Affairs. In AD 1422 a series of Buddhist relics were unearthed from the base of a stupa which led a eunuch named Wang Gui from the imperial court to secure state funds for the construction of the temple's Golden Hall (Jin Ta). It housed scores of Buddhist statues and extensive frescoes typical of Buddhist artistic traditions. There the Buddhist Maha Prajna Paramita Hridaya Sutra (the Heart Doctrine) and the Tri- Pitaka Sutra (the Three Baskets Doctrine) were translated and preserved in gold gilt manuscripts.[7,8]. After having undergone a series of name changes at the behest of successive emperors, one of the temple's older names, Hong Ren (Great Man), was rephrased by the Qing dynasty in 1679 AD and called it the Temple of Great Benevolence, but now it is generally known as the Giant Buddha Temple. In 1966, the temple came under the protection of the provincial government as a national cultural treasure.

One additional legacy of Buddhism in Zangye's religious history that is worthy of note is the Wooden Pagoda Temple. The original of this Chinese pavilion-type pagoda is believed to have been built at the behest of King Ashoka the Great of India as part of his dedication to expand the Buddhist faith throughout Asia. Ashoka belonged to the Indian Maurya dynasty who ruled essentially the entire Indian sub-continent from 269 to 232 BC. However, a more credible history suggests that the original temple – now the grounds of a Middle School in Zangye – was built during the Northern Zhou dynasty then restored in 582 AD by Emperor Wendi of the Sui dynasty but was eventually destroyed during an inclement weather. The present structure with nine progressively diminishing floor areas is a reconstruction completed in 1926. From the pagoda's uppermost level at a height of nearly 33 metres, the snow-capped peaks of the Qilian Mountains to the south-west can be clearly seen.

Yumen and Anxi

The oasis town of Yumen derives its name from two critical passes within the province of Gansu which lie at either end of the Dunhuang extension of the Great Wall about sixty eight kilometres apart. These two westernmost passes of the Middle Kingdom are known as Yumenguan (Jade Gate) and Yangguan.[9] They functioned as two important gates at the frontiers of the Han dynasty and all caravans travelling through Dunhuang either along the northern or the southern branch of the Silk Road were required to pass through one of these gates. The ruins of Yumenguan, which controlled the traffic from the northern branch, are situated eighty kilometres north-west of Dunhuang some four-hundred kilometres west of the city of Yumen. The gate was inserted into the Great Wall as a square enclosure bounded by four mud walls that stood ten metres high. It was constructed in 121 BC during the reign of Emperor Wudi of the Han dynasty. The ruins of its sister gate Yangguan, which controlled the traffic from the southern branch of the Silk Road, lie seventy five kilometres south-west of Dunhuang.

The history of this rather non-descript wind-swept oasis of Yumen, at the doorsteps of the Lop Nor Desert, is unremarkable. The area first came under the direct control of the Middle Kingdom as an outpost frontier territory in the early years of the Han dynasty. In the fifth century AD, Yumen came to be known as Huiji when it was recovered by the Northern Wei dynasty (386–534 AD) during the Chinese periodic occupations of areas around Dunhuang. Subsequently, the name Huiji was reverted to the original, Yumen, by the Sui dynasty in 581 AD. Yumen was dominated for nearly a century by the Tibetan empire in the eighth century AD before it was recovered by the Tang dynasty.

The Settlements of the Silk Road in Gansu Province

The scattered Buddhist sites in the vicinity of Yumen follow the trail of Buddhism that eventually reached the heartland of the Middle Kingdom. Not far from the city centre, just north of the nearby village of Chijin, stands a large, ancient and a magnificent stupa. Stupas are Buddhist religious monuments which originally were simple mounds of mud or clay. They were erected to commemorate the great deeds of the Buddha Siddhartha Sakyamuni Gautama and also to enshrine within them Buddhist relics. With time, stupas gradually evolved into significant structures of various designs and sizes often embellished with bas relief images and complex geometric patterns. Their locations are ususally associated with sites of Buddhist temples, monasteries and institutions and often reflect the size and importance of the Buddhist community in their vicinity.

To the south-west of Yumen against a barren hillside stand a complex of Buddhist caves that contain magnificent Buddhist frescoes with images of Buddhist monks and saints with clearly Indian facial features. Again, these frescoes and murals continue to confirm that Indian Buddhist traditions were brought to the Middle Kingdom not only by the dedicated Chinese monks who travelled along the Silk Road to India but also by a vast army of Indian Buddhist monks and acolytes who impressed upon the land their heritage in spirit and form.

At the north-west extremity of the Hexi Corridor the ancient oasis town of Anxi was nestled between the fading north-western foothills of the Qilian Mountains and the southern reaches of the Gobi desert. The origins of this oasis, situated in the unbounded desolation of north-west Gansu province, go back to the first century BC when the Han dynasty under the reign of Emperor Wudi, progressively began implementing the programme of reinforcing its hold on the commercial significance of the trade along the Silk Road. Although the modern town of Anxi, about forty kilometres north of the ancient oasis, is a non-descript modern development, it nonetheless has become the equivalent of the ancient oasis and serves as an important junction for the overland roads that lead either west to Hami or south to Dunhuang.

Historically, Anxi was also known as Guazhou and Suoyang. Anecdotally, the latter name was acquired when the Han general Xue Rengui during one of his long-lasting campaigns near the western extremities of the Great Wall ordered his men to dig up and eat the locally abundant perennial plant Cynomorium (commonly known as Suo Yang) Thus the oasis came to be known as Suoyang. The name

Guazhou was acquired during the Tang dynasty at a time when the oasis had grown in size to a respectable small city and its use continues to the present.

Mingsha Shan

Mingsha Shan (Mingsha Mountain) is known otherwise as the 'Singing Sand Mountain.' It was known as the Sha Jio Shan during the Later (Eastern) Han dynasty (25-220 AD). Popularly known as Shen Sha Shan (Magical Sand Mountain) it acquired its present name during the Jin dynasty (1115-1234 AD). The Mingsha Shan is so named for the echo created by the wind whipping off at the surfaces of its sand dunes. The southern rocky face of this mountain range is an unlikely place to discover a cornucopia of unimaginable collection of Buddhist art that chronicles in a collage of murals and sculpture a local history of a thousand years. Situated at the edge of the barren Gobi desert southeast of Dunhuang, this mountain range is 40 kilometres long along its east-west axis and twenty kilometres wide from north to south. But its significance to the caravans that followed the trails of the Silk Road was that at its northern foothills near Dunhuang lay an oasis with an inexhaustible source of fresh underground water that surfaces in the form of a crescent pool amidst a sea of sand, hence the name, Crescent Moon Spring (or Crescent Moon Lake). Here amongst the rolling giant sand dunes that reach a height of 250 meters, this small lake with an average depth of 4.2 metres remains clear of sand and its water is always cool and sweet. Although over the centuries it has yielded somewhat to the advances of the all encroaching Gobi desert sands, it nonetheless presently covers a respectable area of 7.8 *Mu* (1 *Mu* = 667 square metres). Over the centuries the lake has earned a number of other descriptive names such as Sha-Jing (Sand Well), Yu Ya Quan (Medicinal Spring) and finally during the Qing dynasty, Crescent Moon Spring. Along the side of the lake is a pagoda in traditional Han Chinese architecture that is now used to serve the visiting guests. Legend has it that a Chinese general while returning from a campaign in the Western Regions had his army camped by the sand dunes beside the Crescent Lake. In the depth of the night as the soldiers quietly slept, a horrific sandstorm erupted and instantly buried the army. It is said the sound of the echoes heard at the dunes are those of the buried soldiers clamouring at their misfortune and struggling to free themselves from their eternal bondage.

The Settlements of the Silk Road in Gansu Province

Splendour of Dunhuang Legacy

For the camel caravans of the Silk Road with an average daily progress that ranged between 20-30 kilometres, Dunhuang marked the start of the long desert crossing westward either along the southern rim of the Taklamakan desert leading to Khotan and Kashgar, or along the less perilous but longer route skirting the northern rim of the desert to Hami as their first oasis destination some 400 kilometres away. This was not a small feat by any standard when one considers that the camel caravans treading the desert sands under burning sun or freezing temperatures yet still had over two thousand kilometres of the unforgiving desert to negotiate before reaching the safety of Kashgar. The etymology of Taklamakan (Tak-la-makan) perhaps lies in the corruption of the Arabic words Tak (gateway/archway), la (no) and makan (place), otherwise meaning a 'place without gateway' that is, once entered an exit is not possible. This fearsome reputation of the desert is well deserved for it stands as the world's second largest desert with howling sub-freezing winter winds and scorching summer heat that create an uninhabitable terrain of constantly shifting sands beneath yellowish opaque air of suffocating sand storms. Scores of beasts and men have lost their lives in their quest to cross the Taklamakan, and many towns and kingdoms have vanished in its bowels and remain buried in its everlasting sands.

With the two natural passes of Yumenguan and Yangguan to its north-west and south-west, respectively, geographically Dunhuang commanded a strategic position that controlled the entrance to the narrow Hexi Corridor leading straight to the heart of the fertile plains of the Middle Kingdom and to its ancient capitals of Chang'an and Luoyang. For this reason, after the Chinese victory (Han dynasty) over the Xiongnu in 121 BC, the Great Wall was extended to Dunhuang and the city was protected by a series of military fortifications. By the second century AD, Dunhuang with a population approaching 100,000 had become a key supply base for those caravans setting out for the arduous trek across the Taklamakan or for those new arrivals from the west with an eye for the lucrative markets further east. The flourishing trade along the Silk Road had made Dunhuang a rather wealthy and an influential town. By the fourth century AD, the Silk Road had brought Dunhuang both commercial prosperity and a growing Buddhist community centred some twenty five kilometres to its south-east along a cliff at the edge of the Mingsha Shan that came to be known as the Mogao Cave Temples. Yet the fortunes of Dunhuang did not remain immune to the prevailing political landscape. It suffered under the occupation of the Tibetans from 781 to 847 AD while the Middle Kingdom was enjoying a renaissance under the Tang dynasty. It came under the domination of the Western Xia dynasty in 1035 AD but in 1226 the victorious Mongol armies decimated the area in the wake of the founding of their empire.

But during the Early Qin dynasty in the year 366 AD here at the edge of the Gobi desert along a two-kilometre long cliff on the rocky southern face of the Mingsha Mountain - the northside of this mountain range slopes down into high rolling sand dunes that meet the south-western edge of the Gobi desert - that a local Buddhist monk and his companion Fa Liang set about carving out a cave for their solitary abode and for the beginnings of a magnificent legacy of Buddhist artistic collection to be consigned to posterity. Over the next one thousand years, they were followed by hundreds of other monks, devout Buddhists and pilgrims who similarly left their imprints in their own caves along this rocky face and endowed them with their visionary images of the holy and the sacred.[10,11] These included some 3,000 murals representative of the Northern Liang (397-439 AD), Northern Wei (386-534 AD), Northern Zhou (557-581 AD), Sui (581-618 AD), Tang (618-690 and up to 936 AD), Western Xia (1032-1227 AD) and Yuan (1279-1368 AD) dynasties. Although no paintings or carvings have survived from the early fourth century period, a significant number from the fifth century can still be seen. Most of the murals and frescoes take their theme from the Jataka stories which refer to a voluminous body of folklore-like literature native to India concerning the previous births of the Buddha. The chosen imagery and the visualizations in the drawings are dynamic and are elevated to celestial plains with swirling clouds, floating ribbons and flying *apsaras* (Buddhist angels) clad in sensuously revealing garments. The frescoes composed during the later centuries are less ethereal and instead express a greater sense of stillness with emphasis on serene iconographic Buddha figures surrounded by Bodhisattvas.

The earliest Buddhist monks arrived at Dunhuang via the Southern branch of the Silk Road. The majority of the arriving monks were Indian in origin who entered the Western Regions either directly at Yarkand or reached Kashgar through the Pamir Mountains before continuing their missions further east along the Southern branch. At the Mogao Caves, they studied and reproduced their scriptures and filled their grottoes with one of the most extensive and exquisite collections of Buddhist paintings and sculptures in the world. Every surface of the walls and ceilings of hundreds of caves was covered with painted clay stucco, some 45,000 square metres in all, and all the voids were adorned with rows upon rows of life-size and miniature images of the Buddha, subtly varied in colouring or dress thus giving the site its popular name the Caves of the Thousand Buddhas. Some 492 decorated caves remain to this day. A small number of Christian relics were also discovered in the Dunhuang grottoes among them a number of documents including one referred to as the 'Jesus-Messiah Sutras' which will be described in a later section.

The sanctuaries at Mogao began to decline around the twelfth century, and slipped into virtual obscurity until the early years of the twentieth century when Wang Yuanlu, an unassuming Taoist monk who lived nearby stumbled into a cave that had been somehow uncovered. His accidental discovery of the artistic trove in the cave would propel many Western archaeologists like Aurel Stein, Albert von Le Coq and Paul Pelliot to take leading roles in unfolding the splendour of Dunhuang's legacy and uncovering its monumental wealth preserved in cornucopia of documentary manuscripts that had remained there unperturbed for centuries.[12-14] These included historical chronicles, treatises on politics and military affairs and also Buddhist sutras, such as the earliest complete printed book of the Diamond Sutra (the Perfection of Wisdom Doctrine). These invaluable manuscripts that are now housed and protected mostly in Western museums and libraries document the history of the political, religious and the cultural changes that affected the course of Buddhism during a thousand-year period.

The artistic heritage of Dunhuang reflects a mixture of cultural influences from the heart of the Middle Kingdom, Central Asia and India. The latter is more apparent in the earlier pre-Tang period where the art is more rigid, appearances severe and the lines follow definitive borders. In contrast, the later art is more fluid, lively and expressive. There are caves which demonstrate repeated or continued occupation of their sanctuaries within. For example, the sculptures of the Buddha and his attendant Bodhisattvas, Ah Nan and Jia Ye, in Cave 328 belong to the Tang period with facial features that reflect Indian heritage but the wall and ceiling murals are of the Song period. Similar contrasts can be seen in Caves 98 and 100. In Caves 325, 321, 285, 249, 35 and 45 beautifully decorated flying apsaras, heavenly musicians and dancers and flying devis (the female aspect of the divine) are seen with long exposed necklines and shoulders and dressed in pastel-coloured transparent silks that cling and highlight the feminine form. Many have been painted with Indian features and reflect Indian artistic patterns but others are unequivocally Chinese in their appearances. A unique feature of Cave 17, perhaps a legacy of the Qing dynasty, is an eight square metre library that housed thousands of scriptural manuscripts produced over a period spanning seven centuries. Collectively, this artistic throve is an amazing record of the extant social hierarchies, traditions and clothing and even of music and dance. Moreover, perhaps fanatical art has also left its imprint in the Mogao grottoes. Cave 96, one of the largest caves, contains a Buddha figure that stands nearly 35 metres high with a width of 10 metres. Typically, such large standing figures were first carved in a preliminary fashion into the sandstone cliff then smoothed over with the local iron-rich clay. This then would allow the artisans to carve the intricate physical details they wished to show. Smaller figures contained wooden cores covered either with wheat husks, reeds or hemp then finished with the iron-rich clay or lime-based plaster. The figures thus produced would then be painted in various colours for their final presentation. A cursory survey of such figures includes the High Tang Bodhisattva statues in Cave 194; the Northern Liang cross-legged Buddha in Cave 275 and the Sui dynasty statues in Cave 419 that include the Buddha's oldest disciple Mahakasyapa. The latter shows the authoritative severely imposing features of the Indian disciple. His exposed collar and chest bones are contrasted with the more serene and resolutely pious figure of a companion monk with clearly Chinese features standing alongside Mahakasyapa. This representation of Mahakasyapa seems to re-tell the legend that he was Buddha's first disciple who was given the authority to compile and record the Buddhist sutras instead of the total reliance on the oral tradition as exercised in the Upanishads. There is also the statue of the elegant disciple Ananda standing gracefully holding a lotus flower in his folded hands and dressed in a meek cassock and hemp shoes. The sharp contrast between him and Mahakasyapa cannot be made clearer. Amongst the Buddha's many disciples, Ananda had the most retentive memory that perpetuated the Upanishads and most of the sutras in the Pitaka Sutras are attributed to his recollection. For that, he was known as the Guardian of the Dharma.

On the less celestial or spiritual subjects, the Tang murals of Cave 45, for example, tell of the age-old stories of merchant caravans encountering highway bandits, and a bribing father paying for the release of his son from confinement, possibly a prison. The murals of Cave 85 illustrate female musicians dressed in Tang fashions sitting in a placid field playing the musical instrument zither. However, of greater interest are the figures in Cave 45. The niche in its western wall contains seven statutes with the Buddha occupying the typical lotus sitting posture flanked on his two sides by three standing figures in a row. The figure of Mahakasyapa can easily be identified standing on Budhha's left side and of Ananda on his right. All of the figures are Chinese in appearance with the exception of the two figures standing at each end of the row. They seem to be Indian monarchs perhaps representing the Northern and Southern Maharajas on a mission to pay homage to a Sinic Buddha or to offer gestures of friendship and peace.

THE SETTLEMENTS OF THE SILK ROADS

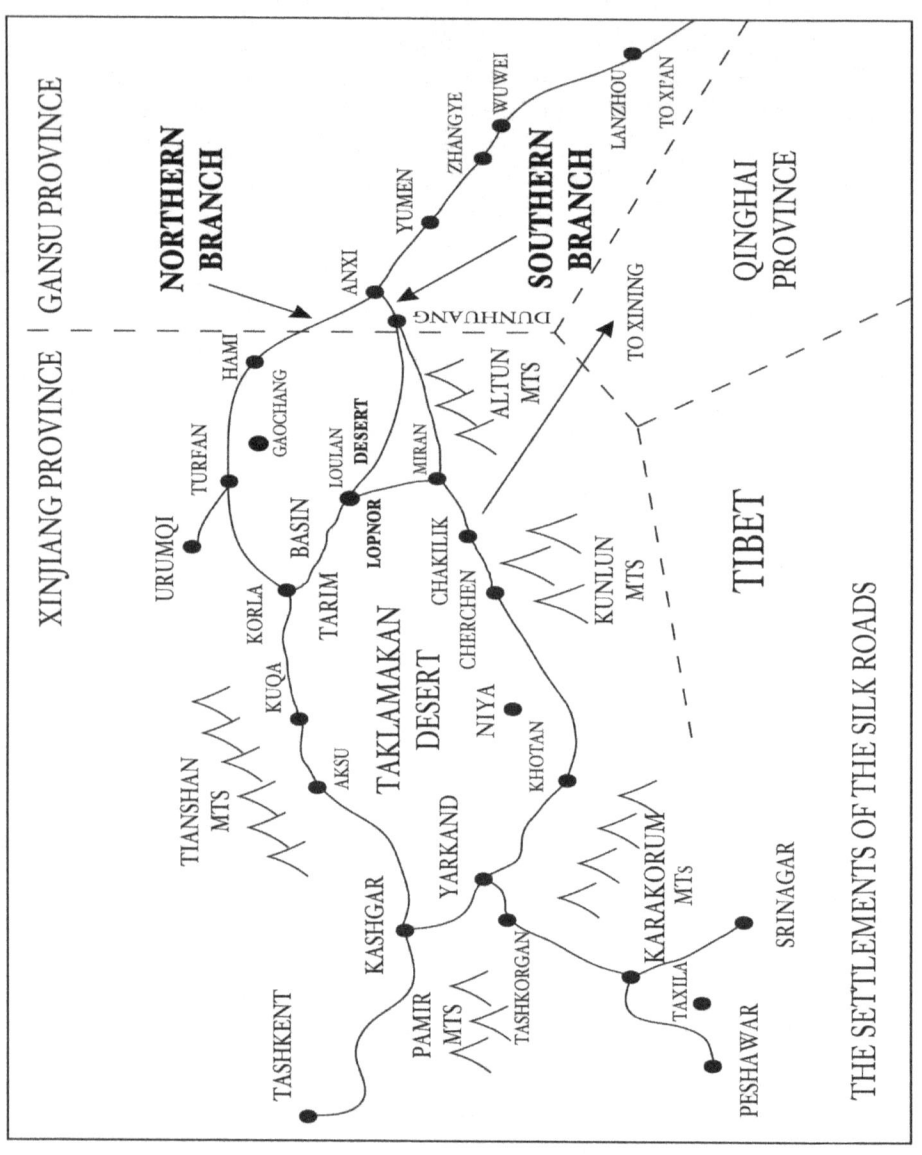

1 cm = 120 Km

The Settlements of the Silk Road in Gansu Province

LAND AND SEA ROUTES FOR SILK AND SPICE TRADE

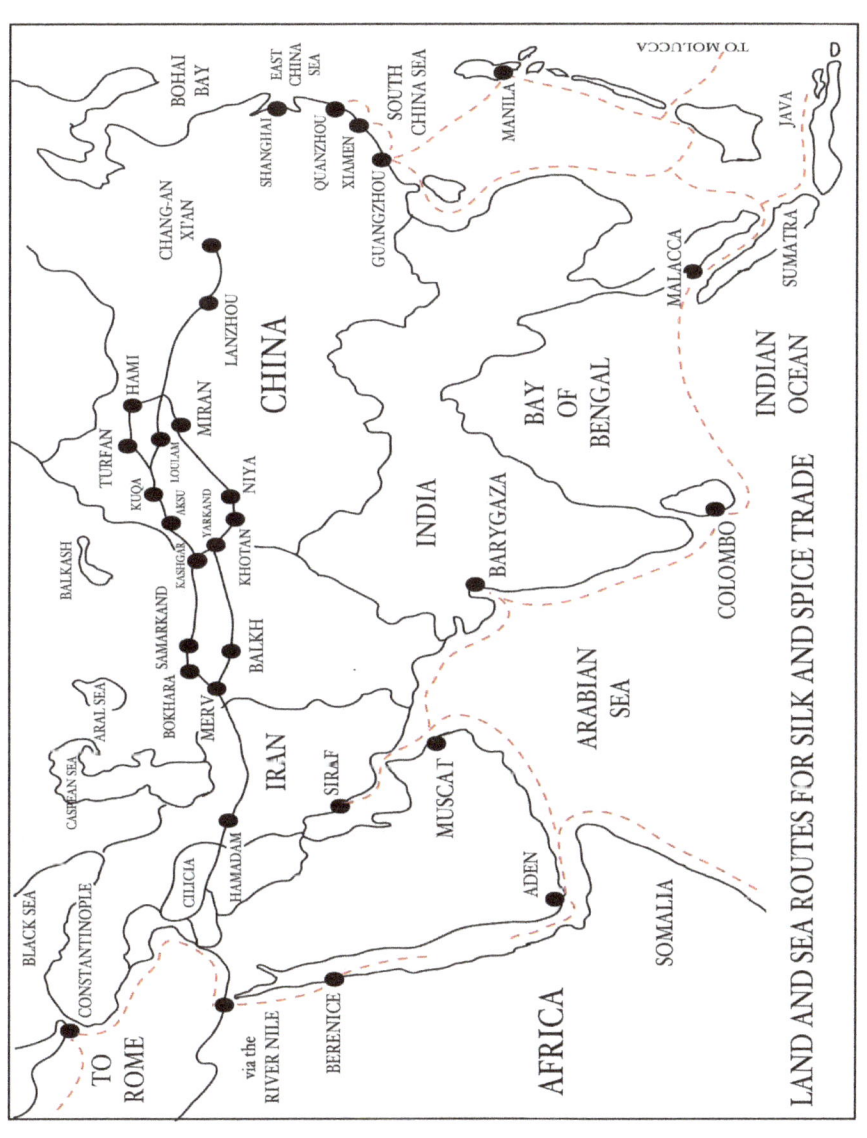

References

1. Whitefield, S. and Sims-Williams, U. (eds.), *The Silk Road: Trade, Travel, War and Faith*. The British Library, London (2004).
2. Bonavia, J., *The Silk Road From Xi'an to Kashgar*. Revised by Christoph Baumer. Odyssey Books and Guides, Hong Kong (2004).
3. Beckwith, C. I., *The Tibetan Empire in Central Asia*. Princeton University Press, Princeton, New Jersey (1987).
4. Chen, K. K. S., *Buddhism in China: A Historical Survey*. Princeton University Press, Princeton, New Jersey (1964).
5. Rhie, M. M., *Early Buddhist Art of China and Central Asia*. 2 vols. E. J. Brill, Boston, Massachusetts (1999-2002).
6. Dillon, M., China's Muslim Hui Community. Curzon, London (1999).
7. Nattier, J., The Heart Sutra: A Chinese Apocryphal Text? *Jour. of Int'l Assoc. of Buddhist Studies*, vol. 15, no. 2 (1992).
8. Waley, A., *The Real Tripitaka, and Other Pieces*. G. Allen and Unwin, London (1952).
9. Hill, J. E., *Through the Jade Gate to Rome: A Study of the Silk Routes During the Later Han Dynasty, 1st to 2nd Centuries CE*. Booksurge, Charleston, South Carolina (2009).
10. Zwalf, V., *Buddhist Art and Faith*. British Museum Publishing, London (1985).
11. Whitefield, R. and Farrer A., *Caves of the Thousand Buddhas: Chinese Art from the Silk Road*. George Braziller, New York (1990).
12. Walker, A., *Aurel Stein: Pioneer of the Silk Road*. John Murray, London (1995).
13. Hopkirk, P., a reprint of *Albert von Le Coq: Buried Treasures of Turkestann*. Oxford University Press, Oxford (1985).
14. Wood, F., Two Thousand Years at Dunhuang. In *Dunhuang and Turfan: Contents and Conservation of Ancient Documents from Central Asia*. S. Whitefield and F. Wood (eds.). The British Library, London (1996).

The Settlements of the Silk Road in Gansu Province

Group 2

9. The Yellow River (Hunag He) course at the far western parts of the city of Lanzhou. Flowing to the right, the river runs its course through the centre of the city then makes a sharp turn flowing directly north into Shaanxi province. Its source is in Qinghai province and after flowing for more than 2,000 miles empties into the Bohai Bay.

10. Qing dynasty Xi Guan (West Gate) Mosque, on Baiyin Road, Lanzhou, is the main mosque of the Hui Muslim community of the city.

11. Heping Peace Mosque; situated in the north-central part of Lanzhou across the Yellow river.

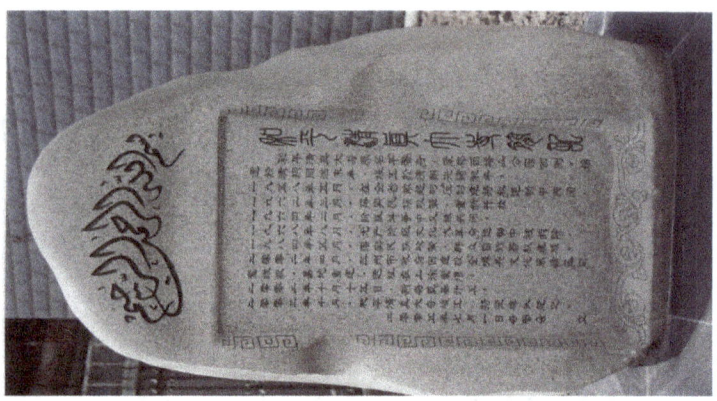

12. '*In the name of Allah, the Merciful and the Benevolent.*' A stelae erected in the courtyard of the Heping Peace Mosque, Lanzhou, commemorating the support the mosque had received from the Ming dynasty Emperor Hongwu in 1368 AD.

The Settlements of the Silk Road in Gansu Province

13. The Hui congregation of the Heping Mosque leaving after Friday's prayers. The mosque was destroyed during the Cultural Revolution but subsequently rebuilt in the 1980s.

14. '*In the Name of Allah, the Merciful and the Benevolent.*' The dedicatory black granite stelae in Linxia delineates the genealogy of Abud al-Kadir al-Jeylani (AH 470-561) and the elements of his Kadariyah Sufism teachings.

15. Huancheng Xi Lu Mosque, one of some 20 Sufi mosques in Linxia.

16. The main dusty thoroughfare running north-south through the centre of Linxia. The two Buddhist monks who belong to the Tibetan Yellow Hat sect were travelers from their Labrang monastery in Xiahe some 50 kilometres south of Linxia.

The Settlements of the Silk Road in Gansu Province

17. The western terminus of Linxia's main thoroughfare. The sharp turn of the road to the left leads to a range of hills in the southerm outskirts of the city. Note the Islamic headgear of the men and the woman, and in the background the silhouette of Xidaotang Machang Mosque.

18. The mausoleum of Hamuz Ali perched atop the southern hills of Linxia overlooking a cemetery below.

19. Recitation of prayers by imams at the shrine of Hamuz Ali at the summit of a hill in the southern outskirts of Linxia. He was one of the first Arab missionaries to bring the teachings of Sufi Islam to southern Gansu province.

20. A group of Hui imams praying in a typical Sufi tradition surrounding the tombs of holy men in the cemetery below Hamuz Ali's mausoleum.

The Settlements of the Silk Road in Gansu Province

21. A tombstone in the cemetery below Hamuz Ali's mausoleum. The header in Arabic is the Islamists profession: '*There is no God but Allah and Muhammad is His Prophet.*' The Chinese inscription identifies the deceased as follows: Feng Pei Xue, born 1927 and died 2001. He was a very strict father; his three sons erected the headstone; they are Se You Bo, Musa and Dong La Hei. His daughters' names are Cui Lan and Cui Ying with one boy grandchild named Yong Bo.

22. The main gate of Labrang Monastery of the Tibetan Yellow Hat sect in Xiahe.

23. The one-room huts which house the monks at Labrang Monastery.

24. The central shrine in Labrang Monastery in Xiahe. The devout, mostly of Tibetan heritage are seen circumambulating the shrine in a clockwise manner.

The Settlements of the Silk Road in Gansu Province

25. The author with the monks of the Yellow Hat sect in Xiahe during their outdoor debating session.

26. A four-year old little Tibetan girl bundled up in traditional clothing to stave off the bitterly cold winds of March that blow in the open plains of Gansu and Qinghai provinces. Behind her is a group novice monks gathered for their afternoon recitations session.

27. The main shopping street in Xiahe. The Tibetan cultural heritage of the people in Xiahe is evident from their manner of clothing.

28. Tibetan residents hurrying about with donkey-drawn carts, walking or on bicycles on a chilli March morning in central Xiahe.

The Settlements of the Silk Road in Gansu Province

29. North-eastern aspect of the Hexi Corridor showing the flat valley contained within the Longshou Mountains (shown) and the opposing parallel Qilian Mountains (not shown).

30. Exquisite bronze 'Flying Horse', 35 cm high, 45 cm long and weighing 7 kilograms that imparts amazingly a life-like vitality. The horse is depicted with three of his legs raised high in the air in a full gallop whilst supported with his fourth leg on the back of a bird in flight. It was excavated in the large brick-chambered Eastern Han dynasty (25-220 AD) Leitai Tomb, in Wuwei, Gansu province.

31. The wooden Pagoda Temple in Zangye.

32. The 'Reclining Buddha' in the Giant Buddha Temple in Zangye. The huge clay delicately-painted statue measures some 40 metres in length and 5 metres in height.

The Settlements of the Silk Road in Gansu Province

33. Buddhist stupa (the sixth century AD), part of the Maijishan Monastery ruins near Tianshui, Gansu province.

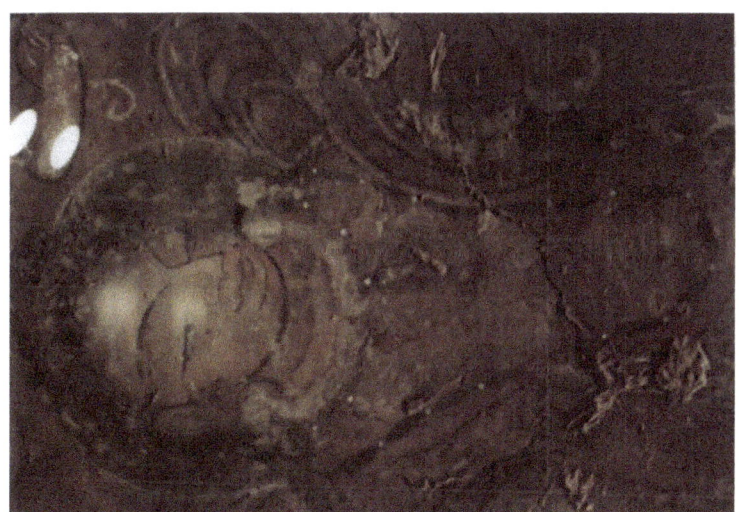

34. Mural with the image of an Indian Bodhisattva. Northern Liang dynasty (397-439 AD). From Tiantishan excavations on the Zangye-Wuwei section of the Silk Road in Gansu province.

35. Wall paintings of Bodhisattvas. Northern Liang dynasty (397-439 AD). From Tiantishan excavations on the Zangye-Wuwei section of the Silk Road in Gansu province. The haloes around their heads were characteristically symbolic of their state of enlightenment.

36. Behind the author is seen the central portion of the vast Dunhuang Buddhist cave complexes.

The Settlements of the Silk Road in Gansu Province

37. Tang dynasty (618-907 AD) clay figures in Dunhuang's Cave 45. The seated Buddha in the centre is flanked on his left by the 'Master of Discipline' Kasyapa, the oldest of the Buddha's ten disciples. The Bodhisattvas on either side are protected by what seem to be two military figures, one on the right of Chinese character and on the left of Indian character.

38. Mural of a 'Flying Devi' from the Western Wei dynasty (535-556 AD) in Cave 285. This gracefully sensual and slender figure of the flying devi is elegantly combined with the undulating airy waves created by the free-hand strokes of the artist.

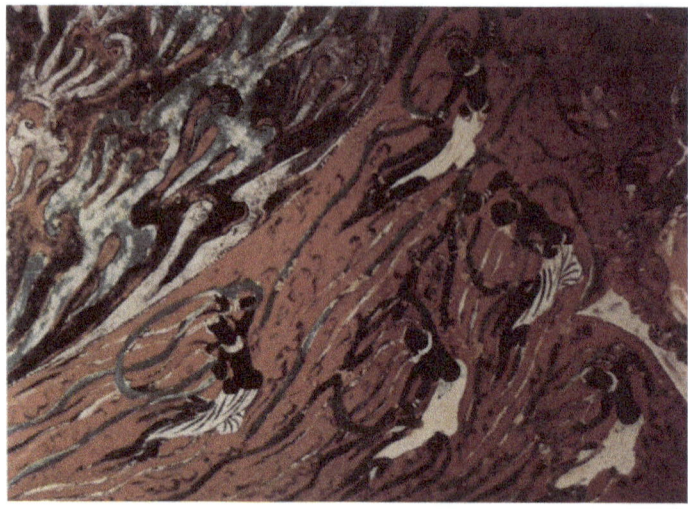

39. Mural of Flying Devis' from the Sui dynasty (581-618 AD) in Cave 206. The images of black devis dressed in white hurling in space in the midst of furling ribbons instantly convey a sense of a heavenly world beyond human experiences.

40. Mural of 'Flying Devis' from the Western Wei dynasty (535-556 AD) in Cave 285. The 'gods of fragrance, music and dance' fly around in an ethereal atmosphere and dance with spread arms whose fingers are held in typically expressive Indian motifs.

The Settlements of the Silk Road in Gansu Province

41. Sui dynasty (581-618 AD) clay figures of Kasyapa accompanied by a Bodhisattva holding an alms cup in his left hand. He was also known as Mahakasyapa to distinguish him from a legendary Hindu sage by the same name.

Treasures of the Silk Road

Chapter Six

Settlements of the Northern Silk Road in Xinjiang Province

Destination Hami قُوْمُوْل

Hami was in ancient times, as is still today, the easternmost gateway to Xinjiang province across from the north-western reaches of Gansu province. It is reached from Lanzhou through the Hexi Corridor which uniquely defines the sole north-western passage of the province. The corridor, which links central China with the Western Regions, is an unremarkable valley formed by the Longshou Mountains to the corridor's north-east that run partly along Gansu's border with the Chinese province of Inner Mangolia, and by the Qilian Mountains to the south-west of the corridor along the border with Qinghai province.[1] The corridor stretches for some 1,000 kilometres from the steep Wushaolin hills near Lanzhou to the Jade Gate at the far north-west corner of Gansu.[2] The village of Liuyuan (Hongliuyuan) is situated at the west-end terminal of the corridor and forms an equilateral triangle with Anxi and Dunhuang, with the former to its east and the latter to the south. Hence Liuyuan was a way station for the camal trains destined for Hami either from Anxi or Dunhuang.

Hami lies in a fault depression well below sea level thus its temperatures are extreme, ranging from a high of 43° C in summer to a low of -32° C in winter. Although the majestic Tian Shan Mountains provide spectacular and picturesque views in the north-western horizons of Hami, the Gobi desert to its north-east in Outer Mongolia and the Taklamakan desert to its south-east define a great contrast to Hami's northern horizons. From the open flat terrain of the Gobi, harsh and unrelenting winds blow throughout the year. They compound and magnify the formidable aridity and the un-forgiving environment associated with the Taklamakan in a way that where the line of planted fields and habitations end, the desert with its constantly blowing sands begins instantly and with a brutal abruptness.

The city is known in Uyghur as Kumul (Qumul). The name "Camul" appears in European maps of the sixteenth century. Also, the Jesuit missionary Matteo Ricci of Rome, in his description of the visit to Hami of the Portuguese Jesuit missionary Benedict Goës in 1605, refers to the city as Camul. During the Han dynasty the city was known as Yiwu and as Yizhou during the Tang dynasty. There is some evidence to suggest that it was founded by the Eastern Jin dynasty in 327 AD at a time when the Northern branch of the Silk Road was coming to its own as an alternate less perilous route than the older more difficult Southern branch. It was not until the Ming dynasty that the city's name officially became Hami. The present population of Hami is about 69% Han, 18% Uyghur, 9% Kazakh and 3% Hui with the remainder represented by other minorities.

During the Later Han dynasty Hami repeatedly changed hands between the Chinese and the Xiongnu both of whom wanted to control this strategic oasis.[3] As early as 111 BC, the Han dynasty had installed military outposts in Hami to protect the safety and security of the trading caravans thereby maintaining China's trade interests throughout the Western Regions. Also, four military garrisons were stationed in Guzang (Wuwei), Zhangye, Jiuquan and Dunhuang reinforcing the security of the caravans passing through the Hexi Corridor. This strategic practice was continued during the Sui and Tang dynasties. Following the unification of China during the Sui dynasty, Emperor Yangdi (604-618 AD) considered trade through the Western Regions important enough to appoint in Gansu a special envoy in the person of Pei Ju for intercepting and administering trade from the Western Regions arriving in Zhangye and Wuwei.

Hami not only was the gateway to the Western Regions but it also serviced as one of the most important east-west routes which extended from the valleys of the Mongolian Altai Mountains to trading posts in areas of present-day southern Kazakhstan. The road starting in Outer Mongolia first ran south to Hami then turned west and ran parallel to the northern slopes of the Tian Shan Mountains passing the rich agricultural grasslands near Lake Barkol in Kazakhstan.

Islam did not, and to this day does not, subscribe to an institutionalized framework of centralized authority as practiced by the Christian denominations, and furthermore China's relative isolation from the

Settlements of the Northern Silk Road in Xinjiang Province

many centres of Islam meant the introduction of Islam into China would be a very slow and gradual process. It is for this reason that a significant credit is accorded to Hami for its role in the history of emergence of Islam in the Western Regions. Although the Islamic faith trickled into the Western Regions in the early centuries of the Christian millennium mostly through the religious practices of the Muslim merchants travelling along the Silk Road, the flowering of Islam in the region owed much to the arrival of missionary work in Hami in the seventh century. According to legend, it was then that a group of Muslim missionaries had brought Islam to China by way of their sailing from Abyssinia (Ethiopia) in 618 AD sent personally by the prophet Muhammad himself from Madina, Arabia (there are no historical records in evidence thus this must be considered anecdotal). Two decades later a second group of missionaries was dispatched to China of which one member was able to reached Hami.

Early Muslim narrative accounts extracted from legends can be replete with confusion, improbability and inconsistencies in names and dates, and often are difficult to accept as factual information. Thus these narratives can either be dismissed as hopelessly inaccurate with little value or can be used as general support for the spirit of a specific point in history. A more practical use of legends however is to extract the meaning they contain as it applies to a specific point in history. This does not mean accepting the early narratives as accurate records of true historical facts, but accepting them as reflections of a social mood for a given society that attempts to reconstruct its past. Therefore, the legends associated with the history of early Arab conquests and Islamic expansionism of the seventh century following the death of the prophet Muhammad are to be taken in the spirit of such reconstructions and in our present discussion of Islam in China the meaning to be extracted from them, or from the Waqqas legend, is that the roots of Islam in China coincide with the astonishing Arab conquests of the seventh century.

There is much confusion regarding the legend of Sa'ad ibn abi Waqqas (Sa'ad son of Abi Waqqas) and his mission to China. Much of his heroic exploits in the Arab conquest of Iran in 637 AD during the reign of Caliph Umar ibn al-Khattab (586-644 AD) can be substantially documented from the Arabic sources.[4] After the battle of al-Qadisiyya in 637 AD Waqqas commanded the military base in Kufa for the defense of central and northern Mesopotamia and for the subsequent conquest of Persia.[5] He was born in Mecca, Arabia, in 595 AD and was a cousin of Aminah bint Wahb (Aminah daughter of Wahb), the mother of the prophet Muhammad, but he is also reputed to have been a maternal uncle of the Prophet. His father Abi Waqqas belonged to the Banu Zuhrah clan of the Quraysh tribe and is alleged to have travelled to China on a number of occasions where he had eventually died sometime in the early decades of the seventh century. Indeed, Chinese Hui accounts maintain that Abi Waqqas (the father) died in Guangdong province (Canton) and was buried in the city of Guangzhou. This account corrects the erroneous belief that the venerated 'Waqqas' tomb in Guangzhou contains the remains of Abi's son, Sa'ad ibn abi Waqqas. The Arabic sources confirm further that Sa'ad ibn abi Waqqas died in 644 AD after returning from his second visit to China and is buried in Madina, Arabia. The said tomb of Abi Waqqas in Guangzhou, which originally lay outside the city walls of the city, now occupies a beautiful park-like setting on Jiefang Bei Road in the heart of the city of Guangzhou just across from the city's North Railway Station. It is constantly visited by the faithful who come on pilgrimage from all corners of the globe.

The Arabic narrative accounts state that at the age of twenty three in 618 AD Sa'ad left Mecca accompanied by his father Abi Waqqas and two other companions named Jafar ibn abu Talib and Jahsh, the latter presumably a father-in-law of the prophet Muhammad. They were dispatched to Abyssinia (Ethiopia) by the prophet Muhammad to escape the persecution of the Quraysh tribe in Mecca for their support of the new faith promulgated by the messanger of Allah, Muhammad. There they were to remain under the protection of the Abyssinian Christian king Najashi until it was deemed safe to return to Arabia. Instead, however, the four sailed east and landed in the port city of Chittagong on the south-eastern shores of far-eastern India (present-day Bangladesh). Their ultimate destination was Canton which they reached overland from Chittagong during the reign of the first Tang emperor Gaozu (618-626 AD). As related above, Abi Waqqas had died in Guangzhou (Canton).

Sa'ad ibn abi Waqqas, after his leadership in the Arab conquest of Persia in 637, returned to China as a member of an embassy authorized by Caliph Umar ibn al-Khattab (586-644 AD). Waqqas was accompanied by Yuwesi (possibly a Chinese corruption of Sa'id ibn Zaid), Qais ibn Sa'ad Ansari (Kayizallahu) known as the 'Helper' and Hasan ibn Thabit taking with them the completed version of the Qur'an. The four missionaries travelled by sea and landed at the port city of Guangzhou in the province of Guangdong (Canton). From Guangzhou their journey continued to Chang'an (Xi'an) where they were received by the emperor Taizong (626-649 AD). The emperor welcomed the embassy and found its members learned and kind in their dealings with his subjects. Although the embassy failed to convert the emperor to Islam, it however obtained the emperor's permission to build the first mosque in Xi'an and to freely proselytize throughout the Middle Kingdom. This early mosque in Xi'an in all probability became the nucleus for the building of the Great Mosque of Xi'an in 742 AD in the tradition of Chinese architecture during the reign of Emperor Xuanrong of the Tang dynasty. The Great Mosque of Xi'an today stands in the heart of the Muslim district in the centre of the walled city of Xi'an. A second mosque, the Huai Sheng Mosque, was later built in Guangzhou upon Waqqas's return journey to Guangzhou on his way back to Arabia where he died in 644 AD. Today, the Huai Sheng Mosque with its atypical minaret in the centre of Guangzhou is a major tourist site for Muslim worshipers.

The compiler of the late Ming dynasty Fujian Gazatteer of 1619, He Qiaoyuan, has described the legend behind the founding of a holy site at the foothills of Mount Ling Shan near Quanzhou (Fujian province) that is dedicated to two Muslim sages:

> In the kingdom of Medina lived a prophet by the name of Muhammad, who was born in the first year of the Kaihuang reign of the Sui dynasty. ....Amongst his disciples were four great sages. In the reign of the Tang dynasty, they came to China to propagate the teaching. The first sage became established in Guangzhou, the second in Yangzhou and the third and fourth taught in Quanzhou where they passed away and were buried.

Although the legends concerning the four sages of the embassy dispatched by Caliph Umar ibn al-Khattab are not clear on the fates of Sa'id ibn Zaid and of Hasan ibn Thabit, it is likely that they are the two missionaries who taught and died in Quanzhou. As for Qais ibn Sa'ad, his venerated tomb is in the city of Hami where he had begun teaching the Qur'an in this oasis town's settlements. It is apparent therefore that whilst Waqqas returned to Guangzhou, Qais had continued his journey westward from Xi'an to Hami passing through the city of Lanzhou where known Muslim traders of the Silk Road had set up their abodes. It is believed that Qais had died in the area of Xingxing Gorge in Hami prefecture where his grave was venerated as a pilgrimage site during the thirteen centuries that followed his death. His remains were later interred in a mausoleum built in 1945 in the city of Hami.

As a matter of interest, there is also a corresponding Hui legend about how Islam was introduced to China, but owing to its origin in China it is replete with events nearly identical to legends found in Song dynasty Buddhist texts describing the birth of Buddhism in China. In the Hui legend, as in the Buddhist legends, the reigning emperor has a disconcerting dream; in the Hui legend the dream is about a turbaned man chasing a demon in the royal court. The emperor's dream is interpreted to mean that the turbaned man is a Hui from the Western Regions who serves a powerful Muslim king and only a Huihui will be able to dispel evils in the royal court. Thus an imperial letter was drafted and sent to the Muslim king who immediately dispatched three of his senior spiritual leaders prepared to present the Qur'anic teachings to the emperor. These men were Qais ibn Sa'ad Ansari, Yuwesi (as mentioned above being possibly a corruption of Sa'id ibn Zaid), or perhaps he was Uways al-Qarani (a Yemeni sage) and a third companion named Husain. While Waqqas and his companions travelled to China by sea, the three men in this Hui legend embarked upon a land journey to the court of the emperor. Travelling east to the Middle Kingdom from the Western Regions, which out of geographic constraints must be overland, the legend conveniently emphasized the underlying heroic dedication of the men to Islam for their arduous and perilous journey across the Taklamakan desert. It is to be expected that legends originating from the southern and eastern coastal areas of China give preference to sea routes and those from inland regions relate journies overland through Asia. In the Hui legend Yuwesi and Husain are dismissed as being unable to cope the the strains of the overland travel and die en route. However Qais survives the hardship of the journey and is received by the emperor in Chang'an. The regional Hui population today in eastern Xinjiang province honours the memory of Qais by the veneration they show at his tomb in Hami.

In more recent years, Hami had become the centre for the preservation and promulgation of Uyghur traditional folk music known as Muqam (Maqam مقام in Arabic). It denotes a modal structure that characterizes the art of music of countries in North Africa, the Middle East and Central Asia. They can be distinguished by four main musical cultures which all belong to the Maqam family, namely the Kurdish, the Persian, the Arabic and the Turkish. The centre for the preservation of

Settlements of the Northern Silk Road in Xinjiang Province

Uyghur Muqam in Hami houses a collection of ancient and modern Uyghur instruments which include the dap (a framed drum), dulcimers, fiddles and lutes. In November 2005 the Art of Uyghur Muqam was named a Masterpiece of the Oral and Intangible Heritage of Humanity by UNESCO.

> Man's fortune is bestowed by Allah,
> He creates high mountains.
> Nothing could be seen between each.
> Then He creates the moon.
>
> From then on, the moon goes before the sun,
> In between lives the cloud.
> The flame of love burning in my heart,
> Guli lives forever in my deep soul.
>
> I cut flowers with colorized paper,
> Which represents my desire in heart.
> I found a ring with gold,
> Which stands for my pure eyes.

[From the 12th Muqam; 2nd Qeibiyate (part)]

Turfan نۇربان

The ancient name of Turfan is now often referred to officially in Chinese as Tulufan and in the Uyghur dialect it is known as Turpan. It has long been the centre of a fertile oasis and an important trade centre on the main Northern branch of the Silk Road heading west to the terminus Kashgar (Kashi). The city lies well below sea level on the northern edge of the deep Turfan Depression directly south of the Bogda Mountains (a part of the larger Tian Shan mountain range). It has the second lowest geologic exposed surface on Earth after the Dead Sea at 154 metres below sea level. As a result of its location and geology, temperatures in Turfan vary extremely from a high of 43°C in summer to a low of -32°C in winter.

From 487 to 541 AD Turfan was an independent kingdom ruled by a Turkish tribe known to the Chinese as the Tiele. Medieval Chinese texts inform us that the Rouran Khanate, referred to as the Tujue (Tūjué), defeated the Tiele and subjugated Turfan, but soon afterwards the Rouran in turn were conquered by the Göktürk, as discussed earlier in Chapter 4. The present population of Turfan is about 69% Uyghur, 22% Han, 7% Hui, 1% Kazakh and the remaining 1% is of Mongol and Tibetan origins. Although the relative Turkic population densities begin to increase in areas progressively moving away westward from the traditional frontiers of the Middle Kingdom, as we shall see, this very high percentage of Uyghurs in Turfan owes its representation to the historic dominance of the Uyghurs in the Tarim basin. Historical fragments of this dominance are dispersed throughout many of the chapters in this book but the details are also discussed at appropriate sections.

During the Tang dynasty (618-907 AD), Turfan was a major commercial centre for Chinese and Sogdian merchants. There appears to have been a significant market activity especially in the slave trade since the official histories report that there were markets in Kucha, Niya and in the kingdom of Khotan for trade in Women. Sogdian documents unearthed at Astana Graves show a young Sogdian girl was purchased by a Chinese merchant in 639 AD. They also show that the recorded pairings between Chinese men and Sogdian women were usually between a male master and a female slave. Other recorded cases include the sale by a Sogdian merchant in 731 AD of an eleven-year-old girl to a resident of the city of Chang'an named Tang Rong, who exchanged forty bolts of silk in the transaction. In this recorded transaction five men were the guarantors and vouched that the young girl was not a free person.[6]

Astana Graves are a series of underground tombs located about 40 kilometres from Turfan.[7] The tombs were the final resting place for the inhabitants of the ancient walled-city of Gaochang in the Mutou Valley during much of the Iron Age from 800-200 BC. Gaochang was a major trading oasis during the first century BC for the merchants of the Silk Road travelling along the Northern branch. It became the centre for the remnants of the Northern Liang dynasty in 439 AD when their capital Guzang (Wuwei, Gansu) fell to the Northern Wei forces and its prince Juqu Mujian was captured. However, subsequently his cousins Juqu Wuhui and Juqu An Zhou managed to settle in Gaochang and held power there until 460 AD when Gaochang finally fell to the Rouran. As mentioned above, eventually the Göktürk emerged as the supreme power in the Tarim basin. The ruins of the ancient oasis town of Gaochang now lie about 30 kilometres south-east of Turfan.

Settlements of the Northern Silk Road in Xinjiang Province

Very early Buddhist influences entered the Middle Kingdom from the Indian sub-continent along the Southern branch of the Silk Road probably as early as the first century AD but certainly there is evidence for its presence in the kingdom by 148 AD as will be shown in a later chapter. This is more than six centuries later from the time of the Buddha's first teachings in his native land India. Nevertheless, the rapid growth of Buddhism in China had to wait until the fourth century when the use of the Northern branch of the Silk Road became prominent. The Buddhist artistry preserved in the Bezeklik Thousand Buddha Caves belongs to this period, probably begun under the patronage of the Northern Wei dynasty (386-534 AD). These Buddhist grottoes are located about 20 kilometres north of Gaochang and are a complex of a series of caves belonging to the Uyghur of the Tarim basin. Buddhism and Shamanism were the main belief systems of the Uyghurs from the fifth to the tenth centuries before Islam became the dominant religion in the region. The history of this religious transformation in the region will be discussed in a later chapter. Nevertheless, the interiors of most of the caves at Bezeklik are rectangular in shape with rounded arched ceilings often divided into quarters, each containing either a mural of a solitary Buddha or surrounded by other figures visibly of Indian and Persian stock. These variable artistic patterns are very much reminiscent of the Buddhist cave complexes at Dunhuang discussed in the previous chapter. Turfan, and no doubt Gaochang, were visited in the seventh century by the famous monk Xuanzang who brought back to China Buddhist sutras from India and translated them in the Big Goose pagoda built specially for him in Xi'an.

The legend of Tuyu valley (Tuyugou), 43 kilometres west of Turfan is a further example of the intermingling of the then prevailing religions of the peoples in the crucible of Xinjiang's shifting sands In this context, the Tuyu valley has four relevant components: Grand Canyon, Mazar Village, Thousand Buddha Caves and the Huojiamu Mazar. In Chinese mythology, the Grand Canyon is part of the Flaming Mountains of Turfan where the Goddess Nuwa created man, collected water from the South China Sea and smelted colourful stones with which she secured the skies. The Mazar Village, on the other hand, is an ever present reminder 'a living fossil' of the ancient Uyghur folklores that have informed the sedentary Uyghur communities of their inherent religious traditions. Central to this is the tomb of the Uyghur sage Huojiamu in the centre of the village which still remains as one of the holiest Islamic sites for the Uyghur people. Yet, Tuyu's Thousand Buddha Caves are a testimony to a millennium of thriving Buddhist heritage in the Western Regions that represented the faith and the religious convictions of the emperors of the Southern and Northern dynasties going back to the fifth century AD.

As discussed earlier in Chapters 3 and 4, in 840 AD the First Uyghur Empire was brought to an end by the Kyrgyz displacing the Uyghur tribes towards the south-eastern parts of present-day Kazakhstan and to areas further south in the Tarim basin in the region of Turfan. The Second Uyghur Empire that ultimately emerged from these areas in the tenth century (see Chapter 11) survived until the early thirteenth century then was absorbed as a vassal khanate into the Mongol Empire of Genghis Khan. Part of this vassalage was founded on the payment of tribute to the Mongols and part on the good-will marriage of the Uyghur khan Bartchouq in 1209 to the daughter of Genghis Khan, Al'altun.

Korla كورلا

The city of Korla was known as Weili in ancient times and served as one of the important oasis stops on the Northern branch of the Silk Road. It is the capital of the Bayin'gholin Mongolian Prefecture, the largest prefecture in China encompassing the eastern half of the Taklamakan desert and extending to the borders of Tibet in the south and of Gansu province in the east. The city lies south-west of Lake Bosten, the largest freshwater lake in Xinjiang province at the doorsteps of the harsh and desolate Gobi Desert of Outer Mongolia. During the Han dynasty there were thirty six kingdoms in the Western Regions (see Appendix) eleven of which were located in the Bayin'gholin Mongolian Prefecture. Korla became the seat of the governing body of the Western Regions during the Sui and the Tang dynasties. Korla's population is composed mostly of Han at about 56% followed by 33% Uyghur, 5% Mongol, 5% Hui and the remaining small fraction is represented by Tibetans and other minorities at less than 0.4% each. The Mongols of this region are the descendents of the Torgut (not to be confused with the Tangut) who had originally migrated from the steppes of western Mongolia in 1630 AD and settled along the Volga River forming the core of the Kalmyk. Today the Kalmyk form a majority in the autonomous Republic of Kalmykia on the western shore of the Caspian Sea.

Settlements of the Northern Silk Road in Xinjiang Province

Korla in the days of the Silk Road served more than an oasis for the travelling merchants. The Iron Gate Pass (Tiemen Pass) leading to Karashahir (Yanqi) before entering Korla is about seven kilometres north of the city and, as it was easily defended, it played a strategic role in providing security and safety to the camel caravans that travelled to Korla south of the gate. At the height of Tang dynasty's commercial interests associated with the Silk Road, the dynasty installed a military garrison at the Iron Gate Pass. The pass follows the gorge of the Peacock River and links Korla with the town of Yanqi, the seat of the Yanqi Hui Autonomous County.

Karashahir means 'Great City' (or perhaps Black City) in Uyghur and its equivalent in Sanskrit is Agni-deśa. Agni in Sanskrit means 'fire' perhaps in reference to the Turkish word for fire 'yagh' hence the local derivation of yanghi (modified yanqi). The combination of yagh with the Turkish word for city 'shahir' thus Yaghshahir (Fire City), in all likelihood may have been once the name of Karashahir. The Buddhist monk Xuanzang in his chronicles regarding his journey to India in the seventh century AD had transliterated 'Agni' to the Chinese pronunciation 'O-ki-ni' perhaps in his efforts at exploring the derivation of the name Yaghshahir.

Karashahir is located on the Kaidu River (also known as the Lius He), the most important tributary of Lake Bosten accounting for about 83% of the water that flows into the lake. The city boasts a large Islamic population with the Yanqi Mosque playing a pivotal role in perpetuating the Islamic heritage of the city. In the early seventeenth century, the Portuguese Jesuit Lay Brother Bento de Góis and his two travelling companions, an Armenian merchant named Sahak (Isaac) and a Greek named Demetrios, on their way from India to China (via Kabul and Kashgar) spent several months in the "Kingdom of Karashahir," which then was also known as the "Kingdom of Cialis." The kingdom was a resting point for the caravans of the Silk Road before continuing their journeys to Turfan and Hami with Jiayuguan gate their immediate destination.

Kuqa كوجار

According to the *Hanshu*, Kuqa, situated on the east bank of the Kuqa River, was the largest of the thirty six kingdoms of the Western Regions. The records of the Han and Tang dynasties refer to Kuqa as Kuchi (or the Kingdom of Qiuci), and the personal memoirs of Mirza Muhammad Haidar Dughlat, describing certain aspects of the history of Xinjiang (see Capter 11), uses the words Kucha and Kujar in reference to this fertile oasis town. Kuqa was the most populous oasis in the Tarim basin and its location at the crossroads of the great cultures (Indian, Persian and Chinese) had significantly impacted upon the social and cultural practices of its Turkic-speaking inhabitants. It was not uncommon to hear Persian or Greek languages spoken in Kuqa's famous markets and bazaars. Also, there is some evidence to suggest that members of Indian houses had at one time reigned in the kingdom of Kuqa.

In the context of religion, Buddhism had come to Kuqa before the end of the first century AD. Here it is worth emphasizing the practice of Buddhism in the various parts of the Western Regions as being distinctly different and follows a separate time frame than the faith's arrival in the Middle Kingdom. The kingdom of Kuqa was a thriving centre of Buddhism in the third century and its institutions were recognized as major contributors to the study of the Shravakayana branch of Mahayana Buddhism. This branch of Buddhism offered the individual the potential to achieve liberation from the cycle of life and death (Nirvana) simply by listening to the teachings of a Bodhisattva. The Chinese Book of Jin (*Jinshu*) confirms the presence of nearly one thousand Buddhist stupas and temples in Kuqa in the third century AD. The *Jinshu* is one of the official Chinese historical works which covers the history of the Jin dynasty from 265 to 420 AD. It was compiled by a number of officials commissioned by the court of the Tang dynasty. They extracted and based their information primarily from official documents of earlier archives and from the memoirs of Kuqa monks who had visited the Middle Kingdom in the third century AD. The Subashi ruins, located twenty three kilometres north-west of Kuqa, are the remains of possibly one of the earliest Buddhist temples founded in the late first century AD in the ancient city of Subashi that flourished during the Wei and Jin dynasties (the third and fourth centuries AD). The walls of the temple contain inscriptions in Tocharian, a language

Settlements of the Northern Silk Road in Xinjiang Province

with roots related to Latin and Greek, indicative of the role Subashi must have played in the cross-fertilization of ideas. The city of Subashi reached its zenith during the Sui and Tang dynasties (the sixth to nineth centuries AD) and became a major centre of Buddhism. The Chinese Buddhist monk Xuanzang in the seventh century AD had spent several months teaching and studying in Subashi during his seventeen-year quest to India for the collection and translation of Buddhist scriptures. Xuanzang was so impressed by Subashi that he is reputed to have said: 'The beauty of the Buddhist images here almost exceed human possibilities and the temples are so beautiful they don't seem to belong to this world.' He had observd that the priests in all the temples of Subashi adhered strictly to their Buddhist laws and were dedicated to their faith but also prayed for their basic sustenance:

> Like the Moon, Like the Sun,
> Oh great benevolent Buddha
> Please bestow upon the Kuqa River
> An eternal flow of water,
> And affluent growth of our crops.

Xuanzang offers us yet a more explicit desscription of the Kingdom of Qiuci as follows:

> The soil is suitable for rice and grain...it produces grapes, pomegranates and numerous species of plums, pears, peaches and almonds...The ground is rich in minerals - gold, copper, iron, lead and tin. The air is soft, and the manners of the people honest. The style of writing is Indian, with some differences. They excel other countries in their skill in playing on the lute and pipe. They clothe themselves with ornamental garments of silk and embroidery.... There are about one hundred convents in this country, with five thousand and more disciples. These belong to the Little Vehicle. Their doctrine and their rules of discipline are like those of India, and those who read them use the same originals. About 40 *li* to the north of this desert city there are two convents close together on the slope of a mountain.

In the context of Kuqa'a local history of Buddhism, the Kuntura Thousand Buddha Caves is a complex of grottoes overhanging the Muzat River about twenty kilometres west of Kuqa. It is a treasure trove of very early fourth century AD Buddhist art. The wall paintings, mostly in black paint, in a cave known as the Music Cave are particulary relevant as they include angelic images playing harps, flutes and lutes but most importantly playing a five-string lute called the *Beewah* which in Japan is considered a uniquely of Japanese origin. One such rare instrument is in the possession of the Japanese National Museum in Tokyo.

The Kuntura caves, as important as they may be, are comparatively small relative to yet another cave complex known as the Kizil Thousand Buddha Caves. They are located on the northern bank of the Muzat River about seventy five kilometres north-west of Kuqa. These are the earliest major Buddhist caves found in East Turkistan (*cf.* Chapter 11) second only in size to the Mogao caves of later ages near Dunhuang. The wall-paintings in the Kizil caves depict mostly Jataka images in relation to the entry of Buddhism into the Western Regions. Jataka stories refer to a voluminous body of folklore literature native to India concerning the previous births of the Buddha. Third and fourth century AD frescoes in cave No. 38 contain the unique images of a double-headed eagle and the Buddha in a lotus posture surrounded by diamond rosettes. None of these dominant themes are seen in the more elaborate and extensive images in the Mogao caves. In Western heraldry, the double-headed eagle symbolism is most commonly associated with the Holy Roman and the Byzantine Empires. In Byzantine heraldry, the heads of the eagle represent the dual sovereignty of the emperor (secular and religious) and/or dominance over his dominions both in the East and in the West. In the heraldry of the Holy Roman Empire on the other hand, it represented the Church and the State. As for the images containing diamond rosettes, this motif is exclusively dominant in Persian paintings of antiquity. Clearly these sybolisms occurring in the Kizil caves point to artistic influences of Roman and Persian origins which must have come along the Northern branch of the Silk Road very early in the course of Buddhism's march towards the Middle Kingdom.

Today, in the old district of Kuqa one can still find the whitewashed traditional Uyghur adobe homes and the distinctively Arabesque style mosques. The Kuqa Mosque is the second largest mosque in Xinjiang, after the Id-Kah Mosque in Kashgar, a living testimony of the enduring impact of Islam in Kuqa. Islam in the Western Regions, including Kuqa, also brought with it and propagated the music native to the Middle East. The music that flourished in Kuqa gained much favour

Settlements of the Northern Silk Road in Xinjiang Province

from the emperors of the Tang dynasty, particularly music which was accompanied by the lute or by the Arabesque string instrument known to the Chinese as the pipa. Through the Middle Kingdom's trade interest across the Yellow Sea, the music of Kuqa had travelled to Japan and also had found favour in the ancient imperial Japanese courts. The Buddhist monk Xuanzang had remarked: 'The instrumental music of Kuqa called *Gookagoo* is superior to that of any other country.' He had more to say about Kuqa's less spiritual attributes:

> The fair ladies and benefactresses of Kizil and Kuntura in their tight-waisted bodicies and voluminous skirts recall - notwithstanding the Buddhic theme - that at all the halting places along the Silk Road, in all the rich caravan towns of the Tarim, Kucha was renowned as a city of pleasures, and that as far as China men talked of its musicians, its dancing girls, and its courtesans.

Lieutenant Colonel Sir Francis Edward Younghusband (1863-1942), a British Army officer, explorer, and spiritual writer, described Kuqa in his memoirs of 1887 as "… a town with some 60,000 inhabitants. The Chinese town was about 700 yards square with walls twenty five feet high. There were no bastions on the gateways, but had a moat about twenty feet deep surrounding it. The houses of the Turkish inhabitants of the town were outside the walls and came right up to the edge of the moat. About 800 yards north of the Chinese town were barracks for 500 soldiers out of a garrison of about 1500 men."

Kuqa today is under the administration of the Aksu Prefecture and its population is 30% Han and 62% Uyghur. The latter during harvest time in July sing the familiar refrain:

> The Sun has given us fine crops.
> The Sun has bestowed upon us its favour.
> That is why we are so happy now.

Aksu ئاقسو

Aksu is juxtaposed between Kuqa and Kashgar along the southern slopes of the Tian Shan Mountains and was one of the many important oasis towns of the Northern branch of the Silk Road in the Tarim basin.

The oasis was situated at the junction of the Northern branch and a road leading directly north through the Muzart Pass in the Tian Shan Mountains to the fertile grasslands of the Ili River. In its native Turkic language the name Aksu stands for ak (white) and su (water), hence, Aksu's reputation as the oasis of 'White (sweet) Water.' This accolade, no doubt, was an important element in the development of Aksu as an oasis not only for the travelling caravans but also as a centre for the expansion of Buddhism into China. The outward expansion of Buddhism through Aksu is best demonstrated by the rapid pace with which nearby Kuqa became a major centre of Buddhism in the early centuries of the Christian era. The monk Xuanzang travelled through Aksu in 629 AD and in his memoirs called it *Baluka.* He recorded that there were many Buddhist monasteries in Aksu with well over 1,000 resident monks with the majority being of Indian heritage. He described the city as being 600 *li* from east to west, and 300 *li* from north to south, and that its written language and laws were the same as that of the kingdom of Qiuci (Kuqa).

In the early history of the Middle Kingdom, Aksu was known as the kingdom of Gumo [Qu-mo].and was described to have had nearly 3,500 households and 24,500 inhabitants of whom 4,500 were able to bear arms. These statistics held great significance to the Middle Kingdom as it struggled throughout the first millennium of the Christian era to contain the unrelenting tribal invasions along its north-western frontiers. Today, nearly 72% of Aksu's population is Uyghur, 26% Han, 1% Hui with the reminder represented by several ethnic minorities including Mongols. The Mongol heritage goes back to the early decades of the thirteenth century AD when Aksu was the capital of the Central Asian Kingdom of Mangalai; a vassal kingdom to the empire of Genghis Khan. In the early years of the thirteenth century Aksu was absorbed into the Mongol Empire and a century later it fell in the portion of the Mongol empire inhereted by Genghis Khan's son Chagatai. Although Aksu was in the early centuries a major conduit for Buddhism, its religious atmosphere was drastically altered with the coming of Islam in the eleventh century.

As Kuqa was visited by Lieutenant Colonel Sir Francis Edward Younghusband (1863-1942), so was Aksu on the lieutenant's overland journey from Beijing to India. He described Aksu as being the largest town he had seen on his way from the Chinese capital which had a population of about 20,000 and a garrison with about a similar number of soldiers. There were large bazaars and several inns – some used by the general visitor and others reserved for merchants who wished to prolong their stay in Aksu to sell their goods.[8]

Kashgar قە شقە ر

Kashgar was the westernmost oasis outpost in the Western Regions and served as a common terminus for both the Southern and Northern branches of the Silk Road. The city stands at the point where traffic along the Silk Road crossed over the high mountain passes into today's Pakistan and on to many of the trading markets beyond the Pamir and the Tian Shan Mountains. Kashgar is bounded in its north by the Tian Shan Mountains, by the Pamirs in the west and by the Hindu Kush and the Karakorum Mountains in the south. To its east is the vast desolate expanse of the Taklamakan Desert which meets the Lop Nor Desert at its eastern end. The latter in effect extends the arid wind-swept lands of the Taklamakan eastward to Loulan and Dunhuang. Kashgar provides access to Kyrgyzstan, Tajikistan, Afghanistan and Pakistan, and is a near neighbour to India. Access to these countries from Kashgar is made possible through several high-altitude mountain passes. Torugart Pass in the Tian Shan range north of Kashgar provides access to Kyrgyzstan, which can also be reached through Irkeshtam Pass in the Pamirs to the west of Kashgar. Likewise, the Khunjerap Pass in the Karakorum Mountains to the south of Kashgar provides access to Pakistan and India whilst the Broghol Pass (Broghil or Boroghil) in the Hindu Kush is the sole access point into Afghanistan. This geographically strategic position of Kashgar has made the city since antiquity a pivotal commercial centre for the trading caravans of Central Asia destined to reach the markets of the Middle Kingdom and those beyond the kingdom's southern limits.

Demographically, 93% of Kashgar's population is Uyghur, 5% Han and the remaining 2% is represented by other minorities. As early as the year 60 BC, Kashgar was a centre for the administrative offices in charge of controlling the Western Regions under the Former Han dynasty.

Perched on a hill and situated in the Haohan village north of the city centre, is Kashgar's ancient enclave known as the "Old Town" which brims with colour and contrast. In Uyghur it is known as the Kozi-qiya-bixi neighbourhood meaning "pottery on the edge of a cliff," the legacy of a native Uyghur who recognized the special qualities of the clay in the hill for making pottery. The centuries-old collection of compressed and congested mud-houses perched on the hill each several stories high to accommodate generations of pottery-making families now are nothing more than a shelter for the 640 families comprising 4,000 souls struggling for survival in a manner not significantly different from their ancestors who lived there during the glory days of the Silk Road. Here the pottery making art in the Uyghur motifs continues along with carpet weaving, shoe and atlas making and the exquisite embroidery much sought after by the traders of bygone days.

Kashgar has a long history going back nearly two millennia. It not only shines in the annals of the history of the Western Regions but, in the later centuries, Kashgar became the gateway for the early entry of Buddhism and Islam into China. Kashgar was also the scene of a battle in the year 90 AD in which the Middle Kingdom defeated the Yuezhi/Kushan Empire described earlier in Chapter 3. Yet Kashgar is now a mesmerizing Muslim city and thoroughly Islamic in character.[9] The residents of Kashgar give the city its unique vitality and charm most evidently a reflection of their multicultural heritage instilled in this community from the early days of the Silk Road. Over a dozen ethnic groups live in Xinjiang province and almost all have also made Kashgar their home. Kashgar is the melting pot of Central Asian faces that mingle in street corners and in the maze of roadside kebab stalls, restaurants and teahouses.

The Islamic character of Kashgar is a direct legacy that took form in the early centuries of the second Christian millennium when the struggle for religious supremacy was waging un-magnanimously between Islam in the ascendancy and the much earlier regional sedentary Buddhist heritage of the entire Tarim basin. Consequently, present-day Kashgar is imbued with the remnants of its monumental Islamic history.

Nestled in the centre of Kashgar is China's largest mosque, the Id-Kah Mosque. Built in 1442 by Sa'id Ali, sultan of the Dughlat tribe of eastern Chaghatai khanate (1435-1458), the beautiful yellow-tiled mosque is a central place of worship for Muslims throughout China. The central dome of the Id-Kah is flanked by imposing minarets more commonly seen in the architecture of the thirteenth century Seljuk mosques that dominate the skylines in Sivas, Turkey. Hence, its exquisite Middle Eastern architecture at once sets it apart from the

Settlements of the Northern Silk Road in Xinjiang Province

Chinese styled mosques which are typically in the shape of woodworked pagodas.

Not far from the centre of Kashgar, towards the north-eastern corner of the city stands the mazar (tomb, mausoleum) of Abakh Khoja (or Afaq Khoja), one of the major Uyghur cultural sites under the protection of the Chinese state. Abakh Khoja (birth name Idayitullah) belonged to a religious group known as the Bai Shan order which thrived in China from the late Ming to early Qing dynasties. This order professed Sufi Islam which was introduced to Xinjiang during the fifteenth century from Bukhara and Samarkand, the two major centres of Islam in Transoxiana. Sufism in Transoxiana had two major divisions which were the Bai Shan (White Mountain) order and the Hei Shan (Black Mountain) order. The significance of these Sufi orders will be described in some detail in Chapter 11. Abakh ruled Kashgar in the seventeenth century and became chief of the Bai Shan order and developed a reputation that exceeded his father's, Muhammad Yusuf Khoja; as a result, the mausoleum which originally bore Yusuf's name, was renamed after Abakh. His father Yusuf was one of the original Sufis who arrived in Xinjiang from Samarkand.

Built in 1640, Abakh's mausoleum is part of a complex which also includes a drawing room, a grand prayer hall and a madrasa. The mausoleum has a green-tiled dome framed by tiled minarets and walls decorated with floral green and brown tiles. Five generations of Yusuf's family, numbering a total of 72 members are interred in the mausoleum. The first generation buried there was the family of Yusuf Khoja, including him. Upon his death, his eldest son Abakh Khoja continued his fathers work and died in 1696. An early missionary Sufi colleague, Haji Muhammad, is also interred in the mausoleum.

Legend has it that among Abakh Khoja's descendants who are buried in a cemetery next to his mausoleum is his great-greatniece, Iparhan. She was known in Chinese as Xiangfei, or more affectionately as the 'Fragrant Maiden.' Xiangfei was inducted by the Qing dynasty's emperor Qianlong to become one of his imperial concubines. She was from Altishahr, a district comprised of the six Muslim Uyghur towns of Kashgar, Yarkand, Khotan, Aksu, Osh (Ush) and Yangi Hisar. Her entry into the imperial harem coincided with the Qing dynasty's 1759 AD conquest of Mughalistan (present-day Xinjiang province; *cf* Chapter 11). Hence, though not permanently, she vowed to remain chaste as a revenge for the loss of her native land and family. However, she ultimately fulfilled her expected sexual role as a concubine and did in fact produce a daughter. Her involuntary removal from Altishahr and entry into the Forbidden City are often interpreted as an allegory for the annexation of Xinjiang by the Qing dynasty and of its incorporation into the Chinese empire.

Iparhan's descent can be traced to Sayyid Makhdum-i-Azam's lineage (*cf* Chapter 11), not through Khoja Abakh (Afaq) but through his brother, Inayat Kiramet. Iparhan's uncle, Khoja Erke Husein, was a descendant of Inayat Kiramet who in 1755 refused to join the two sons of Khoja Ahmad - Khoja Burhan-ud-Din and his younger brother Khoja-i-Jihan, in their resistance and opposition to Qing dynasty's policies towards East Turkistan. Eventually the two brothers lost their struggle and fled from Kashgar and Yarkand and sought refuge in Osh (Ush) (*cf* Chapter 11).

Subsequent to his refusal to join the opposition against the Qing dynasty, Erke Husein left Altishahr with his younger brother Parsa and his two nephews, Turdi and Mahmud, and spent the following three years amongst the Kyrgyz in the valleys of Ferghana. But, in 1759 they were summond to Beijing and were rewarded with ranks and special housings for having remained loyal to the emperor's court and for their seemingly indirect assistance in the conquest of Mughalistan, Within the following year, Turdi's sister Iparhan, left behind in Altishahr, was inducted into Qianlong's harem as a fourth-ranked concubine. Two years hence in 1762 she was promoted to third-ranked concubine whilst her brother Turdi's rank was raised from prince to duke. It was standard practice in the Qing court to promote consorts within the palace concurrently with their male relatives outside the palace. Iparhan's promotion to second-ranked concubine as Xiangfei in 1768 came by a proclamation made by Qianlong's mother Empress Dowager Niuhuru.

Xiangfei died a natural death at the age of 58. There is a tomb bearing Iparhan's name in the Qing Eastern Mausoleum about 125 kilometers east of Beijing, where the emperors Shunzhi, Kang Xi, Qianlong, Xian Feng and Tongzhi are interred along with their consorts. However, Iparhan's final resting place remains uncertain. It is believed that this rather un-customary carnal arrangement between a Chinese emperor and a Uyghur maiden was simply a product of practical reciprocity in action in which the emperor, in exchange, would undertake the repair and restoration of the Abakh Khoja's mazar. Yet it is argued that her entry into Qianglong's palace fits into the pattern of marital alliances that not only was the practice of the Qing dynasty but also of other non-Han dynasties before it that chose consorts for emperors and princes from a pool of strategically important peoples. Furthermore, the accolades bestowed upon Xiangfei's two uncles, her brother Turdi and her two cousins were standard protocols in the Qing dynasty's relations with other important Manchu and Mongol families from whom concubines for the emperor were extracted in order to maintain a modicum of territorial peace and integrity for the Middle Kingdom.

We cannot be certain whether Qianlong was infatuated with the Fragrant Maiden, but various poetic verses written by the emperor seem to suggest that this rather distant Muslim unlikely concubine, who had occupied an influential position in the emperor's palace, may have captured Qianlong's heart-felt fascination:

> Winter's ice looks over the pond to the north;
> The Spring Hall protrudes into the southern city.
> A former record of the Precious Moon-
> Youthful years greeting me today.
>
> A screen inscription tells of new vigor and prosperity,
> The mirror reflects great promise.
> Hard-by reside the Muslim people,
> The pacified West linked through distant sentiments.

Apart from the Islamic religious missionaries who have left their indelible marks throughout Xinjiang, many more personalities have also likewise added much to the rich history of Kashgar. Of particular interest is Yussef Has Hajib, a revered Muslim philosopher, poet and scholar whose teachings are widely recognized and implemented throughout the Uyghur community. His mausoleum in Kashgar is located south of the city centre with its portal quite uniquely inscribed with the poet's immortal verses. He was born in 1019 AD to a Uyghur family in Balasaghun and given the name Yussuf Hajif. Yussef at the age of 51 joined the Royal Islamic Institute in Kashgar where he studied for a year. During his 18-month stay in Kashgar he had written his epic poem entitled 'Sources of Happiness,' a mammoth composition of 13,290 lines, as a tribute to the great khan Hasam Ben Sulayman Taohuashi.[10] The work eulogized the wisdom of past Uyghur rulers and reflected on many aspects of life in the dialogues of the poem's four symbolic characters.

Late in his life, Yusuf Hajif (Haji Yusuf Hajif) was conferred the title 'Has Hajib'. He died late in the eleventh century and was buried in a *'Barigun'* (army camp) on the banks of the Tuman River. In the mid sixteenth century, Abdul-Rashid Khan moved the remains of the scholar to its present location at 'Altunluk' - royal cemetery - just outside the southern gate of Kashgar. His domed mausoleum is part of a complex which includes a domed prayer hall with a ribbed vaulted ceiling and walls bearing inscriptions from the 'Sources of Happiness.' In 1909 a pottery vessel engraved with the poet's verses was unearthed along the banks of Ural River in Kazakhstan suggesting the widespread appeal of Yussef Has Hajib's thoughts and writings.

As a final note to this chapter, we may recall the reference made earlier to the relative increase in the Turkic population densities in areas progressively moving away westward from the traditional frontiers of the Middle Kingdom. By way of a summary therefore, Table 3 is presented to emphasize the population densities of the major demographic components of the communities represented today in the settlements of the Northern branch of the Silk Road discussed in this chapter.

Table 3. Population densities in the settlements of the Northern branch of the Silk Road

Settlement	Percentage					
	Han	Uyghur	Hui	Mongol	Kazakh	Tibetans
Hami	69	18	3	< 1	9	<1
Turfan	22	69	7	< 1	1	<1
Korla	56	33	5	5	< 0.4	< 0.4
Kuqa	30	62	3	4	< 0.5	< 0.5
Aksu	26	72	1	< 0.4	< 0.4	< 0.4
Kashgar	5	93	< 0.5	< 0.5	< 0.5	< 0.5

References

1. Li., Y., Yang, J., Tan, L. and Duan, F., Impact of Tectonics on Alluvial Landforms in the Hexi Corridor, Northwest China. In *Geomorphology*, vol.28 (3-4), Elsevier Science, B.V., Amsterdam (1999).
2. Hill, J. E., *Through the Jade Gate to Rome: A Study of the Silk Routes During the Later Han Dynasty, 1st to 2nd Centuries CE*. Booksurge, Charleston, South Carolina (2009).
3. Yap. J., Wars With the Xiongnu – *A Translation from Zizhi tongjian*. AuthorHouse, Milton Keynes (2009).
4. Frye, R. N., *The Golden Age of Persia: The Arabs in the East*. Weidenfeld, London (1993).
5. Ibid.
6. Millward, J. A., *Beyond the Pass: Economy, Ethnicity and Empire in Qing Central Asia, 1759-1864*. Stanford University Press, Palo Alto, California (1998).
7. Hopkirk, P., *Foreign Devils on the Silk Road: The Search for the Cities and Treasures of Chinese Central Asia*. John Murray, London (1980).
8. Younghusband, F. E., *The Heart of a Continent*. John Murray, London (1896).
9. Shaw, R., *Visits to High Tartary, Yarkand and Kashgar*. John Murray, London (1871).
10. Yusuf Khass Hajib, *Wisdom of Royal Glory*. R. Dankoff, (trans.). University of Chicago Press, Chicago, Illinois (1983).

Settlements of the Northern Silk Road in Xinjiang Province

Group 3

42. Painted brick with double-humped camels. Wei and Jin dynasties (220-420 AD) unearhed at Xincheng, near Jiayuguan City, Gansu province. Jiayuguan was a check- point for the travelling Silk Road caravans either entering or leaving the Middle Kingdom.

43. Tang dynasty (618-907 AD) painted stone figurine of an Arab lute player. Unearthed in Tianshui which is located half-way on the main Silk Road from Lanzhou to Xi'an.

44. The shrine and mausoleum of the seventh century Muslim missionary Qais ibn Sa'ad Ansari in Hami.

45. The draped revered tomb of Qais ibn Sa'ad Ansari inside his mausoleum in Hami and standing by its side is the Uyghur caretaker.

Settlements of the Northern Silk Road in Xinjiang Province

46. The serene and heavily foliaged garden pathway leading to the tomb of Abi Waqqas in Guangzhou. He was possibly the earliest Muslim missionary in China. The inscription on the gated columns in Arabic script read: *'In the Name of Allah, the Merciful and the Benevolent. The path to the tomb of Abi Waqqas.'*

47. The draped revered tomb of Abi Waqqas in Guangzhou.

48. Muslim holy grounds and ancient cemeteries in Turfan with the Bogda Mountain range in the background.

49. A venerated tomb with a prayer *mihrab* in the ancient Muslim holy grounds in Turfan. Names and dates of benefactors are displayed on wall tablets.

Settlements of the Northern Silk Road in Xinjiang Province

50. An original section of the Silk Road meandering through a narrow valley providing access to Korla from Karashahir just north of Korla. The paved fenced section is a recent addition for the benefit of visitors.

51. The Iron Gate (Tiemen Pass), a check-point allowing access to Korla.

Treasures of the Silk Road

52. Kashgar's 'Old Town' perched upon a hill in the village of Haohan.

53. Chinas's largest mosque, the Id-Kah. It faces the central square of Kashgar and was built by Sultan Sa'id Ali in 1442 AD.

54. Abakh Khoja Mausoleum in the north-eastern part of Kashgar.

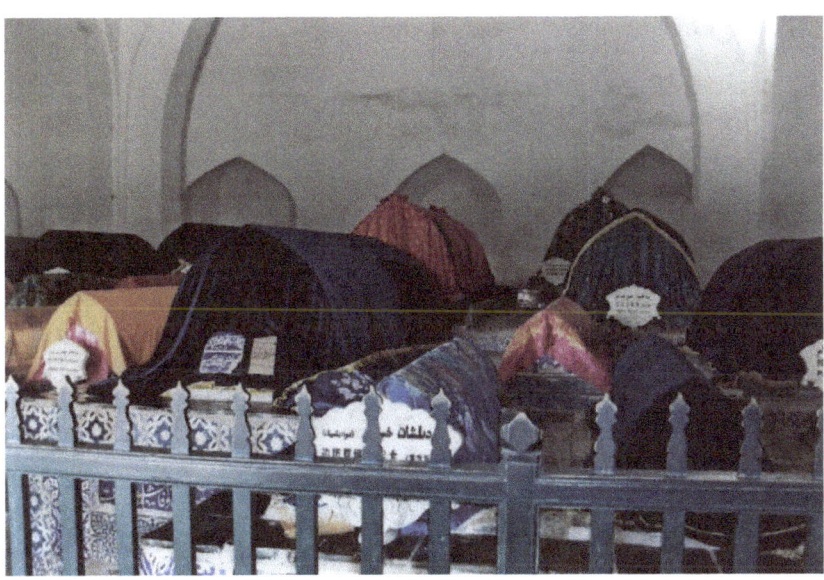

55. The tombs of Abakh Khoja and of his father Yusuf Khoja in Kashgar and the final resting place of their following five generations.

56. The mausoleum of the Uyghur poet and philosopher Haji Yusuf Hajif in Kashgar. His mammoth work was the 13,290-line poem the 'Sources of Happiness.'

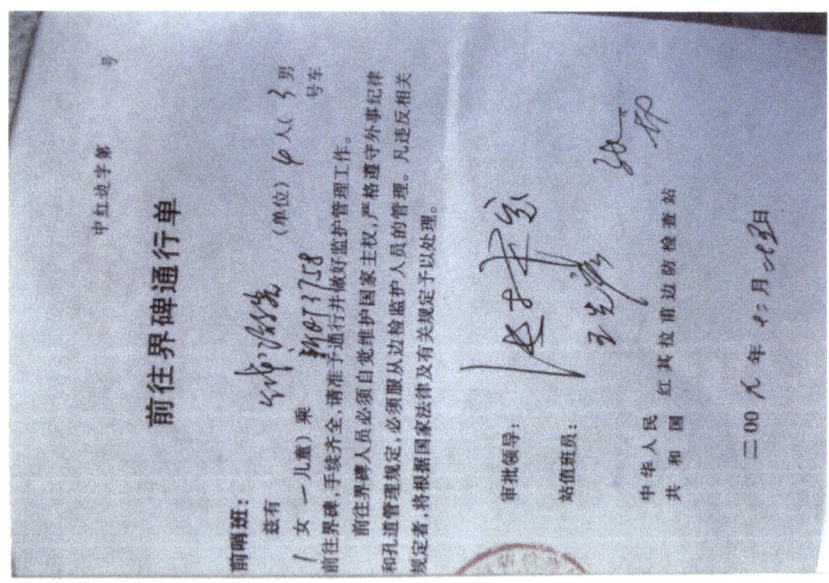

57. Official permit dated 2009/12/25 to travel on the Karakorum Highway from Tashkorgan in Xinjiang province to the Pakistan border.

Settlements of the Northern Silk Road in Xinjiang Province

58. After two millennia it is still an unchanged world along the Karakorum Highway at the foothills of the Pamir Mountains in Xinjiang province.

59. A meandering stream in a barren stony land at an altitude of 3,600 metres in western Xinjiang province on the way to Khunjerap Pass in Pakistan.

60. On the Karakorum Highway at 4,000 metres above sea level in Xinjiang province with snow-covered Mustagh Ata Mountain looming ahead like a threatening giant.

61. A tea break in a Kyrgyz hut in Gez, Xinjiang province. From left: Waheed Karakhan (Uyghur), 80-year old Kyrgyz woman, Chen Jian Wu (Han) and Abdul Keyum (Kazakh).

Settlements of the Northern Silk Road in Xinjiang Province

62. The author with a Kyrgyz family outside their hut in Gez, Xinjiang province.

63. 'Stone Fort' near Tashkorgan. Dating from ancient times the fort has a prominent strategic position in defending Kashgar from the south. and has even served as a palace for Iranian Sasanids when their rule included Central Asia.

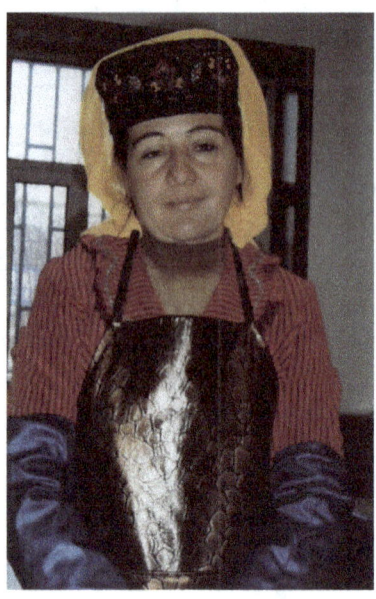

64. Tajik woman in normal everyday headgear working as a kitchen attendant in Tashkurgan.

65. The author at China-Pakistan border at an altitude of 4,900 metres (16,076 feet) just north of Khunjerap Pass.

Chapter Seven

Settlements of the Southern Silk Road in Xinjiang Province

Destination Loulan

From Dunhuang in Gansu province, the oasis of Loulan was a seventeen-day overland journey for the ancient traders of the Silk Road. The first historical mention of the kingdom of Loulan appears in a letter from General Chanyu of the Xiongnu sent to the Chinese emperor in 126 BC in which the general boasts on his conquering the Yuezhi, the Wusun and Loulan. Because of its strategic position connecting the main trade routes, during the Former Han and the Later Han dynasties control of Loulan was regularly contested between the Chinese and the Xiongnu. The *Hanshu* records that:

> It lay close to Han and confronted the White Dragon Mounds. The locality was short of water and pasture, and was regularly responsible for sending out guides, conveying water, bearing provisions and escorting or meeting Han envoys. In addition, the state was frequently robbed, reprimanded or harmed by officials or conscripts and found it inexpedient to keep contact with the Han. Later, the state again conducted espionage for the Xiongnu, often intercepting and killing Han envoys.

Leaving behind the Chinese political sphere in Dunhuang, the camel caravans laden with goods began their ordeal across the waterless, treacherous south-western edges of the Gobi desert and travelled west towards the kingdom of Kashgar at the foot of the Pamir Mountains. Lying west of Dunhuang, Loulan was not only a major trading centre but it also offered a choice to the travelling merchants either to join the Northern branch of the Silk Road at Korla, or the Southern branch at Miran. It was situated on the north-western edge of Lake Lop Nor, now part of Lop Nor Desert in the Tarim River basin.[1] The Tarim River gathered its waters from the Kunlun Mountains in the south, the Pamirs in the west and the Tian Shan Mountains in the north, and flowed in an eastward arc along the northern edges of the Taklamakan towards Lake Lop Nor. Lake Lop Nor most often was nothing more than a group of sandy and salty marshes that were nestled along the southern edge of Lop Nor desert, which defined the eastern edge of the Taklamakan desert. When the Tarim River dried up nearly a century ago, the river's basin turned into the arid wind-swept land which has pesisted to the present.

As mentioned above, Loulan served two alternate routes for the trading merchants arriving from Dunhuang. At Loulan two secondary routes cutting across the Lap Nor Desert joined the Northern branch of the Silk Road either at Turfan or further west at Korla. Another extension ranning south from Loulan led to the oasis towns of Miran on the Southern branch of the Silk Road from which the camel caravans could continue their journey westward towards Khotan, Yarkand and finally Kashgar.[2]

The kingdom of Loulan was a battleground for the warring Han dynasty and the aggressive Xiongnu. Its Uyghur king was obliged to send his sons as hostages to both the Xiongnu and the Chinese to demonstrate his neutrality. In 77 BC, at a banquet held in Loulan to greet the Chinese envoy Fu Jiezi, Chang Gui, the king of Loulan, was stabbed and killed by the envoy's treacherous guards and his severed head was hung from the tower of the northern gate of the city. The kingdom then became integrated into the Han dynasty and was renamed the kingdom of Shanshan with its capital, the city of Loulan, relocated near present-day Chakilik.[3] For nearly three centuries Shanshan served the Chinese repeatedly under many military colonies as under General So Man when he in 260 AD established a military colony of 1,000 men under his direct command. But the Chinese eventually abandoned Shanshan in 330 AD due to lack of sufficient water after the Tarim River, which had supported the colonies over the centuries, became dessicated below the surrounding desert sands. Although the kingdom of Loulan was renamed Shanshan, the name of its capital, the city of Loulan was retained. But ultimately the city of Loulan became the surviving Loulan oasis where the arriving camel caravans over several centuries supported and nourished the growing Buddhist community there. An interesting aspect of the history of the kingdom of Shanshan is related to us through the observations of the Chinese monk, Faxian, who in 399 AD spent a month in the oasis town of Loulan after his seventeen-day journey from Dunhuang. He noted that there were more than four thousand Buddhist monks, all students of the Hinayana Buddhist teachings and that they were all students of Indian books and the Indian language, clearly indicative of Indian religious influences in the region during the fourth century AD.

Loulan became an abandoned oasis in the sixth century due to the chronic lack of water, and was slowly erased from the face of the Earth by centuries of blowing sand. At nearly the end of the nineteenth century, in 1899, the ghosts of the oasis town of Loulan were excavated from the bowels of the desert by Sven Hedin. Sven Anders Hedin (1865–1952) was a Swedish geographer, topographer, explorer, photographer, and travel writer, as well as an illustrator of his own works. The store of cultural relics excavated by him included stone and jade tools and arrowheads dating back to the Neolithic times (10,000 BC-5,000 BC). There were also manuscripts written in the ancient Indian dialect of Kharosthi, Han dynasty coins, Persian perfume and carpets, Greek woollens, and most notably Chinese silk - brocade, damask and embroidery.[4] These relics were a testimony to the forgotten glory of the kingdom of Loulan where the Han and the Uyghur residents had welcomed the trading caravans and, in doing so, had created a melting pot of opportunities not only for the exchange of goods but for the cross-fertilization of cultural nuances in the arts, music religion and languages. The impact of the Indian cultural characteristics upon the sedentary populations of the Western Regions was clearly evidenced by the widespread use of the Kharosthi language as depicted in the discovered manuscripts.[5] Kharosthi was one of the ancient languages used in India between about the third century BC and the fouth century AD. The use of Kharosthi was prevalent in the Kushan Empire and also in Sogdiana until early in the fourth century and there is some evidence to suggest its use may have survived until the seventh century in the oasis towns of Khotan and Niya.

Miran مر ه ن

Because of its proximity and its location south of the brackish Lake Lap Nor, Miran was closely associated with Loulan and often during the Former Han dynasty (BC 206-8 AD) was called the Old Capital of the kingdom of Loulan (or of the kingdom of Shanshan as mentioned above). Other names that the Later Han dynasty associated with Miran included Old Eastern Town or 'Little Shanshan. During the Tang dynasty Miran was called Qitun Cheng (or Tun Cheng). The modern name of Miran was acquired after the collapse of the Tang dynasty. The residents of modern Miran who live adjacent to the ruins of the old oasis town of Miran are the descendents of No.36 Regiment Farm, one of 185 such farms that were formerly prison camps used to help populate Xinjiang province in the second half of the twentieth century. They are almost exclusively Han Chinese in ethnic origin.

Miran, as did Loulan, maintained sophisticated trade connections with centres that ultimately reached the ports of the Mediterranean Sea. Trade from these ports was brisk with the Eastern Roman Empire and its provinces in North Africa including Alexandria in Egypt.[6] Miran had a vibrant Buddhist culture with a large monastery surrounded by several temples. Artistic influences from Greece, and in particular from Rome itself, were brought to Miran and ultimately transmitted to the heartlands of the Middle Kingdom. Archaeological evidence from Miran shows the influence of Buddhism on Miran's artistic work dating to the first century BC. Early Buddhist sculptures and murals excavated in Miran show stylistic similarities to the traditions of Central Asian (Gandharan) and North Indian artistic motifs but, more importantly, many of them contain stunning Greco-Roman motifs, such as angelic wings placed behind the collarbones of Buddhist deities more characteristic of Western cherubs. Also, excavated was a fragment of a woollen textile that featured the Greek god Hermes, a further testimony to the artistic influences of the Greco-Bactrian cultures that had impacted Miran's own heritage.

Miran became a fort town for Tibetan forces which occupied the area in the eighth century AD when the Chinese garrisons from Loulan were withdrawn to Xi'an to deal with the An Lushan rebellion of 755 AD. The fort was a huge circular structure defended by the Tibetan troops who remained there until the mid-ninth century when the last king of the Tibetan Yarlung culture was assassinated bringing an end to the great Tibetan Empire. The Yarlung Valley in Tibet was the cradle of Tibetan civilization and the birthplace of the Tibetan empire which survived for nearly two centuries. A wealth of manuscripts were recovered from the ruins of the Tibetan fort in Miran. They were mostly official Tibetan documents and military information written in early Tibetan script on wood or paper dating to the eighth and ninth centuries. Many of the manuscripts were written in Chinese, Brahmi and Kharosthi and even in a Turkic runic script suggestive of Miran's

Settlements of the Southern Silk Road in Xinjiang Province

vibrant and sophisticated cultural connections.[7] However, Miran had gradually succumbed to the vicissitudes of the Tibetan occupation and was finally abandoned at the end of the ninth century. The desert sands soon engulfed what was left behind and Miran was forgotten.

From the fourth to the ninth centuries a lesser-known but a significant silk route ran south-easterly from Miran destined to reach Xining just east of Koko Nor Lake (today's Qinghai Lake) in Qinghai province. As trade from the Northern and Southern branches of the traditional Silk Road reached the Middle Kingdom primarily through Dunhuang in Gansu, the main purpose of the route to Xining was to evade the bureaucratic costs at Dunhuang and reach the southern markets of China beyond the limits of the Middle Kingdom.

Chakilik جا قلق

The oasis town of Chakilik (modern Ruoqiang) is often referred to as Charklik, Qarklik, Charkilik or Charkliq, however it should not be confused with Karghilik (the Uyghur name for modern Yecheng) most commonly known as Yarkand. Yarkand is another oasis town on the Southern branch of the Silk Road about 240 kilometres south of Kashgar along the western rim of Taklamakan Desert (see below). Today, Chakilik is under the administration of the Bayin'gholin Mongol Autonomous Prefecture, the largest prefecture in China with Korla its capital. The prefecture is the county seat of Chakilik County and of the neighbouring Cherchen County. The word 'Mongol' in the prefecture's designation reflects the large local ethnic Mongol population and is indicative of the area's strong historical connections with Mongolia. Their Buddhist practices common with those of Tibet and the Haixi Mongol Autonomous Prefecture in the adjacent Qinghai province further reinforce their shared inter-cultural socio-religious connections especially in view of the fact that their Buddhist connections have survived long after Buddhism had largely disappeared from much of China.

In his travels in 1273, Marco Polo called the area of eastern Taklamakan the 'Desert of Lop' and passing through Cherchen gave a grim description of Chakilik which he called Lop:

> Upon leaving Charchan the road lies for five days over sand, where the water is generally, but not in all places,

bad. Nothing else occurs here that is worthy of remark. At the end of five days travel you arrive at the city of Lop, on the borders of the great desert. The town of Lop is situated towards the north-east, near the commencement of the great desert, which is called the Desert of Lop. It belongs to the dominions of the Great Khan, and its inhabitants are of the Mahometan religion. The stock of provisions should be laid in for a month, that time being required for crossing the desert in the narrowest part. To travel it in the direction of its length would prove a vain attempt, as little less than a year must be consumed, and to convey stores for such a period would be found impracticable.[8]

From the third to the ninth century the proto-Tibetan nomadic Qiang tribes (e.g. Tuyuhun and Tuoba) had lived in the vicinities of Chakilik in what are now eastern Xinjiang and northern Qinghai provinces. The Qiang, who were related to the Xianbei, had inhabited these areas long before the Silk Road had become a major trading route. During the Eastern Han Dynasty (25-220 AD) and in the periods of the Wei and the Jin kingdoms (220-420 AD) the Qiang were also widely distributed along the mountainous fringes of the northern and eastern Tibetan Plateau. Some of their communities could be found in the valleys of the Kunlun Mountains in northern Qinghai province while others had made their homes in western Sichuan and northern Yunnan. Their collective aggression towards the Middle Kingdom accelerated the collapse of the Eastern Han dynasty. In 663 AD inter-tribal hostilities for supremacy broke out between the Tuoba and the Tuyuhun from which the Tuoba emerged as the dominant power in the Tarim basin. Although fundamentally nomadic in life-style, the Tuoba nevertheless controlled much of the areas east and south of Chakilik and benefited considerably from the trade that reached Xining in Qinghai. Their incessant aggression and growing power gave them the self-confidence to invade and occupy the Hexi Corridor when the Tang dynasty was preoccupied with the An Lushan rebellion. Their total control of the access routes to the Middle Kingdom gave the Tuoba the opportunity to expand and become part of the Tibetan Empire.

The Alternate Route from Chakilik through Qinghai

The commonly reviewed and discussed subjects relating to the Silk Road are mostly focused on the traditional trade routes known as the Northern and the Southern branches that skirt the northern and the

Settlements of the Southern Silk Road in Xinjiang Province

southern rims of the Taklamakan desert, respectively. Throughout the first nine centuries of the Christian era, these traditional routes linked Central Asia almost exclusively with the Middle Kingdom and excluded the vast markets in the southern areas of China beyond the limits of the Middle Kingdom. Later in the early parts of the twelfth century however maritime commerce passing through the Arabian Gulf and the Indian Ocean reached the markets in southern China by trading in the coastal cities on the South China Sea. Yet prior to the active maritime routes of the twelfth century significant trade was nevertheless reaching southern China. This trade often originated in Chakilik and followed the principal Southern route to Miran. From Miran the trade moved in a south-easterly direction and after crossing the Altun Mountains entered the Qaidam Plateau in Qinghai. From the Qaidam plateau the caravans had the option to divert north with Dunhuang as their destination. Alternatively, continuing in an easterly direction the caravans could descend the plateau and reach present-day Xining. The legacy of this alternate route is reflected today in Xining's multicultural population with strong Buddhist and Muslim traditions amongst the city's vast population of Tibetans, Muslims and Hans. This area was the hub of mercantile activities that communicated with Xi'an in the Wei river valley to the east, or with Chengdu in Sichuan province in the south.

There are a number of historical records that provide insight into the extent to which this alternate route was an important passageway. Although there might have been various political circumstances that obligated travellers to consider alternatives to the Southern branch of the Silk Road, such circumstances were not necessarily always the case. For example, we learn from the chronicles of the Buddhist monk Song Yun that in 518 AD he had left for India from Luoyang to bring back Buddhist scriptures for the Empress Dowager Hu. Despite being aware of the familiar routes west to India through Dunhuang, he had elected to follow the alternate Qinghai route. Thus beginning his journey at Luoyang he had travelled to Miran before turning north to reach the great Buddhist community in Loulan.

Other historical sources, such as the *Book of Zhou*, relates that a provincial governor (Cixi) serving the Northern Zhou dynasty had taken advantage of the remoteness of his charge in Qinghai and had in 553 AD raided and plundered a large Tuyuhun royal embassy caravan while returning through the alternate route from its mission to the court of the Northern Qi dynasty (550-577 AD). The dynasty ruled in the lower regions of the Yellow River covering the modern provinces of Shanxi, Shandong and the northern parts of Jiangsu and Anhui. The *Book of Zhou,* which is the official history of the Northern Zhou dynasty, is ranked amongst the official twenty-four historical books of imperial China. It was compiled in 636 AD by the Tang dynasty historian Linghu Defen. One additional reference to the Qinghai alternate route is found in the records of the history of the Southern Qi dynasty (479-502 AD) which informs that travel westward from Sichuan was usually made through Qinghai.

Cherchen چەرچەن

Here we shall begin again with a quote from the travels of Marco Polo, who, to be noted, refers to the area of Cherchen in 1273 as being a province of Turkistan:

> Charchan is also a province of Turkistan, lying in an east-north-east direction from Peyn (*Niya*) [italics author's insert]. ...The country from Peyn to this district, as well as throughout its whole extent, is an entire sand, in which the water is for the most part bitter and unpalatable, although in particular places it is sweet and good. When an army of Tatars passes through these places, if they are enemies the inhabitants are plundered of their goods, and if friends their cattle are killed and devoured. When they collect their harvest, they deposit the grain in caverns amongst the sands; taking monthly from the store so much as may be wanted for their consumption; nor can any person besides themselves know the places to which they resort for this purpose, because the tracks of their feet are presently effaced by the wind.[9]

Cherchen (modern Qiemo) was the largest oasis town east of Khotan spread along the banks of Cherchen River flowing south out of the Kunlun Mountains. In more recent times extensive irrigation canals have been built which have made the lands around Cherchen more arable and agriculturally productive for wheat, oats, corn, watermelons, grapes, peaches, oranges and pears. The oasis is mentioned in the annals of the Early Han dynasty, the *Hanshu,* and purported to have had

Settlements of the Southern Silk Road in Xinjiang Province

at that time a population of near two thousand souls of whom only 320 persons were able to bear arms. Its present population is 85% Uyghur.

The south-eastern region of the Tarim basin, which includes Cherchen, has been a long standing centre for jade trade especially with the Middle Kingdom as evidenced from the personal artefacts recovered from Chinese royal tombs and from similar items buried as funeral offerings unearthed from graves. Natural jade was collected in Cherchen from the wash of the river Cherchen as opposed to that harvested from the river Yurungkash further west in Khotan whose source for jade was also the Kunlun Mountains. These semi-precious stones were thus identified as either Cherchen Jade or Khotan Jade.[10-12]

The recent discoveries of mummies in the graves of Cherchen's adjoining village of Zaghunluq have raised new interests in the regional history. On the vast, empty salt plateau just outside the city limits in the northwest corner of Cherchen, a tiny ornate pink brick building stands housing the Zaghunluq Ancient Mummy Grave. This 2,600-year old grave contains exceptionally well preserved fourteen naturally mummified bodies reclined together in their brightly coloured clothes and funerary offerings that betray their Iron Age date.[13,14]

The Zaghunluq mummies have attracted much attention because of their Caucasian features suggestive of contacts between East and West far more ancient than the Silk Road trade of the Roman times. Based on their Caucasian (Europoid) features – tall statures, white skin, deep-set eyes, prominent noses, facial hair and the fair-colour of the head hair of the men- the possibility has been considered that the mummies are related to the Celts in origin who were part of the Indo-European migrations eastward that began from the surrounding areas of the Caspian Sea during the Iron Age (1000 BC-AD 100). By this account these migrations around 3,000 years ago would have had to cross the Eurasian steppes of Central Asia and enter Xinjiang from the north through the valleys of the Tian Shan Mountains in the vicinities of Urumqi. Alternatively, the migrations may have originated from regions near western Anatolia and cutting across the various parts of the Near East, such as Armenia or further south across Iran and Afghanistan, had eventually reached Kashgar through the Pamir Mountains. Their spoken language has been assumed to have been either proto-Tocharian or an early Iranian language, and they most likely were involved in the extraction and trading of jade. Jade was extensively mined in the Tarim basin and exported to the Middle

Kingdom during the Late Bronze Age (1550-1200 BC). If indeed Tocharian in heritge, the immigrants seem to have lived in what is now eastern Turkistan. They were gradually assimilated into the general population as a result of intermarriages with the sedentary Turkic Mongoloid peoples. The Uyghur population in Xinjiang contains both Mongoloid and Caucasoid phenotypes and therefore possibly are in part descendants of theTocharians.

The buried fabrics worn by the Zaghunluq mummies demonstrate a wide variety of weaving techniques: plain weave, twill weave, woven patterns including tapestry, band plaiting, and nalbinding, as well as non-woven felt and fabric painting. These are all suggestive of an elaborate and advanced textile-dependent culture that was able to produce delicately designed patterned fabrics, shrouds, shirts, trousers, hats, coats, belts and socks.

The ages of the varied mummies unearthed in the vicinity of Zaghunluq belong to three separate time periods suggestive of three separate waves of migrations into the area. The first phase seems to have taken place in the Late Bronze Age (1550-1200 BC); the second phase in the Iron Age (BC 1000-100 AD) and the third phase as recently as the first to the fifth centuries AD. However, these burials are not the oldest in the Tarim basin. A female mummy excavated in 1980 in the Lop Nor desert and known as the 'Loulan Beauty' belongs to the Middle Bronze Age (2200-1550 BC) and is dated 1800 BC.

Niya نيه

The ruins of the ancient oasis town of Niya are located about 150 kilometres north of present-day Minfeng at the southern edge of the Taklamakan desert. The town was the seat of one of the 36 kingdoms that dominated the political landscape of the Western Regions during the first Christian millenium. Archaeological evidence recovered from the lost town has suggested that Niya might have belonged to the ancient Jingjue Kingdom of the Han period. The kingdom had thrived along the Southern branch of the Silk Road just north of the vanished end of the northerly course of the Niya Darya (Niya River). The river's course ran north from the Kunlun Moutains down into the Taklamakan desert and ultimately disappeared below the desert's sands.

Settlements of the Southern Silk Road in Xinjiang Province

Covering an area twenty kilometres in circumference, Niya flourished from the first century BC to the fourth century AD and seems to have occupied the lands around the presently seen ruins a central six-metre high Buddhist stupa. Niya's ruins now are the largest and best preserved of the ancient city kingdoms that were founded along the southern and northern rims of the Taklamakan desert. The stupa in the centre of Niya and the traces of Buddhism which are scattered widely in its surroundings indicate Niya's strong Buddhist heritage. The earlist evidence of this comes from documents found in a red earthenware vessel discovered by Aurel Stein in 1906. These and many other similar historical documents written in Kharosthi on sheepskin and wooden strips have revealed that the sovereign of the kingdom of Loulan had ruled over a number of desert settlements scattered within reach of his kingdom including settlements as far west as Niya. These settlements were administered by the king's appointed chief named Chaboqi who had maintained his headquarters in Niya. His responsibilities were to supervise the commercial activities taking place in the settlements, receive tributes to the king and collect taxes on behalf of the kingdom. His duties surprisingly were much more elaborate and extensive. They included authenticating the adoption of orphaned children, officiating and conducting marriage rites and acting as a marriage counsellor when necessary. His reception room appears to have been a massive 70 square metres in size. These findings collectively have indicated that the kingdom of Loulan was well administered and that Niya was an important centre for the official and the orderly administration of the kingom of Loulan.[15]

In parallel with the historical time frame of the ancient inhabitants of the oasis town of Cherchen, well-preserved excavated copses of the ancient residents of Niya also show Caucasian-Europoid features and have been speculated, amongst many other possibilities, they represent the descendants of the armies of Alexander the Great (356-323 BC) who reached Central Asia through their victories across Anatolia, Iran and Afghanistan. But of particular interest are the corpses of a ruler of the kingdom of Jingjue and his wife wrapped in colourful embroidered silk brocade woven to contain eleven Chinese characters that entreat the royal marriage be blessed with long life and with many offspring. The coffin that contained the corpses has been dated to about the second century AD. Their burial artefacts have included pillows made in the shape of pheasants, a clear Chinese motif of good luck. It appers therefore, that despite the speculated Caucasian origins of the residents of Niya, their proclivities seem to have been cleary imbedded in Chinese traditions.

Amongst other archaeological finds at Niya have been the remains of approximately 100 dwellings, burial sites, sheds for animals, orchards, gardens and cultivated patches. Much of the dwellings seem to have contained many rooms and were built of wooden frames with walls of adobe brick or woven willow branches with applied mud. Their remains have included well-preserved tools such as iron axes and sickles, wooden clubs, fragments of colourful tapestry and woolen clothing, pottery urns and jars full of crop seeds.

Niya fanished from existence in the sixth century AD and the only probable explanation seems to be that it succumbed and capitulated to the all pervasive surrounding desert sands coupled with the diminishing water of the Niya Darya.

INDO-EUROPEAN MIGRATIONS

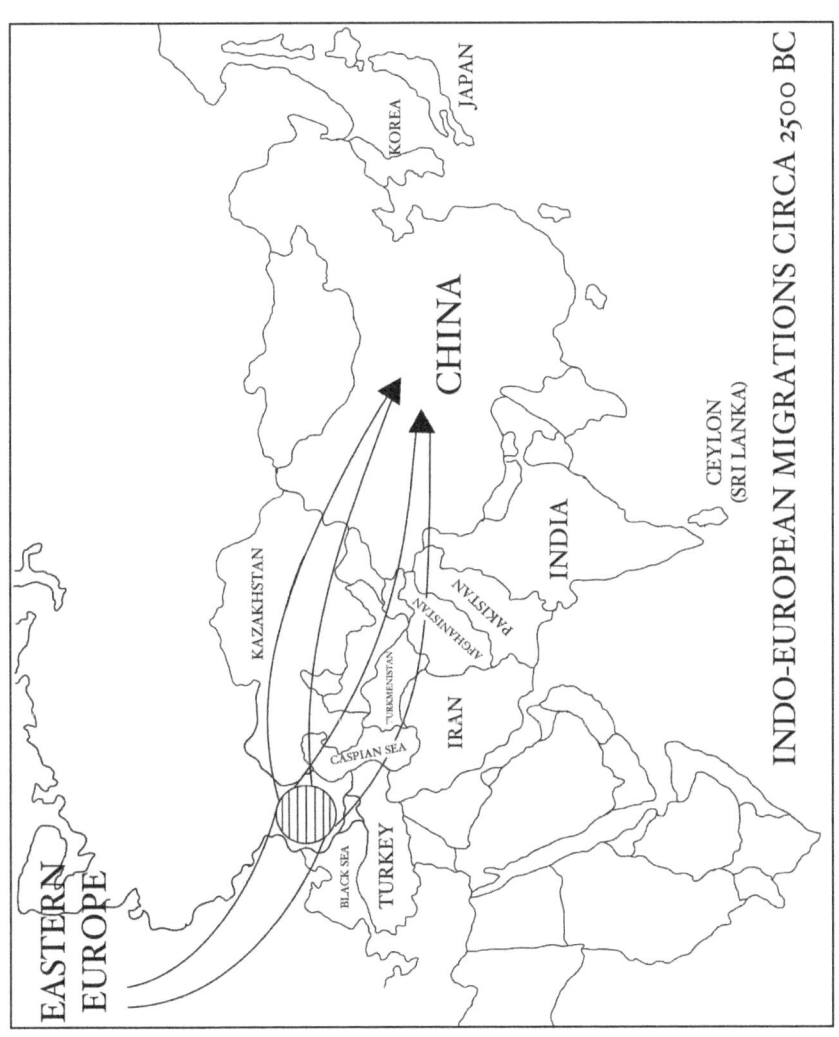

Khotan خوتەن

Beyond the oasis town of Niya travelling west, the ancient trading caravans made their way along the Southern branch of the Silk Road and reached the kingdom of Khotan (modern Hotan). When Marco Polo passed through the kingdom of Khotan in 1271 AD on his way to the court of Kublai Khan at Kanbalu (modern Beijing), he witnessed a prosperous oasis kingdom which had remained vibrant at least as late as the last quarter of the thirteenth century. It is clear from the extent of Marco's observations that the kingdom of Khotan, in addition to its trading and manufacturing business, was cultivating vast areas of arable lands for agricultural produce:

> Following a course between north-east and east, you next come to the province of Khotan, the extent of which is eight day's journey. It is under the dominion of the Grand Khan, and the people are Mahometans. It contains many cities and fortified places, but the principal city, and which gives its name to the province, is Khotan. Everything necessary for human life is here in the greatest plenty. It yields likewise cotton, flax, hemp, grain, wine, and other articles. The inhabitants cultivate farms and vineyards, and have numerous gardens. They support themselves also by trade and manufactures, but they are not good soldiers.[16]

Also, we learn from the *Hanshu* that Khotan, in the early years of the first Chiristian millennium contained 3,300 households with 19,300 living souls of whom 2,400 could bear arms. Khotan's lifeline had always been the rivers Karakash (Black-Stone/Jade) and Yurungkash (White-Stone/Jade), which flow north from the Kunlun Mountains.

Khotan, meaning 'City of Jade' in the Uyghur Turkic lexicon, is a significant midway oasis along the Southern branch of the Silk Road before the caravans set out on their last major trek to reach the kingdom of Kashgar. Khotan lay along an east-west pathway connecting China with several early hybrid civilizations, such as the Yuezhi/Kushan and the Buddhist Gandharan cultures both of which had maintained extensively established commercial interests with the Hellenic, Roman and the Byzantine empires. The present inhabitants of the city of Khotan, mostly of Tukic, Iranian and Indic origins, are almost exclusively Muslims although historically the kingdom of Khotan initially was a major centre of Buddhism and was identified primarily with the Mahayana branch of Buddhism.[17,18] It differed in this respect from the kingdom of Kuqa on the Northern branch of the Silk Road where the dominant practice was Hinayana Buddhism. In essence, the Hinayana practice (the Lesser Vehicle) emphasizes the total detachment from the temporal world as the vehicle for escaping the lower planes of the cycle of birth, death and rebirth. To this end good deeds in addition to detachment were considered helpful for achieving higher states of rebirth within the cycle until Nirvana (eternal bliss) is realized. On the other hand, the Mahayana practice (the Greater Vehicle) emphasizes the interdependence of all things living and considered total detachment unnecessary but maintained that compassion and good deeds will earn the devout merits for a higher state in the rebirth cycle until Nirvana is realized. Inscriptions in Khotanese have suggested that Shravakayana Buddhism first arrived in Khotan from the west across the Pamir Mountains during the second and the third centuries AD and was helped by the flourishing Silk Road trade passing through Khotan before the use of the Northern branch became prevelant. However this early form of Buddhism, unlike the Hinayana and Mahayana forms, was believed to have been based on Buddha's teachings before he had reached his ultimate enlightenment and hence was of lesser doctrinal import. Buddhist histories of Khotan have survived in Sanskrit and Khotanese languages in a large number of documents written from the seventh to the tenth centuries. They were discovered at various sites in the Tarim basin and in a rather unique library at the Mogao ghrottoes near Dunhuang. Their contents have indicated that the more advanced form of the Buddha's teachings, the Mahayana with which Khotan came to be identified, had reached Khotan from Gilgit (Gilit) in northern India. These documents collectively corroborate the widespread contacts that the Buddhist centres in the Western Regions had maintained with Buddhist communities further to their east.

Khotan came under the rule of the Later Han dynasty when it was conquered in 70 AD by General Pan Ch'ao. But during the eighth and ninth centuries, the Tibetans controlled much of the Western Regions including Khotan. In the fourteenth century the Karakhanid dynasty of Kashgar became the new rulers of the western kingdoms within the Western Regions and made Islam the dominant faith displacing or vanquishing the sedentary Buddhist population. In his *Diwanu Lughat at-Turk* (Chronicles of the Turkish Languages), the eleventh century Turkish poet, Mahmud ibn Hussayn al-Kashgari, dedicated several verses in a poem to the memory of the Muslim conquest of Khotan:[19]

> Like river torrents
> We flooded their cities
> We captured their monasteries
> And told them
> Not to worship the statues of the Buddha.

From the days of its early history to the present day, Khotan has produced high-quality nephrite jade which was mostly exported to China. The relationships between the two political centres were cordial enough that in the first century AD (Later Han Dynasty) a Chinese princess was given in marriage to a Khotanese prince. A legend has it that the princess brought with her a silkworm cocoon hidden in her hair as a covert part of her dowry. Henceforth, Khotan became a major producer of silk and it was from Khotan in the sixth century that silkworm eggs were eventually smuggled to the West. In addition to silk production, Khotan also became a major producer of pile carpets that were prized for their fine texture and brilliance of colours. The commercial success and prosperity of the oasis town of Khotan began to decline in the twelfth century as Islam was unable to cope with the Mongol occupations of the Western Regions. But Khotan continued to play major roles in the political developments in the Western Regions that were to come in the succeeding five centuries.

The ruins of the ancient city of Melik Awat are located about 25 kilometres south-east of Khotan but most is buried under several metres of silt brought by the floods of the nearby Yurungkash River (White Stone/Jade River). The city was once a major Buddhist center and today only the tops of a few mud-buildings are seen above the surrounding ground. It was founded in 210 BC and served as the capital of the Udun (ancient name of Khotan) Uyghur Buddhist kingdom under the rule of Buddhist Karakhanid dynasties until their Islamization in 934 AD and the founding of the Karakhanid Uyghur Khanate in 940 AD. The khanate was a unified federation of many Uyghur tribes that functioned as an 'empire' under the sovereignty of the Karakhan clan. Unable to survive in the ensuing conflicts with Islam, the residual Buddhists communities soon abandoned Melik Awat but the Muslim state survived until 1212 AD. The Chinese pilgrim Xuanzang passed through Melik Awat in 644 AD on his way back from India carrying with him the Sanskrit sutras of Buddhism for his soverign. He noted:

> This country is renowned for its music; the men love the
> song and dance. Few of them wear garments of skin and

wool; most wear taffeta and white linen. Their external behavior is full of urbanity; their customs are properly regulated. Their written characters and their mode of forming their sentences resemble the Indian model; the forms of the letters differ somewhat; the differences, however, are slight. The spoken language also differs from that of other countries. They greatly esteem the law of the Buddha. There are about a hundred sangharamas with some 5000 followers, who all study the doctrine of the Great Vehicle.

Yarkand يه که ن

Yarkand (today's Yecheng, also known as Shache, Suoju, Shaju) is strategically located about half way between Kashgar and Khotan at the junction of a recent branch road that leads in a north-easterly direction to Aksu on the Northern branch of the Silk Road. Its fertile soil at the western rim of the Taklamakan desert is nurished by the Yarkand River which flows north from the Kunlun Mountains. This oasis town was the life-line for the caravans travelling north from India through the Karakorum Pass (Black Rock Pass) crossing the Karakorum Mountains in the Wakhan region of what is today northern Pakistan. Caravans from India also reached Yarkand through the Broghol Pass in the Hindu Kush on the frontiers with Afghanistan. The Karakorum mountain range forms a continuum linking the Himalayas to its east with the Hindu Kush in the west and the Pamir Mountains to the north.[20] Today, Yarkand's population is predominantly Uyghur and is imbued with Islamic traditions.

The *Hanshu* of the Later Han dynasty makes reference to Yarkand at a time when the dynasty was interested in establishing trade routes through the Western Regions to reach the western markets of Central Asia. The chronicle states the following in the section pertaining to the Western Regions:

> Going west from the kingdom of Suoju [*Yarkand*, italics by the author], and passing through the countries of Puli and Wulei in the Wakhan, you arrive among the Da Yuezhi. To the east, it is 10,950 *li* from Luoyang.

Marco Polo, in the accounts of his travels in 1273 dismisses Karkan (Yarkand) as a place of any significance perhaps because by the last quarter of the thirteenth century the Mongol invasions had destroyed much of the character of this oasis town as one of the significant centres of Buddhism adjacent to Khotan along the Southern branch of the Silk Road:

> Departing from thence you enter the province of Karkan, which continues to the distance of five day's journey. Its inhabitants, for the most part Mahometans, with some Nestorian Christians, are subjects of the Grand Khan. Provisions are here in abundance, as is also cotton. The people are expert artisans. They are in general afflicted with swelling in the legs, and tumours in the throat, occasioned by the quality of the water they drink. In this country there is not anything further that is worthy of observation.[21]

Yarkand's early Islamic history rests mostly in the period when the region was contested between various Buddhist-Shamanist Mongolic and Islamic Tuekic tribes including in the latter those who allied themselves with Temur (Tamerlane). This history, which will be discussed in detail in Chapter 11, spans over seven centuries. It was culminated with the political and religious leadership of the Khojas in Kashgar and reached its zenith in the seventeenth century. The legacy of Islam in Yarkand is vividly apparent from the vast number of its historic Muslim leaders who are interred in mazars (tombs) and mausoleums within the grounds of the impressive royal cemetery adjacent to the Altunluk Mosque in Yarkand.

The city's other ancient mosque, known as the Jama Masjid (Jama Mosque), dates back to the fifteenth century when the kingdom of Yarkand was founded by Sultan Yunus (Yunus Khan). Yunus had sought refuge in Yarkand from the Chaghatai khanate persecutions of his faith in Bukhara and Samarkand (in present-day Uzbekistan). The mausoleum of his grandson, Sultan Sa'id Khan, in the Altunluk royal cemetery is one of the major revered religious sites in Yarkand. Sa'id Khan was born in Turfan as the great grandson of Temur from his daughter's lineage. A number of Sa'id Khan's successors are also interred within the Altunluk cemetery. His dynasty lasted from 1514-1650.

Settlements of the Southern Silk Road in Xinjiang Province

The Sufi leadership in the mid seventeenth century in Yarkand and Kashgar rested in the hands of the khojas beginning with Khoja Muhammad Yusuf (*cf* Chapter 11) and later gained much prominence under the regime of his son Khoja Abakh. In this context, it is to be noted that the Chaghatai khanate lasted in one form or another from the early decades of the fourteenth century to the middle decades of the seventeenth century. The political power of the western half of the khanate was centred in Bukhara and Samarkand and was lost to Temur in mid fourteenth century. The eastern half of the khanate survived under the Karakhanids in Mughalistan and ultimately in the Tarim basin under the khojas who were periodically allied or were at war with Temur's successors.

Throughout the sixteenth and seventeenth centuries the khans of the Yarkand kingdom were renowned for their love and support of the arts especially music. Sultan Sa'id himself was a poet and a musician. The 'Muqam', the traditional form of Uyghur folk music alluded to in an earlier section, relates partly the national histories of the Uyghur in the form of myths, stories and love songs. These are contained in a collection of muqams known as the 'Twelve Muqams' whose compilation is attributed to Queen Ammanisahan. She was born in Yarkand in 1526 and became the wife of Sa'id Khan's son, Abdul-Rashid Khan. Ammanisahan died giving birth in 1560. She is interred in a modest mazar adjacent to the Altunluk royal cemetery in Yarkand. Her work, the Twelve Muqams, has been declared by the United Nation's Education and Research Organization as 'The third representative work of humans' oral and non-material cultural heritage.'

> At the end of a high blue mountain range,
> The Sun shines silver on the mountain peaks.
> Love is no more.
> You will not return.
> They all whisper about me, but I do not care
> Even if I am given eighty lashes with a whip,
> I am yours forever, forever.
>
> Maiden, lovely as the Moon!
> Your hips as slender as a willow
> Your smiling rouged face like an apple.
> Oh maiden, lovely as the Moon!
> Waiting for your lover;

That heart, like a burning flame,
Dances with desire.
A bird which does not see the rose
Does not know the beauty of Spring.
You are like the glowing Moon in the evening sky.
The shining jewel on your chest,
Like a glowing star in a rift between the clouds.

References

1. Whitefield, S. and Sims-Williams, U. (eds.), *The Silk Road: Trade, Travel, War and Faith*. The British Library, London (2004).
2. Baumer, C. *Traces in the Desert: Journeys of Discovery Across Central Asia*. I. B.Tauris, London (2008).
3. Hulsewé, A. F. P. and Loewe, M. A. N., *China in Central Asia: The Early Stage 125 BC- AD 23: an annotated translation of chapters 61 and 96 of the History of the Former Han Dynasty*. E. Brill Publications, Leiden (1979).
4. Baumer, C., *Southern Silk Road: In the Footsteps of Sir Aurel Stein and Sven Hedin*. Orchid Press, Bangkok (2000).
5. Noble, P. S., A Kharosthi Inscription from Endere. *Bulletin of the School of Oriental Studies*, no. 6 (1931).
6. Young, G. K., *Rome's Eastern Trade: International Commerce and Imperial Policy 31 BC-AD 305*. Routledge, London (2001).
7. Thomsen, V., Dr. M. A. Stein's Manuscripts in Turkish Runic Script from Miran and Tun-huang. *Jour. of the Royal Asiatic Society*, p. 190 (1912).
8. *The Travels of Marco Polo*. Book I, chap. XXXVI. Wordsworth Editions Limited, Ware, Hertfordshire (1977).
9. Ibid, Book I, chap. XXXV.
10. Laufer, B., *Jade: A Study in Chinese Archaeology and Religion*. Dover Publications, New York (1974).
11. Savage, G., *Chinese Jade*. Cory, Adams & Mackay, New York (1964).
12. Till, B. and Swart, P., *Chinese Jade: Stone for the Emperors*. Art Gallery of Greater Victoria, Victoria, British Columbia (1986).
13. Mallory, J. P. and Mair, V. H., *The Tarim Mummies: Ancient China and the Mystery of the Earliest Peoples from the West*. Thames & Hudson, London (2000).
14. Barber, E. W., *The Mummies of Ürümchi*. W. W. Norton and Co., New York (1999).
15. Boulnois, L., *Silk Road: Monks, Warriors and Merchants on the Silk Road*. H.Loveday (trans.), Odyssey Books and Guides, Hong Kong (2004).
16. *The Travels of Marco Polo*. Book I, chap. XXXIII. Wordsworth Editions Limited, Ware, Hertfordshire (1977).
17. Emmerick, R. E., *Tibetan Texts Concerning Khotan*. Oxford University Press, Oxford (1967).
18. Stein, A. M., *Ancient Khotan: Detailed report of Archaeological Explorations in Chinese Turkestan*. Clarendon Press, Oxford (1907).

19. Soucek, S., *A History of Inner Asia*. Cambridge University Press, Cambridge (2002).
20. Rizvi, J., *Trans-Himalayan Caravans: Merchant Princes and Peasant Traders in Ladakh*. Oxford University Press, Oxford (1999).
21. *The Travels of Marco Polo*. Book I, chap. XXXII. Wordsworth Editions Limited, Ware, Hertfordshire (1977).

Chapter Eight

Coming of the Maritime Routes to China

Maritime trade between civilizations can be traced back to at least two millennia. Navigation in waterways was known in Sumerian Mesopotamia between the fourth and the third millennium BC, and the Egyptians had trade routes through the Red sea importing spices and horses from Arabia. Clearly, trade and commerce have been fundamentally linked to societal evolution during much of human history. The commercial endeavours of many societies in the Mediterranean basin, India, Asia, China and the Far East have relied on extensive networks of transportation systems to increase wealth and promote their international political stature.[1] Sea routes were by far the favoured mode of transport for such purposes. The earliest use of sea routes linking the Mediterranean basin and India took place during the Hellenic Era.[2] In 275 BC, Ptolemy II (Philadelphos) who inherited the rule of Egypt from his father Ptolemy I, had founded a shipping port on the western coast of the Red Sea and named it Berenice after his mother, Berenike I. Berenice (Berenike) developed into a vast trading emporium: spices, myrrh, frankincense, pearls and textiles were shipped via Berenice to Alexandria and then on to Rome. The details of this trade come from the first century AD textual evidence recorded in the *Periplus of the Erythraean Sea* which lists the harbours along the Red Sea, on the coasts of East Africa, South Arabia and India and the commodities which were traded in these emporia. From Berenice goods were also shifted inland on the back of camels and delivered to harbours on the Nile River and then dispatched by boats to the seaport of Alexandria on the Mediterranean coast. In this manner goods from India and Africa were delivered to Constantinople and ultimately to the European marketplace.[3]

The port city of Guangzhou on the Pearl River estuary (Canton) China was a major international trading port for vessels sailing mostly in the waters of the South China Sea throughout the Tang and Northern and Southern Song dynasties. Althoug much of Guangzhou's trade during this period was destined for markets in South-East Asia, some goods were also destined for the eastern coast of China. The development of

Guangzhou's sailing potentials towards India and east Africa came later during the period from the late thirteenth to the mid fifteenth centuries. It was during this latter period that the port of Berenice on the west coast of the Red Sea had become an integral link in the chain of sea routes that connected China with the West.

The initial part of the chain involved either vessels leaving the port city of Guangzhou and traversing the waters of the South China Sea in a south-westerly direction, or vessels departing Cochin-China from the port of Chao-Chi at the mouth of the Red River in the Gulf of Tonkin. Portuguese traders (circa 1516) coined the term 'Cochin-China' for the southern third of Vietnam to distinguish it from the city and princely state of Cochin in India. Cochin-China had long been an outlet for goods arriving from inland sources within China. The south-western provincs of Yunnan and Sichuan were major centres for the trade of Chinese products destined for export through Cochi-China to far away foreign markets.

Departures either from Guangzhou or Cochin-China had to negotiate the Straits of Malacca, which separates the Malaysian Peninsula from the Indonesian island of Sumatra, before turning directly west to cross the Indian Ocean en-route to the western coasts of India and Ceylon (modern Sri Lanka)[4,5] Barygaza was a major port in the north-western corner of India from which ships sailed to the next ports of call along the southern coast of the Arabian Peninsula in the Gulf of Aden. There were also branch routes out of the Gulf of Aden which led to the eastern coast of Africa in Somalia and modern Tanzania. These commercial sea routes between Guangzhou, South-East Asia and India became the most preferable and the highly profitable modes of transport system for the merchants of Arabia and Persia, especially during the thirteenth and fourteenth centuries. Initially, silk was by far the most lucrative commodity traded between Asia and the Greco-Roman West, but as trade began to diversify, spices from India and South-East Asia became the West's main import. The spectrum of trade in spices was broad enough and characteristically distinct and interesting enough relative to other commodities that it attracted the attention of many chroniclers, such as Ibn Khurddahbeh (850 AD), al-Ghafiqi (1150 AD), Ishak ibn Imran (907 AD) and, as late as the fourteenth century, of al-Kalkashandi, who left for us their witness of the exotic spice trade.

Coming of the Maritime Routes to China

Apart from the Roman sailings in *Mare Nostrum* (Our Lake, meaning the Mediterranean Sea) and those that occurred within the Roman Empire, early seafaring trade relied upon visual contact with the coastlines for safe navigation hence did not stray far from the coastal contours. Later, with the advances in celestial navigation - the use of the position of the sun, the moon and the stars in the night sky - learned from astronomy, and taking advantage of the monsoon winds, sea-borne vessels ventured farther offshore and reduced the length of their voyages by sailing directly to their destinations between the Arabian Sea and the Bay of Bengal. The port city of Barygaza on the Arabian Sea became a central link between Asia and the Near East. Known as Bharuch City (or Broach) in the Gujarat state in the north-west of the Indian sub-continent, Barygaza was ideally situated at the mouth of the Narmada River that gave the port the capacity to extend its navigational advantages inland towards Central Asia. Through Barygaza a large selection of commodities reached the open markets in Afghanistan and further north in Merv, Bukhara and Samarkand. Much of these commodities were essential for the localized manufacturing industries. For food production wheat, Egyptian corn, wines, fish products and dates were imported. African cotton, Chinese silk and textiles were imported for clothing, and pearl, gold and silver for jewellery making. Timber from Africa and ink, glass and porcelain from China were also imported as essential commodities. Exports from Barygaza were primarily ivory and ebony for China and copper for the African and Middle Eastern houseware industries. With the accelerated dissemination of Buddhism from India in the direction of Central and South-East Asia in the seventh century, Barygaza rapidly expanded its Buddhist institutions and acquired a central position in Buddhist teachings.

During the Middle Ages (the ninth to fourteenth centuries), the wealthy Pisan, Venetian and Genoese city-states monopolized and controlled the bulk of the Mediterranean trading network which linked the commercial interests of Pisa, Venice and Geneoa with the pivotal triad cities of Damascus, Alexandria and Constantinople. They struck alliances with many regional powers and secured exclusive trading charters from coastal countries such as Egypt, Syria, first Byzantine then Lusignan Cyprus and Cilician Armenia. Their imports from China included silk, herbs, spices, lacquer and porcelain. From India sandalwood was imported, and frankincense, aloe and myrrh from Africa. But with the advent of Islam in Arabia in the seventh century and with the rapid conquests it made in the control of territories in the Fertile Crescent, the city-states found themselves disadvantaged and were denied access to much of the overland trade reaching the lucrative markets in the Far East, far afield from their limited Mediterranean markets. This situation was further exacerbated by the proliferation and the increase in the intensity of maritime shipping in the Near East under Muslim control.[6,7] Muslim sailors dominated the maritime routes throughout the Indian Ocean, tapping source regions in the Far East and shipping the goods westward to their home ports around the Arabian Sea. The rise of the Islamic Ottoman Empire subsequent to its conquest of Constantinople in 1453 reinforced hopelessly the exclusion of the European city-states' mercantile ambitions in the the Far East practically until the nineteenth century.

The traditional overland Silk Road traversing the barren deserts and the snow-covered mountains in Central Asia in its more than one thousand year history was the classical example of the extent to which links were essential for societies to forge ahead with trading enterprises. But this example was by no means unique. It was only one consequence of the domestication of pack animals (camels, horses, donkeys and oxen) which permitted traders to increase their capacity to carry heavier loads over greater distances thus bestowing significant merits upon this overland transport system. The singular advantage that the traditional overland Silk Road enjoyed during its time was its low cost of operation. Pack animals consumed vegetation as their source of energy, a commodity provided by the fertile grazing grasslands of Central Asia for most of the way at a minimal cost. Although this pastoral scenario was idyllic for the profit-minded merchants, it, nonetheless, was not without its perils. Adequate source of water throughout the length of the journeys was essential for survival when political circumstances permitted the safe and the un-encumbered passage of the caravans towards their destinations.

Although trade across the Asian continent has existed for several millennia, the history of the traditional Silk Road as we know it is relatively recent. We can trace it back to the Han dynasty (206 BC-AD 220) largely in the context of the mission of Zhang Qian, as was discussed earlier. But by the eleventh century AD the significance of the Silk Road's odysseys had begun to fade into oblivion as alternate routes were sought to circumvent the regional geo-political conflicts that had complicated and plagued the overland passages for over a millennium, if not otherwise had rendered them entirely impassable. In

Coming of the Maritime Routes to China

contrast, sailing the seas was less likely to be hindered by political conflicts and ships were much more accommodating than pack animal caravans in terms of the capacity and variety of goods that could be transported. Moreover, port cities were less dependent on external vital supplies for survival and also less vulnerable to attacks and plunder. Thus, the emergence and the gradual rise in the use of dependable and safe sea routes leading out of Asian and Chinese port cities spelled the certain demise of the overland routes. This demise was complete by the end of the thirteenth century and the memory of the long-cherished routes remained dormant until our romance with their legacy was re-kindled in the twentieth century by Western archaeologists.

Trade arriving or leaving China by sea favoured two interconnecting routes; the first began in the city of Guangzhou at the mouth of the Pearl River that opened into the South China Sea, and the second in the port city of Xiamen on the coast of East China Sea. In the beginning maritime contacts were basically inter-coastal with goods shipped short distances in exchange for other manufactured products or for jewellery, gold and silver. Nonetheless, in this manner, goods and artifacts could travel widely and far. A Han text of 97 AD describes a sea voyage from China to the Near East in the following excerpt:

> The sea is vast and great; with favourable winds it is possible to cross within three months; but if you meet slow winds, it may also take you two years; it is for this reason that those who go to sea take on board a supply of three years provisions. There is something in the sea which is apt to make a man homesick, and several have thus lost their lives.

Contacts between China and the Near East have long been in existence and clearly pre-date the Islamic period. When the Sasanians of the Persian Empire came to power in 226 AD, they became deeply interested in maritime expeditions and by the mid fifth century AD they were well established in Ceylon, and their direct sailings from Ceylon to China had given them the advantage to control the export of Chinese silk to the West.[8] Furthermore, it appears that the Sasanians had impacted significantly on the advances made by the Chinese in the manufacture of various types of ceramics. In this context, analyses have proved that the blue (cobalt) of Chinese Sansai (three coloured) splash glazeware is actually of Persian origin. There can be little doubt that it was introduced to the Chinese potters at the manufacturing sites of Jingdezhen in Jiangxi province by Persian merchants domiciled in the eastern coastal towns of China. Also, pottery in the Sasanian style, mainly as large vases of yellowish ware with a turquoise glaze, have been found in many early tenth century AD tombs near Fuzhou in Fujian province, and more pottery of similar type have been excavated at Yangzhou in Jiangxi province. More evidence of early Persian contacts with China comes from the records of the Arab merchant Sulayman al-Tajer al-Sirafi (Sulayman the merchant from Siraf) who has described a journey from the Persian Gulf to China he had made in 851 AD. His description of the local histories of the production of the yellowish translucent Chinese vases coincides with the period of early Sasanian contacts with China. The production of this type of porcelain represented the height of Chinese craftsmanship which was achieved during the Tang dynasty. Sulayman's contemporary, Ibn Khurddahbeh, on the other hand, provides more evidence for the extent of Persia's contacts with China by giving us the names of the Chinese ports most involved with Persia's foreign trade. The names include the port city of Kanfu (Guangzhou), Kanju (Quanzhou) and Qantu (Yangzhou).

Whilst it appears certain Persian materials and artestry had found their way into China, in return Chinese ceramics were abundantely shipped from the Chinese port cities to Sulayman's own port city of Siraf.[9] The earliest contact between Siraf and China seems to have occurred in 185 AD. The city's location in the center of the Persian Gulf's eastern shorline facilitated its importance in extending the Arabian Sea maritime trade inland into the ancient Abbasid Caliphate capital, Baghdad. In essence, from Siraf goods were transported to Arabia, Meopotamia, the Nile valley in Egypt and East Africa and to Syria. During the height of its commercial activities Siraf was a centre for the trade of ivory from Africa, precious stones from India, lapis lazuli from Afghanistan and Tang dynasty porcelain from China, especially painted stoneware from Changsha in Hunan province. Its role in the import of lapis lazuli from Afghanistan became especially pivotal because the deep blue shade of this mineral dye was used extensively in decorating much of the façades of the Islamic shrines throughout the Middle East. Siraf with its deep commercial heritage suffered near the end of the tenth century at the hands of the invading Tukic Seljuks from the steppes of Central Asia. Thereafter, its prominence began to decline rapidly and was brought to a close by the fifteenth century. The ruins of this ancient port city now lie partly subnerged in the waters of the Persian Gulf.

Coming of the Maritime Routes to China

South China Sea Routes

The earliest settlements in the area of Guangzhou known as Panyu seem to go back to the first decade of the third century BC. Upon the collapse of the Qin dynasty in 206 BC, Panyu became the capital of the Nanyue Kingdom which annexed the modern Chinese provinces of Guangdong, Guangxi, and Yunnan and much of modern northern Vietnam. But within a century of its founding, Nanyue itself was annexed by the Han dynasty which made Panyu its provincial capital in 111 BC. In 226 AD, Panyu became the seat of the Guang prefecture, hence 'Guangzhou' a name later adopted for the city. Today, Panyu generally refers to the region to the south of Haizhu District, which is separated from the central district by the Pearl River.

The city of Guangzhou in Guangdong province (Canton) was the starting point of the South China Sea routes leading to India. Although this route had been in some use for centuries in one form or another as far back as the time of the Han dynasty (206 BC), it nonetheless was considered of secondary importance relative to the overland routes and had not seen much use due to mariners' inability and unwillingness (fear of the sea) to navigate long distance sailings. However, advances in ship design and the application of new technologies to sea navigation opened new possibilities for maritime sailings. Thus by the twelfth century new sea lanes had come into use which were later developed to lead ships to destinations far away from their home ports. At first China's maritime shippings began gradually to venture south into the South China Sea before they developed the confidence to turn west towards the Indian Ocean on their way to India and east Africa. By the end of the Tang dynasty, Guangzhou had become China's greatest international port city for ships trading in South-East Asia. It maintained that status throughout the Northern and the Southern Song dynasties (960-1279 AD). Chinese sailboats known as 'junks' sailed out of the general waters of South China Sea carrying cargoes destined for Java and for the spice islands of Molucca. They traded in cloves, nutmeg, mace, black pepper, silver and gold.

The tempo of challenging long-distance sea voyages from Guangzhou across vast open seas increased rapidly in the thirteenth century and reached a peak in the fifteenth century. The celebrated naval expeditions to east Africa by Admiral Zheng He in the early decades of the fifteenth century involving huge and massive sailboats organized in large fleets demonstrated the high level of sailing sophistication the Chinese had achieved both in commercial and military applications.[10]

In the centuries that followed, however, China lost its seafaring supremacy and capitulated to the technologies achieved by the West as a consequence of the Industrial Revolution in Northern Europe. The Opium Wars of 1839 and 1857 virtually sealed the coffin of the defunct Chinese maritime activities for most of the nineteenth and twentieth centuries.

Direct involvement of seafaring Europeans in trade with China and their physical arrival in China were delayed in a historical sense partly by Islam as discussed above, and partly due to the long and dangerous journey around the African continent which posed great disadvantages to commercial seafaring. Nevertheless, in the fifteenth century, Portuguese navigators under the leadership of their King John II attempted to reach Asia by sailing around Africa. This quest was accomplished in 1488 when Bartolomeu Dias successfully rounded the southern tip of the African continent near the Cape of Good Hope. But the Genoese explorer Christopher Columbus was convinced that by sailing westward across the Atlantic Ocean he could reach the East Indies - Japan in the first instance. After many years of lobbying in Spain for royal patronage and fiancial support he finally succeeded in 1492 in gaining the patronage and support of the Iberian monarchs Ferdinand II of Aragon and Isabella I of Castile. He thus embarked on his first sea voyage in 1492 and instead of reaching Japan as he had intended, he landed in the Bahama Islands. He never admitted that he had reached a continent previously unknown to Europeans rather than the East Indies he had set out to reach. He called the inhabitants of the lands he visited *indios* (Spanish for Indians). Columbus's success set the tone for the rapid emergence of European imperialism and colonization as a *modus operandi* for gaining the upper hand in economic competition over rival powers in the contest for the lucrative spice trade with Asia.

The Portuguese were the first Europeans to arrive in Guangzhou by sea in 1513, establishing a monopoly by 1517 on the trade out of the city's harbour on the Pearl River until the arrival of the Dutch in the early seventeenth century.[11] Portuguese traders had first reached Ceylon in1505 and in their quest to establish a trading empire, a Portuguese fleet in 1509 under the command of Afonso de Albuquerque engaged a combined Ottoman, Gujarat and Egyptian naval forces in a sea-battle that gave him an unprecedented victory and left the control of the Indian Ocean entirely at the disposal of the Portuguese. A year later in 1510 Goa was taken from the Bijapur sultanate and declared the headquarters of the Portuguese State in India. Subsequently, in April 1511, Albuquerque took the Malaysian sultanate of Malacca, the most important eastern point in the trade network where traders from Malaysia, Gujarat, China, Japan, Java, Bengal, Persia and Arabia met to conduct business. Having vanquished the sultanate of Malacca, Albuquerque made Malacca a strategic base under Portuguese rule drawing its power from the Portuguese State in Goa in an attempt to reinforce Portuguese presence closer to mainland China. Thus in May 1513 the Portugese explorer Jorge Álvares under the command of captain Rui de Brito Patalim set sail from Malacca in a mission of reconnaissance along China's southern coastline. He landed on the island of Lantau in the Pearl River estuary and collected information on the regional topography. Confident in the information supplied by Álvares, Albuquerque within the same year dispatched Rafael Perestrello - a cousin of Christopher Columbus's wife Filipa Moniz Perestrello – and ordered him to land on mainland China and to insist on securing trade alliances with imperial China. China's politically reserved response with considerabely measured confidence granted the Portuguese the trade alliances they had sought and within three years of Rafael's mission, Portuguese traders were firmly established on Shangchuan Island near Guangzhou. But after four decades of operating out of the tiny island, the Ming dynasty in 1557 consented to abolishing the island base and replaced it with Macau as an autonomus Portuguese trading authority that made Macau a *de facto* Portuguese colony until it was returned to China in 1999.

With Portugal firmly regulating the trade in South-East Asia, the commercial future of Guangzhou was secure. Traders and merchants from all around the world flocked to Guangzhou and to the markets of South-East Asia. Muslim and Christian merchants alike, especially Christian Armenians from India, took advantage of their renowned trading skills and built their wealth in the lucrative spice and silk markets. The Armenian advantages extended all the way to Constantinople where in the seventeenth century the Armenians of Asia Minor controlled much of the banking, spice, silk and carpet trades on behalf of the sultans of the Ottoman Empire. In the commercial hotbed of Guangzhou soon arrived the French and the British.[12] They convinced the Portuguese they were not to be denied their share of the lucrative Asian markets. The British with their agenda in focus executed with great precision the founding of the famously known East India Company which was granted an English Royal Charter by Queen Elizabeth I on 31 December 1600. It was the oldest among several similarly formed European East India companies for pursuing trade in the East Indies but ultimately traded mainly with the Indian subcontinent and China. The foundations of the company were laid eight years earlier when Queen Elizabeth I had granted a charter on 7 January 1592 to fifty-five English merchants under the name 'Governor and Company of Merchants of London Trading into the East Indies' giving them the monopoly of trade with Venice and Ottoman Turkey. This was the beginning of the Levant Company which ultimately led to the formation of the East India Company of Britain and the advent of the British Empire in India. The company traded mostly in cotton, silk, indigo dye, saltpeter, tea and opium but in time came to rule large swathes of India exercising military power and assuming administrative functions to the gradual exclusion of its commercial pursuits. Under the Government of India Act of 1858, the British Crown assumed direct administration of India that came to be called the British Raj. Many other European East India companies which were founded following the British example colonialized much of the Far East and possessed quasi-governmental powers that included the ability to wage war, negotiate treaties and coin their own currencies. These companies with focused commercial and colonial interests in India and the Far East included the Dutch East India Company (1602); Danish East India Company (1616); Imperial Ostend General India Company of Austria (1717) and the Swedish East India Company (1731). The Spanish, on the other hand, in their pursuit of the spice trade had colonized the Philippine Islands nearly a century earlier when Miguel López de Legazpi of New Spain (Mexico) was installed in 1565 as the first royal governor of the Philippines. He gave the islands their name in honour of King Philip II of Spain and declared Manila the capital of the Spanish East Indies. Spain ruled the Philippines for 333 years enduring intermittent sea battles with the Dutch but ultimately succumbed to the Spanish American War and surrendered the islands to the Americans in 1898.

The trading history of Guangzhou offers us the image of a typical port city metropolis complete with its foreign merchants and sailors. The Muslim traveller-historian Abu Zayid Hasan of Siraf recorded in the ninth century that the rebels of the Chinese Huang Chao Rebellion (874-884 AD) besieged the city of Guangzhou and killed a large number of foreign Muslim merchants residing there. Nonetheless, Guangzhou was a centre for Muslim traders as their home away from home. The Huai Sheng Mosque in the city at No. 56, Guangta Road, the legacy of Sa'ad ibn abi Waqqas, served both as a sacred religious

Coming of the Maritime Routes to China

site as well as a community centre where the devout could pray in its large prayer hall or rest in the cool shades of the centre's ancient Longyan, Sha, Fengyan and Rong trees that stand to this day. Liu Chang, the last emperor of the Southern Han dynasty (907-971 AD) is reputed to have kept a harem of Persian girls, including one he nicknamed 'Beautiful Pearl' (*Meili Zhen Zhu*). Apparently he was notorious for his predilection for Persian girls and had wantonly engaged in carnal activities with them in his palace at Canton.

Guangzhou continued to play its role as an Islamic centre in China throughout the centuries especially with the construction of many additional mosques during the Ming dynasty. The Hao Pan Mosque located at No. 378, Hao Pan Street, off of Tian Cheng Road, was built in 1465 AD and had once housed the Muslim University for the study of Islamic history until it was converted to a factory during the Cultural Revolution. It was re-instituted as a mosque in 1998 and as a centre for the study of the Arabic language. Presently it also serves as the centre for the Guangdong Provincial Islamic Association. The Dong Ying Mosque at No. 1, Yuehua Road and the Nan Sheng Mosque on Danan Road were built sometime during the reign of Emperor Hsien Tsung (1488-1505 AD) of the Ming dyanstay. One final important Islamic feature in Guangzhou is the Xin Shi Mulsim cemetery in the Xin Shi district in the north-west of the city. This site was selected in 1957 for the re-burial of the two-thousand remains of Muslims exhumed from their ancient graves in a cemetary where now stands Guangzhou's North Railway Station. The majority of the remains were burials from the Qing dynasty period; however the oldest was determined paleographyically from a headstone to belong to the Yuan dynasty.

East China Sea Routes

In the geographic monographs of the *Hanshu*, the word Goguryeo was first mentioned in 113 BC as a region under the jurisdiction of the Xuantu. The Xuantu was one of the four administrative districts established by China's Han dynasty in 107 BC. Goguryeo, on the other hand, was one of the ancient Three Kingdoms of the Korean Peninsula, the other two being the Kingdom of Baekje and the Kingdom of Silla.[13] China's trade links with Korea had begun during the Qin dynasty (221-206 BC) primarily through a land route connecting China with the Korean kingdoms of Goguryeo in the north of the peninsula, and Silla in the south. In the present context of China's trade across the East China Sea it is to be noted that from the first to the fourth century AD,

China had maintained extensive trade relationships with its neighbouring Korean kingdoms conducted mostly via overland routes. The regulation of this trade was administred by the Xuantu which for several centuries had been the root cause of a number of conflicts with the Korean kingdoms lasting through the years of the Tang dynasty period. Without belaboring the obvious reasons for the conflicts, they were commonly results of defiance of the vested Chinese authority, disagreements on the payable commercial rates but also included the extent to which tributes were due China payable by the Korean kingdoms as nominal vassal states subject to the authority of the Middle Kingdom. Most of these conflicts had eventually disappeared by the time the Jin dynasty (1115-1234 AD) assumed power in China. Beginning in the twelfth century Japanese merchant ships had begun their journeys to the neutral ports of Cochin-China in the Gulf of Tonkin but had also established significant trading partnerships in Korea, especially with the Korean kingdom of Baekje.[14] It is of interest to note that archaeological finds such as a Vietnamese wooden plate with the engraved date of 1330 recovered in the northern parts of the Japanese Kyushu Island suggest that goods produced in Vietnam had indeed reached Japan. The development of new sea routes out of China's Gulf of Bohai were encouraged by the Japanese trading enterprises and had given China's north-eastern Shantung (Shandong) Peninsula new and relatively conflict-free access to the Korean Peninsula.

China's trade with Japan had begun as early as the Tang dynasty when Chinese merchants had reluctantly crossed the Yellow Sea to Japan. The blossoming of this trade however had to wait until the twelfth century. In the early years of the twelfth century China's eastern port city of Quanzhou (also known as Chinchu or Zaytun) in Fujian province had not yet acquired the trading status enjoyed by the southern port of Guangzhou with its massive international trading establishments operating throughout the south-east Asian archipelago. Quanzhou's trading excellence developed slowly.

Although Quanzhou was founded during the Tang dynasty in the second decade of the eighth century AD, its position as a major eastern port in China was not realized until the arrival of Muslim traders from India and Arabia. The trickle of Muslim traders, who arrived in Quanzhou in the ninth century as part of Tang dynasty's ambitious trade policies for expansion, became the nucleus of the Muslim communities that slowly grew and flourished in Quanzhou.[15] These

Coming of the Maritime Routes to China

non-aggressive trade-focused Muslim communities were tolerated by the Chinese and were allowed to manage the growing commercial traffic in return for a hefty share of the profits in the form of state taxes, levies and tributes. In the centuries that followed, especially in late Song (960–1279) and Yuan (1279–1368) dynasties, Quanzhou became one of the world's largest seaports, and was home for a large population of foreign-born inhabitants from Europe, Middle East, India and the Pacific islands. Their chief legacy was the founding in the late fourteenth century (Ming dynasty) of a second sea port in Fujian province historically known as Amoy (modern Xiamen). In the mid sixteenth century Xiamen was used extensively by Portuguese merchants for the export of tea to Europe. However, the port became the first casualty of the First Opium War of 1839 which by virtue of the Treaty of Nanjing the port became a free zone outside China's jurisdiction.

In addition to its past trading successes in the east, the port city of Amoy also facilitated the administration of the Ryukyu Islands, better known as Okinawa, a chain of islands in the Western Pacific at the eastern limits of the East China Sea. In 1372 AD the islands were a tributary state of the Ming dynasty, but in 1609, Lord Satsuma of Japan invaded the islands and declared their independence from China. In 1879, Japan's Meiji government annexed the Ryukyu Islands as part of territorial Japan.

References

1. Curtin, P. D., *Cross-Cultural Trade in World History*. Cambridge University Press, Cambridge (1984).
2. Lindsay, W. S., *History of Merchant Shipping and Ancient Commerce*. Adamant Media Corp., Boston, Massachusetts (2996).
3. Lunde, P. and Porter, A., Trade and Travel in the Red Sea Region. Proceedings Of Red Sea Project I: British Archaeological Reports International. *Society for Arabian Studies Monographs* Part 2 (2004).
4. Freeman, D. B., *The Straits of Malacca: Gateway or Gauntlet?* McGill-Queen's Press, Montreal (2003).
5. Kearney, M., *The Indian Ocean in World History*. Routlege, London (2003).
6. Tabak, F., *The Waning of the Mediterranean, 1550-1870: A Geohistorical Approach*. The John Hopkins University Press, Baltimore, Maryland (2008).
7. Lunde, P., *The Navigator Ahmed ibn Majid*. Saudi Aramco, Riyadh, Saudi Arabia (2004).
8. Herzig, E., The Iranian Raw Silk Trade and European Manufacture in the Seventeenth and Eighteenth Centuries. *Jour. of European Economic Hist.*, no.19 (1990).
9. Boulnois, L., *Silk Road: Monks, Warriors and Merchants on the Silk Road*. H. Loveday (trans.), Odyssey Books and Guides, Hong Kong (2004).
10. Dreyer, E. L., *Zheng He: China and the Oceans in the Early Ming Dynasty, 1405-1433*. Pearson Longman, London (2006).
11. Donkin, R. A., *Between East and West: The Moluccas and the Traffic in Spices up to the Arrival of Europeans*. Diane Publishing Co., Darby, Pennsylvania (2003).
12. Mungello, D. E., *The Great Encounter of China and the West, 1500-1800*. Rowman and Littlefield, Lanham, Maryland (2005).
13. Byington, M. E., *A History of the Puyo State: Its History and Legacy*. PhD dissertation, Harvard University, Cambridge, Massachusetts (2003).
14. Lee, K. B., *A New History of Korea*", Harvard University Press, Cambridge, Massachusetts (1984).
15. Wang, L., *Return to the City of Light: Quanzhou, An Eastern City Shining with the Splendour of Medieval Culture*. Fujian People's Publishing House, Fujian, China (2000).

Chapter Nine

Buddhism in China

> There one sees a structure of an elevation prodigious in height; it is supported by gigantic pillars and covered with paintings of all the birds created by God. In the interior are two immense idols carved in the rock and rising from the foot of the mountains to the summit...One cannot see anything comparable to these statues in the whole world.
>
> *A description of Afghanistan's Bamiyan Buddhist complex by the Medieval Geographical Sourcebook, Yakut (1218)*

The Middle Kingdom was most receptive to outside influences during the centuries when it was engaged in the creation of wealth and political influence through its control and militarization of the Silk Road. But, apart from the commercial and political aspects of the Silk Road, this ancient network of international highways for transporting goods and products to the four corners of the world also became a conduit for the transmission of cultural as well as religious influences into China.

The first seeds of Buddhism were planted in India in the fifth century BC. For the most part of the following seven centuries this faith and its doctrines remained largely an unknown religious element to the populace of the Middle Kingdom. Moreover, structured Daoism (Taoism) in China would not become a belief practice of its people until the third century BC, and when the very first caravans of the Silk Road might have begun their trek for the riches of the East in the first century AD, Christianity was still in its formative decades. Buddhism made its first appearance in China in the second Century AD but only in a miniscule manner through the involvement of the Parthian monk An Shih-Kao who had come to China in 148 AD to assist in the translation of the scant Buddhist text into Chinese. Despite this, yet still two centuries would lapse before there was a strong Buddhist presence in China. And then but not until the seventh century AD that we witness the first missions of the Christian faith, albeit heretical, setting foot on Chinese soil. As for Islam, the emergence and blossoming a of this faith as a major religion in the Middle Kingdom had to wait until the first Mongol invasions of China in the twelfth century under the leadership of Genghis Khan.

As was briefly discussed in previous sections, Buddhism with its origins in north-eastern India is a system of beliefs and practices based on the '*Sutras*' (the teachings of Siddhartha Sakyamuni Gautama) which instruct the devout the path to liberation from the life's cycle of birth, suffering, death and rebirth until Nirvana – a state of eternal bliss - is realized. It is imbued with a psycho-philosophical approach to the conditioning of the mind that facilitates the achievement of a transcendent and a metaphysical state of harmonious natural existence. This new idea promoted the cultivation of an independent personal mind detached from the temporal physical world instead of being attached to and dependant upon ritualistic intercessions for securing a future eternal life after death. Although the novel teachings of Buddhism were received with great enthusiasm by many, to the Chinese polity and its subordinate society as existed two millennia ago Buddhism was seen as a fundamental threat to the very foundations of their civilization. The cornerstone of Chinese culture, and of many other Far Eastern societies, rested on the expectation and practice of filial piety which demanded of the members of a family their obedience to the living elders within the family, and the veneration and worship of the deceased elders in perpetuity. Buddhism's conflict with the Confucian dictum of filial piety rested in the fundamentals of the new teachings which advocated detachment from the temporal material world in favour of *inventing for oneself a self-conditioned contented existence* throughout the reincarnation cycles of death and rebirth until Nirvana is realized. Detachment from the temporal physical realm - the fundamental prerequisite for Buddhist salvation - was a process which did not distinguish family members from the realm of the physical world. Yet we find Buddhism had not only succeeded in occuping a central position in the Chinese dynastic fabric and of those of many of the other Far Eastern cultures, but it had also bequeathed those societies, and indeed the world at large, with collections of unimaginably wonderous works of art and literature on a scale that few other faiths are able to match.. How did this come about?

Buddhism in China

The impetus for the success of Buddhism in China came from the strong support given to the faith by the emperors of the Wei dynasties which eased Buddhism's acceptance into the Chinese social fabric and ensured the religion's survival. The originally nomadic Wei tribes (the Tuoba) invaded the western frontiers of China in 386 AD and rapidly adopted the Chinese social norms and customs. Their rapid assimilation into the indigenous Chinese society had direct repercussions on the future of Buddhism in China. Monasteries built during this period of Chinese history in the outer western limits of the Middle Kingdom attracted gifts from the faithful, especially gifts of land from the members of the ruling classes. This made the monasteries wealthy and powerful. Moreover, Buddhism's emphasis on self-determination for personal salvation and the renunciation of worldly ties attracted many disciples from the poorer segments of the society where many lived in utter despair and who often were homeless orphans. To such people the new faith offered fellowship but also gave them the power of self-determination for a secure blissful existence in life and death. Thus the ranks of the monastic life swelled as did peoples' spiritual investments and altered lifestyles.

Buddhism

Siddhartha Sakyamuni Gautama, known in the West as the Buddha, 'the awakened one', lived in north-eastern India in the fifth century BC. Born to the noble Gautama family of an ancient Sakya lineage, he came to be known as the Sakyamuni - the sage of the Sakyas. The biographical information concerning his life comes to us mostly from the canonical texts compiled by his devout disciples and by those who followed them. He was born to an aristocratic family in the village of Lumbini in the vicinity of the small city of Kapilavastu on the Indian border with Nepal. Early in his boyhood he was confounded by his observations of suffering, sickness and death. He renounced his life of abundant luxury and set off on a path to find meaningful answers to the causes of these unhappy human conditions. After many years of asceticism and introspective contemplation he achieved 'Enlightenment' beneath the sacred Bodhi Tree, whereupon he was called the Buddha. He expounded his fundamental teachings in what is called Buddha's Four Noble Truths. They are the vehicle by which one can redeem himself from human bondage and develop a transcendent state of existence. The first noble truth reaffirms that all life is sorrowful. 'Now this, O Bhikkus, is the noble truth concerning suffering. Birth is attended with pain, decay is painful, disease is painful, and death is painful...' The second truth gives the reasons for life's sorrowful conditions; they are identified as lust, fear and desire. 'Now this, O Bhikkus, is the noble truth concerning the origin of suffering....that is to say, the craving for the gratification of the passions, or the craving for life, or the craving for success...' The third truth shows the way to emancipation from suffering. 'Now this, O Bhikkus, is the noble truth concerning the destruction of suffering. Verily, it is the destruction in which no passion, no fear and no desire remain...' The fourth truth lists the eightfold path to achieving Nirvana. 'Now this, O Bhikkus, is the noble truth concerning the way which leads to the destruction of sorrow. Verily, it is this noble eightfold path; that is to say: right views; right aspirations; right speech; right conduct; right livelihood; right effort; right mindfulness; and right contemplation.'

The appeal of Buddha's teachings had rested in his apparent condemnation of the greed and the corruption within the Indian society of his time that had dominated and enslaved every aspect of the peoples' lives. In short, *'the way'* of the new faith promised liberation and acceptance of the human condition through the management of the self (self-control) in such a way that the physical flesh of one's self is rendered irrelevant regardless of its condition; what mattered was the quest for the inner peace that gave contentment (transcendent state of existence) and a higher plane of re-incarnation until ultimately Nirvana (eternal bliss) is achieved. The Buddha had claimed no divine inspiration. It is said that on his death-bed at the age of 80, he told his disciples: 'Seek salvation alone in the truth; look not for assistance from anyone besides yourself.' The implicit meaning of these last words is that salvation comes, not from gods or goddesses, but from within the self.

The Buddha died in 484 BC. His body was cremated on a pyre and his ashes as sacred relic were divided equally among his clans who built memorials known as 'stupas' at the sites where the ashes were buried. Two centuries after the Buddha's death, came Buddhism's greatest champion in the person of King Ashoka of India (273-232 BC). During his reign Ashoka brought most of the Indian sub-continent under his rule and his empire extended beyond India's north-western borders and into Ferghana and Bactria where cultural fusion with the Greco-Roman culture had been in progress from the time of the arrival of the Hellenic armies under Alexander the Great in 327 BC. But, saddened by the death and the destruction inflicted upon peoples by his conquests,

Buddhism in China

Ashoka embraced the Buddha's teachings and gave it his royal court's unprecedented support. He sent Buddhist missionaries to all parts of his empire, erected religious structures and monuments in honour of the Buddha and encouraged his people to live by the precepts of the Buddha. Ashoka's missionaries took Buddhism to Ceylon and from Ceylon the new faith spread eastward into Burma, Thailand and then south to the Indonesian archipelago. Buddhism was also introduced into Tibet, India's northern neighbour but, mixed with the local lore, it emerged as Lamaism. From north-western India, Buddhist monks carried Buddhist teachings across the Hindu Kush and the Pamir Mountains into present-day Afghanistan and into the Yuezhi/Kushan Empire centred in Ferghana and Bactria. From these regions of Central Asia, Buddhism entered China, and through China's long standing trade interests in the Korean peninsula, the faith advanced into Korea in the fourth century AD, and within the next two centuries Buddhist teachings would cross the Korean Straits and reach Japan. It is to be noted at this point that a cursory examination of the geographical paths that were instrumental in the dissemination of Buddhism into Central Asia amply reveals the paths' similarity to the contemporaneous geographical networks of travel, trade and transport that connected the Indian sub-continent with Central Asia and the Far East.[1]

The Hellenic Contacts

In the centuries just before the onset of the Christian era, the Yuezhi/Kushan Empire was ideally situated for the control of the overland trade originating from the Greco-Roman Empire destined for Indian and Chinese markets. This was the period when the Silk Road was beginning to be developed centuries before there were any sea routes beyond the Mediterranean Sea that would have made possible for the West to sail directly to the Chinese ports along the South China Sea. The Roman fascination with silk was the impetus that inspired their determination to reach the Far East and share in its wealth. The first Greco-Roman penetration into Central Asia began in the early decades of the fourth century BC following the conquest of the Persian Empire by the Macedonian Alexander the Great. His armies conquered Bactria (including the region of Kabul in present-day Afghanistan) and reached the Indian sub-continent as discussed earlier in Chapter 3.

Bactria and Gandhara were under Buddhist influences from the time of King Ashoka in the third century BC but the new faith only began to expand vigorously in the first century AD. The evidence for the early presence of Buddhism in Bactria and Gandhara comes from the Airtam inscriptions which inform of the restoration of the Airtam complex undertaken during the reign of the Bactrian king Khuvishka in the second century BC. The Buddhist centre at Airtam, consisting of a temple and a monastery, was situated along the Amu Darya (Amu River) in the vicinity of Termez in southern Uzbekistan (near its southern border with Afghanistan). Its buildings were enriched with images of the Buddha and decorated with countless statues of the Buddha sculpted out of the local marble-like limestone. Later with the arrival of the Arabs in the seventh century, Termez became a centre of Islam in Central Asia. But, before the arrival of Islam, Buddhist monastic complexes following the examples of Bactria were also founded in Gandhara at Bamiyan and Hadda. But as a consequence of the fusion of the Western Greco-culture with the Bactrian and Gandharan cultures, the development of Central Asian Buddhist art was influenced by the naturalism of the iconic Greek style. Many of the sculptures, mosaics and friezes in Bamiyan and Hadda assumed highly Hellenic styles. The realistic treatment of the delecate wavy folds of the Greco-Roman toga (robe) covering the representations of the Buddha is apparently derived from equivalent art in the Greco-Roman pantheon. As the faith gradually moved eastward into the Tarim basin and into Dunhuang and the Middle Kingdom, the Greco-Roman influences in Buddhist art were simeltaneously carried forward into these new areas. Inevitably some of these influences came under heavy resistance from local traditions and thus the emerging localized artistic output contained Sinocized images and patterns. For example, elaborate four- or five-clawed dragons were painted or carved around images that clearly possessed Chinese physical characteristics. The faces were usually serene with closed eyes that showed little curvature. At first figurines and painted images were depicted with multi-layered multi-coloured thick robes most commonly Chinese in practice. But the practice of favouring Chinese imagery was abandoned when the Northern Qi dynasty came to power (550-577 AD).

The influence of Indian Buddhist art clearly played a major role in the creation of new Chinese art under the Northern Qi dynasty. The Sinocized stylistic conventions in the art and sculpture adopted in the earlier periods were abandoned in favour of incorporating unusual physical characteristics in the Buddha's imagery. Included in this new wave of artistic expressions was placing the Indian symbolic protrudance, 'ushnisha', on the Buddha's head symbolic of transcendental knowledge and wisdom. This was a distinct diversion from the traditional Chinese practice of presenting their sages either holding a manuscript in hand or an unfolded parchment. The new faces were less serene and projected elements of subtle smile with completely open eyes that showed exaggerated curvatures. The Buddha figures were now distinguished by a greater naturalism, tended to be clad in thin robes that clung to the body and revealed the undulating folds of the human form. Other Indian motifs included placing a swastika on the forehead or the chest of the Buddha symbolic of eternity - everlasting. Moreover, hand gestures, or 'mudras' were also incorporated in the Buddha's imagery; they imparted silent messages of support and encouragement to the devout faithful. The right hand held upright at chest level with palm facing outwards, the 'abhaya mudra', conveyed the message 'Have no fear', while the left hand pointing down at hip level with the palm facing outwards, the 'varada mudra', indicated 'Your wish is granted, or prayers answered'.

Advances into the Tarim Basin

Although there is some evidence to suggest that Buddhist ideas might have reached the western parts of the Middle Kingdom after the death of King Ashoka in the final decades of the third century BC, it is more likely that minor textual elements of Buddhism had reached China from Sogdiana, Gandhara and Bactria through isolated individual traveling traders late in the first century BC. Though we are certain that the introduction of Buddhism into China took place by way of the Northern branch of the Silk Road during the early centuries of the Christian era, Indian missions by and large did not venture east much beyond Dunhuang. Much of the Buddhist missionary works that reacherd deep into the Middle Kingdom in the seventh century AD were conducted by Sogdian monks whose Sogdian merchant families over time had settled in Bactria or further south beyond the Hindu Kush in pursuit of merchantile opportunities.[2] Their offspring naturally belonged to social groups that were accustomed to traveling the routes of the Silk Road; therefore their missions deep into the Middle Kingdom would not have been seen as severely trying ordeals. Many of the Sogdian monks, such as Kang Seng Hui, and Kang Mengxiang who were familiar with the Indian language, were able to translate the Buddhist texts into Chinese without intermediary translators. In contrast, the Indian monks accustomed to the climate of their native tropical homeland might have been less inclined or altogether unwilling to undertake extended journeys into unfamiliar areas with varying linguistic heritage and with which their family traditions lacked historical contact. The Sogdians thus became the leading disseminators of culture and religious traditions from India, and Persia.[3]

Documentary evidence for the arrival of Buddhism in China comes from a number of sources. For example, the *Hanshu* chronicles the visit of a Yuezhi envoy to the court of Emperor Wudi (25-57 AD) for the teaching of Buddhist texts to the members of the court. One exceptional evidence for the very early arrival of Buddhism in China comes from the accounts recorded by the Chinese chronicler Yang Xuanzhi who is credited for translating parts of the Mahayana Buddhist sutras into the Chinese language during the Northern Wei dynasty (386-534 AD). He relates the following regarding the introduction of Buddhism into China around 70 AD, as translated by Ulrich Theobald of the Department of Chinese and Korean Studies, University of Tübingen, Germany:

> The establishment of the Baima Temple (Temple of the White Horse) by Emperor Ming (58-75 AD) of the Han marked the introduction of Buddhism into China. The temple was located on the south side of the Imperial Drive, three leagues (*li*) outside the Xiyang Gate. The Emperor dreamt of the golden man sixteen Chinese feet tall, with the aureole of sun and moon radiating from his head and his neck. A 'golden god', he was known as Buddha. The emperor dispatched envoys to the Western Regions in search of the god, and, as a result, acquired Buddhist scriptures and images. At the time, because the scriptures were carried into China on the backs of white horses, White Horse was adopted as the name of the temple.

The above passage has perhaps drawn its account from earlier legends based on the Emperor's dream in connection with the introduction of Buddhism into China. The legend relates that on a certain night of the year 66 AD, Emperor Mingdi of the Eastern Han dynasty had dreamt of the arrival in his royal court of a golden man but the emperor had no knowledge as to where the man had come from and why. The next morning the emperor summoned his subjects in search of the meaning of his dream. An elderly and a wise minister named Fu Yi had explained that in a far away country there indeed was such a man dressed in gold and is called the Buddha. Hence the minister's interpretation of the dream was that the emperor must have dreamt of the Buddha. The emperor then dispatched his official envoy led by Cai Yin to travel to the far away land west of his kingdom and bring back news of the Buddha. The envoy travelled to India and after three years in the land of the Buddha returned to China laden with Buddhist texts and figurines. To the delight of the emperor, the envoy had also brought along with them several Buddhist monks who according to the legend ultimately founded the first Buddhist community in the capital Luoyang.[4]

Buddhism in China underwent a long and difficult period of assimilation. The new faith which had percolated into China from India was subjected to intense and scrupilous study, and was argued in endless debates about its conflicts with Conficianism and Taoism. Its suitability to the Chinese populace was vehemently rejected by a lobby of a long line of envious Taoist clergy with power to sway royal decisions. Nevertheless after six centuries of endurance, Buddhism succeeded in becoming an important religious force in China even eclipsing its rival Taoism and, during the Tang dynasty, it enjoyed considerable royal patronage. Despite initially being considered a fundamentally foreign religion in China, Buddhism also overshadowed its late arriving Persian rival religions; the Manichaeism of Babylon, the Nestorianism of Edessa and the Zoroasterianism of Persia. There are no unequivocal explanations for these successes. Perhaps even the Buddhists' themselves were surprised of their successes to the extent that in defence of their faith Buddhist monks at court resorted to securing royal edicts declaring Manichaean teachings as being a form of corrupt Buddhism. Yet, Buddhism could not totally escape its image of 'foreignness.' It still had its share of enemies in China. An outspoken critic of Buddhism in the early ninth century was Han Yu who based his attacks against Buddhism on the facts that it was passive against its enemies; that it was not native to China and that it was not known to the ancient Founders and Fathers of the Middle Kingdom. Born in Nanyang in the province of Henan (768-824 AD), Han Yu was a renowned poet and the greatest master of classical prose in the Tang period. During the years of his service to the central government at various posts in Chang'an and Luoyang, he advocated strong central authority in political and military matters and a rigid commitment to the traditional Chinese cultural values. Han Yu's service to the royal courts came abruptly to an end when he wrote in 819 AD his celebrated *Memorial on Bone-relics of the Buddha*. This was a protest against the entrenched Buddhist influence in China in which the language used has been called "belligerently uncompromising and... disrespectful to the edge of personally insulting the emperor." He became an important Confucian intellectual and delineated on the works of Confucius that gave rise to Neo-Confucianism after his death in Chang'an. In his *Memorial on Bone-relics of the Buddha*, he vented his full xenophobic bitterness as follows:

> The Buddha was a barbarian in origin. He was not conversant in the language of the Middle Kingdom and wore clothes of a different fashion. His tongue therefore did not speak the prescribed doctrine of the former Kings, nor did his manner of dress conform to their fashion. He did not recognize the relationship between prince and subject, or the sentiments of father and son. If he were still alive today and came to our court as emissary by the order of his ruler, your Majesty might condescend to receive him but this should amount to no more than one interview in the Hsuan-chang Hall, one banquet in his honour, one gift of clothing and he would be escorted across the frontier so as to prevent him from misleading the masses.

As we shall see later in Chapter 12, when the Tang court finally in 845 AD ordered the suppression of Manichaesim as being foreign and subversive, the way was paved for a full-scale attack on Buddhism and on all other foreign religions including Manichaeism and Nestroianism. The Nestorians in particular suffered the most as a result of these persecutions. Their priests did not have the help and support of educated native collaborators as enjoyed by the Manichaeans. Also, their literature, as opposed to the Manichaeans', was only marginally syncretic which ironically exacerbated their foreignness. Hence the expulsion of the Nestorians from China dealt a severe blow to their work and essentially put Nestorianism into a hiatus that lasted nearly four centuries until its revival with the coming of the Mongols.

The relevance of the Silk Road to the evolution and flowering of Buddhism in China is unequivocal. In the late pre-Christian era and in the first century of the Christian era, the Silk Road was still in its infancy and its blossoming had to wait for yet another century. However, during the zenith of the road's history, principally from the fourth to the ninth century, the Silk Road became an effective and an unparalleled conduit for the entry of the faith into China. As has been discussed throughout this work, and summarized below, the transmission of Buddhism into the Middle Kingdom occurred predominantly via the Northern branch of the Silk Road by way of the Hexi Corridor. These same geographical paths were also used precisely

Buddhism in China

in the reverse direction by a number of renowned Middle Kingdom monks who travelled to contemporaneous centres of Buddhism in the Western Regions and to India for the collection, translation and the delivery of Buddhist documents back to their respective sovereigns.

In terms of a summary, we may recall, Buddhism came to the kingdom of Kuqa - founded on the Northern branch of the Silk Road - before the end of the first century AD. However, it was not until the third century that the kingdom became a major center of Hinayana Buddhism though its schools vacillated also towards the teaching of the Mahayana doctrine. The Subashi temple and the Kizil Thousand-Buddha grottoes not far in the north-west of Kuqa were founded around the first century AD and became great schools of Buddhism and flourished during the Wei and Jin dynasties. As Buddhism advanced towards the Tarim basin its communities in Kashgar, Yarkand and Khotan in the west, Tumsul, Aksu and Kizil in the north, Loulan and Dunhuang in the east and Miran and Cherchen in the south became important centres of Buddhist teachings and art. This prolifration of Buddhism encouraged pilgrimages from the Middle Kingdom to the various Buddhist communities in the above frontier towns of China and also to Buddhist sites in ancient India itself. Although the list of pilgrims must have been very large, the most famous of them were the monks Faxian (Fa Hsien), Dao Zheng, Song Yun, Hui Zheng, Fa Li, Zheng Fouze, Xuanzang and the legend of SunWu Kung, Yi Jing and Hui Chao.[5]

Faxian

A Chinese Buddhist monk named Sehi who adopted the spiritual name Faxian, was born in 337 AD in Wuyang, Shanxi province, when Buddhism in China was enjoying the imperial favour of the Eastern Jin dynasty (217-420 AD). He was pehaps the oldest monk to travel from China to India. Faxian became an exceptionally committed and a deeply devout Buddhist at a very early age. At the age of seven, he fell dangerously ill, and his father took him to a monastery where he was nursed by the monks. Upon his recovery he refused to return home:

> When he was ten years old, his father died; and an uncle, considering the widowed solitariness and helplessness of the mother, urged him to renounce the monastic life, and return to her, but the boy replied, 'I did not quit the family in compliance with my father's wishes, but because I

wished to be far from the dust and vulgar ways of life. This is why I chose monkhood.'

As an ordinaed Buddhist monk at the age of 63, Faxian in 399 AD embarked on an overland trip from the ancient capital Chang'an in the company of several novices as pilgrims to India in search of Buddhist scriptures. They began their journey proceeding west towards Lanzhou and left the Middle Kingdom through the Yumen Gate near the terminal extension of the Great Wall. After a seventeen-day journey from Dunhuang their journey across the Lop Nor desert took them to Loulan in the kingdom of Shanshan where they remained for a month meeting Buddhist resident monks for the first time. Faxian was ultimately separated from his companions and travelling along the Southern branch of the Silk Road he reached Khotan. From Khotan, Faxian continued his journey to Tashkorgan and then crossed the Karakorum Mountains and arrived in Purushapura, a major centre of Buddhist learning until the tenth century. The devout Buddhist Kushan king Kanishka had moved his capital from Pushkalavati (now called Charsadda) to Purushapura in the second century AD. Its current name 'Peshawar' in Pakistan may have been derived from the Sanskrit Purushapura (meaning "city of men"). Faxian described his ordeals in crossing the Pamirs in the following passage:

> The snow rests on them both winter and summer. There are also among them venomous dragons, which, when provoked, spit forth poisonous winds, and cause showers of snow and storms of sand and gravel. Not one in ten thousand of those who encounter these dangers escapes with his life.

From Purushapura, Faxian travelled through Gandhara and eventually reached Taxila and visited Lumbini, the birthplace of the Buddha. On his return journey to China by sea in 409 AD, he first sailed on a mercantile ship to Ceylon where he remained for two years before continuing his jouney home sailing the South and the East China Seas. Faxian was 77 years old when he landed in Shandong province in 414 AD after a fourteen-year absence from China. He spent his last days in Qingzhou, the then capital of Shandong and died in 422 AD.

The opening passages of Faxian's *A Record of the Buddhist Kingdoms* confirm that the purpose of his pilgrimage was to collect Buddhist text regarding monastic rules (*vinaya*) which were badly needed in China for the structural integrity and functioning of the Buddhist communities there. His keen observations detailed in his writings focused on the culture and the practices of the communities in the various multi-ethnic sites he visited. Regarding Khotan, for example, he wrote:

> Throughout the country the houses of the people stand apart like stars...They make rooms for monks from all quarters, the use of which is given to travelling monks who may arrive and are provided with whatever elese they require.

Faxian's accounts included descriptions of Buddhist monks, their teachings and ritual practices which ultimately became the protocols by which many of the early Chinese monasteries operated. Collectively, the narratives of the writings of Faxian revealed many historically relevant facts about the world he lived in.[6] Faxian's narratives have made evident that maritime commercial trading links were in existence in South-East Asia as early as the fourth century AD although it must be emphasized they were infrequent and considered dangerous. His writings were eyewitness accounts of everything relevant to Buddhism from its ritualistic practices to the pilgrims who travelled to holy sites and of their habits, their food, manner of clothing, language and their extreme reverance to Buddhist traditions. Dao Zheng, one of the Chinese monks who accompanied Faxian, was so enthralled and affected by the Buddhist sites and monastic traditions he witnessed on his own travels that he had decided not to return to China. Thus, it is said Dao Zheng had remarked: 'From now until I attain Buddhahood, I wish that I not be reborn in the borderland.'[7]

Song Yun

Chronologically in the order of their travels to India, Song Yun was the next Buddhist monk who in the early decades of the sixth century embarked on a journey to north-western India in search of Buddhist texts. His patron was the devout Buddhist Empress Dowager Hu of the Northern Wei dynasty whose origins were in the Xianbei tribe. Song Yun's journey was of short duration. He left the Wei dynasty's capital Luoyang in 518 AD accompanied by the monks Hui Zheng, Fa Li and Zheng Fouze and returned to Luoyang in the winter of 522 with a large selection of Mahayana Buddhist texts. Song Yun was originally from

Dunhuang and was aware of the existance of the road through Qinghai province that led to the Western Regions. He thus first travelled from Luoyang to Dunhuang and then having chosen to follow the Qinghai route reached Miran in the kingdom of Shanshan. Their journey along the Southern branch of the Silk Road eventually led them to Gandhara. Song Yun's surviving writings are replete with details about dates and names. The following is an example:

> Hui Zheng and the others were sent in the eleventh day of the second month of the second Zhengui year; he and his companions arrived in Karghalik on the twenty ninth day of the seventh month of the second Zhengui year; in the second ten days of the ninth month, they met the king of the Hephthalites; at the beginning of the eleventh, they arrived in Boji; in the second ten days of this month; they entered Chitral and at the beginning of the twelfth month they entered Udyana. Then, during the second ten days of the fourth month of the first Chengkuang year, they arrived in Gandhara. They stayed two years in Udyana and Gandhara until returning at the biginning of the third Chengkuang year.'

Xuanzang

Xuanzang, an early seventh century Buddhist monk, reportedly had had a dream that convinced him of the importance of his mission to India. He was to become a major contributor to the development of correct Buddhist practices in his native Middle Kingdom where the populace was instinctively imbued with Confucianism. He became a proponent of precise translations of the original Butddhist texts as he was dissatisfied and frustrated with the inadequacy of the translations available in his youth. Xuanzang was born in the vicinity of Luoyang in Henan province in 602 AD and was given the name Chen Yi by his parents. He was the yougest of four children in a family whose older members held official state positions in public service and education. In keeping with the Confucian traditions of Louyang, his family life had exposed Xuanzang at an early age to the Confucian teachings of governance and filial piety. After his father's death in 611 AD, Xuanzang lived for a number of years with his elder brother Chen Su who had become a Buddist monk and a member of Jing Tu Monastery in Luoyang which had been founded by the Parthian monk An Shih-Kao. An Shih-Kao had come to China in 148 AD to assist in the translation of the scant Buddhist texts into Chinese and was permitted by the Eastern Han dynasty to found a Buddhist community and a monastery. He was of noble birth and had become a Buddhist monks during the formative years of Buddhism's expansion from India.[8] The monastery he had founded in Louyang became a great beneficiary of endowments from the Sui dynasty but when the Sui dynasty collapsed in 618 AD, the two brothers who were sustained at the Jing Tu monastery through the endowments could no longer remain there and thus were forced to leave the capital and seek residence at Kong Hui Monastery in the ancient city of Chengdu. There Xuanzang immersed himself for several years in the study of Sanskrit and Mahayana Buddhism in preparation of his desire to travel to the very heart of Buddhism in India. At the age of twenty in 622 AD he was ordained a Buddhist monk in Chengdu at a time when Taizong, the reigning Tang emperor, was conducting large scale military campaigns against the Göktürk in the Western Regions. During this time Xuanzang had travelled to the Tang capital Chang'an and it was from there that in 626 AD he made his final preparations for his journey to India. From Chang'an he travelled to the Maijishan Buddhist monastic community near Tianshui on the river Wei in Gansu province.[9] Buddhist monasticism in southern Gansu was well established through the royal supports and benefactions it had received since the time of the Northern Liang dynasty (397-439 AD) and Maijishan was a product of such support. The community was founded in the early decades of the fifth century AD by a monk named Tanhung who was soon joined by another monk named Xuangao and together they expanded Maijishan. At the height of its growth Maijishan housed well over three hundred Buddhist monks.

After Maijishan, Xuanzang passed through Lanzhou and headed for Yumen Gate at the terminus of the Hexi corridor. Permission to travel through the Western Regions would have been refused to Xuanzang due to his emperor's military campaigns in the region. Xuanzang however was able to persuade the Buddhist soldiers guarding the gate of the holiness of his mission to India and that their cooperation would earn them the spiritual merits of a good deed.. They allowed him to pass and thus in 628 AD he was able to leave his native Middle Kingdom via Liangzhou in Gansu and never to see it again for the next seventeen years. Hami (Kumul) and Turfan along the Northern branch of the Silk Road were his immediate destinations. In Turfan he spent a good deal of time studying and teaching at the temples of Bezeklik Thousand Buddha Caves and at the nearby Tuyu valley's Buddhist grottoes. After this short stint in Bezeklik, Xuanzang continued his journey westward and passing through the Iron Gate his next immediate destination was the kingdom of Kuqa. He spent seven months studying and teaching at Kuqa's Subashi Buddhist community before leaving for Aksu where he arrived in 629 AD. In his chronicles Aksu is referred to as Baluka where he spent his time entirely observing the Buddhist community. He remarked on the presence of a large community of resident Buddhist monks whom he described as being extremely well versed in the teachings of the Buddha and studied from texts written in Buddha's native Indian language.

Leaving Aksu in 630 AD Xuanzang's travels westward took him to Tashkent, Samarkand and Balkh and then turning south he crossed the Pamir Mountains and arrived at the Gandharan Buddhist centres in Bamiyan and Hadda. Then turning east Xuanzang crossed the Ganges River and in 637 AD arrived at his ultimate destination, Lumbini, birthplace of the Buddha.[10,11] He spent several years touring the various Buddhist monasteries in India which he described them as in René Grousset's translation: 'whrere an azure pool winds around the monasteries, adorned with the full-blown cups of the blue lotus; the dazzling red flowers of the lovely kanaka hang here and there, and outside groves of mango trees offer the inhabitants their dense and protective shade.' He met Buddhist masters, monks and members of many noble families in their kingly capitals and focused his attention to the further study of Sanskirt grammar and Buddhist logic. He became a leading Indiophile; more of a politician and a good-will emissary of China's emperor than a monk in search of spiritual truth. His writings are abound with descriptions of Indian landscape, its climate, cultural traditions, culinary, economic and legal practices, weights and measures, manner of urban life, architecture and in some detail descriptions of the Indian Brahmins in the context of the Indian caste system. There are also detailed accounts of the kingdoms and towns he visited and especially of an occasion when he was challenged by a host who had questioned Xuanzang as follows: 'Why do you wish to leave after having come here? China is a borderland where the common people are slighted and the Dharma despised: the Buddhas are never born in that country. As the people are narrow-minded, with deep moral impurity, saints and sages do not go there. The climate is cold and the land is full of dangerous mountains. What is there for you to be nostalgic about?' Xuanzang's reply was: 'The King of the Dharma has founded his teachings and it is proper for us to propagate them. How can we forget about those who are not yet enlightened while we have gained the benefit in our own minds?'

On his return journey, Xuanzang crossed the Pamir Mountains and following the old Karakorum trail he reached Kasghar.[12] He had taken this route because his next visit was to be the oasis town of Khotan which in the seventh century had become a major centre for the study of Mahayana Buddhism. There he spent several weeks at Melik Awat monastery where he noted all of the 'sangharamas' studied the doctrine of the Great Vehicle. Leaving Melik Awat, Xuanzang followed the Southern branch of the Silk Road that led him to the great Dunhuang Buddhist community. He ultimately returned to his native home in 645 AD and was honoured with many accolades in the court of Emperor Taizong. This honoured monk, teacher and traveller spent the rest of his life at the Big Goose Temple built specially for him in Chang'an where he studied and translated the mass of Buddhist texts (estimated at 657 Sanskrit texts) that he had brought back with him from India. His frustrations with the paucity of Buddhist texts in China that had motivated him to make his journey to India were succinctly expressed in his memoirs written as a true believer and a scholar. He wrote: 'Though the Buddha was born in the West, his Dharma has spread to the East. In the course of translations, mistakes may have crept into the texts, and idioms may have been misapplied. When words are wrong, the meaning is lost, and when a phrase is mistaken, the doctrine becomes distorted.' He died in 664 AD. His translation of the *Heart Sutra* remains the standard in all East Asian Buddhist sects and his book *The Great Tang Dynasty Record of the Western Regions* has become one of the most thoroughly studies primary sources for the study of medieval Indian and Central Asian history.[13] Before his death, Xuanzang founded the Faxian School of Buddhism to honour the memory of Faxian. Although the school was short lived, its teachings on the meaning of consciousness, perception, death and rebirth were promulgated by Xuanzang's closest student Kuiji.

Disciples for Xuanzang

The journey to India undertaken by Xuanzang had fired the imagination of his people for generations. His legacy clearly was not confined to the pomotion of Buddhism and diplomacy. Although his work is significant both as an account of religious pilgrimage and a historical record of lands and societies neighbouring China, it became the impetus for the creation of many tales as well as of a single classical

Chinese epic novel, all expounding the meaning of Xuanzang's epic accomplishments. Sun Wu Kung, also known as the Monkey King, is a main character in the classical Chinese epic novel *Journey to the West*. In this novel, Sun Wu Kung is depicted as a monkey born from a stone who acquires supernatural powers through Taoist practices. After rebelling against heaven and his subsequent psychological confinement, he proposes to the heavenly powers his offer to serve Master Xuanzang in exchange for his freedom. The epic relates the Bodhisattva Guanyin had searched for disciples who could serve and protect the 'pilgrim from the East' during his journey to India for retrieving Buddhist sutras. Thus Guanyin being made aware of Sun Wu Kung's offer agrees to appoint the monkey as the pilgrim's disciple. But the Bodhisattva having acknowledged the difficulty in securing and maintaining a disciplined service from the monkey had given the pilgrim Xuanzang a gift from the Buddha, a special chant and a magical headband to be tied around the monkey's head. Should it become necessary, Xuanzang would recite the chant that would then tighten the monkey's headband thus constrain his behaviour. In this classical epic Xuanzang and the monkey were ultimately joined by two other characters, Sha Wu Jing and Zhu Ba Jie, as servants for the atonement of their sins. Throughout the perilous journey Xuanzang is constantly exposed to testing ordeals from bandits and demons who believe the pilgrim's flesh once eaten would bring them eternal life. Sun Wu Kung faithfully serves Xuanzang along their journey to India and in return he is granted his freedom and is also given special heavenly powers to protect Xuanzang from the series of eighty-one tribulations he would encounters throughout the rest of his life. In essence, at the end of this ecpic story the Monkey King, Sun Wu Kung, is perceived a Bodhisattva to remain forever in service to humanity.

Yi Jing

The journey of the monk Yi Jing to India, on the other hand was rather unusual in that unlike his predecessors who had travelled overland, Yi Jing travelled by sea. After leaving southern China in 671 AD he sailed through the Straits of Malacca in South-East Asia and crossed the Indian Ocean to India. His returned trip to China in 695 AD after nearly two decades of absence followed a similar maritime route. The focus of Yi Jing's attention was not on the collection and translation of Buddhist texts but on identifying the correct application of the original Buddhist principles and their implementation in the Buddhist monasteries in his native land of China. To this end he dedicated his time while in India to recording his observations of Buddhist practices which were later published as a work of great importance entitled: *The Record of Buddhism as Practiced in India Sent Home from the Southern Seas.* The explicit purpose of Yi Jing's voyage was clearly stated in the closing words of his book: 'My real hope and wish is to build a second Rajagrha City in the Divine Land of China.' A second collection of his works included the compilation of biographical information on fifty-six Chinese Buddhist monks who had made their own pilgrimages in the seventh century often travelling overland across the perilous Tibetan plateau to reach India. Many had decided to stay in India and many others had died before returning to China. These biographies were published under the title: *Memoirs of Eminent Monks who Visited India and Neighbouring Regions in Search of the Law during the Great Tang Dynasty.*

Hui Chao

In the context of Chinese Buddhist monks who had travelled to India, Hui Chao, or Hyecho, would not in principle qualify in the category of Chinese monks. He was a Korean monk from the southern Korean kingdom of Silla but had spent a significant amount of time studying Buddhism in Tang dynasty China before setting out for India in 723 AD to acquaint himself with the language and culture of the land of the Buddha. His journey was by sea and, as the other monks had done before him, he kept a detailed account of what he witnessed about local cultures and diets, spoken languages, climate and the dominant political circumstances. His travelogue was lost for many centuries until a fragment of it was discovered in 1908 by the French orientalist Paul Pelliot while exploring the Dunhuang grottoes in Gansu. The fragment was published as Hui Chao's *Memoir of the Pilgrimage to the Five Kingdoms of India.* Before returning to China in 729 AD via the Southern branch of the Silk Road, Hui Chao visited Lumbini and many other Buddhist sites chronicalling all the while the Buddhist communities and traditions along his way. His account included an interesting observation about cattle roaming freely around the cities and villages of India. As a keen observer of peoples and their local customes, he wrote regarding the territories in Gandhara, Bactria and Ferghana as follows:

> ...under the suzeranity of the Tibetans...The country is narrow and small, and the mountains and valleys very rugged. There are monasteries and monks, and the people

faithfully venerate the Three Jewels. As to the kingdom of Tibet to the East, there are no monasteries at all and the Buddha's teaching is unknown; but in these above mentioned countries the population consists of Hu, therefore they are believers.

The Hu, in the above excerpt, is in reference to the northern nomadic peoples who had continued to harass the Middle Kingdom until they were subdued by the Tang dynasty. Additionally, this excerpt presents unequivocal evidence that in the early eighth century the region described by Hui Chao was clearly under Tibetan suzerainty and that its population was non-Tibetan.

From the accounts of the numerous Chinese monks who had made pilgrimages to the Buddhist centres in India, it is apparent that by the seventh century AD Buddhism had laid a solid foundation in the Western Regions all along the kingdoms and the oasis towns serving the Northern and Southern branches of the Silk Road. From Kashgar to Miran and Loulan along the southern rim of the Taklamakan desert, and from Aksu to Dunhuang along the desert's northern rim, major Buddhist monastic communities were actively propagating the new faith. The Hinayana doctrine prevailed along the Northern branch of the road in the lush green foothills of the Tian Shan Mountains whilest the Mahayana doctrine had found more receptive audiences in the remote and desolate sandy environements of the Southern branch. Nonetheless, in these communities, Indian and native Chinese monks side by side made their individual contributions to Buddhism by their translations of Sanskrit texts, by their teachings, paintings and sculpture. Yet this penetration of Buddhism into China had not taken place directly from the Indian sub-continent. King Ashoka's monumental effort in spreading Buddhism extended the faith first into Gandhara, Bactria, Ferghana and Sogdiana. It was through these Central Asian centres that the Buddhist penetration of China began. We may identify a number of geographical features that may explain this path of Buddhism's progress. Foremost must be the phenomenal natural barrier created by the Himalayan mountain ranges in Tibet stretching along its borders with northern India and Napal. The high altitude and the cold climate of the Tibetan plateau would have made crossing it by the early Indian missionaries, accustomed to the tropical climate of India, nearly impossible. Moreover, beyond the Himalayas, the barren lands of the adjacent Qinghai territory and its extension into the Taklamakan Desert were perilous and formidable barriers to cross. In contrast, crossing the

Hindu Kush and the Pamir mountains was relatively safe with their well established guarded passes that had been in use for centuries. These mountains had played a pivotal role in mediating ancient trade between the sub-continent and the inhabitants of Sogdiana, Bactria, Gandhara and Ferghana. For the Buddhist missionaries the approach to China from these latter areas was secure and free from major concerns about geographical unknowns. Thus the movement of the faith eastward in the direction of China was inevitable. As the Silk Road developed so did the dissemination of Buddhism along the road's trail.

References

1. Liu, X., *Ancient India and Ancient China: Trade and Religious Exchanges AD 1- 600*. Oxford University Press, Delhi (1988).
2. Yoshida, Y., Additional Notes on Sims-Williams' Article on the Sogdian Merchants in China and India. In *Cina e Iran da Alessandro Magno alla dinastia Tang*. A. Cadonna and L. Lanciotti (eds.), Orientalia Veneziana, Florence (1996).
3. La Vaissiere, E. D., *Sogdian Traders: A History*. J. Ward (trans.), Brill, Leiden (2005).
4. Chen, K., *Buddhism in China: A Historical Survey*. Princeton University Press, Princeton, New Jersey (1973).
5. Lahiri, L., *Chinese Monks in India: Biography of Eminent Monks Who Went to the Western World in Search of the Law during the Great Tang Dynasty/ by I- ching*. Buddhist Traditions, no. 3, Motilal Banarsidass, Delhi (1986).
6. Legge, J. (trans.), *A Record of Buddhistic Kingdoms: being an account by the Chinese monk Fa-hsien of his travels in India and Ceylon (AD 399-414) in search of the Buddhist Books of Discipline*. Dover Publications, New York (1965).
7. Sen, S., *India Through Chinese Eyes*. Sir William Meyer Endowment Lectures 1952-53, University of Madras, Madras (1956).
8. Ikemoto, J., Amita. In *Encyclopaedia of Buddhism*. G. P. Malasekera (ed.), Ceylon, pp. 443-56 (1961).
9. Sullivan, M., *The Cave-Temples of Maichishan*. Faber and Faber, London (1969).
10. Bernstein, R., *Ultimate Journey: Retracing the Path of an Ancient Buddhis Monk (Xuanzang) who crossed Asia in Search of Enlightenment*. Alfred A. Knopf, NewYork (2001).
11. Wriggins, S. H., The Silk Road Journey with Xuanzang. Westview Press, Boulder, Colorado (2003).
12. Bellew, H. W., *Kashmir and Kashgar*. Sang-e-Meel Publications, London (1999).
13. Xuanzang, *The Great Tang Dynasty Record of the Western Regions*. R. Li (trans.), University of California Press, Berkeley, California (1996).

Chapter Ten

Christianity in China

The Christian faith with its origins in the lands of the Eastern Mediterranean emerged in Asia Minor, what is today Turkey, through the dedicated personal efforts of Paul of Tarsus. Paul even as a Roman citizen was eventually tried for treason and executed in Rome. He alone was the principal vehicle through which Christianity was brought to Rome. But during the early centuries of the Christian era the new Church was beset with huge doctrinal issues (interpretational) concerning the dogmas (belief system) that it wanted to institutionalize. First the Church struggled with the creation of a unified historical record of its new faith for which a considerable amount of vulgate material was available mostly authored by the disciples of Jesus presumably collated by Saint Jerome (383-405 AD). However apocryphal writings (non-canocical) many of which contradicted the fundamental theses of the new faith created difficulties in how Christianity was to be projected as the true religion of eternal salvation.

Early Church Dogmas

The early Christian Church was administered throughout Christendom from the Sees of Rome, Alexandria and Antioch, and for the most part these were united doctrinally with the common unifying dogmas formulated by the Ecumenical Councils of Nicaea in 325 AD and of Constantinople in 381 AD. But the newly established See of Constantinople, which was the New Rome of the Byzantine (Greek) Empire, was vested with sufficient ecclesiastical powers to make it potentially the dominant See outside of Rome. Although it was apparent to the Byzantines that the historical significance and the legitimacy of their capital, Constantinople, were intimately dependent on the Roman secular heritage, their focus on the use of the Greek language rather than Latin, especially in matters of Christian doctrines, was a significant element in the disharmony that existed between the Latin West and the Greek East. This disparity in the use of a common ecclesiastical language led to divergences in doctrinal understandings and interpretations. As a natural consequence of this, the conceptual development of Christian theology as a discipline diverged badly between the theologians of the East and their counterparts in the West.[1]

The Christology of the Church during the latter part of the fourth century AD had been shaped by influences from two polemical centres each attempting to offer a universally acceptable dogma concerning the human and divine components of Jesus the Man and Christ the Redeemer. The first of the two, known as the Antiochene School, had consistently made a clear distinction between the human and the divine natures in Jesus the Man. Its leading proponents were the theologians Diodorus of Tarsus and his disciple Theodore of Mopsuestia. Their so-called 'Dyophsite' (Diophysite) principle concerning the two natures was carried forward by Nestorius, Patriarch of Conspantinople, who appended to the principle the formula that the two natures of Jesus in his physical manifestation as the Son of God remained also clearly distinct and separate in the divinity of Christ the Redeemer; that is, the Son of God was born human. As an extension of this dogma, Nestorius also rejected the notion of virgin birth. He took special exception to Mary being the 'Mother of God' which he believed was the old pagan expression *Neter Mut* used in the ancient Egyptian pantheon in reference to the goddess Isis. This position taken by Nestorius was reinforced by Priest Anastasius of Antioch, Nestorius's closest supporter, who had declared in one of his many sermons: 'Call ye not Mary, mother of God, for she was but human and God cannot be born of a human being.' This polemical position unequivocally separated the personality of Christ into two separate beings, Christ born of God in eternity, and the human Jesus born as the son of Mary.

Nestorius was adamant in the correctness of his interpretation of the duality in the nature of Christ and never considered his position as heretical. In his installation sermon as Patriarch of Constantinople in the presence of Emperor Theodosius II (408-450 AD), Nestorius had said: 'Give me the earth cleansed of heretics, and I will give you the kingdom of heaven in exchange; aid me in subduing the heretics, and I will aid you in vanquishing the Persians.' But at the Council of Ephesus in 431 AD Nestorius himself was declared a heritic for his dyophysite principles.

In this early Christian polemical warfare, the Alexandrian School which opposed the Nestorian dyophsitism insisted on the intimate inseparable union – fusion - of the two natures in the divinity of Christ the Redeemer (no separate human component) and spoke of one nature in the Word Incarnate.[2] The chief proponent of this 'Monophysite' principle was Cyril of Alexandria who insisted on the 'unutterable union of the Godhead and the manhood of Christ the natural Son of God.' His words in essence meant that the duality in the nature of Christ (Word Incarnate) cannot be verbalized or described in words and that it is the fundamental basis of the Christian faith. During these doctrinal conflicts between the two opposing schools, Cyril's Christology (the study of the nature and the person of Jesus) triumphed at the Council of Ephesus in 431 AD and Nestorius was condemned as a heretic and exiled.[3] His followers were persecuted and, ironically, the Persians whom he had described as the enemy of the Byzantines ultimately became the saviour of Nestorianism and allowed the faith to grow under their protection. We may note here that at the Council of Chalcedon held in 451 AD, the Roman and the Byzantine Churches subscribed to the tenets of the council and thus acquired the term '*Chalcedonian*.' The Churches that disagreed with the Chalcedon tenets remained Monophysites and became known as '*non-Chalcedonian*.' The latter were the Syrian, Armenian, Indian, Coptic and the Ethiopian Churches collectively called the 'Eastern Churches.' But how do these two Churches truly differ in dogmas?

The Church Fathers from both Schools at the Council of Chalcedon, avoiding the extremes of the opposing definitions, compromised their positions and produced the final form of what is now called the Tenets of Chalcedon:

> Following, then, the holy Fathers, we all with one voice teach that it should be confessed that our Lord Jesus Christ is one and the same Son, the Same perfect in Godhead, the Same perfect in manhood, truly God and truly man, the Same of a rational soul and a body; *homoousios* with the Father as to His Godhead, and the Same *homoousios* with us as to His manhood; in all things like unto us, sin only excepted; begotten of the Father before ages as to His Godhead, and in the last days, the Same, for us and for our salvation, of Mary the Virgin Theotokos as to His manhood.
>
> One and the same Christ, Son, Lord, Only-begotten, made known in two natures without confusion, without change,

> without division, without separation; the difference of the natures having been in no wise taken away by reason of the union, but rather the properties of each being preserved, and concurring into one *prosopon* and one *hypostasis*— not parted or divided into two *prosopa*, but one and the Same Son and Only-begotten, the divine Logos, the Lord Jesus Christ; even as the prophets from of old concerning Him, and as the Lord Jesus Christ Himself has taught us, and as the Symbol of the Fathers has delivered to us. (*cf.* Grillmeier, A., *Christ in Christian Tradition,* vol. I, 1988)

The initial draft of the tenets had preserved the principles of St. Cyril of Alexandria, but in order to secure the compromise, the words 'one nature in the Word Incarnate,' (the incarnation of the eternal Son – the Word of God) were removed from the draft. The groups, who opposed this removal and insisted on retaining the wording of St. Cyril, are known as the non-Chalcedonian Monophysites. It appears appropriate, therefore, to say that the difference between the Chalcedonian and the non-Chalcedonian monophysites is only a matter of language.

The Nestorian Church in Mesopotamia

Nestorius died in 451 AD while exiled in the Egytian deserts. But as the persecution of his followers had continued in Byzantium, they had turned their attention to the East. It should be noted here that the term Nestorian(s) is a misnomer. The adherents of Nestorian dualistic dyophysite principle were primarily Syrians and Assyrians. The spiritual and religious centre of the Syrians was in Edessa in Mesopotamia under the sovereignty of the Byzantine Empire. However, early in the fourth century AD small centres of Syrian Christianty existed also in Nisibis in the regions of the Upper Euprates River in Persian-controlled Mesopotamia. Soon after his return from the Council of Nicaea, held in 325 AD, James of Nisibis had established the first theological school in Nisibis followed in 330 AD by the founding of the first Syrian monastery there by Mar (Saint) Augin. Thus Persian Mesopotamia had been a home to the Syrian Christians who were faithful to the Western Church and were identified as Syrian Chalcedonians. They coexisted with the Monophysite (non-Chalcedonian) Orthodox Syrian Church in Persia and together they were called the 'Persian Church.' However, both of these Syrian communities were persecuted by the Zoroastrian majority in Persia which suspected the Syrians of harbouring allegiances to the Persian's primary enemy, the Byzantine Greeks. In an effort to ward off such allegations against the Persian Church, many Syrian communities in Persia increasingly aligned themselves with Nestorian beliefs as their expression of anti-Byzantium sentiments. And, in 424 AD, at the Third General Synod of Mar Dadiso* the Persian Church amidst much disharmony and disagreements, created the office of 'Patriarchate of the East' with its Seat in Seleucia and, in defiance to Byzantium, declared it equal in authority to the Patriarchates of Rome, Alexandria, Antioch and Constantinople. Moreover, in 486 AD, the Bishop of Nisibis, Bar Sauma, publicly declared Nestorius's mentor, Theodore of Mopsuestia, as the spiritual authority of his Church thus creating the Nestorian-dyophysite Syrian Church in Nisibis that made them the third denomination of the Syrian Church in Persia. In retaliation to these developments, the Byzantine emperor Zeno in 489 AD ordered the closure of the Syrian schools in Edessa that taught the Nestorian tenets. The emperor's decision almost immediately precipitated a wave of Nestorian Syrian immigrations east into Persia.

The Assyrians in Persian Mesopotamia, on the other hand, had their roots in ancient Babylonia and were the indeginous Christians in northern Mesopotamia (Mosul in present-day northern Iraq). Their native Church followed Nestorian-dyophysite principles but remained a distinctly separate sect from its Syrian counterparts in Persia. Their second denomination known as the Assyrian Chaldean Roman Church was only created in 1681 AD when the patriarch of Amida (Diyarbakir in present-day Turkey) submitted to the authority of the Roman papacy and was consecrated Patriarch of the Chalcedonian Chaldean Assyrian Church. These denominational divisions in the early Christian Church in Mesopotamia are summarized in Figure 3. It should be noted that the Chalcedonian Catholic Church as indicated in the figure is doctrinally dyophysite and subject to the authority of the Roman papacy. However, the fundamental difference between this Church and the Nestorians is in the latter's insistence that Christ was born human and in their rejection of Mary as the Mother of God.

---

* The Third General Synod of AD 424 was held at the behest of the fourteenth Sasanian King Bahram V. The synod was chaired by Mar Dadiso and decided that the authority of a patriarch cannot be challenged and that he was answerable to God alone.

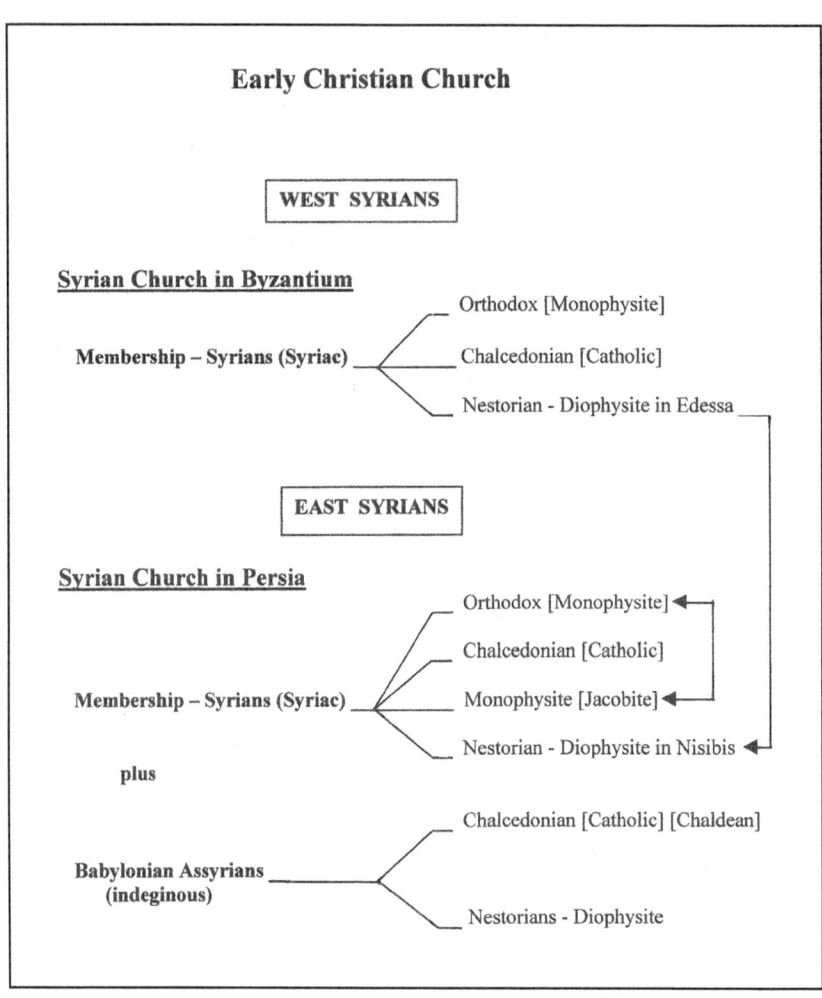

Figure 3. The early Christian Church in Mesopotamia

At this point we may also note the existence of the Jacobites in the Persian Churuch. The Orthodox Syrian Church in Byzantine Mesopotamia was Monophysite. It was persecuted by Byzantium during the reign of Emperor Justinian I (527-565) for being anon-Chalcedonian Church. In response, the bishop of Edessa, Jacob al-Baradi (Baradaeus) challenged the persecutions and actively defended Monophysitism by his vigorous campaigns both in Edessa and in Persia. His efforts became instrumental in revitalizing the Monophysite communities and his Monophysite supporters came to be known by their alternate designation, the Jacobites.

The persecution of the Syrians forced them to abandon Edessa and settled in Persian Mesopotamia as carpenters, smiths, weavers and as the best of the artisan classes. They established industries and laid the foundations of prosperity in the land they had adopted. Here, the zeal and the devotion of the peoples who were exiles for their faith enriched the churches they founded. In their former homes in Byzantine Mesopotamia they had been denounced as heretics; but in their new homes in Persia they emerged possessed with the spirit of enthusiastic evangelism for the spread of the gospel of Christ. They became very successful, winning converts in one district after another as they penetrated further and further into the unknown lands of Asia.[4]

The Nestorian Church in Persia became a widely active evangelistic church more so than her sister Chalcedonian and Monophysites Syrian Churches and quickly expanded with major centres in Nisibis, Ctesiphon and Gundeshapur. It grew beyond the Persian Sasanid Empire and reached Armenia, Azerbaijan, India, Tibet and China. To illustrate the extent of this Church's growth and the level of its evangelical zeal, it is only necessary to list a number of the locations where the Nestorians founded churches away from their homes in Persia as shown in Table 4.

The most interesting aspect of the Nestorian expansion becomes apparent when the distribution of the widely founded churches is examined. This will instantly reveal that almost all of the sites where the churches were founded in Central Asia and China coincided with the major destinations of the Silk Road in these lands.

Table 4. Distribution of the early Nestorian churches

Mesopotamia	Persia	India	Central Asia	China	South-East Asia
Arbil	Hamadan	Ceylon	Balkh	Aksu	Ayuthya
Antioch	Hormuz	Gaya	Bukhara	Beijing	Java
Baghdad	Isphahan	Ladak	Ghazni	Chengdu	Pegu
Ctesiphon	Shiraz	Madras	Herat	Cherchen	
Damascus	Tabriz	Malabar	Issy-Kul	Dunhuang	
Jerusalem		Patna	Kabul	Fuzhou	
Mosul			Merv*	Guangzhou	
Nisibis			Samarkand	Hami*	
Seleucia			Tashkent	Hangzhou	
Tripoli				Kashgar*	
				Khotan	
				Lanzhou	
				Shanghai	
				Yangzhou	
				Yengishahir	
				Yumen	
				Xi'an*	
				Zaytun	
				Zangye	

* Bishoprics in the context of this book.

But despite these heroic acts of faith demonstrated by the Nestorians from the time of their exile in the fifth century AD, their Christian legacy, with the exception of the tiny communities that still survive in present-day northern Iraq, has all but disappeared from the lands of their worlwide evangelism. Their successes in China were mostly restricted from the time of their arrival in Chang'an in the mid seventh century until they were expelled along with the Manichaeans and the Zoroastrians in the mid ninth century. Although for the next four centuries the Nestorians were active in Central Asia and Mongolia their religion for the most part remained dormant in China until it was resurrected in 1279 AD during the reign of Emperor Kublai Khan of the Mongol Yuan dynasty. The period of the Yuan dynasty saw a significant revival of Nestorian evangelism in China but after the Ming dynasty's total expulsion of the Mongols from China in 1376, Nestorian Christianity was forced to make a permanent and a decisive exit from China. Thereupon, the adherents of the Nestorian faith in

Christianity in China

Central Asia and China, despite of their accomplishments, seemed to have lost their significant presence. The adherents of this Christian sect in China and Central Asia being mostly of Mongolic stock, it is presumed that over many centuries they gradually slipped back to their native and traditional Shamanic or Buddhistic practices, or were simply overpowered by the invasive Islam. But, what is relevant in the context of our present subject is the nature of the Nestorian contribution to China's Christian history.

Nestorians in Central Asia

The records in connection with the Council of Mar Dadiso mention that ancient Merv (Mary or Mari in present-day Turkmenistan) was the seat of a Nestorian bishopric and that a bishop named Bar Shabba presided over Nestorian evangelical affairs in Merv and in its adjacent territories. Merv was an Iranian, originally Parthian, city and the gateway to Central Asia. The local religion was Zoroastrianism but there was also a Buddhist presence from the second century AD. In addition to the records of the council, the official acts of the East Syrian Church (Persian Church) include matters related to the bishopric of the city of Merv and a number of other Christian centres west of the Oxus River (Amu Darya). Mingana, who has compiled similar information, mentions over twenty such centres.[5] For each of the centres, the number of the bishops and of the archbishops are listed by name. We might assume therefore, that Merv was the point from which missionary activity was carried further east and eventually beyond the Oxus. What better confirmation of this assumption of the progression of the faith than the request by the Hephthalites (White Huns) inhabiting the region of Bactria for the installation of a bishop in their homeland. Indeed, their request was granted in 549 AD when the Nestorian Patriarch Mar Aba I sent them a bishop.

As discussed in Chapter 3, the eastern Iranian people known as Sogdians had taken advantage of the strategic location of their homeland in Sogdiana north of Iran and had been involved in wide-reaching trading activities. From their cities like Samarkand and Bukhara (in present-day Uzbekistan) their trading activities with neighboring cities to their west or to their east were facilitated by a string of settlements the Sogdians constantly maintained on the Central Asian routes leading east to Mongolia and China, or south to Iran and India. They were originally Zoroastrian but their trading activity had exposed them to many foreign religions especially to Nestorian evangelism. Thus many were converted to Nestorianism, Manichaeism and Buddhism. In turning to Nestorian Christianity in the sixth century, they spread Syriac literature to their east, often translating many texts into their own language and into Chinese. They became the vehicle with which Nestorianism was transmitted from Merv along the Silk Road to Mongolia and China. Through them we witness the penetration of Nestorian Christianity amongst the nomadic Turkic and Mongolic peoples. In 781 AD, the Nestorian Patriarch Timothy I in his letter to the monks of the monastery of Mar Maron affirms the conversion of certain Turks to the Christian faith:

> The king of the Turks, with nearly all his country, has left his ancient idolatry, and has become Christian, and he has requested us in his letters to creat a Metropolitan for his country; and this we have done.[6]

There is good reason to suggest (*cf.* Chapter 11), the Turks in Timothy's letter may be inferred to be the Mongolic Tiele Turks whose homelands were in the southern regions of Lake Baikal in north-central Mongolia. They were the Uyghurs, who at that time were subjugated and held in servitude by the Göktürks and would have been very receptive to foreign religious influences which may have been seen as emancipatory. In 840 AD they were displaced by the Yenisei Kyrgyz and, as was discussed earlier, were forced to migrate south and west and settle at the fringes of the Tarim basin and the Tian Shan Mountains in the north-western parts of China. The successes of Nestorian and Manichaean Christianity amongst the various Mongolic peoples and of their impact on the Christian history of China will be discussed in Chapter 12. But presently we will continue with the Nestorians in China.

Nestorians in China

In their progress eastward, Nestorian missionaries had finally succeeded in reaching Chang'an (Xi'an). It was the *Pax Sinica* of the Tang Period (618-907 AD) that allowed access to China by trade and travels through Central Asia. Hence it is not surprising that in the early decades of the seventh century a Nestorian missionary, named Olopun (or A-lopân) had actually arrived in the court of the Tang emperor. His presence in China is confirmed by the much celebrated stone monument (stelae/stele)) discovered in Xi'an in 1625. This engraved stelae which stands 279 cm high, 99 cm wide and 28 cm thick is a slab of hard black limestone that stands upright on the back of a tortoise, symbolic of longevity and stability; and is known as the Nestorian Monument (*Jingjiaobei*).[7,8] It contains at the very top of its front side a 'Maltese cross resting on a Taoist cloud with a Buddhist lotus flower beneath it.' The inscriptions contain more than 1,756 Chinese ideographs and some 70 odd Syriac names written along the sides with additional Syriac inscriptions appended at the foot of the stone. The tone of the inscriptions is syncretic - an attempt to reconcile contrary beliefs by combining their practices and in this case of Christianity, Buddhism and Taoism of which the latter two were flourishing in China. This was a synthesis to facilitate communication amongst the various communities. It states the text was composed by a Syrian priest named Ching-ching (*Jingjing*, or Adam in the native Syriac) and the engraver was Lu Xiuyan.

The ancient stone monument had remained buried as a protection from Emperor Wuzong's (840-846 AD) Imperial Edict of 845 AD which had barred the practice of Buddhism and all foreign religions in China. But before its discovery in 1625 the Nestorian stelae had stood erect for several centuries in the open near the wetsern gate of Chang'an (Xi'an). Presently housed in Bailin Museum in Xi'an, the Nestorian stelae is arguably one of the most important historical relics of Christianity's commune with the Far East. It was erected during the reign of Emperor Dezong (779-805 AD) but alludes to the arrival of Nestorians in China in the year 635 AD well within the period of the reign of Emperor Taizong (626-649 AD) of the Tang dynasty. Immediately after its excavation, the stelae was housed in Jin Sheng Temple in western Xi'an but was moved to its present location in 1907 during the Qing dynasty. The monument was inscribed both in Chinese and Syriac and was originally commissioned by Lord Yazedbouzid (also know as Issu), the son of Priest Milis and a military general during the reign of three emperors – Suzong (756-762 AD), Daizong (762-779 AD), and Dezong (779-805 AD). His father Milis was the Nestorian missionary from Balkh, as mentioned in the Syriac part of the inscriptions which states:

> My lord Yazedbouzid, the Presbyter and Chorepiscopus of Khumdan, city of the King, who is the son of the late Presbyter Milis from Balkh, city of Tahounstan, erected this stone monument in which the Law of our Saviour was

written and that our forefathers preached to the Rulers of China.⁹

The composition of the text is mostly self-explanatory, well-versed and is presented in three parts. The first briefly relates the Biblical creation, the Christian (*Jingjiao*) doctrine of the trinity and the coming of the Missiah. The second describes various historical anecdotes regarding the entry of the Christian faith into China and the patronage it received from the emperors. It describes the arrival of a priest named Olopun [A-lopân], from Syria in 635 AD who had brought with him the True Scriptures. He had been favourably received by Emperor Taizong who then sanctioned the translation of a portion of the scriptures and proclaimed it in his Imperial Edict of 638 AD to be available freely throughout the empire. The third and final part is an ode in praise of the liturgical and the secular practices of the Nestorian Illustrious Religion.

Perhaps the one singular significance of the Nestorian stelae lies in the revelation that many centuries before the arrival of Roman Catholic Franciscan and Jesuit missionaries in China there indeed was a vibrant and a zealous Christian evangelism brought to China by the Nestorians.¹⁰ Although the Chinese socio-cultural characteristics drew their essence from the native Chinese Confucian, Menciusian and Laozian philosophies, as described in the earlier chapters of this book, the Nestorian legacy in China still was able to inculcate in the Chinese psychy the Christain concretized concept of the personal deity. Below is given the complete translation of the Nestorian stelae inscriptions as produced in 1855 by A. Wylie of the London Mission at Shanghai.¹¹ The two reasons for this inclusion are, first, to acquaint the reader with the actual contents of the stelae despite any previous descriptions or analyses of its attributes in order that its message and appeal are read and experienced at a personal level, and second, given the historical age of the subject matter, it is uncommon to find the translation made available in readily accessible publications. Hence, the translation of the text of the Nestorian stelae is given below.

Nestorian Monument of Xi'an

> Tablet Eulogising the Propagation of the Illustrious Religion in the Middle Kingdom [China], Composed by King-Tsing [Ching-ching] or Adam in Syriac, a priest of the Syrian Ta-ch'in [Da Qin] monastery.

Christianity in China

BEHOLD the unchangeably true and invisible, who existed through all eternity without origin; the far-seeing perfect intelligence, whose mysterious existence is everlasting; operating on primordial substance he created the universe, being more excellent than all holy intelligences, inasmuch as he is the source of all that is honourable. This is our eternal true lord God, triune and mysterious in substance. He appointed the cross as the means of determining the four cardinal points, he moved the original spirit, and produced the two principles of nature; the sombre void was changed, and heaven and earth were opened out; the sun and moon revolved, and day and night commenced; having perfected all inferior objects, he then made the first man; upon him he bestowed an excellent disposition, giving him in charge the government of all created beings; man, acting out the original principles of his nature, was pure and unostentatious; his unsullied and expansive mind was free from the least inordinate desire; until Satan introduced the seeds of falsehood, to deteriorate his purity of principle; the opening thus commenced in his virtue gradually enlarged, and by this crevice in his nature was obscured and rendered vicious; hence three hundred and sixty-five sects followed each other in continuous track, inventing every species of doctrinal complexity; while some pointed to material objects as the source of their faith, others reduced all to vacancy, even to the annihilation of the two primeval principles; some sought to call down blessings by prayers and supplications, while others by an assumption of excellence held themselves up as superior to their fellows; their intellects and thoughts continually wavering, their minds and affections incessantly on the move, they never obtained their vast desires, but being exhausted and distressed they revolved in their own heated atmosphere; till by an accumulation of obscurity they lost their path, and after long groping in darkness they were unable to return. Thereupon, our Trinity being divided in nature, the illustrious and honourable Messiah, veiling his true dignity, appeared in the world as a man; angelic powers promulgated the glad tidings, a virgin gave birth to the Holy One in Syria; a bright star announced the felicitous event, and Persians observing the splendour came to present tribute; the ancient dispensation, as declared by the twenty-four holy men, was then fulfilled, and he laid down great principles for the government of families and kingdoms; he established the new religion of the silent operation of the pure spirit of the Triune; he rendered virtue subservient to direct faith; he fixed the extent of the eight boundaries, thus completing the truth and freeing it from dross; he opened the gate of the three constant principles, introducing life and destroying death; he suspended the bright sun to invade the chambers of darkness, and the falsehoods of the devil were thereupon defeated; he set in motion the vessel of mercy by which to ascend to the bright mansions, whereupon rational beings were then released, having thus completed the manifestation of his power, in clear day he ascended to his true station. Twenty-seven sacred books have been left, which disseminate intelligence by unfolding the original transforming principles. By the rule for admission, it is the custom to apply the water of baptism, to wash away all superficial show and to cleanse and purify the neophytes. As a seal, they hold the cross, whose influence is reflected in every direction, uniting all without distinction. As they strike the wood, the fame of their benevolence is diffused abroad; worshiping toward the east, they hasten on the way to life and glory; they preserve the bread to symbolize their outward actions, they shave the crown to indicate the absence of inward affections; they do not keep slaves, but put noble and mean all on an equality; they do not amass wealth, but cast all their property into the common stock; they fast, in order to perfect themselves by self-inspection; they submit to restrains, in order to strengthen themselves by silent watchfulness; seven times a day they have worship and praise for the benefit of the living and the dead; once in seven days they sacrifice, to cleanse the heart and return to purity.

    It is difficult to find a name to express the excellence of the true and unchangeable doctrine; but as its meritorious operations are manifestly displayed, by accommodation it is named the Illustrious Religion. Now without holy men, principles cannot become expanded; without principles, holy men cannot become magnified; but with holy men and right principles, united as the two parts of a signet, the world becomes civilized and enlightened.

In the time of the accomplished Emperor Taitsung, the illustrious and magnificent founder of the dynasty, among the enlightened and holy men who arrived was the Most-virtuous Olopun, from the country of Syria. Observing the azure clouds, he bore the true sacred books; beholding the direction of the winds, he braved difficulties and dangers. In the year A.D. 635 he arrived at Chang'an; the Emperor sent his Prime Minister, Duke Fang Hiuen-ling; who, carrying the official staff to the west border, conducted his guest into the interior; the sacred books were translated in the imperial library, the sovereign investigated the subject in his private apartments; when becoming deeply impressed with the rectitude and truth of the religion, he gave special orders for its dissemination. In the seventh month of the year A.D. 638 the following imperial proclamation was issued:

'Right principles have no invariable name, holy men have no invariable station; instruction is established in accordance with the locality, with the object of benefiting the people at large. The Greatly-virtuous Olopun, of the kingdom of Syria, has brought his sacred books and images from that distant part, and has presented them at our chief capital. Having examined the principles of this religion, we find them to be purely excellent and natural; investigating its originating source, we find it has taken its rise from the establishment of important truths; its ritual is free from perplexing expressions, its principles will survive when the framework is forgot; it is beneficial to all creatures; it is advantageous to mankind. Let it be published throughout the Empire, and let the proper authority build a Syrian church in the capital in the I-ning May, which shall be governed by twenty-one priests. When the virtue of the Chau dynasty declined, the rider on the azure ox ascended to the west; the principles of the great Tang becoming resplendent, the Illustrious breezes have come to fan the East.'

Orders were then issued to the authorities to have a true portrait of the Emperor taken; when it was transferred to the wall of the church, the dazzling splendour of the celestial visage irradiated the Illustrious portals. The sacred traces emitted a felicitous influence, and shed a perpetual splendour over the holy precincts. According to the Illustrated Memoir of the Western regions, and the historical books of the Han and Wei dynasties, the kingdom of Syria reaches south to the Coral Sea; on the north it joins the Gem Mountains; on the west it extends toward the borders of the immortals and the flowery forests; on the east it lies open to violent winds and tideless waters. The country produces fire-proof cloth, life-restoring incense, bright moon-pearls, and night-lustre gems. Brigands and robbers are unknown, but the people enjoy happiness and peace. None but Illustrious laws prevail; none but the virtuous are raised to sovereign power. The land is broad and ample, and its literary productions are perspicuous and clear.

The Emperor Kautsung respectfully succeeded his ancestor, and was still more beneficent toward the institution of truth. In every province he caused Illustrious churches to be erected, and ratified the honour conferred upon Olopun, making him the great conservator of doctrine for the preservation of the State. While this doctrine pervaded every channel, the State became enriched and tranquillity abounded. Every city was full of churches, and the royal family enjoyed lustre and happiness. In the year A.D. 699 the Buddhists, gaining power, raised their voices in the eastern metropolis; in the year A.D. 713, some low fellows excited ridicule and spread slanders in the western capital. At that time there was the chief priest Lohan, the Greatly-virtuous Kie-leith, and others of noble estate from the golden regions, lofty-minded priests, having abandoned all worldly interests; who unitedly maintained the grand principles and preserved them entire to the end.

The high-principled Emperor Hiuentsung caused the Prince of Ning and others, five princes in all, personally to visit the felicitous edifice; he established the place of worship; he restored the consecrated timbers which had been temporarily thrown down; and re-erected the sacred stones which for a time had been desecrated.

In 742 orders were given to the great general Kau Lih-sz', to send the five sacred portraits and have them placed in the church, and a gift of a hundred pieces of silk accompanied these pictures of intelligence. Although the dragon's beard was then remote, their bows and swords were still within reach; while the solar horns sent forth rays, and celestial visages seemed close at hand.

In 744 the priest Kih-ho, in the kingdom of Syria, looking toward the star, was attracted by its transforming influence, and observing the sun, came to pay court to the most honourable. The Emperor commanded the priest Lo-han, the priest Pu-lun, and others, seven in all, together with the Greatly-virtuous Kih-ho, to perform a service of merit in the Hing-king palace. Thereupon the emperor composed mottoes for the sides of the church, and the tables were graced with the royal inscriptions; the accumulated gems emitted their effulgence, while their sparkling brightness vied with the ruby clouds; the transcripts of intelligence suspended in the void shot forth their rays as reflected by the sun; the bountiful gifts exceeded the height of the southern hills; the bedewing favours were deep as the eastern sea. Nothing is beyond the range of the right principle, and what is permissible may be identified; nothing is beyond the power of the holy man, and that which is practicable may be related.

The accomplished and enlightened Emperor Suhtsung rebuilt the Illustrious churches in Ling-wu and four other places; great benefits were conferred, and felicity began to increase; great munificence was displayed, and the imperial State became established.

The accomplished and military Emperor Taitsung magnified the sacred succession, and honoured the latent principle of nature; always, on the incarnation-day, he bestowed celestial incense, and ordered the performance of a service of merit; he distributed of the imperial viands, in order to shed a glory on the Illustrious Congregation. Heaven is munificent in the dissemination of blessings, whereby the benefits of life are extended; the holy man embodies the original principle of virtue, whence he is able to counteract noxious influences.

Our sacred and sage-like, accomplished and military Emperor Kienchung appointed the eight branches of government, according to which he advanced or degraded the intelligent and dull; he opened up the nine categories by means of which he renovated the illustrious decrees; his transforming influence pervaded the most abstruse principles, while openness of heart distinguished his devotions. Thus, by correct and enlarged purity of principle, and undeviating consistency in sympathy with others; by extended commiseration rescuing multitudes from misery, while disseminating blessings on all around, the cultivation of our doctrine gained a grand basis, and by gradual advances its influence was diffused. If the winds and rains are seasonable, the world will be at rest; men be guided by principle, inferior objects will be pure; the living will be at ease, and the dead will rejoice; the thoughts will produce their appropriate response, the affections will be free, and the eyes will be sincere; such is the laudable condition which we of the Illustrious Religion are labouring to attain.

Our great benefactor, the Imperially-conferred-purple-gown priest, I-sz', titular Great Statesman of the Banqueting-house, Associated Secondary Military Commissioner for the Northern region, and Examination-palace Overseer, was naturally mild and graciously disposed; his mind susceptible of sound doctrine, he was diligent in the performance; from the distant city of Râjagriha, he came to visit China; his principles more lofty than those of the three dynasties, his practice was perfect in every department; at first he applied himself to duties pertaining to the palace, eventually his name was inscribed on the military roll. When the Duke Koh Tsz'-I, Secondary Minister of State and Prince of Fân-yang, at first conducted the military in the northern region, the Emperor Suhtsung made him his attendant on his travels; although he was a private chamberlain, he assumed no distinction on the march; he was as claws and teeth to the duke, and in rousing the military he was as ears and eyes; he distributed the wealth conferred upon him, not accumulating treasure for his private use; he made offerings of the jewellery which had been given by imperial favour, he spread out a golden carpet for devotion; now he repaired the old churches, anon he increased the number of religious establishments; he bonoured and decorated the various edifices, till they resembled the plumage of the pheasant in its flight; moreover, practising the discipline of the Illustrious

Religion, he distributed his riches in deeds of benevolence; every year he assembled those in the sacred office from four churches; and respectfully engaged them for fifty days in purification and preparation; the naked came and were clothed; the sick were attended to and restored; the dead were buried in repose; even among the most pure and self-denying of the Buddhists, such excellence was never heard of; the white-clad members of the Illustrious Congregation, now considering these men, have desired to engrave a broad tablet, in order to set forth a eulogy of their magnanimous deeds.

ODE

The true Lord is without origin,
Profound, invisible, and unchangeable;
With power and capacity to perfect and transform,
He raised up the earth and established the heavens.

Divided in nature, he entered the world,
To save and to help without bounds;
The sun arose, and darkness was dispelled,
All bearing witness to his true original.
The glorious and resplendent, accomplished Emperor,
Whose principles embraced those of preceding monarchs;
Taking advantage of the occasion, suppressed turbulence;
Heaven was spread out and the earth was enlarged.

When the pure, bright Illustrious Religion
Was introduced to our Tang dynasty,
The Scriptures were translated, and churches built,
And the vessel set in motion for the living and the dead;
Every kind of blessing was then obtained,
And all the kingdoms enjoyed a state of peace.

When Kautsung succeeded to his ancestral estate,
He built the edifices of purity;
Palaces of concord, large and light,
Covered the length and breath of the land.

The true doctrine was clearly announced,
Overseers of the church were appointed in due form;

Treasures of the Silk Road

The people enjoyed happiness and peace,
While all creatures were exempt from calamity and distress.

When Hiuentsung commenced his sacred career,
He applied himself to the cultivation of truth and rectitude;
His imperial tablets shot forth their effulgence,
And the celestial writings mutually reflected their splendours.

The imperial domain was rich and luxuriant,
While the whole land rendered exalted homage;
Every business was flourishing throughout,
And the people all enjoyed prosperity.

Then came Suhtsung, who commenced anew,
And celestial dignity marked the imperial movements,
Sacred as the moon's unsullied expanse,
While felicity was wafted like nocturnal gales.

Happiness reverted to the imperial household,
The autumnal influences were long removed;
Ebullitions were allayed, and rising suppressed,
And thus our dynasty was firmly built up.

Taitsung the filial and just
Combined in virtue with heaven and earth;
By his liberal bequests the living were satisfied,
And property formed the channel of imparting succour.

By fragrant mementoes he rewarded the meritorious,
With benevolence he dispensed his donations;
The solar concave appeared in dignity,
And the lunar retreat was decorated to extreme.

When Kienchung succeeded to the throne,
He began the cultivation of intelligent virtue;
His military vigilance extended to the four seas,
And his accomplished purity influenced all lands.

His light penetrated the secrecies of men,

And to him the diversities of objects were seen as in a mirror;
He shed a vivifying influence through the whole realm of nature,
And all outer nations took him for example.

>The true doctrine how expansive!
>Its responses are minute;
>How difficult to name it!
>To elucidate the three in one.

>The sovereign has the power to act!
>While the ministers record;
>We raise this noble monument!
>To the praise of great felicity.

This was erected in the 2nd year of Kienchung, of the Tang dynasty (A.D. 781), on the 7th day of the 1st month, being Sunday.

Written by Lu Siu-yen, Secretary of Council, formerly Military Superintendent for Taichau; while the Bishop Ning-shu had the charge of the congregations of the Illustrious in the East.

Translation of the Syriac along the sides:

>Adam, Deacon, Vicar-episcopal and Pope of China.
>In the time of the Father of Fathers, the Lord John Joshua, the Universal Patriarch.

Translation of the Syriac at the foot of the stone:

>In the year of the Greeks one thousand and ninety-two, the Lord Jazedbuzid, Priest and Vicar-episcopal of Cumdan the royal city, son of the enlightened Mailas, Priest of Balach a city of Turkestan, set up this tablet, whereon is inscribed the Dispensation of our Redeemer, and the preaching of the apostolic missionaries to the King of China.

Translation of parts following the end of the Chinese characters;

The Priest Lingpau.
Adam the Deacon, son of Jazedbuzid, Vicar-episcopal.
The Lord Sergius, Priest and Vicar-episcopal.
Sabar Jesus, Priest.
Gabriel, Priest, Archdeacon, and Ecclesiarch of Cumdan and Sarag.
Assistant Examiner: the High Statesman of the Sacred rites, the Imperially-conferred-purple-gown Chief Presbyter
and Priest Yi-li.

On the left-side edge of the stelae are listed the Syriac names of sixty-seven priests of whom sixty-one are also given in Chinese.

The Olopun Documents

The importance of the Nestorian monument's mention of the Syrian priest Olopun lies in the association of this priest with a collection of the seventh century Christian documents discovered by the French archaeologist Paul Pelliot in 1908 in a small cubical side-library (Cave No. 17) within the larger Cave No. 16 in Dunhuang. Four of the collection's documents are called the 'Bishop Olopun Documents' which are a discourse on Monotheism. Drawing from the socio-philosophical imageries of Confucian, Taoist and Buddhist treatises, these documents attempt to define the religious message and teachings of the 'Jade-Faced One', a metaphor for immortality and symbolic of Christ. Thery were written between 635 amd 638 AD and were intended for Emperor Taizong's edification in the very early years of the Nestorian missions arriving in China (*cf.* Moule, A. C., 1977). Each of the four documents dealt with a separate subject; they were 1) The Parable; 2) The Oneness of the Ruler of the Universe; 3) The Lord of the Universe's Discourse on Alms-giving and 4) The Jesus-Messiah Sutras, which contain a complete outline of the fundamental doctrine of Christianity clearly intended for teaching purposes. A discussion of these sutras is beyond the scope of the present work however for the reader who is interested in exploring this aspect of Christian history, there are a number of publications worth exploring.[12,13] Nevertheless, it is to be noted that the Bishop Olopun Documents constitute a substantial testament to their author's, Olopun's, travel itinerary and that his journey to China had indeed been by the Silk Road. We may

Christianity in China

therefore safely conclude that the Silk Road caravans were the main conduit by which many Nestorian evangelists had travelled to China.

The library of Dunhuang's Cave No.17 offers further evidence connected with the movement of Christianity along the ancient Silk Road. A fragment of a painting in colour on silk depicting a blue-eyed Bodhisattva recovered from the library by Aurel Stein in 1908 was noted to show the Bodhisattva bearing two Maltese crosses, one on his headdress and another on his breast. It has been suggested on reasonable grounds that the image may have been originally that of a Christian saint whose features at some point in time were altered by a resident Buddhist monk and was made to resemble a Bodhisattva.[14] There are many other calloborative materials which further confirm the presence of Nestorians in Xi'an. Such materials include, for example, a Buddhist document written in 788 AD which identifies the Syrian Ching-ching (Priest Adam, the composer of stelae's text) as 'Persian priest of the Nestorian Monastery.'

The Nestorian legacy soon after their first missions to the East is quite apparent from many sources and not least from the travel records of Marco Polo who during his travels in Central Asia and China beween 1271 and 1295 AD mentions no less than eight times his encounters of Nestorian churches, Nestorians and Jacobites and of their presences at various places he visited. The first mention appears in Book I, chapter VI while he was passing through Mosul where he also noted that many of the indeginous Kurds were Christians. Also in Book I, Nestorians and Jacobites in Baghdad (Baldach) are mentioned in chapter VIII; in Kashgar in chapter XXX; amongst the race of Prester John, in chapter LIV and in Samarkand in chapter XXXI which also relates the captivating story of the erection of the church of Saint John the Baptist.

Although the Nestorian evalgelical efforts were thrusted into the heart of the Tang dynasty, Mongolia in the seventh century seems to have also attractd a considerable attention from the Nestorians. It was mentioned in an earlier chapter that although Christianity never achieved a prominent position amongst the Mongol as it did in China, many Great Khans and their families were exposed to a great deal of Christian teachings. Genghis Khan's daughter-in-law, the Nestorian Kereit princess, Sokaktani-beki, was a Christian force in the lives of her sons Kublai Khan (Emperor of China), Mongke (the Great Khan) and the Il-khan Hulagu whose wife Tokuz Khatun was proselytized to Nestorian Christianity. We should note however that these leaders of the Mongol Empire ruled in the thirteenth century therefore the greater Nestorian impact on the Mogol is significantly later than its history in pre-Yuan dynasty China. In this context, of some interest are the personal experiences of the Nestorian Mongol monk turned diplomat, Rabban Bar Sauma (1260–1313 AD) (not to be confused with Bar Sauma of Nisibis). He is known for embarking on a pilgrimage from Mongol-controlled China to Jerusalem with one of his students, Rabban Markos. Due to military conflicts along their way, their journey was truncated in Baghdad where they spent many years in the Mongol-controlled Baghdad. Markos was eventually chosen as Nestorian Patriarch of Baghdad who subsequently suggested that his teacher Rabban Bar Sauma be sent as the Mongols' ambassador to Europe. Consequently, the elderly monk met with many of the European monarchs, as well as Pope Clement V (1305-1314 AD) in attempts to arrange a Franco-Mongol alliance against the Turkic Mamluks' power rising in the Near East. The mission bore no fruit, but in his later years in Baghdad, Rabban Bar Sauma documented his lifetime of travels that give an illuminating viewpoint of the Eastern perceptions of the West.

Nestorian presence in China extended east to the port city of Quanzhou as evidenced by tombstones decorated with the typically Nestorian Cross-on-Lotus symbol discovered in Quanzhou in the seventeenth century by Catholic missionaries. The Nestorian legacy in Quanzhou dates only from the period when China was ruled by the Mongols (Yuan dynasty) during which Quanzhou became a sea-port of major international significance. The seventeenth century Catholic missionaries in Quanzhou represented the renewed evangelical spirit of the Catholic Church especially towards the Mongol sector of China's population. The same evangelical spirit continues to occupy the attention of the Vatican heirarchy to the present day. Below is a letter from Pope John Paul II sent on 22 August 2003 to Cardinal Crescenzio Sepe from the papal summer residence in Castel Gandolfo. The contents of this letter give us a rare insight into the Church's internal workings, its hierarchal lexicon and its focused mindset on issues of evangelism and expansion. The letter also reviews briefly the history of Catholic missions to Mongolia:

> To His Eminence Cardinal Crescenzio Sepe:
> Prefect of the Congregation for the Evangelization of Peoples

Christianity in China

With great joy I write to you, Venerable Brother, as you prepare to visit for the second time the young Christian community which dwells in the vast Asian country of Mongolia, rich in history and cultural traditions.

Last July you visited Ulaanbaatar, the capital of the Mongolian nation, in order to celebrate the anniversary of the establishment of diplomatic relations between Mongolia and the Holy See and to highlight the lively presence in the region of a Christian community of relatively recent foundation. Although the first evangelization of Mongolia was due to the arrival of Nestorians from Persia in the seventh century, it was only in the first half of the twentieth century that a mission in that distant region was entrusted to the *Congregatio Immaculati Cordis Mariae* (Congregation of the Immaculate Heart of Mary). The pro-Communist regime of the time at first prevented the missionaries from entering the region. With the end of Communist dictatorship the doors were finally opened to the Gospel, and from 1991 the first evangelizers began to arrive: priests, men and women religious and laypersons, actively engaged in the Lord's vineyard.

To demonstrate the fruitful and positive advances made in this decade, last year witnessed two events fundamental for the life of the Church: the elevation of the Mission *sui iuris of Urga*, Ulanbator, to the rank of Apostolic Prefecture with the new name of Ulaanbaatar, and the subsequent appointment of the first Apostolic Prefect in the person of the Reverend Father Wenceslaw Padilla, CICM, as well as the first ordination of three priests and a deacon who, while not natives of the country, consider Mongolia as their adopted homeland. They represent a promising sign of hope for the future of the local ecclesial community.

Your Eminence's return to that beloved land a little more than a year later is prompted by two other no less important and happy events: the episcopal ordination of the Apostolic Prefect and the blessing of the Cathedral Church dedicated to the Apostles Peter and Paul. These events consolidate the spiritual edifice being built up by the 'little flock' of a young missionary Church which is growing in confidence, sustained by the renewing power of the Holy Spirit.

I would dearly have liked to be present in person for these significant and historic liturgical celebrations. Since this was not part of the Lord's plan, I now entrust you with the responsibility of conveying my paternal and affectionate greetings to the new Bishop in that chosen portion of the People of God, to the other Bishops, and in a special way to Archbishop Giovanni Battista Morandini, Apostolic Nuncio in Mongolia and Apostolic Administrator. My greetings also go to the priests, the women religious, the other pastoral agents and those engaged in different charitable and humanitarian activities. I also offer a cordial greeting to all the members of the Catholic community, the baptized, the catechumens and the 'sympathizers', especially the children, adolescents and young adults, who are the future and the hope of the Church and the society of that noble country.

Finally, I ask you to present my respectful greetings to the Authorities and to all the Mongolian people, who are ever close to my heart, as well as to the representatives of the various religions, with which the Catholic Church hopes to cooperate in fruitful service to the common good. I assure everyone of a special remembrance in my prayers, and I ask Almighty God to bless the efforts being made to spread his kingdom.

To Mary, Mother and Queen of Mongolia, I entrust the expectations and the hopes of the Church and the Mongolian nation, and having emerged from the long winter of the Communist oppression may they look to the future with renewed confidence.

May the light of Christ accompany everyone along the journey which lies ahead. I willingly seal these good wishes with my special Apostolic Blessing which I now entrust to you, Venerable Brother, as my special representative.

Christianity in China

Later Christian Missions to China

The history of Christianity in China several centuries after the arrival of the Nestorians was froth with competitiveness. Roman Catholic missionaries began their evangelism in China late in the thirteeth century after contacts were successfully established with the court of Kublai Khan.[15,16] In 1253, the Franciscan friar William of Rubruck was sent by King Louis IX of France to convert the Tatars, a sort of medieval incorrect collective reference to the Mongol with no distinction made between the true ethnic Tatars, the Mongols or the Chinese. The Tatars were a group of nomadic tribes with distinct ethnicity who inhabited far-eastern Mongolia, northern Inner Mongolia and northern Manchuria and were known from the time of the Northern Wei dynasty (386-534 AD). They were closely related to the Khitan people to their south. As various of these nomadic groups became part of Genghis Khan's empire in the thirteenth century, they were widely fused with the Mongols hence the names 'Mongol' and 'Tatar' were used interchengeably to denote all the Shiwei tribes.

On his journey eastward, William first met Sartaq Khan, ruler of the Kipchak Khanate and son of Batu Khan, and his wife Khatun Boraqcin of Alchi Tatar. Sartaq was reputed to have been a Christian proselyte. There are several stories of Sartaq's conversion. Armenian writers, for example, alleged that Sartaq was brought up and baptized among the Russians. Also, Muslim chroniclers described Sartaq as hostile towards his second cousin Mongke because of tensions between their religious proclivities. Nevertheless, upon meeting Sartaq, William was sent to the khan's father Batu at Sarai, the seat of Batu from where he ruled parts of Russia in the thirteenth and fourteenth centuries. Located on the Akhtuba River, a channel of the lower Volga River, ancient Sarai now lies some distance north of present-day Astrakhan.

Batu, being a Shamanist by tradition, had refused William's overtures to convert to Christianity and instead had sent William to the Great Khan Mongke in his capital Karakorum. William was received courteously, staying there until July 10, 1254, and then returning to the West in 1255. He was followed by John of Montecorvino (Giovanni da Montecorvino) (1246-1328) an Italian Franciscan missionary and founder of the earliest Roman Catholic missions in India and in China. In 1289 John was commissioned by the papal court of Nicholas IV (1288-1292) and sent as a Roman legate to meet the Great Khan,

Kublai, the Il-khan of Persia, Hulagu and other leaders of the Mongol Empire. He started his journey in 1289 carrying official letters to Kublai Khan, to Il-Khan Arghun and to Kaidu, Prince of the Tatars. He was accompanied by the Dominican friar Nicholas of Pistoia and a merchant named Peter of Lucalongo. After reaching Tabriz (in Persian Azerbeijan) Corvino travelled south to the coast on the Arabian Sea and sailed to India landing in the vicinity of Madras in 1291 where he proselyted for two years before his embarkation in Bengal to sail to China reaching there on 1294. His missionary work in China was met with great success despite constant opposition from the Nestorians who hampered his work whenever they could, but he was able to build the first Catholic Church in Kanbalu (Beijing) in 1299 and a second church opposite the imperial palace in 1305. Corvino also established a mission in Xiamen, the port city which also became an early entry point for Protestant missions in China.

Corvino was elevated to the ecclesiastical position of archpishop in the bishopric of Kanbalu before his death in 1328. Following the death of Corvino, an embassy to Pope Benedict XII (1334-1342) in Avignon was sent by Toghun Temur, the last Mongol emperor in China (Yuan dynasty). The embassy was led by two Genoese in the service of the Mongol emperor. They were Andrea di Nascio and Andalò di Savignone. They carried a letter from Toghun for delivery to the pope in which Toghun claimed his people had been without a spiritual guide for eight years and thus earnestly desired a priest to fill the void left by Corvino's death. In reply, the pope obliged by appointing four ecclesiastics as his legate to the khan's court accompanied by a large Franciscan mission headed by John of Marignolli who reached Kanbalu in 1342. Marignolli returned to Avignon in 1353 to deliver a letter of gratitude from the great khan to Pope Innocent VI (1352-1362).

Much of the Roman Catholic mission work in China appears to have been productive especially as it had received royal support and subsidy. A letter written in January 1326 by St. Andrew of Perugia, the third Bishop of Zaytun (Xiamen) confirms the philanthropic generosity of the imperial court in Beijing:

> Friar Andrew of Perugia, of the Order of Minor Friars, by Divine permission to the Bishop, to the revered father the Friar Warden of the Convent of Perugia, health and peace in the Lord for ever.

'...through much fatigue and sickness and want, through sundry grievous sufferings and perils by land and sea, plundered even of our habits and tunics, we got at last by God's grace to the city of Camballech (*Beijing*), which is the seat of the Emperor the Great Khan, in the year of our Lord's incarnation 1308, as well as I can reckon.

There, after the Archbishop was consecrated...we obtained an Alafa from the emperor for our food and clothing. An Alafa is an allowance for expenses which the emperor grants to the envoys of princes, to orators, to warriors, different kinds of artists, jongleurs, paupers, and all sorts of people of all sorts of conditions. And the sum total of these allowances surpasses the revenue and expenditure of several of the kings of the Latin countries.

As to the wealth, splendor, and glory of this great emperor, the vastness of his dominion, the multitudes of people subject to him, the number and greatness of his cities, and the constitution of the empire, within which no man dares to draw a sword against his neighbour, I will say nothing, because it would be a long matter to write, and would seem incredible to those who heard it. Even I who am here in the country do hear things averred of it that I can scarcely believe...

There is a great city on the shores of the Ocean Sea, which is called in the Persian tongue Zaytun; and in this city a rich Armenian lady did build a large and fine enough church, which was erected into a cathedral by the Archbishop himself of his own free-will. The lady assigned it, with a competent endowment which she provided during her life and secured by her Will at her death to Friar Gerard the Bishop, and the friars who were with him, and he became accordingly the first occupant of the cathedral.

I caused a convenient and handsome church to be built in a certain grove, quarter of a mile outside the city, with all the offices sufficient for twenty-two friars, and with four apartments such that any one of them is good enough for a church dignitary of any rank. In this place I continue to dwell, living upon the imperial dole before-mentioned... Of this allowance I have spent the greatest part in the construction of the church; and I know none among all the convents of our province to be compared to it in elegance and all other amenities...

Tis a fact that in this vast empire there are people of every nation under heaven, and every sect, and all and sundry are allowed to live freely according to their creed. For they hold this opinion, or rather this erroneous view, that everyone can find salvation in their own religion. However we are at liberty to preach without let or hindrance. Of the Jews and Saracens there are indeed no converts, but many of the idolators are baptized; though in truth many of the baptized walk not rightly in the path of Christianity....

"Farewell in the Lord, father, now and ever.

A hiatus of more than two centuries followed the Roman Catholic missions to China until new missionary zeal to China was ignited by the priests of the Society of Jesus, the Jesuits, who were the powerful and often controversial religious order in the history of the Roman Catholic Church. They were founded by St. Ignatius of Loyola, a Basque soldier who had a vision in March 1522 at the shrine of Our Lady of Montserrat while recuperating after his left leg was shattered by a French cannonball during the wars of King Charles V (king of Spain as Charles I, 1516-1556 AD). The order was organized on military protocols of soldier-priests and was approved in 1540 AD by Pope Paul III (1534-1549 AD) in his Bull *'Regimini militantis ecclesia'* of 27 September 1540. Throughout their almost 500 years of history, the Jesuits have at tmes had difficult relations with the papacy as they were often seeen as political and religious rivals. The Society was even dissolved by a papal Bull in 1773 but was rescinded in 1814.

The Jesuits were/are dedicated to bold missionary activities. They evangelized much of Asia in the Sixteenth century, particularly acting as emissaries to the emperors of China. The first attempt by the Jesuits to reach China was made in 1552 by St. Francis Xavier, a Spaniard Basque priest and founding member of the Society of Jesus. Xavier never reached the mainland; he died after only a year on the Chinese island of Shangchuan. Three decades later, in 1582, Jesuits once again initiated mission work in China, led by several figures including the Italian Matteo Ricci (1552-1610). Matteo was an Italian priest and one of the founding figures of the Jesuit missionary work in China. In 1583 Ricci and and his brother in faith Michele Ruggieri, who joined Ricci from Portuguese India, obtained permission to settle in Zhaoqing where jointly they undertook the compilation of their Portuguese-Chinese dictionary - the first ever European-Chinese dictionary, for which they developed a consistent system of transcribing Chinese words into the Latin alphabet. In 1601 Ricci was invited by emperor Shen Tsung as an advisor to the imperial court in Beijing thus became the first Westerner to be invited into the Forbidden City though he actually never had a personal audience with the reclusive emperor. Nevertheless, Ricci became quite influential in the imperial court that gave him the resources to build the Cathedral of the Immaculate Conception in Beijing, the oldest Catholic church in the capital. He died on May 11, 1610 and was inturred in Macau as required by dynastic law but by special permission granted by Emperor Wanli his mortal remains were transferred in the same year to Beijing and interred in Zhalan Cemetery where the remains of other missionaries were also interred. The cemetery now is part of the grounds of Beijing Administrative College in the Xicheng District of Beijing. Although the tombstones of Matteo Ricci, Ferdinand Verbiest and Johann Adam Schall von Bell can be seen in the Zhalan grounds, the actual burial sites were lost during China's Cultural Revolution.

Although Roman Catholic missionary work in China continued to take place periodically and only when political circumstances were condusive, they were mostly brief and fragmanted periods of activity. However, as discussed earlier in connection with the Boxer (Uprising) Rebellion, Christian mission work both of Roman Catholic and Protestant denominations, returned with great force in the nineteenth century and penetrated with some determination from the southern coast city of Guangzhou into the hallowed imperial areas around Xi'an and Beijing. Beginning with the English missionary Robert Morrison in 1807 of the London Missionary Society,[17] who spent twenty five years of intense work translating the whole Bible into Chinese, a new generation of missionaries undertook extended religious works amongst the Chinese populace. Morrison himself worked with contemporary missionaries, generally representing Protestant denominations. They included Walter Henry Medhurst, William Milne, Samuel Dyer and Peter Parker. Other notable missionaries were Hunter Corbett, Gladys

Aylward, Pearl S. Buck, Jonathan Goforth, Eric Liddell, Robert S. Maclay, Lottie Moon, Timothy Richard and Hudson Taylor.[18] Although many of the missions at first were restricted to Guangzhou and Macau, the area of their work gradually expanded both geographically and socially. A musician and an engineer named James O. Fraser was the first to bring the Gospel message late in the nineteenth century to the Lisu tribes in the province of Yunnan in south-west China. His efforts produced a phenomenal number of conversions among the various tribes in the area despite severe opposition and frequent physical violence by the local Buddhist community monks.[19]

The majority of the Chrisian missions to China in the nineteenth century entered China at the time when the political power wielded by the British East India Company in the Indian sub-continent was growing rapidly. But with the slowly escelating internal political struggles in China in the early twentieth century, and in the face of a rapidly deteriorating religious progress, most of the Christian institutions lost their initiative to continue. In more recent years, however, renewed but much subdued interest in Christianity has been revived in China with the tacit consent of the national government.

As a closing remark in the context of the present chapter, we may reflect upon the widely diversified populations of the East whose ethos had been impacted by the Christian ideals of morality and worship. And to appreciate this diversification, we need only refer to the inscriptions typical on the many Christian tombstones erected in China, in Semirechensk (Kazakhstan), in Frunze (the ancient capital of Kyrgyzstan), and in India, Mongolia and Persia. We find, for example, the following, all inscribed both in Syriac and in their native Turkish scripts: 'Terim the Chinese'; 'Banus the Uigurian'; 'Sazik the Indian'; 'Kiamata of Kashgar'; 'Tatt the Mongol' and 'Shah Malison of George of Tus'. Some inscriptions mention the occupation of the interred: 'Zuma, priest'; 'General Amir'; 'Shliha the celebrated commentator and teacher who illuminated all the monasteries with light'; 'Pesoha, exegetes and preacher'; 'Julia, the charming maiden, the betrothed of the Bishop Johanan'; 'Sabrisho, the Archdeacon, the blessed old man and the perfect priest' and 'This is the grave of Chorepiscopus Ama. In the year 1566, (or 1255 according to our time), he departed from this world in the month of July on the Sabbath. May our Lord unite his spirit with those of the pious and the righteous; Amen.'.

References

1. Ghazarian, J. G., *The Armenian Kingdom in Cilicia during the Crusades: The integration of Cilician Armenians with the Latins 1080-1393*. Curzon Press, London (2000).
2. Dupuis, J. (ed.), *The Christian Faith in the Doctrinal Documents of the Catholic Church*. Alba House, New York (2001).
3. Atiya, A. S., *A History of Eastern Christianity*. Methuen and Co., London (1968).
4. Garsoian, N. G., Mathews, T. F. and Thomson R. W. (eds.), *East of Byzantium, Syria and Armenia in the Formative period*. Dumbarton Oaks, Washington, D.C., pp. 35-43 (1982).
5. Mingana, A., The Early Spread of Christianity in Central Asia and the Far East: A New Document. *Buuletin of the John Raylands Library*, no. 9, pp. 297- 371 (1925).
6. Ibid, p. 306.
7. Saeki, P. Y., *The Nestorian Documents and Relics in China*. The Maruzen Co., Tokyo (1951).
8. Saeki, P. Y., *The Nestorian Monument in China*. The Macmillan Co., New York (1928).
9. Moule, A. C., *Christians in China before the Year 1550*. Octagon Books, New York (1977).
10. Mungello, D. E., *Curious Land: Jesuit Accommodation and the Origins of Sinology*. University of Hawaii Press, Hawaii (1989).
11. Couling, C. E., *The Luminous Religion: a study of Nestorian Christianity in China*. Carey Press, London (1925).
12. Drake, F. S., Nestorian Literature of the Tang Dynasty. *Chinese Recorder*, vol. 66, pp.608-617 (1935).
13. Palmer, M., *The Jesus Sutras: Rediscovering the Lost Religion of Taoist Christianity*. Piatkus, London (2001).
14. Whitefield, S. and Sims-Williams, U. (eds.), *The Silk Road: Trade, Travel, War and Faith*. The British Library, London, p.124 (2004).
15. Elia, P. M. d', *The Catholic Missions in China. A Short Sketch of the History of the Catholic Church in China from the Earliest Records to our own Day*. Commercial Press, Shanghai (1934).
16. Rachewiltz, I. de, *Papal Envoys to the Great Khans*. Faber and Faber, London (1971).
17. Townsend, W., *Robert Morrison: The pioneer of Chinese Missions*. S. W. Partridge, London (1890).
18. Wylie, A., *Memorials of Protestant Missionaries to the Chinese*. American Presbyterian Mission Press, Shanghai (1867).

19. Taylor, H. Mrs., *Behind the Ranges: Fraser of Lisuland, S.W. China*. Lutterworth Press, Cambridge (1944).

Chapter Eleven

Islam in China

The earliest dedicated Islamic missions to China seem to have begun in the seventh century when Arab holy men riding the monsoon winds across the Bay of Bengal arrived in the coastal cities of China and devoted themselves to the promulgation of the new faith. Although the general consensus might be that this was the primary path by which Islam was introduced into China, it falls short of taking into account the extensive historic elements both physical and textual that show Islam in China is the legacy of the Muslims who had travelled the ancient Silk Road(s) soon after the advent of Islam in the seventh century. They were truly the first champions of Islam who had planted the seeds of their new faith in the hearts and minds of those they encountered whilst trading along their travels from the western reaches of China to the heart of the Middle Kingdom in Xi'an. They unwittingly transmitted the virtues of Islam by their daily rituals of ablution as part of the purification of their bodies before the offering of their prayers to Allah. These early activities of the Muslim men of the Silk Road might therefore be ascribed as the roots of Islam in China from which the faith continued to grow, blossom and flourish unabated throughout the second millennium of the Christian era. Much of the blossoming of Islam in China and the impact it had made on this ancient land occurred during the ascendancy of the power of the Mughals in Central Asia and under the subsequent rule of their historic lands by the Islamic Karakhanid and Dughlat dynasties. A thorough discussion of this aspect of Islam in China is presented later in this chapter. With the above brief on the origins of Islam in China in mind, the present chapter will focus on the history of the various ways Islam had entered China and the impact of their entry on the longevity of the practice of Islam in China. But in this discourse we must remain cognizant of the fact that the majority of China's Muslims who reside in the far western provinces of Gansu and Xinjiang are Turkic in origin. This will become amply clear as we delineate the subject of this chapter in the pages that follow. Nevertheless, Muslims today of all heritage and denominations live and prosper as farmers and merchants throughout the vast expanse of modern China.

Distribution

Amongst the 56 ethnic groups that make up China's population today (inclusive of the Han), ten proclaim Islam as their national faith and according to a number of population surveys, about 1-2 percent of the total population of China is Muslim, or approximately 20.5 million. Of this number the Sufi Hui represent 48% (9.84 million), the Turkic Sun'ni Uyghur 41.7% (8.55 million), Kazakh 6.1% (1.25 million), Dongxiang 2.5% (514,000), Kyrgyz 0.8% (161,000), Salar 0.5% (105,000), the Tajik of Iranian stock who are Shi'a Muslims 0.2% (41,000), Bonan 0.08% (16,000), Uzbek 0.06% (12,300) and finally the Tatar 0.03% (6,150). The majority of these minorities live in the vast emptiness of Xinjiang, Gansu and Ningxia provinces in north-west China. The Hui are either the descendants of mixed marriages between Muslim Arab or Persian traders of the ancient Silk Road and native Chinese, or are the descendants of intermarriages between Central Asian Muslims of Turkic/Iranian origins and native Chinese. The former assimilated into the general Chinese population keeping only their distinctive Islamic religion, and by adopting the mainstream traditional social norms became indistiguishable in their social environments. They settled mostly in the industrial cities and ports on the eastern coast of China. There they have, from the time of Tang dynasty, kept the practice of their ethnic Qur'anic heritage in focus and successfully apart without confusion from the Confucian social norms. The latter Hui, on the other hand, claim their genealogy from the convergence of Turkic/Iranian Central Asian Muslims with the native Chinese of the south-western and the north-western provinces of China, such as Yunan and Ningxia, respectively.[1] They are strongly influenced by Central Asian mystical Sufism in their practice of Islam coupled with the spirituality of Taoism (Daoism). Taoist personal philosophy, as opposed to Confucian social philosophy, focuses on the well-being of the individual and strongly promotes health and vitality. Perhaps for this reason the practice of the martial arts is a common social activity amongst the north-western Hui. The Hui of Ningxia constitute a third (2 million) of the province's sedentary population of six million. The province is located in the upper reaches of the Yellow River and is bordered by the Gobi Desert and the Helan Mountains on its north and by the Liupan Mountains along its south. The Tengger Desert, practically at door-steps, extends along the entire western border of the province paralleling the course of the Yellow River which flows in a northerly direction shadowing the province's capital Yinchuan before entering the pasturelands of Inner Mongolia. Despite Ningxia's endless sands and sandstorms, the province is still able to boast its three treasures; the medicinal Chinese Wolfberry (Goji), the exceptionally sweet Zhongwei's Xisha melon and the semi-precious Helan Stone.

In the desolate bleakness and wind-swept remoteness of Ningxia, the history of this province, apart from its past involvement in the trade along the ancient Silk Road, was surprisingly important in the eleventh century's political events of the Middle Kingdom. It was in Ningxia that in 1032 AD the Tangut chieftain Li Yuanhao founded the Western Xia dynasty. A large number of secluded tombs of Xia kings and princes that lie at the foot of the Helan Mountains stand to this day as reminders of the richness of the history of Ningxia province.

Although many early adversarial contacts between Arabs and Chinese can be cited, such as the contingent of Arab forces that fought against the Chinese at the battle of Talas River in 751 AD, Arab impact on the Middle Kingdom became more substantial after the arrival of Arab forces in 755 AD sent by the Abbasid caliph Abu Jafar al-Mansur to help Emperor Xuanzong quell the An Lushan Rebellion. Following the recovery of the capital Chang'an from rebel hands, the Arab soldiers settled in China, married Chinese women and founded scattered inland Muslim colonies analogous to those established by the earlier Muslim travellers of the Silk Road or by the later Muslim traders who arrived in China by sea and settled along the east coast of China.

The history of Islam in Xinjiang province and its impact on the regional sedentary population at a more significant level than that of the earliest Muslim missionary efforts, or that of the Silk Road traders' religious contributions, began early in the tenth century (circa 920s) with the conversion of the Karakhanid Sultan Satuq Bughra Khan to Islam.[2] The Bughra khans were one of the original Turkic Uyghur peoples who after the collapse of their First Uyghur Empire in 840 AD had established settlements fashioned as regional kingdoms (khanates) centred in Balasaghun and were known as the Karakhans. Balasaghun was an ancient Sogdian city in present-day Kyrgyzstan founded by a people of Iranian origin It was located in the Chu River valley between the city of Bishkek and Issyk Köl (Hot Lake).

Satuq Bughra Khan (909-956 AD) was first introduced to Islam at the age of twelve by Abu al-Nasir Mansur, a Samanid governor of Bukhara in Transoxiana. The Iranian Samanid dynasty was an Islamic Sun'ni dynasty founded during the rule of Iran and parts of Central Asia by the

Abbasid caliphate of Baghdad. The dynasty had been granted the rule of the territories in Transoxiana for its many years of faithful service to the caliphate. Ahmad, a son of the dynasty's founder Saman (hence the Samanid), was awarded the rule of Ferghana and his son Nasir appointed governor of Bukhara. The Samanids of Tansoxiana were eventually ousted in 1008 AD by Satuq's grandson, Iliq Mazi (Iliq Nasir). But early in the tenth century (circa 920 AD) Nasir had befriended the Karakhan of Kashgar, Satuq's uncle Oghul Chaq, and was granted special permission to build a mosque in the town of Artux (Artush) in the region of Kashgar south of Torugart Pass. Satuq, it is said: 'would often go to the mosque to watch the arrival of the camel caravans and witness the ablution of the Muslim traders in preparation of their thanksgiving prayers.' His eventual profession of Sun'ni Islam during his teenage years had brought his uncle's displeasure and the punishment of a brief incarseratiom. But by the time Satuq reached the age of twenty five in 934, he had gathered enough supporters to overthrow his uncle and establish himself as the sole ruler of Kashgar and of the Silk Road oasis towns of Yarkand and Khotan. This may be said, to constitute the earliest varifiable date for the presence of Islam in Xinjiang. But the development of a more substantial history of Islam in Xinjiang required four additional centuries before its full glory was firmly expressed first by the Karakhans and the Dughlats then by the Khojas – the influential Islamic Naqshbandiyah Sufis who secured the permenance of Islam in China.

Emergence of Islam

In essence, Islam emerged in China during the Tang dynasty and began a journey that was characterized by many successes and persecutions spanning the Song, Yuan, Ming and Qing dynasties. During the Tang dynasty (618-907 AD), Islam was referred to as the *'Dashi Jiao'* (religion of the Dashi, the traders). During the Ming dynasty (1368-1644 AD) it acquired the name *'Tianfang Jiao'* (religion of Arabia), or *'Hui Hui Jiao'* (religion of the Hui Hui). At the beginning of the Qing dynasty (1644-1911 AD) Islam came to be known as the true religion (*Qingzhen Jiao*). Although the term *'Hui Jiao'* (religion of the Hui) was in use during the intervening years from 1912 to 1949, this restrictive term in reference to Islam was dropped in favour of the all-inclusive generic word 'Islam.' Yet to this day the identity of a Han remains unchanged regardless of the person's native or acquired religion unless Islam is the acquired faith in which case, in most circumstances, a Han Muslim, and indeed any Muslim in China, is simply referred to and is

Islam in China

identified as a Hui. Despite these vacillating references to Islam and their corresponding social connotations, Islam's golden age in China came during the Yuan dynasty (1279-1368 AD). It was during this period that Muslims in China began to leave their indelible mark on the Chinese social structure of the time. Although the rulers and the nobility of this Mongol dynasty refrained from professing the Islamic faith, they nonetheless supported their Muslim populace by appointing many into high state-positions of authority and many Muslims were given prominent roles in official and state ceremonies. Indeed as early as the Song dynasty (960-1279 AD) the office of the Director General of Shipping was held by a Muslim until the closing decades of the Ming dynasty. The Hui, especially in the east, were seen as being fair tradesmen, law-abiding and self-disciplined. Their assimilation into the majority Han population was accelerated by their adoption of Chinese names closest to their own Muslim roots. In this context, Muhammad (or Mohammad) became Mo; Mustafa. Mu; Masoud, Mai; Hasan, Ha; Husain, Hu and Sa'id became Sai. Many Muslim communities thrived in the coastal cities Guangzhou and Quanzhou as well as in the interior of China as in Hangzhou, Yangzhou, Kaifeng and Chang'an. Today, many of these cities contain the tombs of early Muslim missionaries revered for their legendary roles in bringing Islam to China. Discussed earlier are the presumptive tombs of Abi Waqqas in Guangzhou and of Qais ibn Sa'ad Ansari in Hami. However, substantially better dated tombs can also be found. The tomb of Husain ibn Muhammad al-Khalat in Quanzhou, Fujian province, reads in Farsi: 'This is the tomb of Husain ibn Muhammad al-Khalat. May God show mercy upon him. Died on the 13th of the fourth month of the year 567 (1171 AD).' Similarly, tombs of later missionaries associated with the Ming dynasty (1368-1644 AD) are preserved and revered and have become attractive sacred pilgrimage shrines for the devout Muslims who come not only from within China and Hong Kong but from many nearby Asian countries such as Pakistan, Malaysia and Indonesia. Many of these shrines are located in the traditionally Muslim sectors of western, southern and eastern China. For example, the most important Sufi shrine in Lanzhou is that of Abud al-Kadir al-Jeylani credited with the founding of Kadariyah Sufism. The shrine of Hamza (Hamuz Ali) Isfahani stands on the summit of a local hill in the small village of Xiaonan in the outskirts of the city of Linxia in Gansu province. His epigraph in Persian states he had come to China from Isfahan, Iran (as his name implies) during the sixteenth century and became a major figure in promoting Sufism in Hezu and Dongxiang regions of Gansu. Hezu (present-day Linxia) became one of the most important centres of

Sufi Islam in China thus came to enjoy the accolade 'Little Mecca.' In a sandy desert environment outside Khotan in Xinjiang provine, the dvout Uyghurs consider the mazar (tomb) of a sixteenth century legendary imam called Asim a holy shrine thus make metaphoric offerings of animal hides or of coloured handkerchiefs. The devout who visit this tomb throughout the seasons come and stand or kneel in the sand in reverent prayers seeking blessings and inspiration whilst the baking hot sands in summer or the punishing icy winds of the Taklamakan desert in winter would make such visits most unthinkable to many us mortals. There are many more such shrines scattered throughout China too numerous to mention but collectively they are a testament to the old Islamic deeply rooted heritage of the numerous Muslim communities that exist today in China. The importance of these vastly scattered shrines in China actively generating a fundamental worldwide sense of Islamic brotherhood and unity cannot be underestimated.[3]

Under the patronage of the Yuan dynasty (1279-1368 AD) large numbers of Middle Eastern Muslims were allowed to settle in China and equally large numbers of Muslims were relocated into China from Central Asia to redress the imbalance of Mongol minority numbers against the majority Hans in the Mongols' newly conquered land. The large Muslim populations especially in the larger urban cities diminished the impact of the native Han populations and offered the Mongols alternative sources of impartial and mostly politically neutral manpower. Thus the Muslims became to the Mongols a reliable ally and helped administer the rapidly expanding Mongol empire.[4,5] The ranks of the Muslim administrators included Persians, Arabs and Uyghurs who mostly held administrative posts in the offices of finance and taxation. They continued to enjoy a tranquil co-existence well into the Ming dynasty (1368-1644 AD) but the new isolationist tendencies of this dynasty restricted the influx of new immigrants. Furthermore beginning with the rise of the Qing dynasty (1644-1911 AD) new difficulties faced the Muslim communities. These difficulties included the prohibition of the Islamic lawfully permitted ritual slaughter commonly known as 'Halal' and also a freeze on the construction of new mosques. The consequent increase in social tensions and unrest gave the Manchu rulers of the Qing dynasty opportunities to exploit the sectarian divisions amongst the Muslims in an effort to overcome a number of Islamic resistance movements that had erupted in Yunnan, Xinjiang, Gansu, Shaanxi and Guizhou provinces. The list of notable Muslims who allied themselves with the Manchu General Zuo

Islam in China

Zongtang and defeated fellow Muslim revolutionaries of the Jahariyah Order included Ma Zhan'ao, Ma Anliang, Dong Fuxiang, Ma Qianling and Ma Julung - all members of the rival Khufiyah Order.[6]

For the purposes of a fuller appreciation of the above comprehensive review of the history of Islam in China, a more detailed history will now be presented which divides the history of Islam in China into four major periods.[7] They are the Gedimu; Sufi Tariqas; Yihewani and, finally, the Period of Nationalism. However, it should be borne in mind that as we progress into this chapter it will become progressively clear that the Chinese Muslims in the main are the descendants of people with Altaic Turkic, Mongolic, Central Asian and Middle Eastern heritage and the majority are of Sufi persuasion (circa 51%) followed by the Sun'ni at 44%. The percentage of the Shi'a is very small and is mostly practiced by the Tajik. It is important to note in the present context that Hanafi is one of the four schools of legal thought within Sun'ni Islam. The other three are the Shafi'i, Malik'i, and Hanbal'i schools. The Hanafi was the sole school of Islamic thought in China until the widespread introduction of Sufism during the Ming dynasty, but worldwide it has the largest followers - principally in Central Asia, Afghanistan, Pakistan, Bangladesh, India, most of the Middle East with the exception of Iran, Turkey, Albania, Bosnia, Kosovo, the Balkans and the Caucasus. The Mughal Empire practiced the Hanafi Sun'ni tradition. Perhaps it should be stated here that the followers of Sun'ni Islam believe in the righteousness of the Muslim leadership that lived during the lifetime of the prophet Muhammad whilst the followers of Shi'a Islam rever only the family and the direct descendants of the Prophet as the rightful hairs to leadership.

The word Gedimu is a corruption of the Arabic word *qadim* قديم ' which means 'old'. The term is applied to the period of Islam in China when the first Muslim merchants, official envoys and soldiers began to arrive in China from Arabia, Persia, and Central Asia. From the seventh to the fourteenth centuries, these immigrants formed mostly small isolated communities in the southern and eastern coastal cities of China. The eastern Hui in particular, as mentioned earlier, are the desecendants of the earliest immigrants of the Gedimu period.

The Sufi Tariqa period began in the seventeenth century and is described as the period during which Sufism in China evolved into two distinct, often rival, major sects known as the Kadariyah and Naqshbandiyah Sufism, each with its own independent branches and sub-branches. The former's sub-branch is the Kubriyah order whilst the latter's major branches are the Khufiyah and the Jahariyah orders. They all share the common theological fundamentalism which links their separate belief systems with descendants of early Sufi saintly personas 'holy men.' The Arabic word *'Tariqa'* means 'path' and stands in the present context for 'sect' and the word 'order' is used in reference to the sect's many branches and sub-branches. The shrine of the founder of the Kadariyah sect, Abud al-Kadir al-Jeylani is preserved in Linxia, Gansu province. The sect's precepts are focused on the combination of a simple ascetic mysticism with a non-instutionalized form of worship that is centred around the tomb of a saintly holy man rather than in the practice of the traditional devotional rituals at a mosque. The personal saintly powers of the Sufi holy men are derived from the continuum of their inherited holiness from the time of the prophet Muhammad. The simplicity of this new worshiping, where individuals regardless of gender can independently visit a tomb or a shrine for devotional worship, was seen amongst the Hui as a spiritual renewal movement thus gained much appeal in the Hui communities.

The Kadariyah Tariqa was the first to become established among the Hui through the efforts of a student of Abu Abd-Allah who entered China in 1674 AD and promulgated his Sufi beliefs in the provinces of Guangdong, Guangxi, Yunnan, Gansu and Guizhou. He died in 1689 and was buried in Guizhou. His student, Hilal al-Din known amongst the Hui as Qi Daozu 'great master', preached amongst the Hui in Lanzhou and Linxia. He died in 1719 and was buried in Linxia's complex of the shrines of Sufi masters that ultimately became the centre of the Kadariyah sect in China. Linxia's location along the ancient trade and communication routes allowed it unhindered opportunities to interact with the West and, particularly, with the Islamic centres in Arabia and Iran. Almost every major Islamic movement in China has its origins amongst Muslims, who after pilgrimage to Middle Eastern and Iranian Islamic centres of study, had come to Linxia disseminating new doctrines. Thus Linxia's theological heritage embodied the importance of Mecca's spirituality along with the Islamic teachings that have emanated from Qum in Iran.

The Kubriyah order of the Kadariyah sect is believed to have been introduced in China in 1370, much earlier than the later teachings of the Sufi holy men who arrived in the sixteenth and seventeenth centuries. It was promulgated in the provinces of Qinghai, Gansu and Henan from which an inference can be made that a descendant of the prophet

Muhammad, Muhuyindeni, who is credited for teaching the tenets of the Kubriyah order, must have almost certainly entered China from Kashgar and travelled along the Silk Road(s) to his intended destinations. His identity remains obscure but it is claimed he reached Linxia and died in Dawantou village in Dongxiang prefecture of Gansu province.

Naqshbandiyah Sufism, on the other hand, was successfully established through its two major orders, the Khufiyah and the Jahariyah. The word *Naqshbandi* is Persian taken from the name of the founder of the sect, Baha-ud-Din Naqshband Bukhari (of Bukhara). The Khufiyah order was established in China in the eighteenth century by Ma Laichi (1681-1766) and was centred in Linxia. Its practices in China were taken from an earlier Central Asian and Yemeni Naqshbandiyah Sufism that emphasized the veneration of saints, the seeking of inspiration at tombs, and most importantly, maintaining a 'silent remembrances' – the constant awareness of Allah's divine presence along with the silent repition of the Qur'anic verses and supplications taken from the hadith texts (the original words and deeds of the prophet); thus the individualized devotional activities are conducted entirely silently. Most of its adherents are the Hui of the provinces of Gansu, Ningxia and Qinghai. They are often referred to as the 'Silent Ones.'

In distinct contrast to the Khufiyah order, the Jahariyah order (Derwishes) was founded under the leadership of Ma Mingxin (1719-1781) who after two decades of study under Naqshbandiyah Sufi masters in Yemen and Saudi Arabia returned to China in 1744 with militant fundamentalist reforms in mind that instituted 'vocal and loud remembrances' during worship and engaged in ritualized recitations, singing and dancing. The prevalence of the Jahariyah order extended from Yunnan northwards to Qinghai, Gansu and Ningxia and then crossing over towards Beijing it reached the easternmost parts of China. Essentially all of the revolutionary dissidents in the Qinghai, Gansu and Ningxia provinces during the eighteenth and nineteenth centuries were members of this order.[8]

The third period of Islam in China is the Yihewani period, a term drawn from the Arabic word '*Ikhwan*' meaning 'brotherhood.' This was a period of reformist movements which arrived in China in the late nineteenth century and focused its objectives on Islamic fundamentalism. It was established in Linxia late in the nineteenth century by Ma Wanfu (1849-1934) upon his return from Mecca. Its advocates were Sun'ni who promoted the Hanaf'i school of thought.

The final period of the history of Islam in China is the period of nationalism which, for the most part, began in 1979 as a result of central government's efforts in classifying its non-Han citizens into minorities based on ethnicity relative to the majority Han population, which draws its historic identity firmly from the Middle Kingdom. The minorities were defined as a group of people who speak a common language, occupy a common region in China and share a set of common values. Based on this definition the central government divided China's population into fiftyfive ethnic minorities with the majority Han population representing the fiftysixth group. For a number of reasons which are beyond the scope of the present work, the effort invested in the classification of China's minorities was the impetus that crystalized Muslim nationalism in China whose legacy still lingers quietly to the present day amongst certain segments of Chinese Muslims.[9]

The people of Uyghuristan

China's ethnic minority group known as the Uyghur, have a history that superimposes the story of their heritage with the evolution and importance of Islam in China. Turkic in origin, Uyghur diasporic communities also exist in many parts of Central Asia. Their ancestors were nomadic pastoralists belonging to the Tiele tribe who roamed the pasturelands in the valleys of the Altai Mountains in Mongolia.[10,11] They covered territories that encompassed the shores of Lake Baikal and the southern floodplains of the Yenisei River in north-central Mongolia. In the early periods of their history the Uyghur were either subjugated or served as vassals to a number of regional states that included the Xiongnu, the Rouran and the Göktürk. The Uyghur of present-day China are settled Turkic urban dwellers and farmers who live along the periphery of the vast sandy emptiness of the Taklamakan Desert in Xinjiang province. Their main produce is wheat, vegetables and a variety of fruits such as apples, grapes, raisen and melons. Animal husbandry is their major industry but is restricted by their Islamic faith to the production of sheep, mutton and limited amounts of beef. Although it is argued that the Yugur and the Salar ethnic minorities in China represent sub-groups of the general Uyghur population on the basis of their linguistic and part historical roots, they were recognized as separate ethnic groups in a census conducted by the Chinese central government.

The *Suishu*, the official history of the Sui dynasty which ruled China from the city of Chang'an (581-618 AD) relates the following concerning the Uyghur under the Chinese ethnonym *Gaoche*, literally meaning 'Wheel-Wagon' in reference to the ox-drawn carts with two distinctive high wheels used for transport, which, ironically, are still prevalent in Xinjiang province:

> The names of these tribes differ, but all of them can be classified as Tiele. The Tiele do not have a master, but are subject to both the Eastern and Western Tujue (Göktürk). They do not have a permanent residence, and move with the changes of grass and water. Their main characteristics are, firstly, they possess great ferocity and yet show tolerence; secondly, they are good riders and archers and, thirdly, they show greed without restraint for they often make their living by looting. The tribes towards the west are more cultivated for they breed cattle and sheep but fewer horses. Since the Tujue had established a state, they (Uyghur) are recruited as auxiliary for the empire.

Upon the disintegration of the Xiongnu dominance in the Western Regions in the third century AD, a group of Turkic peoples with the largest tribal divisions, all previously subjugated by the Xiongnu, emerged to prominence. They collectively became known as the Tiele tribes.[12] The Tiele were ruled by the Göktürks during the mid sixth and early seventh centuries and many of their tribal chiefs were expelled and some were killed during this period. A century earlier however, twelve clans from the Tiele tribes had gathered enough power and leasership to create their independent kingdom in 481 AD. But the leadership was unable to maintain an effective unity and thus the kingdom copitulated to the power of Göktürk tribes in 520 AD. Nearly three decades later in 546 AD the Tiele renewed their struggle against the Göktürks by forming a tribal coalition called the *Tokuz-Oghuz* (Nine Ttibes) that included clans from nine separate Tiele tribes (these were the Xue, Yantuo, Basmyl, Oghuz, Khazar, Alan, Kyrgyz, Tuva and Yakut). Several revolts by the coalition against the Göktürk were attempted in 600, 603, 611, 615 and 627 AD but all had failed to deliver them from subjugation. But when the Tang emperor Taizong took Gaochang, the seat of the Göktürk khanate in 648 AD, the Uyghur tribes who had fought as allies of the emperor against their common foe were given the authority to establish their rule over the lands that comprised the western Göktürk khanate. Despite these political power shifts, the struggle between the Uyghurs and the Göktürks continued for more than a century under the watchful eyes of the Tang dynasty. But capitalizing on their victory over the Tang dynasty at the battle of Talas River in 751 AD, the Uyghurs used their newly-acquired confidence and engaged their arch-enemy the Göktürks in a final battle that terminally ended their struggle with a victory. This victory gave the Uyghur the ability to found their First Uyghur Empire (Orkhun Uyghur Empire) in the mid eighth century with its capital in Ordunbaliq, in the original Uyghur homelands in north-central Mongolia. The new empire now covered vast lands which contained the original homelands of the Uyghur in north-central Mongolia and areas as far west as the north-western foothills of the Tian Shan Mountains.[13] This empire survived until the mid ninth century (840 AD) when it was defeated by the Yenisei Kyrgyz as these nomadic tribes began to move westward from their native lands in the upper plains of the Yenisei River.[14]

During the century following the collapse of the First Uyghur Empire in 840 AD, the Uyghur tribes concentrated, enlarged and organized their settlements and fashioned them into three separate kingdoms in the regions they had previously occupied along the periphery of the Tian Shan Mountains. These kingdoms included areas, first, west of Tian Shan Mountains in the fertile plains around Bishkek, irrigated by the Chu River (fed by the Issyk Köl); second, in areas that later came to be referred to as East Turkistan and, finally, in the western parts of Gansu province. The Yugur, mentioned above, are conventionally referred to as the Yellow Uyghur and are one of the oldest nomadic Uyghur tribes who settled in parts of Gansu province. Their ancestors lived in the Hexi Corridor around present-day Zhangye but also moved westward and settled in Dunhuang area. Unlike their Uyghur kin who settled further west, the Yugur maintained their Buddhist heritage and did not convert to Islam.

The Uyghur tribes that settled in East Turkistan sometime in the 850s AD around the oasis towns of Beshbalik, Kucha (Kuqa), Turfan and Kumul (Hami) ultimately became the predecessors of the Islamic Dughlat dynasty that reigned in East Turkistan during much of the sixteenth century.[15] Before their emergence as a major Islamic force, they supported and maintained Buddhism as their native majority faith.

But free from persecution, Manichaean communities in these areas also flourished alongside Buddhism and became centres of religious, artistic and economic activities. The dynasty's Islamicization was gradual. Its members in Hami were the first to convert to Islam in the early decades of the tenth century whilst those living further west in Turfan, Kucha and Beshbalik remained multicultural until their conversion to Islam was complete by the fifteenth century.

In contrast to the Uyghur tribes of East Turkistan, many other Uyghur tribes in the 850s settled in the floodplains of the Chu River. In time, the Karakhans emerged as the dominant tribe and established the Karakhanid (Great Khans) dynasty. The dynasty's founder was Kül Belgae Kadir Khan whose sons were Bazir Arslan Khan and Öghul Chaq. The latter son was the uncle of Sultan Satuq Bughra Khan (909-956 AD). From their khanates in Balasaghun the Karakhanids earnestly allied themselves with the Islamic Sun'ni Samanids of Samarkand (Iranian stock) and thus extended their influence into Transoxiana. But the Samanids eventually ended their alliance with Kül Belgae Kadir Khan who, driven eastward, designated Kashgar as the new capital of his Karakhanid dynasty. From their native faith (partly Buddhist and Shamanist), the Karakhanids converted to Islam early in the tenth century after the founding of their khanate. Their conversion to Islam was complete in 934 AD under Satuq Bughra Khan. Together with their kin in the Tarim basin a new coalition was created that fashioned itself as the Second Uyghur Empire. Until 1212 AD this empire remained the regional bearer of the Turkic heritage and Islamic culture as examplified by Mahmud ibn Hussayn al-Kashgari's legacy as a scholar and a historian of Turkic languages. His father, Hussayn, was related to the Karakhanid dynasty and his mother, Bibi Rabiya al-Basri, drew her heritage from the marshes of southern Arabia. In 1072 al-Kashgari (meaning 'of Kashgar') compiled the first comprehensive dictionary of the Turkic languages of his time intended for use by the caliphs of Baghdad. The dictionary which contained the words of the most commonly spoken Turkic languages by the Uyghur, demonstrated that well over half of the words in their lexicon had Persian roots and that their use follows Persian syntax. His contemporary, Yusuf Has Hajib Balasaghuni (meaning 'of Balasaghun'), was also a great Islamic writer and a philosopher, as mentioned earlier in Chapter 6.

The Mughals

Mughal, or Maghul (مغول), also Mogul, is the Persian word for 'Mongol' which in our present usage applies to an ancestral descent from the Mongol armies that invaded China, Central Asia and Iran under Genghis Khan (1162-1227 AD) in the thirteenth century, and Temur (Tamerlane) in the fourteenth century. The two main Mongolian nomadic clans were the Chagataids and the Barlas. The former claimed descent directly from Chagatai Khan (son of Genghis Khan,).[16] The mother of Babar Khan, the founder of the Mughal dynasty in South Asia, was a Chagataid (a member of the Chagatai clan). In colonial India, the centre of Chagataid power was in Delhi with marginal power centres in Lucknow and Punjab. The Barlas, on the other hand, traced their origins to the Timurids of Bukhara and Samarkand who founded their Mughal Empire in the far north-western regions of the Indian subcontinent and ruled much of Central Asia and Iran. Hence, the peoples of present-day Pakistan and North India of Mughal origin may share their ancestry with the Uzbek, the Tajik and the Kipchak. The more recent settlers in the latter areas area from Turkey and Iran are referred to as the Qazilbash.

The great Mongol conqueror Genghis Khan died in 1227 and the empire he left behind, which contained nearly the whole of northern Asia, was partitioned among his sons. Jochi, the eldest son had died before his father, hence his share of the empire was inherited by his son, Batu, the grandson of Genghis Khan. Chagatai and Ogotai, the two eldest of the remaining four living sons of Genghis became the major inheritors of their father's empire. Chagatai's share was the largest division and included the greatest diversity of races and tribes who were flanked by Batu's domain in the west and by Ogotai's in the east. The distribution of the shares rested more on tribal lines rather than on territorial boundaries because in most cases the tribes were nomadic who often shifted their abodes or were dislocated by political conflicts. Nevertheless, in territorial terms which reflected the tribal-based partition of the empire, Chagatai's central domain consisted of lands that were confined by the Syr Darya (Jaxartes River, or the Sayhun) and the Amu Darya (Oxus River, or the Jihun). It extended from Ferghana - in the lower course of the Jaxartes - in the north, to lands in southern Afghanistan in the south; and from the Tarim basin in its easternmost parts to the eastern shores of the Aral Sea in the west. In present-day geographical context this would contain the territories of southern Khazakhstan, Uzbekistan, the eastern half of Turkmenistan,

Islam in China

Tajikistan, Kyrgyzstan and Afghanistan. Chagatai's domain was indeed a large political entity and was ruled as a khanate by Chagatai himself. After his death in 1241 the khanate became a Mongol ruling autocracy that inherited Chagatai's legacy.

The second share of the Mongol Empire inherited by Ogotai was represented mostly by territories north of the Tian Shan Mountains defined in the west by the shores of the river Chu and Lake Balkash in present-day eastern Kazakhstan, and extended east into the Mongol original homelands in the valleys of the Altai Mountains.

Batu's share of the Mongol Empire was mostly confined to lands immediately north of the Caspian Sea and west of the Volga River. He joined his uncle Ogotai in military campaigns against the Jin Dynasty in northern China and after the end of the Mongol-Jin wars he undertook the conquest of Russia in 1237 and within a year he successfully completed his mission by burning the cities of Kolomna, Moscow and Vladimir.

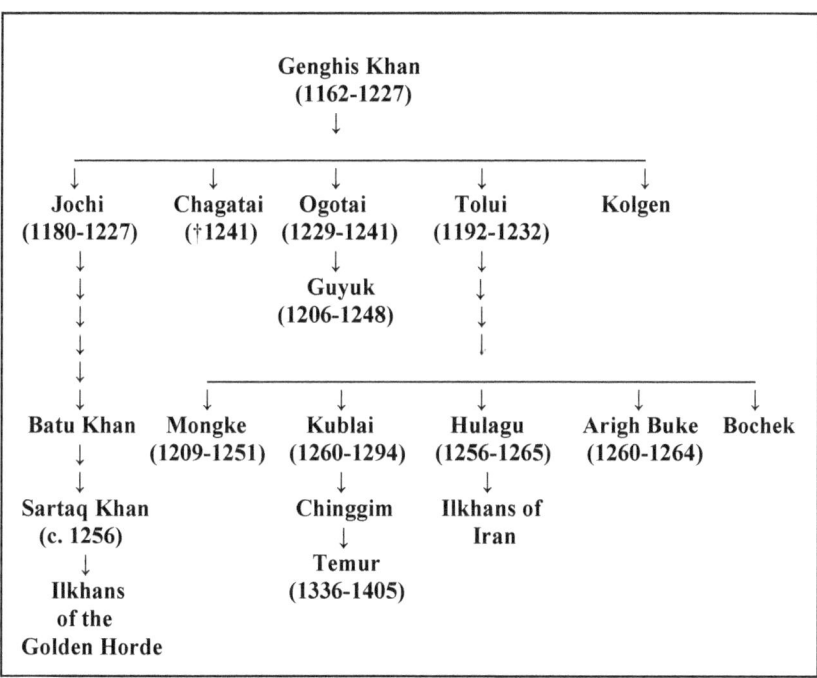

Figure 4. The lineage of Genghis Khan

A century after Chagatai's death his khanate in 1346 AD was divided into western and eastern halves. The western half, known as Transoxiana (present-day Uzbekistan and eastern Turkmenistan; a region confined by the rivers Amu Darya to its south and Syr Darya to its north) with its capital in Samarkand, was conventionally also referred to as West Turkistan as opposed to the eastern half of the khanate named Mughalistan with its capital in Almaliq (present-day Yining in Xinjiang province of China). This latter half included the eastern highlands of the Pamir Mountains (the fertile lands of historic Ferghana), the Tarim river basin and the southern foothills of the Tian Shan mountain range. Mughalistan was home for a family of Uyghur tribes but was ruled by the khans of the dominant Karakhan tribe. Early in the sixteenth century (circa 1514 AD) Mughalistan was divided along tribal lines into eastern and western halves with the khans of the Karakhan tribe (descendants of the Karakhanid dynasty - see their histroy discussed above) exercising dominion over both halves and ruled from their capital in Kashgar. The khans of the Dughlat tribe were given dominion over the eatern half of Mughalistan (often referred to as East Turkistan) and ruled as 'Emirs' from the seat of their power in Turfan but only as vassals to the Karakhans. Emirs were rulers who did not have genealogical linkage to Genghiz Khan. In this instance, their domain included the whole of the Tarim basin. The sedentary inhabitants in these areas of the Tarim basin were and remain to this day overwhelmingly Uyghur in heritage. In this context, it is of interest to note that starting in the twentieth century the politically controvertial term Uyghuristan had come into use synonymously with East Turkistan. Although the Han dynasty had used the term Xiyu for this region of China, which the dynasty had controlled, the term Xinjiang (meaning New Territory) was adopted only in the eighteenth century by the Qing dynasty.

The political power in the western half of Chagatai khanate (Transoxiana) devolved into the hands of many tribal leaders who appointed puppet khans for delivering spesific self-serving agendas. In mid fourteenth century Transoxiana came under the fold of the Mongol leader Temur.[17] Our present topic of discussion, however, will remain focused on Mughalistan. Mughalistan as mentioned above was home for a family of Uyghur tribes but ruled by the dominant Karakhan tribe. The Dughlats, on the other hand, had often attempted to end that relationship and had raised frequent rebellions against the Karakhans. One such attempted rebellion was pursued by Mirza Abu-Baker in1465 AD. Abu-Baker crossed the tribal divisional lines of rule in

Mughalistan and launched his own rebellion by occuping the oasis towns of Khotan and Yarkand. He declared himself an independent ruler of his State of Yarkand and designated Yarkand his capital. However, after five decades of quasi independence, the Karakhanid Sultan Sa'id Khan captured Yangi Hisar citadel in 1514 AD (which had defended Yarkand from the south) and brought Abu-Baker's rule to an end. This in effect fixed a line in the sand and upon the division of Mughalistan into two halves confined the Dughlats' rule to East Turkistan. Sa'id Khan's dynasty survived until 1670 AD.

In the final analysis, it should be borne in mind that all the various Turkic tribal confederations of the Asian steppes, including the Kipchak and the Oghuz, were major players in the shaping of the Islamic history of Central Asia. The Kipchak Turks, who lived in the fertile plains of the Irtysh River, began advancing in the late tenth century and displaced the Oghuz Turks from their homelands north of the Jaxartes River. The advancing Kipchak then turned westward into south Russia and entered the eastern reaches of Europe. Many Oghuz tribal groups, forced out of their native lands by the Kipchak, migrated in waves into the surrounding territories that were Islamicized under the Abbasid caliphate. The Seljuks were one Oghuz tribal group that ultimately settled in Bukhara and embraced Sun'ni Islam. In time their leaders Tughrul and Chagri advanced into Khurasan and vanquished the Iranian Ghaznavids south of the Oxus River. By 1079 AD the Seljuks had dominated Mesopotamia, Iran, Syria and Palestine. Their victories gathered momentum again in the late thriteenth century sparked by Osman (Othman) who had succeeded his father Ertughrul as the tribal leader of Bithynia situated along the southern shores of the Black Sea. He successfully challenged the Byzantine Empire in Asia Minor and in 1326 AD established his capital in Bursa on the coast of the Sea of Marmara. His descendants came to be known as the Othmanli, or the Ottomans, whose unparalleled commitment to Islam succeeded in raising the crescent of Islam in 1453 on the ramparts of the defeated and pillaged Constantinople, the city that was once the jewel of Christiandem and the creation of the Byzantine emperor Constantine the Great.

CHAGATAI KHANATE	
WESTERN DIVISION	**EASTERN DIVISION**
TRANSOXIANA OR WEST TURKISTAN Capital: Samarkand Under the rule of Temur 1347 AD	MUGHALISTAN Capital: Almaliq & Kashgar Ruled by the Karakhanids Divided in the 16th century

	WESTERN	EASTERN
	Ruled by the Karakhanids until 1680 AD	also called EAST TURKISTAN Vassal to the Karakhanids Ruled by the Dughlat Emirs until 1565 AD
	The Khojas ruled Mughalistan from 1680 until Chinese takeover in 1759 AD	

Figure 5. Chagatai khanate after 1346 AD

Islam in China

Later Islamic History of Xinjiang Province

This section begins with an elaboration on the early dynastic divisions as discussed above and provides the framework for understanding how Islam evolved in East Turkistan. The first important reference to be cited in this regard is the *Tarikh-i-Rashidi* (History of Rashid), a history in two volumes by Mirza Muhammad Haidar written as his personal memoires over the period 1541 to 1546 AD. It is basically a partial history of the Mughals of Central Asia. Mirza, a cousin of Sultan Sa'id Khan, was a Turkic-speaking Dughlat prince who wrote in Persian. His subject embraced the history of many Turkic tribes but its central focus constitutes a part of the history of the Chagatai khanate. This is presented as a running account of the hisorical events surrounding two parallel Muslim Turkic dynasties, which were 1) the khans of the western half of Mughalistan and 2) the vassal Dughlat Emirs of East Turkistan.[18] The two dynasties in reference are those that resulted from the division of the family of khans of Mughalistan into the two branches as discussed above.

The history of the khans of Mughalistan begins with Khan Tughluk Temur (1347-1362 AD) while that of the Dughlat emirs of Eastern Turkistan begins with Emir Bulaji, Mirza's ancestor who had supported Tughluk Temur in his bid to khanship. Mirza's ancestral relationship had given him the facility to record authoritavely the parallel histories and genealogies of the khans of Mughalistan and of the emirs of his Dughlat tribe. Here it should be emphasized that the accounts detailed below are not drawn from the *Tarikh-i-Rashidi* but have been cross-referenced with Mirza's text for historical reliability.

The dawn of Islam in Xinjiang province dates back nearly two centuries before the Uyghur dynasties were founded in the mid ninth century. Their Islamicization was gradual from their original Buddhist and Shamanic origins either as a result of proselyting, as was in the case of Karakhanid Satuq Bughra Khan (920s), or driven into accepting Islam by virtue of vassalage, as was the case with the Doughlats of Hami, Turfan and Kuqa. Therefore, it was not until early in the sixteenth century when political events in Mughalistan began to have major impact on the shaping of Xinjiang's future Islamic history. This period began with the founding of the State of Yarkand by Mirza Abu-Baker, as discussed earlier, and his demise in the hands of Sa'id Khan in 1514 AD. It is at this time that a major chapter in the Islamic history of Xinjiang province begins to emerge prompted by the political events emanating from East Turkistan.

Sultan Sa'id Khan was born in 1487 in Turfan as a member of the Karakhan tribe. His grandfather was Sultan Yunus Khan When Sa'id was fourteen years old, his father Sultan Ahmad Khan (son of Yunus Khan) took the young Sa'id to Tashkent in 1508 to join his uncle Sultan Mahmud Khan in a battle with Shahi Beg Khan of Akhsi (near Bamiyan, Afghanistan). The battle was lost and Mahmud Khan was killed. Sa'id's older brother Mansur Khan (1482-1543) was then ruling Mughalistan from Turfan and thus forced Sa'id to remain in exile. Several years later, at the age of seventeen, Sa'id joined his cousin Babar Padishah in Kabul. It was from there that Sa'id, relying on his extensive experiences in warfare at an early age, launched his campaign against Mirza Abu-Baker defeating him in 1514 and capturing Yarkand, as mentioned above. He thus established himself as ruler of Yarkand and Kashgar. In 1516 Sa'id made his peace with his brother Mansur who shared the rule of Mughalistan from Turfan and Karashahir but allowed Sa'id to gradually take control of most of Mughalistan. Sa'id Khan became a devout patron of the arts of poetry and music until his death in 1534 AD. He was succeeded by his son Sultan Abdul Rashid Khan I, whose death had come in 1565 after having succeeded in repelling several attacks by the Kyrgyz in Kashgar. However his most enduring accomplishment as a Karakhan ruler was the dismanteling of the power of the Dughlats and ending their dominance and political opposition in East Turkistan Sultan Sa'id Khan's dynasty continued in Abdul Rashid's sons, first under Sultan Abdul Karim Khan in Yarkand (1565-1591 AD) and then under Sultan Muhammad Khan in Kashgar. Although formally Kashgar was considered the seat of the khanate, Yarkand was the khanate's real source of authority.

Under Muhammad Khan the khanate reached its peak of glory with its territories extending east to the edges of Ming dynasty's fronteirs, and north to the territories populated by Kyrgyz and Kazakh tribes. But after his death, a series of struggles amongst the grandsons of Abdul-Rashid Khan for ascendancy in Yarkand resulted in the assassination of Shuja-ud-Din Ahmad (1609-1619 AD) (son of Muhammad Khan). Then, Ahmad Khan (1631-1636 AD), who had briefly succeeded his uncle Abdul Latif Khan I (1619-1631 AD) was dispatched swiftly by a grandson of Abdul Rashid, and instead Abdu-llah Khan (1636-1667 AD), a son of Sultan Abdul Rahim was installed. Abdu-llah was the assigned governor of Turfan and Karashahir, the latter just north of Korla, at the time of Muhammad Khan's death.

Towards the later years of Abdu-llah Khan's reign the pressure from Kyrgyz and Kazakh tribes was mounting rapidly and the regional stability was coming under new threat from the quarrels within the Sufi Naqshbandiyah sect. The Bai Shan (Aq Taghliq - White Mountain) order and the Hei Shan (Kara Taghliq - Black Mountain) order were the two dominant religious orders of Naqshbandiyah Sufism. These designations did not refer to localities where their members lived as they were members of tribal coalitions who prided themselves with loyalty but lived throughout Mughalistan. Their affiliations were in reference to the alliances they had established with Kyrgyz or Kazakh tribes of the neighbouring mountains hence those in the vicinity of the Tian Shan Mountains were known as the 'White Mountain' order and those of the region of the Pamir Mountains as the 'Black Mountain' order. These competing parties made their alliances with the Kyrgyz and Kazakh tribes and subsidized them to fight their opponents. The motivation of the Kyrgyz or the Kazakh tribes to fight mercenary wars in bahalf of the khans rested in part on their animosity towards the Chagataid khans who had long been converted to Islam whilst the tribes saw theselves as non-Muslim sedentary populations.

Abdu-llah Khan's political circumstances were further complicated by the increased pressure from the Kalmyks in their effort to gain territorial concessions from the khanate. This led to a battle between the khanate and the Kalmyks which ended in a truce. Perhaps it should be noted here that the Kalmyks, also known as the Dzunghars, were a confederation of several pastoral nomadic tribes that included the Choros, Dorbet and Khotis tribes, collectively referred to as the Oirats.[19] They migrated from the upper Irtysh River in Siberia to the lower Volga in the early seventeenth century and established a homeland in the Altai region of western Mongolia along the borders of present-day China and Kazakhstan.

With the truce of the battle still fresh in their minds, the Kalmyks began to encourage Abdu-llah's son Yolbars to rebel against his father. During Abdu-llah's reign the Aq Taghliq had begun to challenge the power of the Kara Taghliq who had been amassing a considerable political and religious power from the time of Sultan Muhammad Khan. The political influence of the Kara Taghliq, particularly under the leadership of Muhammad Abdu-llah Khoja (for Khoja see below), had infilterated every level of life in Kashgar and Yarkand. However, from the 1620s, prior to Abdu-llah's reign, the Aq Taghliq had slowly strengthened their position under the leadership of Muhammad Yusuf Khoja, son of Khoja Ishan-i-Kalan. Muhammad, an influential leader of the Aq Taghliq with roots in Samarkand, was living in Hami and had married the daughter of the local religious leader Sayyid Jalali Khoja. Their son, born in 1626 AD, was named Idayitullah, who came to be better known as Abakh (Afaq) Khoja. In the 1630s Muhammad Yusuf Khoja with a mission to expand the Aq Taghliq influence in East Turkistan moved his family and settled in Kashgar. By the time Abdu-llah Khan's political situation was being weakened by the regional conflicts mentioned above, his son Yolbars (1667-1670 AD) was the governor of Kashgar. Under the constant encouragements by the Kalmyks (Dzungars) to rebel against his father, and in an effort to increase his own power-base, Yolbars began to patronize the Aq Taghliq in opposition to the powerful Kara Taghliq. Hence in 1667 AD, Yolbars in his bid to power rose in rebellion against his father in Yarkand and led his troops to the seat of the khanate. Abdu-llah abandoned Yarkand and escaped to Kashmir. Muhammad Abdu-llah Khoja and most of the Kara Taghliq community retreated to Aksu but their relatives left behind in Kashgar and Yarkand were put to death by Yolbars. However Yolbars' political situation deteriorated rapidly as he capitulated to renewed attacks by the Kalmyks. His demise came swiftly in 1670 AD with a successful conspiracy to assassinate him. After a short period of rule by his son Adul Latif Khan II, the succession was passed to a patron of the Kara Taghliq, Isma'il Khan (1670-1680 AD) who was the then governor of Aksu. With the demise of Yolbars the rule of Mughalistan shifted mostly into the hands of the Khojas.

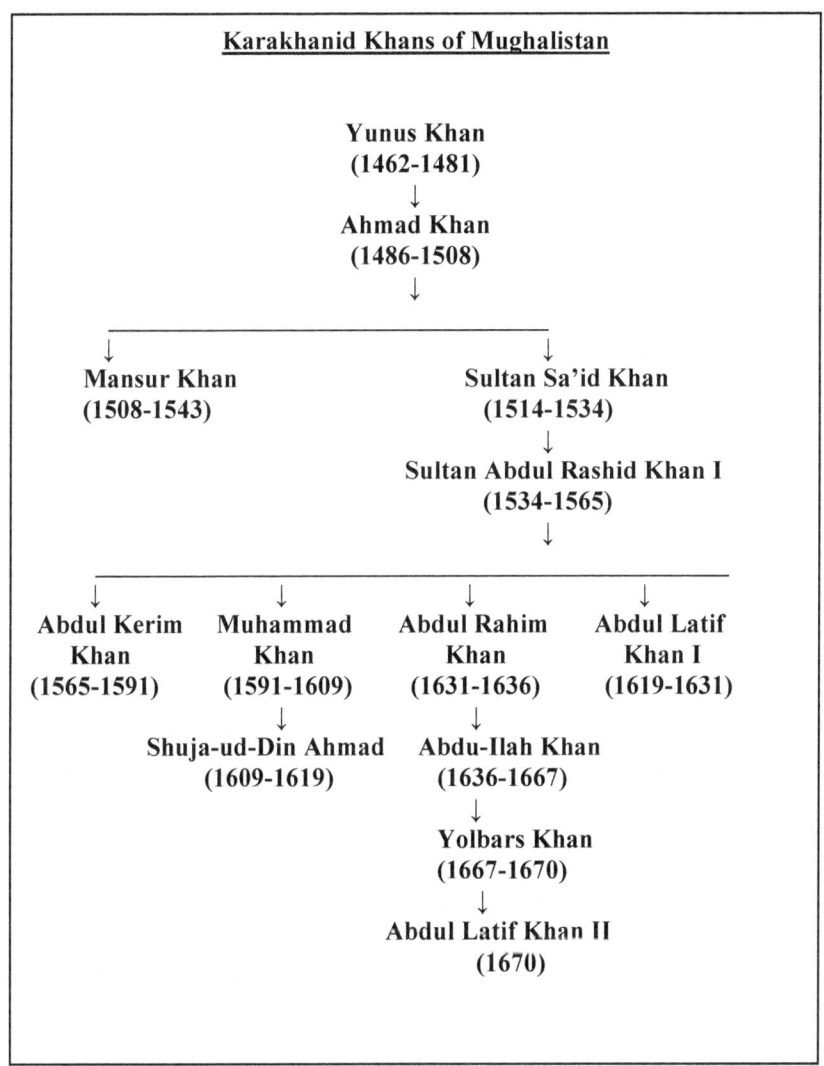

Figure 6. The lineage of Yunus Khan

The Khojas

The 'Khojas' were the influential Islamic Naqshbandiyah Sufis who secured the permanence of Islam in China. The word 'Khoja' is derived from the Persian honorary title 'Khwaja' which stood for 'Glorious Leader, or Great Master.' There have been a number of interpretations as to who was entitled to be called a 'Khoja.' One such interpretation described the khojas as those who claimed descent from the bloodline of the two grandsons of the prophet Muhammad, Hasan and Husain. They differed from the 'Sayyids' in that the latter connected their origins specifically to the bloodline of the Prophet's daughter Fatima and her husband Ali, as well as to Ali's offsring borne to him by women other than by his wife Fatima. Nevertheless, in most instances, these strict interpretations did not seem to have been followed and thus the term 'Khoja' was synoymous with 'Sayyid' although both required descent from the Prophet.

A history of the khojas written in the nineteenth century by Muhammad Sadiq traces the identity and the origins of the Khojas of East Turkistan. Muhammad Sadiq was a descendant of Caliph Uthman ibn Affan, the third successor of the prophet Muhammad. His ancetors migrated from Arabia to Iran and afterwards settled in Bhera in the Sargodha District of Punjab in India during the reign of Sultan Mahmud Ghaznavi (979-1030 AD). There the family served as religious scholars and judges to the local authorities. Sadiq's history therefore describes authoritatively that Sayyid Kamal-ud-Din Majnum, a descendant in the sixteenth generation from the Prophet's daughter Fatima, had travelled from Medina to Osh (Ush) in Ferghana (present-day Kyrgyzstan) and married the daughter of Sultan Iliq Mazi, a descendant of Sultan Satuq Bughra Khan. Kamal-ud-Din Majnum then returned with his wife to Medina where his son Sayyid Burhan-ud-Din Kilic was born, who ascended to the throne of his maternal grandfather in Osh. His son Sayyid Jalalu-ud-Din in turn fathered a son born in 1461 AD and named him Ahmad Khoja Kasani, otherwise also known as Makhdum- or Maujdum-i-Azam. He hailed from Kasan, a town in northern Ferghana near present-day Chust (Uzbekistan). Makhdum gradually gained fame as a devout saintly Muslim and a holy man who spread his faith to the frontiers of China. He married Bibica al-Kashgari who bore him two sons, Ishan-i-Kalan and Ishaq Wali. Makhdum was invited to Yarkand by Sultan Abdul-Rashid Khan (1542-1565 AD) and although Makhdum himself never seems to have accepted the invitation, he instead sent his two sons who became the vehicles for the expansion of Naqshbandiyah Sufism into East Turkistan.

Makhdum-i-Azam died in 1542 AD and today his venerated tomb is a shrine in Dahpid, a village just north of Samarkand. In memory of Makhdum, a symbolic grave of this holy man, perhaps containing an amulet from him, has become a shrine in a patch of sandy desert just outside of Khotan where many pilgrims today seeking blessings brave the blowing sands and pay homage to Makhdum's holiness. A short visit there and of its adjacent humble mosque will immediately impress upon the casual visitor or the devout pilgrim the power of his legacy.

In the remote sand-covered wildernesses of Xinjiang there are a number of traditional practices by which a shrine, as Makhdum's, is held holy and venerated. A rough wooden low fence usually surrounds the shrine and at its edge in the direction facing Mecca an arch is erected made of long tree branches symbolic of a gateway. Almost all arches have large numbers of swatches of fabric tied to them that sway in the wind. Such fragments of fabric are also tied to poles made of tree branches and stuck in the sand around the fencing adding a colourfull array of floating motions. Animal skins, fleece, feathers, skulls of sacrificed animals and various amulets fashioned from bones or wood are also commonly placed at the shrine as votive offerings. To the praying devout, these tokens of worship in the bleakness of the desert collectively create a sense of true holinees and a spiritual communion with the interred saint. A modest fenced-off mosque built of mud-bricks attached to a covered porch may also be found next to a venerated shrine, and often it will contain a few simple wooden platforms for the pilgrims to sleep or refresh from the searing heat of the summer sun.

It is not known when precisely in the sixteenth century a division had taken place among the Khojas in Transoxiana, which had resulted in one faction becoming the allies of Makhdum's elder son Ishan-i-Kalan, and another attaching themselves to the younger son Ishaq Wali. The party of Ishan belonged to the Bai Shan (Aq Taghliq - White Mountain) order of Naqshbandiyah Sufism and that of Ishaq Wali to the Hei Shan (Kara Taghliq - Black Mountain) order.

This struggle for religious ascendancy between the two brothers led the younger brother Ishaq Wali to leave his abode in Ferghana in 1622 AD and take refuge amongst the Kazakhs associated with his order Kara Taghliq many of whom were converted to Islam by Ishaq. The elder brother Ishan-i-Kalan took his father's religious authority and led his flock from Samarkand. His son Muhammad Yusuf, who lived in Hami, established his religious leadership in Kashgar during the reign of Abdu-llah Khan (1637-1667 AD) before Yusuf's son Abakh Khoja replaced his father as a major influence in the growth of Sufism in East Turkistan. Yusuf died in 1640 AD and was interred in Kashgar's Abakh Mausoleum that initially bore his name, as was described ealier.

Presently we will return to Isma'il Khan who had taken over the rule in the Tarim basin after the assassination of Yolbars in 1670. Isma'il was a descendant of Sayyid Makhdum-i-Asam from the latter's younger son Khoja Ishaq Wali. As described above, Isma'il Khan patronized the Kara Taghliq and his animosities against the Aq Taghliq is traced to the deeply rooted sibling rivalry for the leadership of Mughalistan that existed between his great grandfather Khoja Ishaq Wali and Ishaq's brother Khoja Ishan-i-Kalan, the sons of Sayyid Makhdum-i-Asam. So, it is not surprising that under Isma'il Khan a devastating persecution of the Aq Taghliq was undertaken by the Kara Taghliq throughout East Turkistan. Abakh Khoja, a distant paternal cousin of Isma'il, had now taken over the leadership of the Aq Taghliq in Kashgar from his father, Muhammad Yusuf Khoja, and was fighting for survival. In desperation, Abakh fled to Kashmir and sought the help of the Dzungars as part of his plan for a come-back.

Despite Abakh's great religious and political leadership in Kashgar and his contributions to Sufism in East Turkistan, Sufi rule of Mughalistan fell short of its political aspirations and became a victim to the incessant encroachments by the Dzungars. Under the leadership of Galdan Boshughtu (1644–1697 AD) the Dzungars' homeland was exdended from Lake Balkash eastward to the valleys of the Altai Moutains and their plans for further expansion included taking possession of the many towns of East Turkistan lying to their south, which included the oasis towns of Hami and Turfan. To this end their opportunity came when Abakh sought their help to fight and dislodge Isma'il Khan.

Galdan led a large cavalry into East Turkistan supported by Abkha and his Aq Taghliq supporters. They were met by Isma'il's son Babak Sultan who was immediately killed in an ensuing battle. The Dzungars were able to quickly occupy Kashgar and then Yarkand, respectively and took Isma'il and his family as prisoners and confined them in Ili, the Dzungar capital north of the Tian Shan Mountains. With Dzungars' great design in mind for their expansionist plans, they seemed reluctant to return their victories to Abakh and instead chose to install in Yarkand Abdul Rashid Khan II (1680-1682) of Turfan, a relation of the Chagataid khanate and a distant cousin of the Dzungars. This was not only an effort to pacify the Kara Taghliq but also fulfilled part of the Dzungar plan to occupy Turfan and hold it as a vassal territory. This, no doubt, led to a series of conflicts between Abdul Rashid and Abakh. Disenchanted and disappointed with the treatment he had received from the Dzungars, Abakh left the area for the second time. In 1682, riots and social discord amongst the residents of Yarkand forced Abdul Rashid Khan II to abandon Yarkand in favour of his brother Muhammad Amin Khan (1682-1694). Despite Muhammad Amin's efforts to re-establish authority, the increased dominance of the Dzungars led to a series of further revolts in which Muhammad Amin was killed by Abakh Khoja's loyalists. In trimuph Abakh returned to Kashgar and helped his son Yahya Khoja take control of Yarkand in 1694. But Abakh's and the Aq Taghliq's victory was short lived. Only two years later in 1696, Abakh and his son Yahya were killed in local rebellions.

Following these tragic internal conflicts in Yarkand, Abdul Rashid Khan's second youngest brother, Muhammad Mu'min took the throne in Yarkand but the powerful Aq Taghliq in Kashgar refused to acknowledge him as their leader and allied themselves with the Kyrgyz and attacked Yarkand taking Muhammad prisoner back to Kashgar. As anticipated, the Kara Taghliq turned to the Dzungars for help. However, the Dzungar system of administration generally remained unattached with their vassal states and did not interfere with their religious or cultural life. Posting of permanent troops was not the norm thus allowing the locals to conduct their own internal political affairs provided they met their obligations to pay taxes to the Dzungar khanate. Hence Muhammad Mu'min was dislodged, and the rule of East Turkistan quietly continued first under Yahya's son Khoja Ahmad and then of Ahmad's two sons Burhan-ud-Din and Khoja-i-Jihan. Nonetheless the latter two brothers continued to engage internally in their own struggles for ascenaency to rule in Yarkand until the rebellions of 1755 against the Dzungars.

Amursana (1722-1757 AD), one of the sovereign princes of the Oirats, having lost the power struggle to a rival, allied himself with the

Chinese emperor Qianlong (1736-1796 AD), the fourth emperor of the Qing (Manchu) dynasty (1644-1911 AD). He then formed a coalition force of Kalmyks and Chinese that marched into East Turkistan against the two brothers, Khoja Burhan-ud-Din and Khoja-i-Jihan. They were pursued by the Chinese General Chao Huei who captured the two brothers and sent them to Ili as prisoners. Amursana subsequently became the overlord of East Turkistan and a vassal to the Qing dynasty. But Amursana's successes were short lived. Unable to cope with the political restrictions placed upon him as a vassal to the Chinese emperor, and in pursuit of his own independence, he revolted against many of the small Chinese garrisons stationed in his territories. The two imprisoned brothers in Ili were released as they agreed to join Amursana's revolt. But after a few brief successes against a massive invasion launched by the Chinese in 1759, the revolt was decisively crushed. Burhan-ud-Din and Khoja-i-Jihan were able to make their escape and take refuge in Osh where they remained until their death. Amursana temporarily took refuge with the Kazakh and Kyrgyz tribes in northern Ferghana and finally found his way into Russia where he almost immediately died of smallpox. Thus, the year 1759 marked the end of the Dzungar power in Mughalistan and its full possession by the Qing dynasty and incorporation into the Chinese empire. .

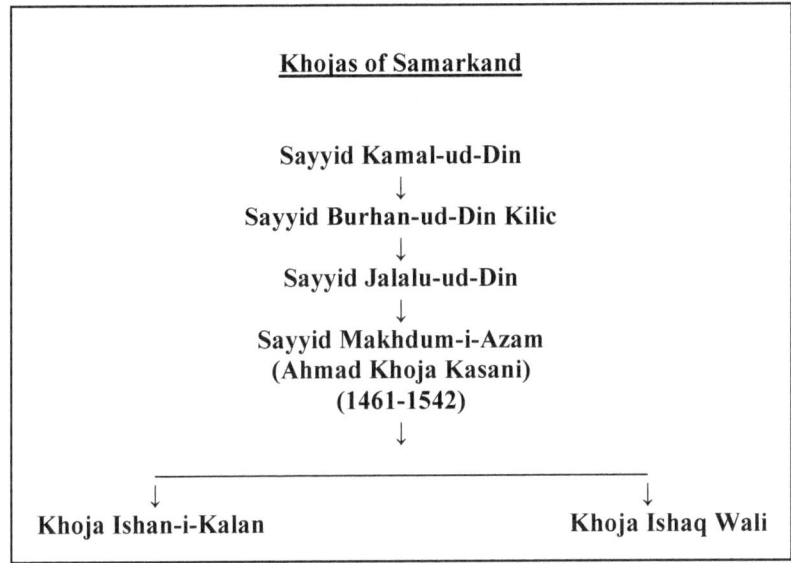

Figure 7. The lineage of Sayyid Kamal-ud-Din

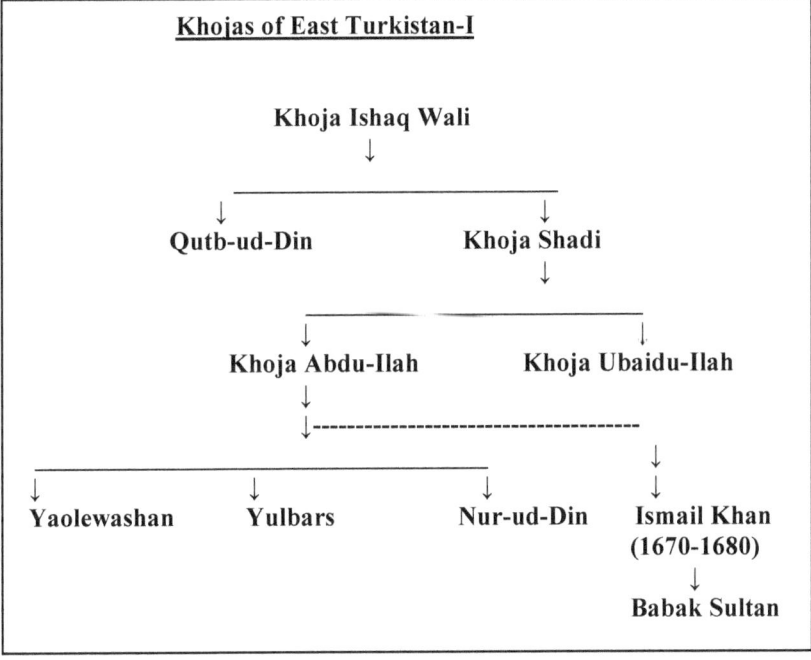

Figure 8. The lineage of Khoja Ishaq Wali

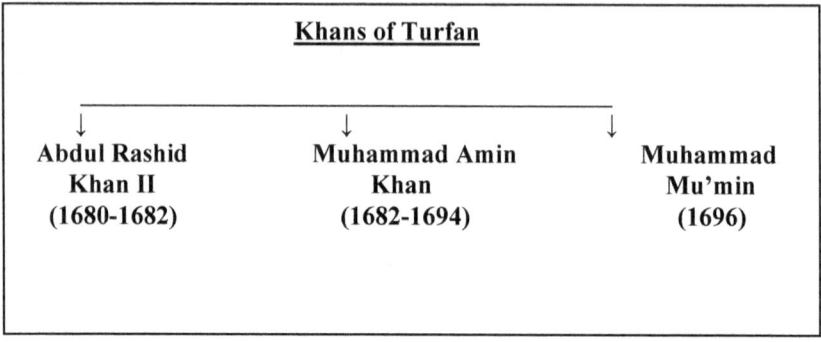

Figure 9. The last of the Chagataid khans

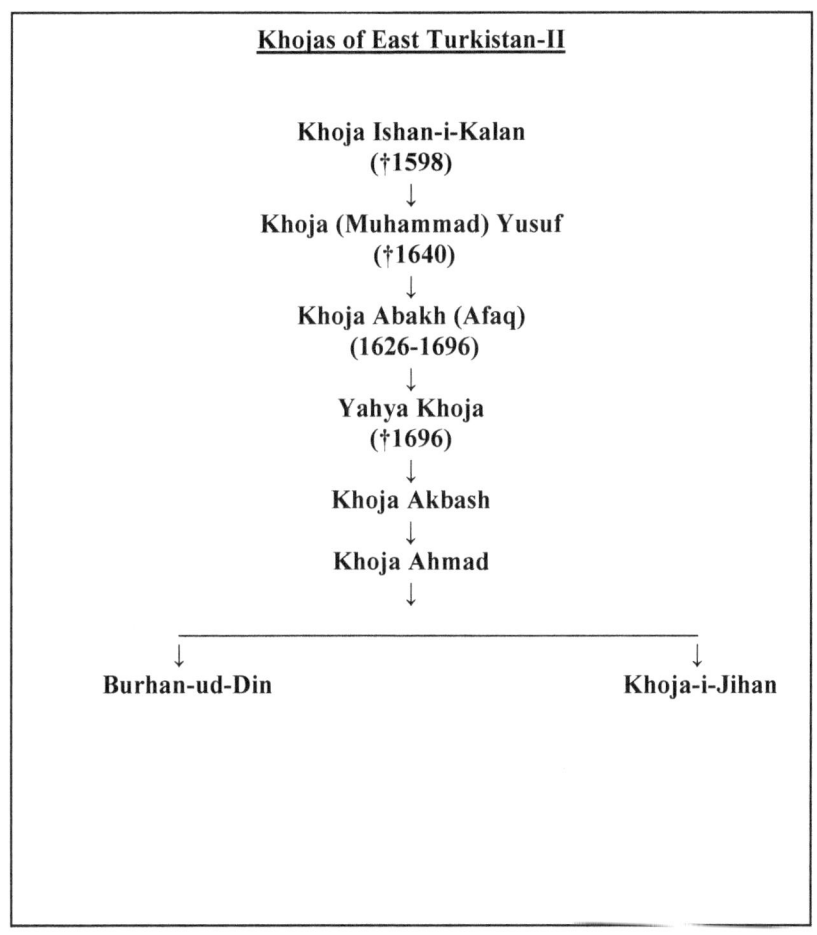

Figure 10. The lineage of Khoja Ishan-i-Kalan

References

1. Dillon, M., *China's Muslim Hui Community: Migration, Settlement and Sects.* Curzon Press, London (1999).
2. Lipman, J. N., *Familiar Strangers: A History of Muslims in Northwest China.* University of Washington Press, Seattle, Washington (1997).
3. Gladney, D. C., Muslim Tombs and Ethnic Folklore: Charters for Hui Identity. *J. of Asian Studies*, vol. 46 (3), pp. 495-532 (1987).
4. Leslie, D., *Islam in traditional China: A Short History to 1800.* Canberra (1986).
5. Israeli, R., *Islam in China.* Lexington Books, Lanham, Maryland (2002).
6. Gladney, D., The Salafiyya Movement in Northwest China: Islamic Fundamentalism among the Muslim Chinese? In *Muslim Diversity: Local Islam in Global Context.* L. Manger (ed.), Curzon Press, London (1989).
7. cf. Dillon, M. (1999).
8. Gladney, D. C., *Muslim Chinese: ethnic nationalism in the People's Republic.* Harvard University Press, Cambridge, Massachusetts: (1996).
9. Rossabi, M., Muslim in Central Asian Revolts. In *From Ming to Ch'ing Conquests, Region, and Continuity in Seventeenth-century China.* J. D. Spence and J. E. Wills, Jr. (eds.), Yale University Press, New Haven, Connecticut (1979).
10. Mackerras, C. and Clarke, M. (eds.), *China, Xinhiang and Central Asia: History, transition and crossborder interaction into the 21st century.* Routledge, London (2009).
11. Bugra, Muhammad A., *Sĕrki Turkistan tārihi.* Ofset Reproductions, Ankara, Turkey (1987)
12. Gladney, D. C., The Ethnogenesis of the Uighur. *Central Asian Survey,* vol. 9 (1), pp.1-28 (1990).
13. Mackerras, C. (ed. & trans.), *The Uighur Empire according to the T'ang Dynastic Histories: a study in Sino-Uyghur relations 744–840.* University of South Carolina Press, Columbia, South Carolina (1972).
14. Legg, S., *The Barbarians of Asia.* Dorset Press, New York (1970).
15. Shaw, E., The History of the Khojas of East Turkistan. *Supplement to the J. of the Asiatic Society of Bengal,* vol. 66 (I0) (1897).
16. Kim, H., The Early History of the Moghul Nomads: The Legacy of the Chagatai Khanate. In *The Mongol Empire and Its Legacy.* R. Amitai-Preiss and D. Morgan (eds.), Brill, Leiden (1998).
17. Manz, B. F., *The Rise and Rule of Tamerlane.* Cambridge University Press, Cambridge (1989).

18. Ross, E. D. (trans.), *A History of the Moghuls of Central Asia: being the Tarikh-i-Rashidi of Mirza Muhammad Haidar, Dughlát.* Curzon Press, London (1972).
19. Guchinova, E. B. L., *The Kalmyks.* D. C. Lewis (trans.), Routledge, London (2006).

Treasures of the Silk Road

Group 4

66. A typical residential street in Cherchen with the occasional Muslim prayer hall identified with the semicircular portico flanked by miniature minarets topped with the familiar crescent of Islam.

67. Uyghur woman in Cherchen.

68. Entrance to a mosque and its enclosed courtyard adjacent to the shrine of Sayyid Makhdum-i-Azam in a patch of the Taklamakan desert in the outskirts of Khotan.

69. The fenced-off shrine of Sayyid Makhdum-i-Azam.

70. Town Centre of Yarkand. The portico of the ruins of the Jama Mosque built by Yunus Khan in the fifteenth century dominates the town centre.

71. A group of Uyghur men passing the day on a crisp sunny January morning seated near the entrance to the Altunluk Mosque and to its adjacent royal cemetery in Yarkand.

72. The mausoleum of Sultan Sa'id Khan in the cemetery of Altunluk Mosque in Yarkand.

73. The draped tomb of Sultan Sa'id Khan within his mausoleum bearing the inscription in Arabic script: '*In the Name of Allah, the Merciful and the Benevolent. Tomb of Sultan Sa'id Khan.*'

74. The tomb of Queen Ammanisahan near Altunluk Mosque in Yarkand.

75. The calligraphy in Arabic script on the tomb of Queen Ammanisahan: *'Compiler of the Muqams, Poetess Ammanisahan.'*

76. Huai Sheng Mosque at.56 Guangta Lu, Yuexiu District, Guangzhou.

Islam in China

77. A Yuan dynasty (1279-1368 AD) Islamic tombstone removed from the ancient cemetery in central Gunagzhou when the cemetery was relocated to the Xin Shi District of Guangzhou in 1957. It is preserved at the Huai Sheng Mosque in Guangzhou.

78. The Islamic cemetery at Xin Shi District of Guangzhou where the remains of 2,000 corpses were re-interred after their exhumation from central Guangzhou in 1957. Although most of the epitaphs are in Chinese pictographs, some are identified in Arabic script for example as husband and wife.

79. Three undated Islamic tombstones in Xin Shi cemetery with epitaphs entirely in Arabic script. All three headers proclaim: *In the Name of Allah, the Merciful and the Benevolent,* and their identities are given from left; Muhammad Zamn, al-Sharief Kharyani and Mujar Khan.

80. Glass-encased Xi'an stelae of Nestorian Christianity (635 AD) in Beilin Forest of Stone Museum, Xi'an, Shaanxi, province.

81. Gilded bronze Christian cross with Abrahamic motif seen on the left and right transepts. Eastern Han dynasty (25-220 AD) unearth in Gangu County, Gansu province.

Islam in China

82. The 'Christian Church of Our Saviour' at 184 Wanfu Lu, Yuexiu District, Guangzhou, Guangdong province.

83. A Chinese mother and child and a Bible inside Zion Christian Church at 392 Renmin Zhong Lu, Liwan District, Guangzhou.

Treasures of the Silk Road

Chapter Twelve

Gnostic Religions in China

In this final chapter a few of the religions which have had a lesser impact on the development of the ancient history of China will be reviewed.

Apocryphal texts of early Christian writings belong to a group of doctrines known as Gnosticism[1] which describe the human condition as a struggle between light and darkness, or otherwise between good and evil. Manichaean teachings, for example, attempted to explain how the soul which is of divine origin came to reside in the body matter of man which is evil. This view emphasized that the human body was intrinsically evil and therefore cannot be the creation of God. The teachings of a number of the so-called Christian heretics of the early centuries subscribed to this dogma. They included, for example, the Paulicians and the Bogomils in Byzantium and the Cathars (Albegensians) in central Europe. But such dogmas were not only the fundamentals of early Christian Gnostic teachings, but were also the common denominator of several non-Christian mainstream religions, such as Zoroastrianism[2,3] in Iran and the Greco-Roman Mystery Religions in Europe.[4] However, none of the Gnostic religions which reached the orient was able to permanently invade the ethos of the Far Eastern populations who were imbued with the core tenets of Shamanism, Buddhism or Confucianism. Even the Nestorians, who had enjoyed widespread successes with their missions as we have seen, were obliged to use syncretism in their efforts in order to assuage the Chinese and the nomadic tribes into accepting the Nestorian concepts of Christianity. This was the same approach, ironically, employed by their co-religionists, the Manichaean missions, who used syncretism to extreme limits. To illustrate this point, the myth of the Buddha Mani as an avatar (reincarnation) of the Chinese sage Lao Tse was used to present Manichaeism as a form of Buddhism or as Taoism depending on circumstances. Yet, not surprisingly, the Nestorian as well as the Manichaean successes have, for all intended purposes, evaporated from China without much significant legacy. It must be said, however, that the Manichaean achievements during the sixth and seventh centuries prior to the arrival of the Nestorians in Central Asia were prodigious despite the pressures their evangelists had to endure. They became the unprecedented recipients of praise for their success in having a nation declare Manichaeism as its state religion (see below). Many of their generations, unlike the Nestorians, struggled without a centralized political or financial backup in the face of diplomacy and deep-rooted religious rivalry. Yet, despite all the glory and pomp, the Manichaean golden era lost its luster in the fourteenth century contemporaneous with the decline of the Nestorian Church in China. Astonishingly, it had survived in the East longer than the Nestorian Church. No doubt, it is appropriate for us at this point to review the Manichaean Church in the East and explore its modes of survival despite the ordeals it withstood against severe Zoroastrian and Buddhist persecutions.

Manichaeism

> When I was four and twenty years old, in the year in which Dariadaxir [Ardashir], the King of Persia, subjected the city of Hatra, and in which Sapores [Shapur], his son assumed the mighty diadem, in the month of Pharmuthi on the eighth day according to the moon, the most blessed Lord had compassion on me and called me to his grace and immediately sent to me from there my Syzygos... He remembered and passed on all the noble counsels which came from our Father and from the Good Right which is from the beginning.[5]

The above words regarding the calling to a personal divine revelation were spoken by a man named Mani (216-276 AD) who founded a new religion at a time when the sphere of influence of the Persian Sasanian dynasty was expanding. The new religion which bears his name, Manichaeism, found widespread acceptance in the West, in Mesopotamia and especially in Iran. In the latter part of the fourth century the new faith established a stronghold in eastern Iran and from there it was ultimately carried forward along the Silk Road to Central Asia. In a manner quite analogous to the manner Nestorian Christianity was conveyed to China, Manichaeism likewise entered China through the Tarim basin after crossing the lands of Sogdiana, Ferghana and Bactria.

Mani was born in Ctesiphon, Babylonia, when Mesopotamia was part of the Sasanid Empire. He was not of Babylonian origin but of Iranian descent. His parents belonged to the religious sect Elchasaites whose Judaeo-Christian writings significantly influenced Mani's ideas of good and evil. His father, Patik, was a native of Hamadan, and his mother, Maryam (Mary), came from the princely family of the Iranian Ardashir dynasty. The biographical notes of the tenth century Muslim scholars, Muhammad ibn Is'haq al-Nadim of Baghdad and Muhammad ibn Ahmad al-Biruni of Khwarazm, relate that Mani had received his divine revelations from his Syzygos, a word synonymous with 'kindred spirit' who brought Mani the divine gift of self-realization thus making him a Gnostic spiritualist – one with divine knowledge and liberating insight (somewhat similar to the Buddha's Enlightenment). Mani was educated in the Judaeo-Christian traditions and was well aware that Zoroaster was the prophet of the Persians in his native land of Mesopotamia and that the Buddha was the prophet of the Indians. Thus his religious inclinations had led him to formulate the theological basis of a new Church that would unite the beliefs of all the peoples of his time, and he presented his theology as divine revelations brought to mankind through him - the messenger of God.[6] He wrote:

> Wisdom and deeds have always from time to time been brought to mankind by the messengers of God. So in one age they have been brought by the messenger called Buddha, to India, in another by Zaradust to Persia, in another by Jesus to the West. Thereupon this revelation has come down and this prophecy has appeared in the form of myself, Mani, the envoy of the true God in the Land of Babylon.[7]

In the years that followed his death, Mani's new religion of the struggle between good and evil in which good will ultimately triumph spread with extraordinary speed and reached Rome in 280 AD but within two decades it was to face severe persecutions by Rome and ultimately vanished from the Roman Empire by the end of the sixth century. In the course of a visit to Egypt in 302 AD, Emperor Diocletian had received a disturbing report from the proconsul of Africa concerning Manichaean activities in areas within his jurisdiction. Diocletian's alarm rested in the fact that the Manichaean cult operating in Egypt was Persian in origin who's King Shapur I (240-270 AD) had dealt the Roman armies some of their worst defeats in the east. Diocletian's response to the proconsul was immediate and had the full force of an imperial decree:

We have heard that the Manichaeans, concerning whom your Carefulness has written to our Serenity, have set up new and hitherto unheard of sects in opposition to the older creeds so that they might cast out the doctrines vouchsafed to us in the past by divine favour for the benefit of their own depraved doctrine. They have sprung forth very recently like new and unexpected monstrosities among the race of the Persians – a nation still hostile to us – and have made their way into our empire, where they are committing many outrages, disturbing the tranquility of the people and even inflicting grave damage to the civic communities: our fear is that with the passage of time, they will endeavour, as usually happens, to infect the modest and tranquil Roman people of an innocent nature with the damnable customs and the perverse laws of the Persians as with the poison of a malignant serpent... Those who introduce new sects or religions unknown to reason by which the minds of men were perverted should be punished. Those who are of high status shall be exiled while those who are of low status shall be executed.[8]

Expansion to the East

Manichaean movements eastward into the heartland of Iran and Central Asia began when Mani secured the friendship of Peroz; the governor of Khurasan and brother of King Shapur I. Through Peroz, Mani obtained the permission of King Shapur to preach freely throughout the king's empire. This was a great opportunity for Mani to expand because the eastern parts of the Sasanian Empire had been virtually unexposed to Judaeo-Christian teachings. Mani proceeded with his mission accompanied by his closest disciple Mar Ammo who not only knew the language and the Parthian script but was also well connected with the Parthian aristocracy in the east. Mar Ammo's assistance was complemented by the fact that much of the Central Asian territories under the suzerainty of the Sasanians remained substantially independent. Although Mani, early in his mission, made substantial progress in gaining converts to his faith (which included the conversion of Peroz), the degree of Iranian royal favour he enjoyed during Shapur's reign was beginning to deteriorate. His ardent supporter King Shapur died in 272 AD and the reign of his successor Hormizd I was indeed short-lived (272-273 AD). The successor to the diadem was Shapur's eldest son Vahram I who yielded to his Zoroastrian hierarchy's demands to limit Manichaean activities. The Zoroastrians regarded the Manichaeans as heretics because the latter in the course of their missionary work had adopted some Zoroastrian concepts and names of deities into their religious teachings. Mani had travelled far and wide, and after forty years of intense missionary work in places as far away as India and Turkistan, he returned to Ctesiphon to confront the challenges of the Zoroastrian resistance and seek a renewed royal favour from the new king. Instead, Mani was imprisoned and tortured to death.

The severe persecutions of the Manichaeans in Sasanian Iran that followed the death of Mani in 276 AD gave rise to mass exodus of Manichaeans eastward to lands as far away as the valleys north of the Oxus River. This pattern of migrations continued sporadically for many centuries. For example, although the Arabs with their successful eastward military campaigns into Sasanian territories were at first tolerant of non-Muslims, the caliphate of al-Muqtadir (908-932 AD) was less sympathetic.[9] Thus the flow of Manichaeans eastward from Mesopotamia was generally a continuous process. But in the third century, through the evangelical efforts of many Manichaean missionaries including Mar Ammo, the faith became well established in Transoxiana and brought the Manichaeans into intimate contact with the Sogdians. The Sogdians in the third century had already established their chain of trading colonies along the Silk Road that stretched form Merv to the western frontiers of the Middle Kingdom. Sogdian contacts with the Middle Kingdom was quite extensive at this time which provided lucrative trade in the sale of silk in exchange for horses that the Chinese needed for their cavalry. It was inevitable that the Manichaean religion would soon find its way into China. However, this process of the transmission of the faith into China had to wait until the sixth century before the Middle Kingdom would hear of the teachings of Mani. As was discussed in Chapter 3, the period from the third to the sixth centuries Sogdiana was pillaged, first by the Huns in the third century followed by the Hephthalites in the fifth century. The Mongolian Turks (Tatars) were next to plunder Sogdiana in the sixth century. These events had brought Sogdian trade along the Silk Road to a virtual standstill. The success of the Tatars was facilitated through the support they received from the Sasanians who were concerned that the Hephthalites might eventually reach the Sasanian bastion of Merv.

It was amongst the Sogdians who traded from oasis to oasis in the Tarim basin that the displaced Manichaeans found some measure of security and ardent proselytes. The resumption of secure and safe trade along the Silk Road in the sixth century lessened the pressure on Manichaean plight and substantially aided their enthusiasm for the eastward spread of their religion. The Sogdian language came to be used by the Manichaeans alongside Persian in their religious literature, and, in anticipation of proselytizing the Chinese, the Manichaeans began to assimilate and adopt many features of Buddhism. The use of Buddhist phrases, concepts and motifs for forging ahead with their syncretic teachings became frequent in Manichaean writings. Thus in their literature, Jesus was referred to as 'the Buddha Jesus' or 'the Messiah Buddha.' Also, Jesus, after his crucifixion and death, was described as having attained the highest transcendental state, 'Nirvana.'

In essence, the first converts to Manichaeism in its push towards China were the Tatars of the frontier settlements who became the essential link between the Manichaeans and the Turkic tribes of the Tarim basin. The Sogdian traders in these circumstances were indispensable because they were multilingual, Khotanese in particular, and served as interpreters not only in business transactions but also in the dissemination of religious literature. Once the Tarim basin was reached, contacts with the Chinese would be facilitated through the basin's inhabitants who were expected to be more fluent in Chinese. In this manner the Manichaean traditions have implied that the entry of their religion into the Middle Kingdom was inaugurated by the arrival in China of a *Mozak* (teacher) during the reign of Emperor Gaozong (649-683 AD) of the Tang dynasty. However, the Manichaean fortunes were soon to face severe difficulties. After the emperor's death the throne was usurped by his talented wife Empress Wu Zetian (690-705 AD). However, as the Chinese social hierarchy did not recognize a woman as head of state, Wu Zetian took pleasure in accepting an audience with Manichaean teachers and asked them to explain their scriptures hoping she might find a justification for her role as a female ruler. She had earlier failed to produce such a justification from Buddhist scriptures and in doing so had alienated many of the royal court's senior monks. Despite this, Wu Zetain was determined to rule with an iron fist and it was inevitable that after her death the Manichaeans would be barred from receiving any favours from the royal court. And so it was; and included limiting their religious activities. The Buddhist monks of the royal court who had harboured more than a decade of vehement resentment and animosity against the Manichaeans convinced the successor of Empress Wu, Emperor Xuanzong (712-756 AD) that limiting the rights of the Manichaeans among the indigenous population would isolate the dangerous foreigners and prevent them from perverting and adulterating the sacred Buddhist doctrines. Thus, the emperor's edict addressing these concerns was decreed in 732 AD:

> The doctrine of Mo-mo-ni is basically a perverse belief and fraudulently assumes to be a school of Buddhism and will therefore mislead the masses. It deserves to be strictly prohibited. However since it is the indigenous religion of the Western Barbarians and other foreigners, its followers will not be punished if they practice it among themselves.[10]

Transmission of Manichaeism by the Uyghurs

As described previously, the court of Emperor Xuanzong was beset with political unrest and frontier wars. Furthermore, the An Lushan rebellion had prompted the emperor to seek assistance from the First Uyghur Empire whose predominantly Buddhist tribes were at home from the pasturelands south of Lake Baikal in north-central Mongolia to Balasaghun in the valleys of the western Tian Shan Mountains. With the Uyghurs' assistance the emperor succeeded in quelling the rebellion and liberating his capital Chang'an and the historical eastern capital Luoyang. But the effects of the rebellion on the royal court had been debilitating leading to Xuanzong's abdication and death in Chengdu. Hence his edict was unlikely to have been rigidly enforced. Those who had greeted the Uyghur armies which had helped quell the rebellion included scores of Manichaean priests and laymen; they immediately impressed upon the commanding Uyghur khan named MuoYu the virtues of Manichaeism. Dazzled and bewildered by the priests' enthusiastic description of their faith, the khan was quick to accept the faith on behalf of his people and in him Manichaeism found the support of the highest reliable political brotherhood hitherto denied to it in China. The narrative of Khan Muo Yu's conversion is inscribed on the famous trilingual stelae in Balasaghun on the river Orkhon in which Manichaeism is praised for its positive influence on the Uyghur people:

> ...who previously practiced the abnormal custom of blood sacrifices but now changed into a people of vegetarians, and whose state which indulged in excessive killing into a nation which beheld righteousness.

It was no secret the Uyghur-backed Manichaean activities deep in

Chinese soil were a symbol of foreign imposition and a constant reminder to the Chinese of their military weakness. Therefore the collapse of the First Uyghur Empire in 840 AD at the hands of the Yenisei Kyrgyz was a welcome opportunity for the Middle Kingdom to take a renewed and a decisive action not only against the Manichaeans but also against the followers of all non-native belief systems that included the Nestorians, Zoroastrians and Buddhists. The native Chinese social philosophies of Confucius and Lao Tse were the paramount guiding principles of Chinese culture and civilization. Presently, the reigning Emperor Wuzong (840-846 AD) succumbed to the power of the Taoist priests who demanded the suppression of their Buddhist rivals and in doing so set a pogrom in motion against all foreign influences. The persecutions were intensified in the late spring of 843 AD and with the emperor's Edict of 845; large-scale killings of priests occurred during which some three thousand priests lost their lives:

> An imperial edict was issued, ordering the Manichaean priests of the Empire to be killed. Their heads are to be shaved and they are to be dressed in Buddhist robes and are to be killed looking like Buddhist *sramana.*[11]

But, as Manichaeism had been declared the quasi religion of the Uyghur people who had helped the Tang dynasty in its hour of need, the dynasty now found itself obliged to become more sympathetic to the needs of the Manicheans within China. Consequently, the Manichaeans secured the necessary permission to establish several temples deep in the Yangtze river basin and in this manner Manichaeism was introduced into south China and thrived there from the tenth to the end of the thirteenth century. The central Manichaean activities formally conducted from the large mostly Buddhist cities of the north were now based in a number of the coastal cosmopolitan cities, such as Quanzhou (Zaytun) in Fujian province and Ningbo in Zhejiang province.[12] There, the Manichaeans took advantage of the eclectic Taoist traditions prevelant in the eastern populations of China. Taoist teachings, which were found to manifest far greater degree of doctrinal diversity than Buddhism had contained in the west, allowed the Manichaeans to quickly assimilate Taoist dogmas into their own teachings and offer them as the Manichaean 'Religion of Light.' Often mistaken for a form of Taoist sect, the Manichaeans became the beneficiaries of royal favours from the members of the Song dynasty and, from a pragmatic point of view, their places of worship were often mistakenly seen as Taoist temples.

Manichaeism maintained a presence in south China well into the sixteenth century. They orchestrated an approach to evangelism that narrowed the cultural and the ideological divides, to some extent deceptively, between the Chinese and the Manichaean ways of life. Their impact on the Chinese social fabric was more fundamental than that of the Nestorians or the Zoroastrians which were quite separately viewed as the religions of foreign lands. Manichaeism, on the other hand, had gained the accolade of being the only one of the three foreign faiths to have enjoyed a more lasting presence in China.

Manichaean Literary and Artistic Legacy

The study of the history of Manichaeans in China underwent a renaissance in the early decades of the twentieth century as a result of discoveries made in Dunhuang's Thousand Buddhas Caves and also in Turfan (East Turkistan) by three European archaeologists; British explorer Sir Aurel Stein, French Sinologist Paul Pelliot and German archaeologist Albert von Le Coq. In 1907 Aurel Stein discovered a large hoard of Manichaean texts along with many thousands of scrolls written in Buddhist script which were sealed in the small library (Cave 17) at Dunhuang. This was followed by the discoveries of Paul Pelliot whose collection of manuscripts from the same small library included religious discourses on the rules governing the organization of the Manichaean sect, hymns in praise of Mani and a compendium of the teachings of the sect. Pelliot, being appreciative of the scope of the documents held in the cave, took advantage of his time and selected texts in Chinese, Tibetan, Khotanese, Sogdian and Uyghur, which were safely transported to Paris before the Chinese authorities ordered the closure of the caves to foreign expeditions. One manuscript in particular, interestingly, shed light on the myth of the Buddha Mani mentioned above. It purported the reincarnation of Lao Tsi as Mo-mo-ni. In similar expeditions, the German Le Coq reached Turfan in 1907 and collected Manichaean literature relating to the history of the sect.[13] He then moved to Bezeklik Thousand Buddha Caves where he found wall frescoes carved into the soft cliffs largely untouched for centuries. He removed many artifacts and frescoes and had them shipped to Berlin only to be destroyed or badly damaged by the bombing of Berlin in the Second World War.

As would be expected, essentially all the recovered fragments of manuscripts and miniature Manichaean art from East Turkistan have religious motifs.[14] The texts of the manuscripts were written in Middle Persian, Parthian, Sogdian, Uyghur, Tocharian and Bactrian. The miniatures depicted high priests surrounded by Manichaean clergy clad in all-white monastic robes and with headgears that reflected their ecclesiastical ranking. Some of the miniatures depicted rows of laymen distinguished by their high conical black hats. But one miniature in the German collection which has raised a great deal of controversy depicts a high ranking Manichaean priest in full vestment kneeling before a man in full armour accompanied by three attendants. There are also several Manichaean laymen standing to the left of the priest. The most striking aspect of this miniature is that its background contains the images of the Hindu god Ganesha and those of the Hindu trinity, Vishnu, Brahma and Shiva. Many interpretations of this miniature are possible but most likely it was intended to be a record of paying homage to the Mughals of northern India whose Turkic ancestors of the Tarim basin, the Uyghurs, were instrumental in preserving Mani's religion.

Although Manichaeism became extinct by the end of the sixteenth century, the artistic legacy of its followers has left us their murals and miniatures which have allowed us to reconstruct various aspects of its colourful history. By the time of the Mongol conquest of the Tarim basin in the mid thirteenth century, Manichaeism was already in its twilight years. The majority of the areas inhabitants had remained Buddhist but also the Mongols introduced Islam, which soon became the predominant religion of the region that remains so to the present.

Zoroastrianism in China

The first inklings of the manner of transmission of Zoroastrianism into China were extracted from a collection of materials held by the Palace Museum in Beijing which had been first discovered in Luoyang and Anyang in the 1920s.[15] The Beimang Shan area of Luoyang in particular was known for its high concentration of ancient tombs which had been a chronic target for grave robbers and criminals causing significant historic losses from the local heritage. In an attempt to safeguard the history of the region, the first director of the museum, Ma Heng (1881-1955 AD) had begun systematically making rubbings of images and their inscriptions existing in Luoyand and Anyang which for the most part were related to the history of the Jin dynasty. This dynasty had its roots in China's frontier barbarian Tuoba tribe; they were the descendants of the Xianbei people from the north and northeast who soon after their settlement in China had adopted the mainstream culture of the central plains and ruled from their capital in Luoyang. In 1999 while catalouging the massive number of rubbings bequeathed to the museum by Ma Heng, a staff member named Shi Anchang had the keen eye to notice the monuments associated with the Jin tombs were embellished with images of haloed deities, fire altars and winged horses. Similar observations later emerged from studies of tombs of the Northern Wei dynasty, of the Liang dynasty and of the Northern Qi dynasty tombs in Anyang. The relevance of the images of the haloed deities, the fire altars and the winged horses was that they were all manifestations of Iranian and Central Asian Zoroastrian motifs. They are quite similar in their artistic rendition to arrangements seen in Persian miniatures and in the Persian Book of Kings. This realization confirmed for the first time the previously speculated manner with which Zoroastrianism must have been transmitted into China. There have been other more recent discoveries in China bearing similar motifs. In 1999, near the city of Taiyuan, in Shanxi province archaeologists uncovered a Sui dynasty (581-618 AD) tomb that held a marble sarcophagus with inscriptions describing the deceased as a Sogdian chieftain named Yu Hong who had settled in China during the Sui dynasty and died in 592 AD. There were also the spectacular uncovering of two other tombs both discovered in Chang'an, the first in 2000 of a Sogdian priest named An Jia, and the second in 2003 of a Sogdian landlord named Shi who had lived during the Northern Zhou dynasty (557-581 AD). It has become clear therefore that Zoroastrianism was brought and practiced in China by immigrants of Iranian stock from Central Asia, in particular, by Sogdians who had settled in the Middle Kingdom as far east as Luoyang, the traditional centre of Chinese autocracy. Furthermore, the presence of these immigrants in China in the sixth century was later reinforced in the seventh century by the arrival of the fleeing nobles and their followers from the disintegrated Sasanian court in the face of the conquering Arabs, alluded to in various parts of this book.

Zoroastrianism (known in China as Xianjiao) was one of the two Iranian religions which had based its dogmas on the cosmic dualistic relationship between light and darkness and good versus evil.[16] It was founded a millennium before the birth of Jesus by the prophet Zoroaster (also known as Zarathustra) who exalted the uncreated creator he called Ahura Mazda, hence the usage of Mazdaism synonymously with Zoroastrianism. The central physical feature of the Zoroastrian religious practice was the Fire Altar which signified not only the good light of the world but also as the source of life-giving warmth. Their pantheon included a host of lesser gods through whom the creation of Ahura Mazda was to be revealed to humanity. The opposing force of darkness was the devil Ahriman symbolizing evil in opposition to the forces of good.[17]

Zoroastrianism was the long-standing state religion of the pre-Islamic Iranian people.[18] It received vast support from the ancient Iranian dynasties which gave the faith a heightened state of prestige. But the religion suffered a set-back at the time of the invasions by Alexander the Great and much later by the Arab conquest of Iran of the seventh centruy, which decimated Zoroastrianism to virtual extinction.[19] What survived of the faith initially took refuge in the Iranian vassalages in Central Asia but soon the Arabs were there to force the faith flee further east and south-east into China. The fleeing Zoroastrians were neither experienced in evangelical work nor did their religion encouraged evangelism. They made no attempts to win Chinese converts, and no Zoroastrian literature was produced in Chinese. Hence the practice of Zoroastrianism in its waning centuries particularly in China remained limited to the expatriated Iranians. Their ensuing unavoidable incestuous practices made the sect's situation even more untenable. Also, because of their limited numbers, they sustained the greatest loss under the persecutions of Emperor Xuanzong's decree of 732 AD. This hastened the demise of Zoroastrianism in China when it finally came as a result of Emperor Wuzong's decree of 845 AD.[20]

References

1. King, C. W., *Gnostics and their Remains Ancient and Medieval*. Bell and Daldy, London (1998).
2. Boyce, N. E. M., *A History of Zoroastrianism*. Vol. 1 (Handbuch der Orientalistik Series). Brill, Leiden (1975).
3. Boyce, N. E. M., *A History of Zoroastrianism*. Vol. 2 (Handbuch der Orientalistik Series). Brill, Leiden (1982).
4. Angus, S., *The Mystery Religions: A Study in the Religious Background of Early Christianity*. Courier Dover Publications, New York (1975).
5. Lieu, S. N. C., *Manichaeism in the Later Roman Empire and Medieval China: A Historical Survey*. Manchester University Press, Manchester, p. 5 (1985).
6. Widengren, G., *Mani and Manichaeism*. Weidenfeld and Nicholson, London (1965).
7. *Cf* Lieu, S. N. C., p. 60.
8. Ibid, p. 91.
9. Ibrahim, M., Religious inquisition as social policy: the persecution of the Zanadiqah in the early Abbasid Caliphate. In *Arab Studies Quarterly*, vol. 16, p. 5 (1994).
10. *Cf* Lieu, S. N. C., p. 190.
11. Ibid, p. 197.
12. Zhuang, W. J., *Quanzhou Monijiao Chutan (Tentative studies on Manichaeism at Quanzhou*. In Journal of Studies on World Religions, vol. 3, pp. 72-82, Beijing (1983).
13. Chao, H., New evidence of Manichaeaism in Asia. A description of some recently discovered Manichaean temples in Turfan. In *Monumenta Serica*, no. 44, pp. 267-315 (1996).
14. Haetel, H., *Along the ancient silk routes: Central Asian art from the West Berlin State Museums : an exhibition lent by the Museum fur Indische Kunst, Staatliche State Museen Preussischer Kulturbesitz, Berlin, Federal Republic of Germany*. The Metropolitan Museum of Art, New York, 1982.
15. Shi, A. C., Fire Altars and Avian Deities as Sacrificial Officiants. Forbidden City Publishing House, Beijing (2004).
16. Runciman, S., *The Medieval Manichee: a study of the Christian dualist heresy*. Cambridge University Press, Cambridge (1947).
17. Boyce, N. E. M., *Zoroastrians: Their Religious Beliefs and Practices*. Routledge, London (1979).
18. Dhalla, M. N., *History of Zoroastrianism*. Oxford University Press, New York (1938).

19. Lieu, S. N. C., *Manichaeism in the Later Roman Empire and Medieval China: A Historical Survey*. Manchester University Press, Manchester, p.191 (1985).
20. Zaehner, R. C., *The Dawn and Twilight of Zoroastrianism*. Phoenix Press, London (1961).

Epilogue

The emergence of a centralized authority that ruled China's Middle Kingdom from the third to the seventh centuries had made the control of the silk trade routes a state priority. The constant flow of silk and luxury goods passing through the Western Regions represented wealth and also a conduit by which strategic advantages could be gained over the various tribal insurgencies that constantly threatened the stability and security of the Middle Kingdom. The silk trade was in many ways equivalent in value to that involving gold and precious stones thus often victorious troops after their successful battles were rewarded with silk. Unlike gold, silk offered many tantalizing benefits to the traveling traders. Silk was unique in its thinness, translucency and durability. It was light and usually produced in bright colours of red, blue, yellow and green. These qualities of silk had made it the fabric of choice for the making of ceremonial dresses, ritual garments and burial capes; it thus enjoyed a special significance in many cultural traditions. We can safely assume that the basis for the term 'Silk Road' in use conventionally since 1877 rests in the context of silk's prominence in social perspectives and not for the Road's exlusive use for the trade of silk. The 'Road' was characterized by a multitude of activities that included a wide spectrum of commercial, cultural, artistic and religious aspects.

Although the traditional Silk Road mercantile movements across the Western Regions had mostly ceased by the early thirteenth century with the Mongol invasions of Central Asia, the Mongols, ironically, had serendipitously created for Europe opportunities for trade and commerce that unfolded the politically-focused European objectives. The prosperous Pisan, Venetian and Genoese merchants had been denied access to the lucrative markets in the East by the impenetrable barrier of the Middle Eastern Islamic world. Hostile towards the Christians who had constantly waged war against Islam from the time of the Crusades of the late eleventh century, the Islamic powers had effectively prevented the Europeans from enjoying much commercial advantages east of the Mediterranean Sea. The Muslim Seljuk Turks of Asia Minor and the Mamluks of Egypt were the prime force and barrier that resolutely prohibited the Europeans from proceeding east overland.

Neither the crusading march of the Christians, nor the diplomatic maneuvering of European statesmen could lower this trade barrier. Yet the Turks happily traded with the Europeans in cities like Alexandria, Aleppo and Damascus which reinforced and perpetuated their political interests and determination to maintain the integrity of the imaginary trade wall they had created.

Therefore, the rapid military successes of the Shamanic Mongol did not go un-noticed by the anxious European Christian states. They were quick to recognize that a Christian-Mongol alliance against the Islamic powers of the Middle East could achieve their commercial objectives. In an attempt to establish such an alliance, John Carpini (John of Plano) headed a mixed diplomatic-missionary envoy to Mongolia at the behest of Pope Innocent IV (1243-1254 AD). John Carpini was a Franciscan friar who left Lyon, France in April 1245, and crossing the rivers Dnieper and the Don met Batu Khan on the banks of the Volga River. As he was allowed to proceed to the court of the supreme khan, John continued his journey and after crossing the rivers Ural and the Jaxartes reached the imperial Mongol camp near the capital Karakorum in the summer of 1246. The supreme khan, Guyuk (1206-1248), who had just been installed after the death of his father Ogotai, received the envoy but declined the envoy's invitation to become a Christian. Instead, he held the envoy until November of that year then dismissed them with a letter to the pope asserting that alliances are sealed between rulers and demanded that the pope along with other leaders should come to Karakorum and swear allegiance to him. The following is a version of Guyuk's letter to the pope written in Persian. The original letter written with ink on paper is kept in the Vatican Secret Archives in Rome:

منکو تنکری کو چنداکور الغ اولوس ننگ تالوی نونک خان یرلغمز

این مثالیست بنزدیک پاپاء کلان فرستاده شد بداند و معلوم کند ما نبشت دو زفان ولایتهاء کرل کنکا ش کردست اوتک ایلی بندگی فرستاده از ایلچیان شما شنوده آمد و اگر سخن خویش برسید توکی پاپاء کلان با کرل لان جمله بنفس خویش بخدمت ما بیائید هر فرمان یاساء کی باشد آن وقت بشنوانیم.

دیگر گفته‌اید کی مرا در شیلم درآی نیکو باشد خویشتن مرا دانا کردی اوتک فرستادی این اوتک ترا معلوم نکردیم دیگر سخن فرستادی «ولایتهای مجار و کرستان را جمله گرفتیت مرا عجب می‌آید ایشان را گناه چیست ما را بگوید» این سخن ترا هم معلوم نکردیم - فرمان خدای را چنگیز خان و قاآن هر نو شنوانیدن را فرستاد - فرمان خدای را اعتماد نکرده‌اند هم چنان که سخون توایشان نیز دل کلان داشته‌اند - گردن کشی کرده‌اند - رسولان ایلچیان ما را کشتند - آن ولایتها مردمان را خدای قدیم کوشت و نیست گردانید - جز از فرمان

Epilogue

خدای کسی از قوت خویش چگونه کوشید چگونه گیرد – مگر تو همچنان میگوئی که من ترسایم خدای را میپرستم زاری میکنم مییابم – تو چه دانی که خدای که را میآمورزد، در حق که مرحمت میفرماید – تو چگونه دانی که همچنان سخن میگوئی - بقوت خدای آفتاب بر آمدن و تا فرو رفتن جمله ولایتها را ما را مسلم کرد است میداریم - جز از فرمان خدای کسی چگونه تواند کرد – اکنون شما بدل راستی بگوئید کی ایل شویم کوچ دهیم - تو بنفس خویش بر سر کرل لان همه جمله یک جای بخدمت و بندگی ما بیائید - ایلی شما را آنوقت معلوم کنیم و اگر فرمان خدای نگیرید و فرمان ما را دیگر کند شما را ما یاغی دانیم همچنان شما را معلوم میگردانیم و اگر دیگر کند آنرا ما میدانیم خدای داند - فی اواخر جمادی الاخر سنه اربعه اربعین و سته میه

> You must say with a sincere heart: 'We will be your subjects; we will give you our strength'. You must in person come with your kings, all together, without exception, to render us service and pay us homage. Only then will we acknowledge your submission. And if you do not follow the order of God, and go against our orders, we will know you as our enemy.

A second mission was undertaken in the name of King Louis IX of France in 1253 by the Franciscan friar William of Rubruck. William had in 1248 accompanied the king on the Seventh Crusade to Egypt which the king had thought the land's wealth and supply of grain would keep the crusaders fed and equipped, and also would provide a base from which to attack Jerusalem. William, in this instance, accepted to lead the mission not because of service to his king's political interests but because he was still motivated by his religious objectives and by the present occasion that would give him the opportunity to meet the Mongol prince Sartaq Khan, a supposed Christian convert (Nestorian). William and his entourage set out from Constantinople and, unlike his predecessor, he travelled across the Black Sea and the Crimea then onward across the Don River where he met Sartaq Khan who politely sent William onward across the Volga to meet the khan's father, Batu Khan. Batu was not receptive to William's proselyting and sent him forthrightly to the supreme khan, Mongke Khan in Karakorum where the envoy enjoyed an audience with the great khan on 4 January 1254. Soon thereafter, William began his return journey by way of the Caucasus, Armenia, Persia and Asia Minor arriving in Tripoli in 1255.

The missions of John Carpini and William of Rubruck to the courts of the great Mongol khans had not been entirely fruitless. With the defeat of the Abbasid caliphate in Baghdad in 1258 AD by the Mongol Il-khan Hulagu, the above efforts by Christian Europe ultimately secured for them un-hindered passage throughout the Mongol Empire. Under the Mongol Empire's hegemony, the so-called *Pax Mongolica*, or *Mongol Peace*, the European city states enjoyed a safe land passage from the eastern shores of the Mediterranean Sea to lands far in the east. The travels of the Venetian merchants Niccolo Polo and his brother Maffeo in 1260 AD, and later of Niccolo's son Marco in 1271, are early examples of those who took advantage of these new opportunities. Their trading missions initially took them from Venice to Bukhara and ultimately to the court of Kublai Khan in Beijing.

The dialogues regarding Christian-Mongol alliances were soon to take a different turn. In about a decade after their conquests over the caliphate in Baghdad, the Mongol themselves had begun sending a series of embassies to England and Europe seeking support for ousting from Asia Minor their archetypal enemy, the Egyptian Mamluks, who under the command of Baybars had defeated Hulagu at the battle of Ayn Jalut (Palestine) in 1260 AD. This was an intolerable setback for the Mongols' ambitious plans for adding Asia Minor to their list of conquests. Their efforts for securing European alliances were to continue for nearly two decades. The first of the Mongol embassies that sought a European alliance was sent by the Il-khan Abaqa of Iran in 1270 AD to meet King Edward I of England in Tunis whilst the king was on his way to the Holy Land for his first crusade. The king had his own agenda at the time and did not consider the embassy's mission a priority. A final embassy which arrived in the summer of 1290 AD was dispatched by Il-khan Arghun (Abaqa's grandson). On this occasion Edward was delighted by the embassy because in the same year he had made a pact with Pope Nicholas IV (1288-1292 AD) to take the cross for a second crusade. However, the death of Edward's wife Eleanor put an early end to the king's enthusiasm for a second adventure to Jerusalem. Ultimately, the Mongols' prospects for achieving their major objective concerning Asia Minor slowly faded as their centralized authority began to wane in the wake of the progressive loses of their Il-khanates to local dynasties. The conquest of Asia Minor, then, had to wait until the coming of the great Mongol khan Temur (Tamerlane) in 1380.

The mid ninth century was a watershed for the Middle Kingdom; it defined the end of several centuries of political and religious conflicts but was also a time for China to take stock of itself and assimilate the endless variety of foreign influences within its borders. These ranged from art, music and astrology to the unfamiliar religious doctrines that

Epilogue

were constructed on metaphysical concepts of light versus darkness and of good versus evil. This was also a time when the Chinese masses had been exposed to Buddhism, a yet another alien religion which advocated detachment from the temporal world in a manner that contradicted the Chinese fundamental belief in their obligatory practice of ancestral worship. Such metaphysical concepts in reality were unfathomable by the Chinese populace imbued with the centuries-old philosophies of their native sages. Although some portion of the population may have legitimately subscribed to the foreign teachings of good and evil, their subscription however sincere brought upon their nation divisions, unrest, hatred and civil disorder. These events, collectively and inevitably encouraged the Chinese to take stock in their cultural and Confucian heritage and reassess their attitudes and the direction their social order should follow. In the final analysis, their conclusions were unequivocal and were clearly inwardly self-centred which served the Chinese well during the following four centuries but came to an end only with the rise of the Jurchen and the Mongols.

The political turmoils of the thirteenth century which stretched from the steppes of Central Asia to the shores of the Mediterranean Sea were the outcomes of the ambitious visions perpetrated and pursued by pragmatic Asiatic tribal men who were propelled to acquire territorial gains, political power and social dominance by simply killing. The carnages that followed their wars, and the devastations that inflicted indiscriminant pain and suffering, were expected to create opportunities for material gains and prosperity for the nations of such men, either as the spoils of war and pillage or as tributes that soon followed. Unfortunately, however, international trade and cultural traditions frequently suffered in such circumstances and often spelled the demise of the human habitations that had been marginally surviving. Unable to recover from the ravishes of wars, such habitations were reduced to ghost towns and gradually faded into history as romanticized folkloric memories. Once thriving and profit-making centres, the vanished emporia of the traditional Silk Road(s) like images in a faded photograph, are the prime examples of such memories that have continued to fascinate us and dazzle our imagination for a millennium.

On the religious aspects of Central Asia, centuries before the demise of the Silk Road's emporia, the lands of Islam stretched from the eastern coasts of the Atlantic Ocean to the shores of South China Sea, and from the Mediterranean coast of Africa to the frontiers of the steppes of Central Asia. In reterospect, we are now aware that the Arab conquests of the seventh and eighth centuries shaped the world we live in today. Following the life of the prophet Muhammad, Islam was confined to Arabic-speaking tribesmen living in the deserts of Arabia. In contrast, the peoples of Mesopotamia and Syria spoke Greek, Aramaic or Persian; in Egypt they spoke Greek and Coptic; Christian Alexandria was the hub of Christian theology and was the home of the early Church Fathers; in North Africa the people spoke Latin, Greek and Berber. In Iran and to its north-east in Afghanistan their inhabitants spoke various dialects of Persian, such as the Farsi of Iran or the Pahlavi (Middle Iranian) of the Parthian Empire. None of these peoples professed Islam and few if any spoke Arabic. Within a century of the Prophet's death however all these lands, along with Spain, Portugal, Central Asia and western India came under the rule of Arabic-speaking elite, and in all of them Islam became the majority dominant religion. In the centuries that followed, North Africa became a bastion for the defense of the Islamic Empire and Egypt, the pride of Christian heritage, became the heart of fundamental Islamic thought. This was a monumental achievement unparalleled in human history; the Islamic victories not only were remarkably swift and total but also left permanent effects on the social orders, the languages and the religions of the lands they conquered.

The speed with which the Islamic faith had entered the hearts and minds of the nomadic peoples of Central Asia early in the tenth century is best exemplified by the un-provoked holy wars waged by the newly converted Turks north of the river Jaxartes (in present-day Uzbekistan) against their own pagan kinsmen, and no brother or father was to be spared the edge of a scimitar unless they professed 'There is no God but Allah' and witnessed that 'Muhammad is the prophet of Allah.' Their identity as the armies of Islam meant their religious identity had replaced their ethnic identity. Such universal identity with Islam had never been equaled either by the Arabs or the Persians, and the legacy of Turkic devotion to Islam continues today in the hearts and minds of the poples of the Fertile Crescent and of those of Turkish heritage all over the globe. Islam was undoubtedly the most profound religious and social revolution in the history of the world that achieved its objectives by the edge of the sword. It was a revolution that affirmed a Muslim was no longer bound to his tribe by loyalty and property ownership; his personal duties towards his faith were to replace tribal solidarity. The individual Muslim was obligated to defend the entire Islamic community, the *'umma,'* and, if necessary, by war of attrition, *'jihad'*. Often in the history of Islam jihad is mentioned as the sixth pillar of the

Epilogue

faith equivalent to the main five namely, profession of the faith *'shahada'*, prayer *'salat,'* fasting during the month of Ramadan *'saum,'* the offering of alms *'zakat'* and finally pilgrimage to Mecca, the *'hajj.'*

The growth of the Silk Road and the emergence of the sea-borne spice trade across South-Eastern Asia and northern India brought the luxuries of the Far East to a generally less civilized Northern Europe ravaged by barbarian invasions and by the self-serving ambitions of a Papal Roman Empire, which in the ninth century had installed Charlemagne as its puppet emperor. The caliphate of Baghdad in the ninth century championed the benefits of science, art and literature and sponsored translations of texts from Sanskrit, Greek and Syriac. Their discoveries in medicine, mathematics and astronomy became the bed-rock for the later social development of the West. Thus, as a direct result of these advances and through the wealth produced from the bold voyages of the European 'Age of Exploration' in the late fifteenth and sixteenth centuries, the balance of international power shifted in favour of Europe. Despite the glory days of the Ottoman, Mughal and the Safavid empires in Turkey, North India and Iran, respectively, Islamic power was gradually eclipsed first by the Portuguese, then by the Dutch and finally by the British. However, despite the loss of their economic power and the dominance of European colonialism, the Islamic culture in time acquired a new resilience. Today, the Islamic sphere of influence extends from the shores of the Atlantic Ocean in the west to the edge of the forbidding sands of the Gobi Desert in China in the east, and from the Turkic lands of Central Asia in the north to the heart of the Indonesian archipelago in the south. In the face of this new awakening of Islam, Buddhism in China and Central Asia has become a novelty of the past for the visiting traveler, and Christianity has lost the opulence it once enjoyed many centuries ago. Although the future of the latter faith in the East is in the ascendancy, it is doubtful that the gospel of Christ will make a monumental impact.

It is therefore, a source of great virtue for the practiced mind to learn, bit by bit, first to change about in visible and transitory things, so that afterwards it may be able to leave them behind altogether. The person who finds his homeland sweet is a tender beginner; he to whom every soil is as his native one is already strong; but he is perfect to whom the entire world is as a foreign place. The tender soul has fixed his love on one spot in the world; the strong person has extended his love to all places; the perfect man has extinguished his.

Hugh of the Augustinian Abbey of Saint Victor
Paris (1096-1161 AD)

Bibliography

General Reading

Burns, T. S., *Rome and the Barbarians*, 100 BC-AD 400. John Hopkins University Press, Baltimore (2003).
Eberhard, W., *A History of China*. Routledge and Kegan Paul, London (1977).
Frye, R. N., *The Golden Age of Persia: The Arabs in the East*. Weidenfeld, London (1993).
Hedin, S. A., *Through Asia*. Harper and Brothers, New York (1898).
Hopkirk, P., *Foreign Devils on the Silk Road: The Search for the Cities and Treasures of Chinese Central Asia*. John Murray, London (1980).
Kennedy, H., *The Great Arab Conquests: How the Spread of Islam Changed the World We Live in*. Weidenfeld and Nicolson, London (2007).
Keverne, R., *Jade*. Anness Publications, London (1991).
Liu, X., *Ancient India and Ancient China: Trade and Religious Exchanges AD 1- 600*. Oxford University Press, Delhi (1988).
Markel, S. (ed.), *The World of Jade*. Marg Publications, Bombay (1992)
Walker, A., *Aurel Stein: Pioneer of the Silk Road*. John Murray, London (1995).
Warner, L., *The Long Old Road in China*. Page and Company, Garden City New York (1926)
Whitefield, S. and Sims-Williams, U. (eds.), *The Silk Road: Trade, Travel, War and Faith*. The British Library, London (2004).
Wood, F., The Silk Road: Two Thousand Years in the Heart of Asia. The British Library, London (2003).
Zhao, F., *Treasures in Silk: An Illustrated History of Chinese Textiles*. Costume Squad Ltd., Hong Kong (1999).

Treasures of the Silk Road

Appendix

Selected Glossary

AD: anno domini (Our Lord); year in the Christian era
Adobe: compacted mud
Analects: Confucian commentaries on social philosophy
Apocryphal: writings excluded from canonical literature because of their Contradictory nature
Artush: a city situated south of the Tian Shan mountains, in the north-western part of the Tarim basin
Artux: see Artush
Aspara: beautiful females (angels) in Buddhist tradition with celestial attributes
BC: year before the Christian era
Bei: north
Bodhisattva: an enlightened person with great compassion to assist others achieve enlightenment
Bronze Age: circa 3000-1000 BC
Caliph: successor to the prophet Muhammad
Canton: southern Chinese province of Guangdong
Christology: the study of the human and divine natures of Jesus Christ
Consort: non-bloodline related wife or spouse of a ruler
Concubine: unmarried woman kept in a harem
Dawager: a widow or consort of deceased emperor or ruler
Devi: female aspect of the divine
Doctrine: is the interpretation and legalization of Dogma
Dogma: belief system, religious, political or social
Dong: east
Dughlats: Mongolic tribes with no genealogical links with the great khans who ruled in East Turkistan as vassals to the Karakhans
Dzungars: confederation of several Mongolic tribes with genealogical links with the great khans who inhabited the plains north of the Tian Shan mountains from the sixteenth to the eighteenth centuries. They were destroyed by the Qing dynasty.
East Turkistan: generally considered to represent most of present-day Xinjiang province
Fang: tribe; clan
Farsi: spoken Persian dialect of the trading bureaucracy in Central Asia

Gnostic: about understanding the oneness with God
Han Shu: history of the Later Han dynasty
He: river
Hellenic: relating to Greek language, culture, religion, etc.
Huang: yellow
Hun: nomadic peoples who inhabited regions near the Caspian Sea
Imam: Muslim clergy
Iron Age: circa BC 1000-AD 100
Il-Khan: title of a Mongol with bloodline relation to the great khan ruling a land conquered by him
Jataka: folkloric literature native to India about the lives of the Buddha
Kalmyks: see Dzungars
Karakhans: Mongolic tribes with genealogical links with the great khans who ruled in Mughalistan
Karluqs: or Karluks, see Qarluqs
Kazakh: Kipchak tribes that populated the territory between Siberia and the Black Sea
Khan: title of a ruler in Mongolia, and also of his descendants, with bloodline relation to the great khan
Khanate: territories under the rule of a khan
Khoja: secular leader with direct descent from the prophet Muhammad or from his daughter Fatima
Kipchak: ancient Iranian-speaking Turkic nomadic tribes related to the Qarluqs. Kyrgyz and Kazakh tribes are descendants of the Kipchak
Kyrgyz: Kipchak tribes that lived in Siberia. By processes of migration, conquest, intermarriages and assimilation with the Kazakh, many of the Kyrgyz who now inhabit Central Asia and China are of mixed origins.
li: 0.4158 kilometres
Madrasa: or Madrassa, school
Manichaeans: a gnostic Christian sect with origins in Sasanid-era Babylonia
Masjid: mosque
Nestorians: a Christian sect with origins in Constantinople considered heretical by the early Church
Mazar: tomb; mausoleum
Mihrab: semicircular niche in the wall of a mosque that indicates the direction of Mecca and more specifically, the Qa'ba
mu: 667 square metres

Mughals: Mongolic descendants of the armies of Genghis Khan who

Appendix

    ruled in the plains of the Tian Shan mountains
Mughalistan: generally considered to represent the plains of the Tian Shan mountains and the Tarim basin
Nan: south
Osh: city in southern Kyrgyzstan in the historical Ferghana valley
Parthia: province in north-east of Iran which was the political base of the Arsacid dynasty of the Parni tribe
Parthian empire: founded after Arsaces I of Parthia rebelled against the Seleucid Emprire
Pashtun: Pashto (Persian dialect)-speaking Sun'ni Muslims of Afghanistan and Pakistan
Patrilineal: descent calculated through men
Patrilineage: descent calculated from a specific male ancestor
Pictograph: writing or painting with pictorial symbols such as the Egyptian or Chinese hieroglyphics
Qarluqs: Turkic tribe residing north of the Tian Shan mountains in the region between the Kara-Irtysh and the Altai mountains - the latter is in western Outer Mongolia
Ren: person; people
Sayyid: Muslim holy person with direct descent from the prophet Muhammad or from his daughter Fatima
Shamanism: a religious practice aimed at interacting with the spirit world through trance
Shan: mountain
Shiji: Han dynasty chronicles
Stupa: Buddhist religious monument that covers a relic of the Buddha
Sutra: a Buddhist scripture
Tajik: a Iranian-speaking native Sh'ia Muslim of Tajikistan
Tarim basin: generally considered to represent most of the north-western part of present-day Xinjiang province south of the Tian Shan mountains
Tian: heaven
Ush: see Osh
Uzbek: a Turkic-speaking native of Uzbekistan
Vassal: a person or an administrative body that vows political allegiance and pays taxes and tributes to a conqueror
West Turkistan: western half of the divided Chagatai khanate that came under the rule of Temur in 1347 AD - generall includes present-day Uzbekistan, Turkmenistan and parts of western Kazakhstan

Western Regions: territories directly west of the western frontiers of the Middle Kingdom that was hostile until their subjugation was completed in the ninth century with the removal of the Tibetans

Xi: west
Xia: land
Xianbei: nomadic federation of Mongolic tribes who livid in Manchuria in north- eastern parts of China
Xiongnu: confederation of nomadic steppe people of Mongolia
Yuezhi: Indo-European tribes related to Tocharians; Da Yuezhi: great Kushan Empire
Zungar: see Dzungar

Appendix

Detailed dynasties of ancient and imperial China

Xia$_1$	22nd – 17th century BC
Xia$_2$	2070 – 1000 BC
Xia$_3$	2207 – 1766 BC
Xia$_4$	17th – 1122 BC
Shang$_1$	1600 – 1046 BC
Shang$_2$	1765 – 1122 BC
Shang$_3$	1134 – 771 BC
Western Zhou$_1$	1046 – 771 BC
Western Zhou2	1121 – 771 BC
Western Zhou$_3$	770 – 256 BC
Eastern Zhou$_1$	770 – 249 BC
Eastern Zhou$_2$	722 – 481 BC
Spring & Autumn$_1$	770 – 476 BC
Spring & Autumn$_2$	403 – 221 BC
Warring States	476 – 221 BC
Qin State$_1$	900 – 221 BC
Qin State$_2$	221 – 206 BC
Qin	248 – 207 BC
Western Han$_1$	206 BC – 23 AD
Xin	9 – 23 AD
Western Han$_2$	23 – 25 AD
Eastern Han	25 – 220 AD
Three Kingdoms	
Wei	220 – 265 AD
Shu	221 – 263 AD
Wu	222 – 280 AD
Western Jin	265 – 316 AD
Eastern Jin	317 – 420 AD
Sixteen Kingdoms	
Cheng Han (Di)	301 – 347 AD
Hun Han (Zhao)	304 – 329 AD
Former Liang	317 – 376 AD
Later Zhao (Jiehu)	319 – 352 AD
Former Qin (Di)	351 – 394 AD
Former Yan (Xianbei)	337 – 370 AD
Later Yan (Xianbei)	384 – 409 AD
Later Qin (Qiang)	384 – 417 AD
Western Qin (Xianbei)	385 – 431 AD

Later Liang (Di)	386 –	403 AD
Southern Liang (Xianbei)	397 –	414 AD
Northern Liang (Hun)	397 –	439 AD
Southern Yan (Xianbei)	398 –	410 AD
Western Liang	400 –	421 AD
Xia (Hun)	407 –	431 AD
Northern Yan	409 –	436 AD
Northern Dynasties		
Northern Wei	386 –	534 AD
Eastern Wei	534 –	550 AD
Western Wei	535 –	557 AD
Northern Qi	550 –	577 AD
Northern Zhou	557 –	581 AD
Southern Dynasties		
Liu Song	420 –	479 AD
Southern Qi	479 –	502 AD
Liang	502 –	557 AD
Chen	557 –	589 AD
Sui	581 –	618 AD
Tang$_1$ (Early)	618 –	690 AD
Wu Zhou	690 –	705 AD
Tang$_2$ (Middle)	705 –	907 AD
Five Dynasties		
Later Liang	907 –	923 AD
Tang$_3$ (High)	923 –	936 AD
Later Jin	936 –	946 AD
Later Han	947 –	950 AD
Later Zhou	951 –	960 AD
Ten Kingdoms		
Wu (Nanking)	902 –	937 AD
Shu (Sichuan)	907 –	925 AD
Nan-Ping (Hubei)	907 –	963 AD
Wu-Yue (Zhejiang)	907 –	978 AD
Min (Fukien)	907 –	946 AD
Southern Han (Canton)	907 –	971 AD
Chu (Hunan)	927 –	956 AD
Later Shu (Sichuan)	934 –	965 AD
Southern Tang (Nanking)	937 –	975 AD
Northern Han (Shanxi)	951 –	979 AD
Khitan Liao	907 –	1125 AD

Appendix

Northern Song	960 – 1127 AD
Southern Song	1127 – 1279 AD
Western Xia	1032 – 1227 AD
Jurchen Jin	1115 – 1234 AD
Yuan (Mongol)	1279 – 1368 AD
Ming	1368 – 1644 AD
Qing (Manchu)	1644 – 1912 AD
Republic of China	1912 – 1949 AD

Dynastic emperors of imperial China

Qin Dynasty (221 - 207 BC)

Qin Shihuangdi (221-210 BC)

Western Han Dynasty (206 BC-23 AD)

Kao Ti [Gaodi] (206-195 BC)
Hui Ti [Huidi] (195-188 BC)
Empress Kao as regent [Lu Hao] (188-180 BC)
Wen Ti [Wendi] (180-157 BC)
Jingdi (157-141 BC)
Wu Ti [Wudi] (141-87 BC)
Zhaodi (87-74 BC)
Xuandi (74-49 BC)
Yuandi (49-33 BC)
Chengdi (33-7 BC)
Aidi (7-1 BC)
Pingdi (1 BC-6 AD)
Ruzi (7-9 AD)

Xin (Hsin) Dynasty (9-25 AD)

Cia Huang Ti (regent) (9-23 AD)
Huai-yang Wang (23-25 AD)

Eastern Han Dynasty (25-220 AD)

Guang Wudi (25-57 AD)
Mingdi (57-75 AD)
Zhangdi (75-88 AD)
Hedi (88-106 AD)
Shangdi (106 AD)
Andi (106-125 AD)
Shundi (125-144 AD)
Chongdi (144-145 AD)
Zhidi (145-146 AD)
Huandi (146-168 AD)
Lingdi (168-189 AD)
Xiandi (189-220 AD)

The Three Kingdoms Period (220-280 AD)
Wei Dynasty (220 - 264 AD)

Wendi (220-226 AD)
Mingdi (227-239 AD)
Shaodi (240-253 AD)
Gao Gui Xiang Gong (254-260 AD)
Yuandi (260-264 AD)

Shu Han Dynasty (221-263 AD)

Chao Lieh/Liu Pei [Xuande] (221-223 BC)
Hou Zhu (223-263 BC)

Wu Dynasty (222-280 AD)

Wudi (222-252 AD)
Feidi (252-258 AD)
Jingdi (258-264 AD)
Modi (264-280 AD)

Appendix

The Disunion Period (265-589 AD)
 Southern Kingdoms

Western Jin Dynasty (265-316 AD)

Wudi (265-289 AD)
Huidi (290-306 AD)
Huaidi (307-312 AD)
Mindi (313-316 AD)

Eastern Jin Dynasty (317-419 AD)

Yuandi (317-322 AD)
Mingdi (323-325 AD)
Chengdi (326-342 AD)
Kangdi (343-344 AD)
Mudi (345-361AD)
Aidi (362-365 AD)
Hai Xi Gong (366-370 AD)
Jian Wendi (371-372 AD)
Xiao Wudi (373-396 AD)
Andi (397-418 AD)
Gongdi (419 AD)

Liu Song Dynasty (265-316 AD)

Wudi (420-422 AD)
Ying Yang Wang (423 AD)
Wendi (424-453 AD)
Xiao Wudi (454-464 AD)
Cang Wu Wang (473-476 AD)
Shundi (477- 479 AD)

Qi Dynasty (479-501 AD)

Gaodi (479-482 AD)
Wudi (483-493 AD)
Mingdi (494-498 AD)
Dong Hunhou (499-500 AD)
Hedi (501 AD)

Liang Dynasty (502-556 AD)

Wudi (502-549 AD)
Jian Wendi (550 AD)
Yu Zhang Wang (551 AD)
Yuandi (552-554 AD)
Jingdi (555-556 AD)

Chen Dynasty (557-589 AD)

Wudi (557-559 AD)
Wendi (560-566 AD)
Lin Hai Wang (567-568 AD)
Xuandi (569-582 AD)
Hou Zhu (583-589 AD)

The Disunion Period (265-589 AD)
Northern Kingdoms

The Sixteen Kingdoms (304-439 AD)
Northern Wei Dynasty (386-534 AD)
Eastern Wei Dynasty (534-550 AD)
Western Wei Dynasty (535-557 AD)
Northern Qi Dynasty (550-577 AD)
Northern Zhou Dynasty (557-581 AD)

Sui Dynasty (581-618 AD)

Wendi (581-604 AD)
Yangdi (604-617 AD)
Gongdi (617-618 AD)

Tang Dynasty (618-907 AD)

Gaozu (618-626 AD) (Kao Tsu)
Taizong (626-649 AD)
Gaozong (649-683 AD)
Zhongzong (684, 705-710 AD)
Ruizong (684 - 690, 710-712 AD)
Wu Zetian (690-705 AD)
Xuanzong (712-756 AD)
Suzong (756-762 AD) (Su Tsung)
Daizong (762-779 AD)
Dezong (779-805 AD)
Shunzong (805 AD)
Xianzong (805-820 AD)
Muzong (820-824 AD)
Jingzong (824-827 AD)
Wenzong (827-840 AD)
Wuzong (840-846 AD) Wu Tsung
Xuanzong (846-859 AD)
Yizong (859-873 AD)
Xizong (873-888 AD)
Zhaozong (888-904 AD)
Aidi (Zhaoxuan) (904-907 AD)

Five Dynasties Period (907-960 AD)
Later Liang Dynasty (907-923 AD)

Taizu (907-910 AD)
Modi (911-923 AD)

Later Tang Dynasty (923-935 AD)

Zhuangzong (923-926 AD)
Mingzong (926-934 AD)
Feidi (934-935 AD)

Later Jin Dynasty (936-947 AD)

Gaozu (936-944 AD)
Chudi (944-947 AD)

Later Han Dynasty (947-951 AD)

Gaozu (947-948 AD)
Yindi (948-951 AD)

Later Zhou Dynasty (951-960 AD)

Taizu (951-954 AD)
Shizong (954-960 AD)

Liao Dynasty (907-1125 AD)
Former Shu (907-960/76 AD)

Wang Yen (918-924 AD)

Southern Han Dynasty (917-942 AD)

Liu Yen (917-942 AD)

Southern Tang Dynasty (907-978 AD)
Northern Han Dynasty (950-976/97 AD)

Yuan Tsung (960-961 AD)

Appendix

Liao Dynasty (907-1125 AD)

T'ai Tsu (907-926 AD)
Hsing Tsung (1031-1054 AD)
Tao Tsung (1055-1100 AD)
T'ien Cha (1101-1125 AD)
Tsao Wang (died 1143 AD)

Western Hsia Dynasty (982-1227 AD)

Jen Tsung (1140-1193 AD)
Hsiang Tsung (1206-1212 AD)
Shen Tsung (1212-1222 AD)

Chin Dynasty (1115-1260 AD)
(Nu-chen Tatars)

Wan-yen Liang (1149-1161 AD)
Shih Tsung (1161-1189 AD)
Chang Tsung (1190-1208 AD)

Northern Song Dynasty (960-1126 AD)

T'ai Tsu [Taizu] (960-976 AD)
Chen Tsung [Zhenzong] (998-1022 AD)
Jen Tsung [Renzong] (1022-1063 AD)
Ying Tsung [Yingzong] (1064-1067 AD)
Shen Tsung [Shenzong] (1068-1085 AD)
Che Tsung [Zhezong] (1086-1101 AD)
Hui Tsung [Huizong] (1101-1125 AD)
Ch'in Tsung [Qinzong] (1126 AD)

Southern Song Dynasty (1127-1279 AD)

Kao Tsung [Gaozong] (1127-1162 AD)
Hsiao Tsung [Xiaozong] (1163-1190 AD)
Kuang Tsung [Guanzong] (1190-1194 AD)
Ning Tsung [Ningzong] (1195-1224 AD)
Li Tsung [Lizong] (1225-1264 AD)
Tu Tsung [Duzong] (1265-1274 AD)
[Gongzong] (1275 AD)
[Duanzong] (1276-1278 AD)
[Bing Di] (1279 AD)

Yuan Dynasty (1279-1368 AD)

Khublai Khan [Shizu] (1279-1307 AD)
Temur Oljeitu/Cheng Tsung [Chengzong] (1294-1307 AD)
Khaishan/Wu Tsung [Wuzong] (1308-1311 AD)
Ayurbarwada/Jen Tsung [Renzong] (1311-1320 AD)
Shidebala [Yingzong] (1321-1323 AD)
Yesun Temur [Taiding] (1323-1328 AD)
Tugh Temur [Wenzong] (1328-1329; 1329-1332 AD)
Khoshila [Mingzong] (1329 AD)
Toghon Temur/Shun Ti [Shundi] (1333-1368 AD)

Yuan Rebels (1355-1368 AD)

Han Lin-erh of Sung (1355 AD)
Ch'en Yu-liang of Han (1358-1363 AD)
Chang Shi-ch'eng of Chou (died 1367 AD)

Ming Dynasty (1368-1644 AD)

T'ai Tsu (1368-1398 AD)
Hui Ti (1399-1402 AD)
Ch'eng Tsu (1403-1424 AD)
Jen Tsung (1425 AD)
Hsuan Tsung (1426-1435 AD)
Ying Tsung (1436-1449; 1457-1464 AD)
Tai Tsung or Ching Ti (1450-1457 AD)
Hsien Tsung (1465-1487 AD)
Hsiao Tsung (1488-1505 AD)
Wu Tsung (1506-1521 AD)
Shih Tsung (1522-1566 AD)
Mu Tsung (1567-1572 AD)
Shen Tsung (1573-1620 AD)
Kuang Tsung (1620 AD)
Hsi Tsung (1621-1627 AD)
Chuang Lieh (1628-1644 AD)

Ming Rebels (1644-1681 AD)

The Ming Prince of Lu (ousted in 1657 AD)
The Prince of Fu (1644 AD)
The Prince of T'ang (died 1646 AD)
The Prince Yung Ming (died 1662 AD)
Li Tzu Ch'eng (1606-1645 AD)
Chang Hsien Chung (circa 1644 AD)
Sun K'o Wang (circa 1665 AD)
Wu San Kuei (died 1678 AD)
Wu Shih Fan (died 1681 AD)
Keng Ching Chung (died 1681 AD)

Qing Dynasty (1644-1911 AD)

Tian Ming (1616-1626 AD)
Tian Xong (1626-1643 AD
Shun Zhi (1642-1661 AD)
Kang Xi (1661-1722 AD)
Yong Zheng (1722-1735 AD)
Qian Long (1735-1796 AD)
Jia Qing (1796-1820 AD)
Dao Guang (1820-1850 AD)
Xian Feng (1850-1861 AD)
Tong Zhi (1861-1875 AD)
Guang Xu (1875-1908 AD)
Xuan Tong (1908-1911 AD)

Appendix

Alphabetical list of the Thirty-Six Kingdoms

1. The Kingdom of Alanliao
2. The Kingdom of Anxi
3. The Kingdom of Chaghatai (Eastern & Western)
4. The Kingdom of Chakilik
5. The Kingdom of Chu
6. The Kingdom of Da Qin
7. The Kingdom of Da Yuezhi (Kushan)
8. The Kingdom of Dere
9. The Kingdom of Dongli (Eastern Kushan)
10. The Kingdom of Gaofu (Kabul)
11. The Kingdom of Jingjue
12. The Kingdom of Jumi (Keriya)
13. The Kingdom of Jushi (southern) (Turfan)
14. The Kingdom of Jushi (northern)
15. The Kingdom of Karakhanid
16. The Kingdom of Karghalik (Xiye)
17. The Kingdom of Khotan (Yutian)
18. The Kingdom of Korla
19. The Kingdom of Kuqa
20. The Kingdom of Liyi (Sogdiana)
21. The Kingdom of Loulan
22. The Kingdom of Niya
23. The Kingdom of Pueli
24. The Kingdom o Qi
25. The Kingdom of Qiemi
26. The Kingdom of Qiuci
27. The Kingdom of Shule (Kashgar)
28. The Kingdom of Suoche (Yarkand)
29. The Kingdom of Tianzhu
30. The Kingdom of Tiaozhi
31. The Kingdom of Wuyishanli
32. The Kingdom of Yan
33. The Kingdom of Yanqi (Karashahir)
34. The Kingdom of Yerqiang
35. The Kingdom of Yizhi (Barkol)
36. The Kingdom of Zihe (Shahidulla)

List of the officially recognized 56 ethnic groups in China and their relative numbers*

Han	1,225,933	Zhuang	16,179	Manchu	10,683	Hui	9,817
Mio	8,941	Uyghur	8,400	Tujia	8,029	Yi	7,763
Mongol	5,814	Tibetan	5,417	Buyei	2,972	Dong	2,961
Yao	2,638	Korean	1,924	Bai	1,859	Hani	1,440
Kazakh	1,421	Li	1,248	Dai	1,159	She	710
Lisu	635	Gelao	580	Dongxiang	514	Gaoshan	459
Lahu	454	Sui	407	Va	397	Nakhi	309
Qiang	307	Tu	242	Mulao	208	Xibe	189
Kyrgyz	161	Daur	133	Jingpo	133	Maonan	108
Salar	105	Blang	92	Tajik	42	Achang	34
Pumi	34	Ewenki	31	Nu	29	Gin	23
Jino	21	De'ang	18	Bonan	17	Russian	16
Yugur	14	Uzbek	13	Monba	9	Oroqen	9
Derung	8	Tatar	5	Hezhen	5	Lhoba	3

*From 2010 census rounded to the nearest whole number in 1000s

Appendix

List of Mongol khans

<u>Great Khans</u>

Genghis Khan (1206-1227)*
Tolui (1227-1229)
Ogotai (1229-1241)
Guyuk (1246-1248)
Mongke (1251-1259)
Kublai (1260-1294)

<u>Khans of the Golden Horde</u>

Batu (1227-1255)
Berke (1256-1267)
Uzbek (1313-1341)

<u>Khans of the Yuan Dtnasty</u>

Kublai (1260-1294)
Temur Oljaitu (1294-1307)
Toghan Temur (1333-136

<u>Khans of the Chagataid Khanate</u>

Chagatai Khan (1227-1242)
Taliku (1308-1309)
Kebek (1318-1326)
Il-Chigidai (1326)
Tamashirin (1326-1334)
Buzan (1334)
Chingshi (1334-1338)

<u>Il-Khans</u>

Hulagu (1256-1265)
Abaqa (1265-1282)
Tegudur (1282-1284)
Arghun (1284-1291)
Gaykhatu (1291-1295)
Baydu (1295)
Ghazan (1295-1304)
Oljaitu (1304-1316)
Abu Sa'id (1316-1335)

*Reigning dates

Chronology of the Popes
4th - 20th centuries

Marcellus I	(306-309)
Eusebius	(310)
Miltiades	(311-314)
Silvester I	(314-335)
Mark	(336)
Julius I	(337-352)
Liberius	(352-366)
Damasus I	(366-384)
Siricius	(384-399)
Anastasius I	(399-401)
Innocent I	(401-417)
Zosimus	(417-418)
Boniface I	(418-422)
Celestine I	(422-432)
Sixtus III	(432-440)
Leo I	(440-461)
Hilarus	(461-468)
Simplicius	(468-483)
Felix II	(483-492)
Gelasius I	(492-496)
Anastasius II	(496-498)
Symmachus	(498-514)
Hormisdas	(514-523)
John I	(523-526)
Felix III	(526-530)
Boniface II	(530-532)
John II	(533-535)
Agapitus I	(535-536)
Silverius	(536-537)
Vigilius	(537-555)
Pelagius I	(556-561)
John III	(561-574)
Benedict I	(575-579)
Pelagius II	(579-590)
Gregory I	(590-604)
Sabinian	(604-606)
Boniface III	(607)
Boniface IV	(608-615)
Adeodatus I	(615-618)

Appendix

Boniface V	(619-625)
Honorius I	(625-638)
Severinus	(640)
John IV	(640-642)
Theodore I	(642-649)
Martin I	(649-653)
Eugene I	(654-657)
Vitalian	(657-672)
Adeodatus II	(672-676)
Donus	(676-678)
Agatho	(678-681)
Leo II	(682-683)
Benedict II	(684-685)
John V	(685-686)
Canon	(686-687)
Sergius I	(687-701)
John VI	(701-705)
John VII	(705-707)
Sisinnius	(708)
Constantine	(708-715)
Gregory II	(715-731)
Gregory III	(731-741)
Zacharias	(741-752)
Stephen I	(752)
Stephen II	(752-757)
Paul I	(757-767)
Stephen III	(768-772)
Hadrian I	(772-795)
Leo III	(795-816)
Stephen IV	(816-817)
Paschal I	(817-824)
Eugene II	(824-827)
Valentine	(827)
Gregory IV	(827-844)
Sergius II	(844-847)
Leo IV	(847-855)
Benedict III	(855-858)
Nicholas I	(858-867)
Hadrian II	(867-872)
John VIII	(872-882)
Marinus I	(882-884)
Hadrian III	(884-885)

Stephen V	(885-891)
Formosus	(891-896)
Boniface VI	(896)
Romanus	(897)
Theodore II	(897)
John IX	(898-900)
Benedict IV	(900-903)
Leo V	(903)
Anastasius III	(911-913)
Lando	(913-914)
John X	(914-928)
Leo VI	(928)
Stephen VII	(928-931)
John XI	(931-936)
Leo VII	(936-939)
Stephen VIII	(939-942)
Marinus II	(942-946)
Agapitus II	(946-955)
John XII	(955-964)
Benedict V	(964)
Leo VIII	(963-965)
John XIII	(965-972)
Benedict VI	(973-974)
Benedict VII	(974-983)
John XIV	(983-984)
John XV	(985-996)
Gregory V	(996-999)
Silvester II	(999-1003)
John XVII	(1003)
John XVIII	(1003-1009)
Sergius IV	(1009-1012)
Benedict VIII	(1012-1024)
John XIX	(1024-1032)
Benedict IX	(1032-1045)
Silvester III	(1045)
Gregory VI	(1045-1046)
Clement II	(1046-1047)
Benedict IX	(1047-1048) (re-elected)
Damasus II	(1048)
Leo IX	(1049-1054)
Victor II	(1055-1057)
Stephen IX	(1057-1058)

Appendix

Nicholas II	(1058-1061)
Alexander II	(1061-1073)
Gregory VII	(1073-1085)
Victor III	(1086-1087)
Urban II	(1088-1099)
Paschal II	(1099-1118)
Gelasius II	(1118-1119)
Callistus II	(1119-1124)
Honorius II	(1124-1130)
Innocent II	(1130-1143)
Celestine II	(1143-1144)
Lucius II	(1144-1145)
Eugene III	(1145-1153)
Anastasius IV	(1153-1154)
Adrian IV	(1154-1159)
Alexander III	(1159-1181)
Lucius III	(1181-1185)
Urban III	(1185-1187)
Gregory VIII	(1187)
Clement III	(1187-1191)
Celestine III	(1191-1198)
Innocent III	(1198-1216)
Honorius III	(1216-1227)
Gregory IX	(1227-1241)
Celestine IV	(1241)
Innocent IV	(1243-1254)
Alexander IV	(1254-1261)
Urban IV	(1261-1264)
Clement IV	(1265-1268)
Gregory X	(1271-1276)
Innocent V	(1276)
Adrian V	(1276)
John XXI	(1276-1277)
Nicholas III	(1277-1280)
Martin IV	(1281-1285)
Honorius IV	(1285-1287)
Nicholas IV	(1288-92)
Celestine V	(1294)
Boniface VIII	(1294-1303)
Benedict XI	(1303-1304)
Clement V	(1305-1314)
John XXII	(1316-1334)

Benedict XII	(1334-1342)
Clement VI	(1342-1352)
Innocent VI	(1352-1362)
Urban V	(1362-1370)
Gregory XI	(1370-1378)
Urban VI	(1378-1389)
Boniface IX	(1389-1404)
Innocent VII	(1404-1406)
Gregory XII	(1406-1415)
Martin V	(1417-1431)
Eugene IV	(1431-1447)
Nicholas V	(1447-1455)
Callistus III	(1455-1458)
Pius II	(1458-1464)
Paul II	(1464-1471)
Sixtus IV	(1471-1484)
Innocent VIII	(1484-1492)
Alexander VI	(1492-1503)
Pius III	(1503)
Julius II	(1503-1513)
Leo X	(1513-1521)
Adrian VI	(1522-1523)
Clement VII	(1523-1534)
Paul III	(1534-1549)
Julius III	(1550-1555)
Marcellus II	(1555)
Paul IV	(1555-1559)
Pius IV	(1559-1565)
Pius V	(1566-1572)
Gregory XIII	(1572-1585)
Sixtus V	(1585-1590)
Urban VII	(1590)
Gregory XIV	(1590-1591)
Innocent IX	(1591)
Clement VIII	(1592-1605)
Leo XI	(1605)
Paul V	(1605-1621)
Gregory XV	(1621-1623)
Urban VIII	(1623-1644)
Innocent X	(1644-1655)
Alexander VII	(1655-1667)
Clement IX	(1667-1669)

Appendix

Clement X	(1670-1676)
Innocent XI	(1676-1689)
Alexander VIII	(1689-1691)
Innocent XII	(1691-1700)
Clement XI	(1700-1721)
Innocent XIII	(1721-1724)
Benedict XIII	(1724-1730)
Clement XII	(1730-1740)
Benedict XIV	(1740-1758)
Clement XIII	(1758-1769)
Clement XIV	(1769-1774)
Pius VI	(1775-1799)
Pius VII	(1800-1823)
Leo XII	(1823-1829)
Pius VIII	(1829-1830)
Gregory XVI	(1831-1846)
Pius IX	(1846-1878)
Leo XIII	(1878-1903)

Chronological history of the Silk Road

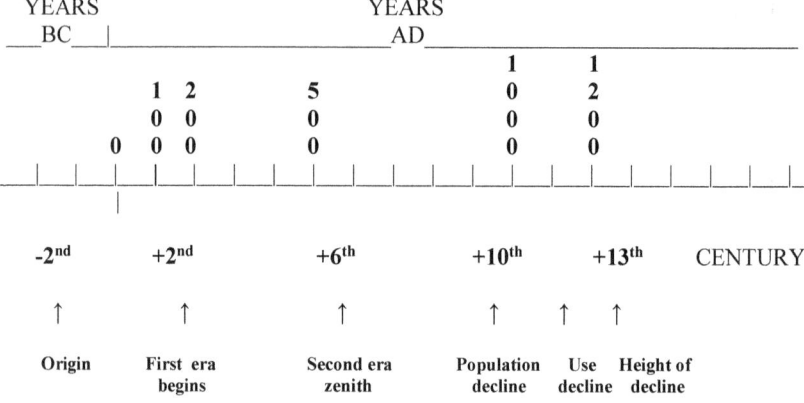

Index

A

Abakh (Afaq), Khoja 161, 197, 292, 296, 297, brother 162, son 297
Abaqa, Il-Khan 54, 334
Abbasid, caliph(ate) 99, 206, 273, 274, 287, fall 333
Abdu-llah Khan 290, 292, 296, son 291
Abdul Karim Khan, Sultan 290
Abdul Latif Khan I, 290
Abdul Latif Khan II, 292
Abdul Rahim Khan, Sultan 290
Abdul Rashid Khan I, Sultan 164, 197, 290, 294
Abdul Rashid Khan II 297, brothers 297
Abi Waqqas 146, 275
Abu Abd-Allah
Abu al-Nasir Mansur, Samanid 273, 274
Abu Jafar al-Mansur, Caliph 273
Abu Zayid Hasan, historian 210
Abud al-Kadir al-Jeylani, Sheikh 110, 275, 278
Abyssinia (Ethiopia) 145, king 146
Achaemenid, Empire 67, 68, 73, 74, 77
Adam, Syrian priest (see Ching-ching) 247
Aden, Gulf 202
Adijan 76
Afghanistan 41, 72-74, 91, 101, 109, 159, 187, 189, 195, 203, 219, 220, 284, 285, 290, 336, lapis lazuli 206
Afonso de Albuquerque 208
Africa 55, 319, North 182, 336, coast of east 201-203, ivory 206, coast of 335
Ah Nan (Bodhisattva) 119
Ahmad, son of Saman 274

Ahmad Khan 290
Ahmad Khan, Sultan 290
Ahmad, Khoja 162
Ahmad Khoja Kasani 294 (see Makhdum)
Ahriman, devil 328
Ahura Mazda, deity 49, 327
Aidi, Emperor 42, 347
Airtam, inscriptions 220
Akhsi 290
Akhtuba, river 263
Aksu 97, 98, 106, 161, 195, 225, 234, (Baluka) 230, Prefecture 157, Population 158, monasteries 158, capital 158, governor 292
A-lopân (see Olopun)
Al'altun 152
al-Ghafiqi, chronicler 202
al-Hira 80
al-Kalkashandi, chronicler 202
al-Muqtadir, Caliph 321
al-Qadisiyya 80, 145
Alan, tribe 281
Albegensians 317
Albert von Le Coq 119, 325
Alchi, Tatar tribe 263
Aleppo 332
Alexander the Great 69, 70, 72, 73, 77, death 71, 189, 218, 219, 328
Alexandria 182, 201, 203, 332, See of 237, 241, 336
Alexandrian School 238
Ali 294
Almaliq 286
Altai, mountains 100, 144, 280, 285, 296
Altaic Turks 97
Altishahr, district 161, 162
Altun, mountains 94, 106, 185
Altunluk, mosque 196

American(s) Spanish War 210
Amida (Diyarbakir) 241
Aminah bint Wahb 146
Ammanisahan, Queen 197
Amoy 86, 213
Amu Darya, river (see Oxus) 68, 72, 92, 220, 284, 286
Amursana, Oirat prince 297, lord and vassal 298, in Russia 298
An Jia, Sogdian priest 327
An Lushan 51, 52, 99, 182, 184, 273, 323
An Shih-Kao, monk 215, 228
Ananda, (Guardian of the Dharma) 120, 121
Anastasius of Antioch 238
Anatolia 187, 189
Ancestral worship, reverence 16, 17, 19, 22
Andalò di Savignone 264
Andrea di Nascio 264
Andrew of Perugia, Saint 264
Anhui, province 44, 186
Antioch 54, See of 237, 241
Antiochene School 238
Antiochus III 68, defeat 68
Anxi (Parthia) 95, 105, 106, 115, 143, Four Garrisons 98,
Anyang, capital 17, 326, 327
apsaras 118, 119
Arab(s)(ia) 55, 71, 72, 80, 86, 109, 145, 201, 206, 209, 220, 327, missionaries 110, 145, 146, connections 110, conquest of Iran 145, 321, 328, Gulf 185, south 201, peninsula 202, sea 203, 204, 264
Arabic 85, 92, 117
Aral, lake 78, sea 97, 284
Aramaic 336
Ardashir, dynasty 319
Arghun, Il-Khan 264, 334
Armaments 24, 88
Armenian(s) 71, 78, 187, 265, 333, Sahak 153, Cilician 203, of India 209, Church 239, 243, writers 263
Arsaces I 68, 77
Arsaces II 68, son 68
Arsacid, Empire 68
Artabanus I, King 73
Artush 274
Artux (Artush) 274
Aryan 93
Ashina She'er, commander 97
Ashoka the Great 74, 113, 218, 219, 234, missionaries 219, 221
Ashoka Bindusara Maurya 74
Asia 55, 67
Asia Minor 71, 74, 80, 209, 331, 333, 334
Asim 276
Assyrians
Astana Graves 150
Astrakhan 263
Atlantic Ocean 208, 335
Augin, Saint (Mar Augin) 240
Augustus, Emperor 1
Aurel Stein 119, 189, 259, 325
Austria 56, 210
Avignon 264
Ayn Jalut, battle 334
Azerbaijan 81, 243, Persian 264

B
Ba, tribe 19
Babak Sultan 296
Babar, Khan 284, Padishah 290
Babylon(ia) 71, 74, 223, 241, 318
Bactria(n) 41, 67, 71, 72, 74, 76, 101, 218-221, 233-235, 245, 318, texts 326
Baekje, kingdom 211
Baghdad 107, 206, 274, 283, 319, 333, 334, 337, (Baldach) 259, patriarch 260
Baha-ud-Din Naqshband Bukhari 279
Bahama Islands 208
Bai Shan, order 161
Baikal, lake 97, 246, 280, 323

Bailin, museum 247
Balasaghun, 163, capital 100, 273, 283, 323
Balkh 69, 72, 82, 107, 230, Milis 247
Balkash, lake 285, 296
Baltic 78
Bamiyan 109, 220, 230, 290
Ban Chao, General 96
Bangladesh 146
Bar Sauma, bishop 241, 260
Bar Shabba, bishop 245
Baradaeus 243
Barkol, lake 144
Barlas, clan 284
Bartchouq, Khan 152
Bartolomeu Dias 208
Barygaza, port 202, exports 203
Basmyl, tribe 100, 281
Basra 80, 82
Batu, Khan 263, 284, 332, 333
Bay of Bengal 203, 271
Bayan Hai, mountains 19
Baybars, 334
Bayin'gholin Mongolian Autonomous Prefecture 152, capital 183
Bazir Arslan Khan 283
Beautiful Pearl, Persian concubine 211
Beewah, Japanese lute 156
Beijing 8, 39, 40, 45, 53, 56, 58, 86, 162, 192, 267, 334, support of Roman church 264, cathedral 267, Administrative College 267, Xicheng district 267
Beimang Shan, area 326
Benedict XII, Pope 264
Benedict Goës, Jesuit 144
Bengal 209, 264
Bento de Góis, Jesuit 153
Berber 336
Berenice, port 201, 202
Berenike I 201
Berlin 325

Beshbalik 282, 283
Bezeklik Thousand Buddha Caves 151, 229, 325
Bharata 74
Bharuch, city 203
Bhera, Punjab 294
Bhutan 91
Bibi Rabiya al-Basri 283
Bibica al-Kashgari 294
Bible, translation 267
Big Goose pagoda 151, temple 231
Bijapur, sultanate 208
Bing Di, Emperor 113, 354
Bingling, caves 109
Bishkek 273, 282
Bithynia 287
Black Sea 79, 107, 287, 333
Bodhi Tree 217
Bodhisattvas 118-120, 154, 232, blue eyed 259
Bogomils 317
Bohai Bay 7, 19, 58, gulf 212
Bohemond 54
Bonan 90, 108
Book of Zhou 185, 186
Bosten, lake 152, 153
Boxer Uprising 40, 58, 267
Brahma 326
Brahmi 182
Britain 8, 57 British 8, 40, 56, 58, 209, Raj 210, 337, Empire in India 210
Broghol, pass 195
Bronze Age, cultures 88, Late 188
Buddha 50, 118-120, living Ngawang-tsondru 110, disciples 120, births 156, 217, awakened 217, death 218, prophet 319, Messiah 322
Buddha Jesus 322
Buddha Mani 317, 325
Buddhism 69, origin 50, 216, in China –birth and entry 4, 148, 151, 335, 337, support 217, Golden Age 49, Shravakayana

369

154, 193, Mahayana 75, 154, 193, 225, 227, 231, Hinayana 96, 181,193, 225, Tibetan (Gelugpa) Yellow Hat 110, Four Noble Truths 217
Buddhist 4, 17, 101, 258, monks 17, 69, 96, 115, 118, 119, 185, 215, 219, 221, 225, beliefs 49, 216, grottoes 89, temples 112, 225, Tutor 112, Regional Religious Affairs Office 113, art 116, 220, angels 118, Bodhisattvas 118-120, 154, caves 109, 117, 119, 151, 155, 156, 225, 229, 325, Airtam inscriptions 220, gestures (abhaya mudra, varada mudra) 221
Bukhara 82, 107, 161, 196, 197, 203, 245, 284, 287, 334, capital 100, governor 273, 274
Bumin, Khan (Göktürk) 97
Burhan-ud-Din, Khoja 162, 297, prisoner 298, in Osh 298, brother 162
Burhan-ud-Din Kilic, Sayyid 294
Burma (Myanmar) 219
Bursa 287
Byzantine, Empire 49, 192, 237, 240, in Palestine 80, in Asia Minor 80, 287, symbolism 156, Cyprus 203

C

Cai Yin 222
Campichu (see Zhangye) 111
Canton 55, 56 (see Guangzhou)
Cao Cao, General 43
Cape of Good Hope 208
Caspian Sea 69, 74, 78, 79, 91, 92, 107, 152, 187, 285
Cathars 317
Catholic, Church 260
Caucasus 67, 69, 333
Caves of the Thousand Buddhas 119

Celts 187
Central Asia 2, 41, 49, 51, 67, 68, 72, 85, 88, 91, 94, 99, 100, 119, 219, art 220, 318, 336, 337, Nestorians in 244, 245, steppes 335
Ceylon 93, 202, 205, 208, 219, 226
Chaboqi 189
Chach 70 (see Tashkent)
Chagatai, Khan 284, death 286
Chagatai(ds) 158, 284, khanate 160, 196, 289, duration 197
Chagri 287
Chakilik 106, 180, 184, 185, (Yarkand) 183
Chalcedon, Council of 239
Chalcedonian (vs. non-Chalcedonian) 239, Syrian 240, 243
Chandragupta, Emperor 74 (see Sandracottus), Mauryaian Empire 74
Chang Gui, King 180
Chang'an 1, 19, 20, 41, 49, 71, 85, 87, 89, 98,105, 108, 117, 147, 148, 150, 223, 224, 226, 229, 231, 323, Nestorians expelled 244, missionaries 246, Muslims 275, Sogdian tombs 327
Changsha 206
Chanyu, General 179
Chao-Chi, port 202
Chao Huei, General 298
Charlemagne, Emperor 337
Charles I, King 266
Charles V, King 266
Charsadda (see Pushkalavati)
Chen Mu, General 96
Chen Su 228
Chen Yi (see Xuanzang), brother 228
Cheng Tsu, Emperor 55, 113, 355
Chengdi, Emperor 42, 347
Chengdu 44, 51, 185, 229, 323

Cherchen 106, river 186, 189, population 187, jade 187, 225
Chiaochow (Qingdao) 58
Chijin, village 115
China, ancient 9, imperial 7, 9, 19, modern 9, unification 144, Cochin 202, exports 203, Nestorian evangelism 243, Roman missions 264, ethnic groups 272, ethnic definition 280, Islam terms 274, Hui 275, Islam distribution 277
Chinese, history 15, classic histories 8, 150, literary classics 21, dynasties 9, kingdoms 9, dating and succession to rule 15, social hierarchy 16, characters 17, language 49, heaven 20, governance 21, classes 23, 53, nationalism 40, silk 41, 203, 205, legalism 87, Bronze Age cultures 88, Book of Jin 154, Book of Zhou 185, 186, historical books 186, dictionary 267, Bible 267
Ching-ching (Jingjing) 247, 259
Chittagong, port city 146
Chong Zong, Emperor 112
Choros, tribe 291
Christian, calendar 9, tombstones 268, Mongol alliance 332, 334
Christianity 4, doctrine vs. dogma 237, in China 337
Christopher Columbus 208, wife 209
Chu, state 22, 23, tribe 44, river 92, 95, 273, 282, 283, 285
Chuang Lieh, Emperor 56, 355
Chust, Uzbekistan 294
Cimmerians 79
Cixi (Tsu-Hsi), Empress Dowager 59
Cixi, governor 185
Clan 16
Clement V, Pope 260

Cochin-China 202, 212, India 202
Confucianism 21, 223, *Analects* 21, filial piety, 22, 216, Neo- 224
Confucius 87, 324, Confucian philosophy 20, 22, 23, 40, 258
Constantine the Great, Emperor 287
Constantinople 1, 49, 71, 106, 107, 201, 203, 204, 209, 333, See of 237, 241, 287
Coptic, Church 239, spoken 336
Crescent Moon Spring (lake) 116
Crusades 331, seventh 333
Crescenzio Sepe, Cardinal 260
Crimea 333
Ctesiphon 243, 318, 321
Cultural Revolution 267
Cyril of Alexandria 239
Cyrus the Great, King 67, 72, 74

D

Dadiwan, culture 88
Dahpid, village 295
Daizong, Emperor 247
Dalian, port of 58
Damascus 107, 203, 332
Danieper, river 332
Danish East India Company 210
Dao Zheng, monk 225, 227
Daoism 87, 89, 215, 223, 258, 272
Darius I, King 70, 73, 74
Darius III, King 70, 72, 74, 80
Datong 41
Dawantou, village 279
Daxia (see Bactria) 92, 95
Dayuan 75, 76, 92, 94, 95 (see Ferghana)
Delhi 284
Demetrios, traveller 153
Demetrius, King 72, 74
Derwishes 279 (see Jahariyah)
Devis 119
Dezong, Emperor 247, 351
Dharma 230, 231, guardian of 120
Diamond Sutra 119

Diocletian, Emperor 319
Diodorus of Tarsus 238
Divine Right 19, 20
Divining 17
Diwanu Lughat at-Turk 193
Diyarbakir 241
Don, river 332, 333
Dong Fuxiang 277
Dongxiang 90, 108, 275, 279
Dorbet, tribe 291
Drum Tower (see Gulou) 112
Du Fu, poet 46
Dughlat 154, 271, 274, 282, 289, 290, tribe 160
Dujiangyan, canal 44
Dunhuang 90, 96, 106, 109, 112, 114-119, 143, 144, 159, 185, 193, 220, 221, 225, 226, 228, 231, 233, 234, 258, 259, 282, texts 325
Dutch 56, 208, 210, 337
Dutch East India Company 210
Dyophsite (Diophsite) 238, 240
Dzunghars 296 (see Kalmyks), tribes 291

E

East China Sea 4, 56, 205, 213, 226
East India Company 8, 57, 209, 210, British 268
East Indies 208, 210
East Turkistan 156, 162, 282, 283, 286, 287, 295-297, 325, Islam in 289, 290, 292, Khojas 294, fall 298, art 326
Eastern Churches 239
Edessa 223, 240, 243
Edward I, King 334, wife 334
Egypt(ians) 70, 74, 182, 201, 203, 206, 208, 319, 331, 334, 336, corn 203, , crusade 333
Elchasaites, sect 319
Elizabeth I, Queen 209, 210
Emir Bulaji 289
Emirs, of Turfan 286, 289

England 19, 334
English, missionaries 267
Ephesus, Council 238, 239
Eric Liddell, Scottish missionary 268
Erkashtam, pass 107
Erke Husein, Khoja 162, brother 162, nephews 162
Ertughrul of Bithynia 287
Ethiopian, Church 239
Euphrates, river 70, 240
Europe (European) 1, 8, 24, 40, 45, 54-56, 58, 71, 287, 331, 333, society 22, goods 57, alliance 59, markets 201, seafaring 208, East India companies 210, central 317, archaeologists 325, city-states 334, Age of Exploration 337, colonialism 337
Euthydemus, King 72

F

Fa Li, monk 225, 227
Fa Liang, monk 118
Fan Zhongyan, minister 53
Fars 81
Farsi 336
Fatima 294
Faxian, monk 69, 96, 180, 225-227
Ferdinand II, of Aragon 208
Ferdinand Verbiest, Jesuit 267
Ferdinand von Richthofen 105
Ferghana 41, 67, 76, 101, 162, 218, 219, 233-235, 274, 284, 286, 294, 295, 298, 318
Fertile Crescent 336
Feudal, Fiefdoms 18, 20, 23, 24, 37, bureaucratic 39
Fez 54
Filial piety 22, 216, 228
Filipa Moniz Perestrello 209
Fire altars 327, 328
First Emperor 38, 87, 95, death 39
First Opium War 57, 213

First Uyghur Empire 100, 273, 282, 323, fall 152
Five Dynasties, period 52
Florus, historian 1
Forbidden City 162, 267
Formosa (Taiwan) 58
Four Garrisons of Anxi 98, 99
Fragrant Maiden 161, 163
France (French) 19, 54, 56, 58, 209, 258, 332
Francis Edward Younghusband 157, 158
Francis Xavier, Saint 266
Fu Hao, wife 18, Queen 18, 19, capital 18
Fu His, Emperor 7
Fu Jiezi 180
Fu Xi (Fu His), Emperor 7, sister 89
Fu Yi 222
Fujian, province 86, 206, 212, 213, 275, 324, gazetteer 147
Fuzhou 57, 206

G

Galdan Boshughtu 296
Gandhara(n) 41, 67, 74, 107, art 70, 109, 182, 192, 219-221, 226, 228, 230, 233-235
Gandhaka, river 74
Ganges, river 74, 230
Ganesha 326
Gansu, province 19, 20, 39, 41, 44, 58, 85, 88, 89, 95, population 90, names in antiquity 90
Ganzhou (Zhangye) 91, 98, 111
Gaochang 97, 100, 151, fall 150, 281
Gaodi, Enperor 41, 347
Gaolan, mountains 108
Gaozong, Emperor 50, 322, 351
Gaozu, Emperor 146
Genghis, Khan 3, 4, 53, 76, 100, 101, 108, 158, 215, 259, 263, 284, 286, daughter- in-law 54, 259, son 100, 158, daughter 152, death 284
Genoese 54, 203, 264, 331
George III, King 8
Germany 56, 58
Ghaznavids 287
Giant Buddha Temple 112
Gladys Aylward, English missionary 267
Gnostic(ism) 317, spiritualist 319
Goa 208, 209
Gobi Desert 42, 76, 85, 90, 111, 115, 116, 118, 143, 179, 272, 337
Goguryeo, kingdom 211
Göktürk 80, 92, 93, 150, 229, 246, 280-282, Celestial Turks 97, Eastern khanate 97, Western khanate 97, defeated 99
Gong, Prince 57
Grand Canal 15, 45
Great Wall 55, 90, 111, 112, 114, 115, 117, 226
Greco-Bactrian Kingdom 72, 73, 79, culture 182
Greco-Roman, culture 218, 220, Empire 219, mystery religions 317
Greek, artistic style 220, spoken 336, texts 337
Guang, prefecture 207
Guangdong, province 39, 57, 58, 86, 146, 147, 207
Guangxi 207
Guangzhou 4, 55-58, 86, 146, 147, 202, 205, 206, 208-212, mosques 147, 210, 211, 267, port 201, Xin Shi district 211, missionary work 268, Muslims 275
Guanyin, Bodhisattva 232
Guazhou (see Anxi) 98, 105, 115
Gui, river 92, 94, 95
Guishuang 76
Gujarat, state 203, 208, 209
Gulou (Drum Tower) 112
Gundeshapur 243

Guo Xiaoke, commander 97
Guyuk, Khan 332
Guzang (Wuwei) 144, 150

H
Hadda 220, 230
Hadrian, Emperor 1
Hainan, island 37
Haixi Mongol Autonomous Prefecture 183
Haizhu, district 207
Haji Muhammad, missionary 161
hajj (pilgrimage) 337
Hajji Ma Laichi 108
Haloed deities 327
Hamadan 67, 81, 107, 319
Hami 106, 115, 117, 143, 147, 229, 275, 282, 289, 292, 296, other names 144, Population 144
Hamuzeli (Hamuz Ali) 275, (Han Zeling) 110
Han, use of word 40
Han, dynasty 20, 22, 39, 42, 43, 51, 85, 114, 211, state 23, Western (Former) 40, 42, 111, Eastern (Later) 42, 96, 116, 184, 222, 229, Golden Age 42, commercial interests 94, Book of Han 95, fall 108, Southern 211
Han Fei Zi, thinker 87
Han Yu, critic and poet 223
Hangzhou 4, 45, 52, 53, 86, Muslims 275
Hanshu 73, 75, 76, 154, 179, 186, 192, 195, 211, 222
Hasam Ben Sulayman Taohuashi, Khan 163
Hasan ibn Thabit, Arab missionary 146, 147
He Qiaoyuan, gazetteer 147
He Zun (see Bing Di) 113
Heart Doctrine 113, sutra 231
Heaven 20
Hebei, province 17

Hegemony, political 54, Tibetan 99
Hei Shan, order 161
Helan Mountains 272
Hellenic, Empire 71, 74, 192, 218, era 201
Henan, province 17, 19, 52, 89, 223, 228
Hephthalites (White Huns) 71, 245, 321
Herd-boy and the Weaver 48, 49
Herodotus, historian 69, 79
Hexi Corridor 88, 90, 98, 108 111, 115, 117, 143, 144, 184, 224, 229, 282, Hexi Zoulang 105
Hezhou (see Linxia) 108
Hilal al-Din 278
Himalayas 195, 234
Hinayana Buddhism 96, 181, 193, 234
Hindu Trinity 326
Hinduism 70
Hindu Kush, mountains 72, 107, 195, 219, 221, 235
Hittite 78
Holy Land 334
Holy Roman Empire 156
Hong Kong 57, 275, convention 58
Hong Wu (Wu Tsung), Emperor 109
Hongliuyuan 143
Hongwu 55
Hormizd I, King 320
Horse 204, lore and legend, 42, heavenly (Celestial) 42, domestication 78, import 201, 321, Baima (White Horse) Temple 222, winged 327
Horse's Hoof Temple 112
Hou Gao 19
Hou Junji, commander 97
Hu, Empress Dowager 185, 227
Hu, people 234
Huang, Emperor 7
Huang Chao 52, rebellion 210

Huangdi 7
Huangtu, plateau 85
Hubei, province 38, 44
Hudson Taylor (James), English missionary 268
Hui Chao, monk 225, 233, 234
Hui Zheng, monk 225, 227
Hui 85, muslims 58, 110 origins 85, Autonomous Prefecture 110, legend 148
Huihui 85
Huiji (see Yumen) 114
Huizong, Emperor 53, 353
Hulagu , Il-Khan 54, 264, 333, wife 54, 259, son 54, mother 259, defeat 334
Hun(s) 69, 71, 321, white 71, 321
Hunagling, county 7
Hunan, province 44, 206
Hungary 56
Hunter Corbett, American missionary 267
Huo Qubing, general 111
Huoshaogou, culture 89, 90
Husain ibn Muhammad al- Khalat 275
Hyecho, Korean monk (see Hui Chao) 233

I

Ibn Battuta, historian 54
Ibn Khurddahbeh, chronicler 202, 206
Id-Kah, mosque 156, 160
Ignatius of Loyola, Saint 266
Ili, capital 297, 298
Ili, river 158
Iliq Mazi (Iliq Nasir), ousted the Samanids 274, sultan 294
Il-khanates 100, northern, southern, eastern and western 100, population 101
Imperial Ostend General India Company of Austria 210
Inayat Kiramet, Khoja 162
India(n) 2, 41, 49, 50, 54, 70, 74, 76, 91, 95, 107, 115, 118, 119, 121, 146, 234, 245, 284, western 336, opium 57, sea links 201, Cochin 202, Portuguese state 209, Armenians 209, British Empire 210, Act of Government 210, society 218, *ushnisha* 220, missions 221, 263, 264, Church 239, 243, Mani 321
Indian Ocean 55, 185, 202, 204, 207, 232, control 208
Indies, East 210, Spanish 210
indios 208, 210
Indo-European 41, 74, 78, 88, 91, migrations 187
Indonesia(n) 202, 275, archipelago 219, 337
Indus, river 74
Industrial Revolution 208
Innocent IV, Pope 332, 363
Innocent VI, Pope 264, 364
Iparhan (Xiangfei) 161, uncle 162, brother 162
Iran(ian) 49, 54, 67, 80, 101, 187, 189, 245, 287, 318, 336, stock 92, Arab conquest 145
Iraq 70, 80, 241, 244
Irkeshtam, pass 159
Iron Age 187
Iron Gate (Tiemen), pass 153, 230
Irtyish, river 287, 291
Isabella I, of Castile 208
Isfahan 275
Ishak ibn Imran, chronicler 202
Ishan-i-Kalan, Khoja 292, 294-296, son Yusuf 296
Ishaq Wali 294-296
Islam(ic) 67, 71, 76, 81, 86, in China 4, 145, distribution in China 272, khanates 100, Sun'ni 108, Middle East 110, resistance 276, parts 277, Schools 277, Sun'ni vs. Shi'a 277, in East Turkistan 289, lands 335, in Egypt 336,

five pillars 336
Isma'il Khan 292, 297, son 296
Issus, Cilicia 70
Issyk Köl, lake 75, 273, 282
Italy 56
Ivory 19

J
Jacob al-Baradi (Baradaeus) 243
Jacobites 243, 259
Jade 19, 88, 95, 105, tools181, Tarim basin 187, nephrite 194
Jade-Faced One 258
Jade Gate, pass 90, 143 (see Yumenguan)
Jafar ibn abu Talib 146
Jahariyah, order 277-279
Jahsh 146
Jalalu-ud-Din, Sayyid 294
Jama Masjid (mosque) 196
James O. Fraser, English missionary 268
James of Nisibis 240
Japan (ese) 49, 56, 58, 208, 209, 219, governance 21, Lute 156, music 157, trade 212, Kyushu Island 212, Lord Satsuma 213, Meiji government 213
Jataka stories 118, 156
Java 207, 209
Jaxartes, river (see Syr Darya) 68, 284, 287, 332, 336
Jerome, Saint 237
Jerusalem 260, 333, 334
Jesuits, 267, society dissolution 266
Jesus 237, 238, 322, 327
Jesus Messiah Sutras 119, 258
Ji Bonqin, 21, son of Ji Dan 21
Jia Ye (Bodhisattva) 119
Jiaguwen 17
Jiangsu, province 44, 86, 186
Jiangxi, province 44, 206
Jiankang, capital 43
Jiayuguan, fort (gate) 90, 111
jihad 336

Jin Sheng, temple 247
Jin, dynasty, 116, 154, 212, 225, 285, Western 43, 109, clan 43, Eastern 43, 144, 225, Northern 53, Jin, kingdom 184, tombs 326
Jing Tu, monastery 228, Sui support 229
Jingdezhen, 206
Jingjue, kingdom 188, 189
Jinshu 154
Jishi, hill 109
Jiuquan 144
Jochi 100, 101, 284
Johan Gunnar Andersson 88, 89
Johann Adam Schall von Bell, 267
John II, King 208
John Carpini 332
John Marignolli 264
John Montecorvino (Giovanni) 263
John Paul II, Pope 260
Jonathan Goforth, Canadian missionary 268
Jorge Álvares, explorer 209
Juqu Mujian 150, cousins Wuhui and An Zhou 150
Jurchen 4, 53, 335
Justinian I, Emperor 243

K
Kabul 107, 219, 290
Kadariyah 275, 277, 278
Kaidu, Khan 76, river 153, Prince 264
Kaifeng 4, 19, 52, 53, Muslims 275
Kalmyks 152, 291, 292, 298 (see Dzunghars)
Kanbalu 53, 192, 264, (see Beijing), bishopric 264
Kang Mengxiang, monk 221
Kang Seng Hui, monk 221
Kang Xi, Emperor 162, 356
Kangju 75, 95
Kanishka, King 72, 75, 226

Kapilayastu, city 217
Kara-Irtysh, river 100
Karakash, river 192
Karakhanid(s), dynasty 100, 193, 271 (see Il- khanates), Uyghur khanate 194, in Mughalistan 197, sultans 273, karakhans 283, 286
Karakhojas 100
Karakorum, mountains 72, 107, 159, 226, pass 195, 231, capital 263, 332, 333
Karashahir (Yanqi) 97, 153, 290
Karluk, tribe 100
Kasan, 294 (see Chust)
Kashgar (Kashi) 97, 98, 100, 101, 106, 107, 117, 118, 149, 161-163, 180, 187, 193, 225, 231, 234, 259, 283, 286, 296, population 159, kingdom 179, 192, Kara Taghliq in 292
Kashmir 296
Kazakhs 90, 92, 291, 296, 298
Kazakhstan 41, 71, 73, 75, 91, 92, 99, 144, 284, 285
Kerala 54
Kerbogha, General 54
Keriya 106
Kharosthi 181, 182, 189
Khatun Boraqcin, wife of Sartaq 263
Khazar, tribe 281
Khitan, tribe 96, 97, 263
Khoja(s) 196, 197, 274, 292, 294, division 295
Khoja Ahmad 297
Khoja-i-Jihan 162, 297, prisoner 298, in Osh 298, brother 162
Khotan (Hotan) 98, 105, 106, 117, 161, 180, 181, 187, 225-227, 231, 276, 287, 295, Darya (river)107, kingdom 107, 150, 192, jade 187, population 192, Mahayana 193, decline 194, conquered 193, ancient Udun 194

Khotanese 193, 322
Khotis, tribe 291
Khufiyah, order 277, 279
Khunjerap, pass 107, 159
Khurasan 68, 287, 320
Khuvishka, King 72, 220
Khwarazm 319
Kipchak, 284, 287, khanate 263
Kizil Thousand Buddha Caves 156, 225
Koko Nor, lake 183
Kolomna 285
Kong Fuzi 21, 87 (see Confucius)
Kong Hui, monastery 229
Korea(n) 45, 97, governance 21, peninsula 42, 49, 58, 211, 212, 219, kingdoms 211, 233
Korla 106, 107, 179, 180, 183, population 152
Kowloon 58
Kublai, Khan 53-55, 113, 192, 244, 264, 334, mother 259
Kubriyah, order 278
Kufa 80, 145
Kuiji, student 231
Kül Belgae Kadir Khan, 283, sons 283
Kunlun, mountains 89, 94, 106, 179, 184, 186-88,192,195
Kuntura Thousand Buddha Caves 155
Kuqa (Kucha) 96, 98, 106, 107, 150, 154, 225, 282, 283, 289, mosque 156, population 157, kingdom 193, 230
Kurds 259
Kurgan, culture 78, 79
Kuruk Darya (river) 107
Kushan (Guishuang), Empire 76, 181
Kyrgyz 91, 92, 100, 152, 162, 290, 291, 298, tribe 281, allies of Aq Taghliqs 297
Kyrgyzstan 76, 91, 92, 159, 164, 273

Kyushu, island 212

L
Labrang (Labuleng Si), monastery 110
Lamaism 219
Lantau, island 209
Lanzhou 19, 39, 89, 90, 105, 108, 109, 110, 147, 226, 229, 275, Jincheng (Golden City) 108, mosques 109
Lao Zi (Lao Tse) 89, 317, 324, Daoism 87
Lapis lazuli 206
Latin 336
Levant Company 210
Li Bo, poet 46
Li Chongrun, Prince 50
Li Rong, sage 89
Li Xi'an 50
Li Xian Hui (see Yongtai)
Li Yuanhao, chief 273
Li Zhong 50
Liang, dynasty (Former) 108, Northern 118, 120, 229, 327
Liangshan, mountain 50
Liangzhou 98, 229
Liangzhu, culture 18
Liaodong, peninsula 37
Liaoning, province 58
Lin Zexu 57
Lin Tse-hsu 57
Lineage 16
Ling Shan, mount 147
Linghu Defen, Tang historian 186
Lintong, county 39
Linxia 111, 275, Arab connections 110, mosques 110, Hezu 275, Little Mecca 276
Lisu, tribe (Yunnan) 268
Liu Bang 39, 40, 87
Liu Chang, Emperor 211
Liu Xuan, 42
Liujiaxia, reservoir 109
Liupan Moutains 272
Liuyuan (Hongliuyuan) 143

Loess, plateau Shaanxi 85 (see Huangtu)
London, mission 248, 267
Longshan, culture 89
Longshan (Longshou) mountains 90, 111, 143
Lop Nor Desert 94, 107, 114, 159, 179, 188, 226
Lop Nor, lake 95, 107, 179, 180, 181
Lop Nor, river 92
Lottie Moon, American missionary 268
Louis IX, King 263, 333
Loulan, oasis 94, 106, 107, 159, 185, 226, 234, kingdom 95, 179-181, 189, garrison 96, 182, Beauty 188
Lu Xiuyan, engraver 247
Lu, state 21, founder 21
Lucknow 284
Lumbini, village 217, 226, 230, 233
Luoyang 19-21, 42, 43, 117, 185, 223, 225, 227, 228, 323, 326, 327
Lyon 332

M
Ma Anliang 277
Ma Heng 326, 327
Ma Julung 277
Ma Laichi 279
Ma Mingxin 279
Ma Qianling 277
Ma Wanfu 280
Ma Zhan'ao 277
Macartney, George, Lord 8
Macau, Portuguese authority (colony) 209, 267, 268
Macedonia(n) 70, 219
Madina 145-147
Madras 264
Maffeo Polo 334
Maghreb 54
Magical Sand, mountain

(see Mingshan) 116
Mahabharata 74
Mahakasyapa, first disciple 120, 121
Maharajas 121
Mahayana Buddhism 75, 154, 193, 227, 229, 231, 234, sutras 222
Mahmud 162, al-Kashgari 193, parents 283
Mahmud Ghaznavi, Sultan 294
Mahmud Khan, Sultan 290
Maijishan, grottoes 89, monastery (founder) 229
Majiayao, culture 88
Makhdum 294, 296 (see Sayyid Makhdum-i-Azam), wife 294, sons 294, death 295
Malacca, straits of 202, 232, sultanate 209,
Malaysia(n) 275, peninsula 202, sultanate 209
Maltese, cross 259
Mamluks 260, 331, 334
Manchu 40, 56, 59, 90, 163, 276, 298
Manchuria(n) 4, 42, 44, 53, 55, 56, 58, 96, 263
Mandate of Heaven 19, 20, 23, 42
Mangalai, kingdom 158
Mani, prophet 49, 325, origin 318, parents 319, *syzygos* 319, preaching 320, 321, death 321
Manichaeism 49, 69, 71, corrupt Buddhism 223, 317, Taoism 317, state religion 318, decline 318, 326, impact 325
Manichaen(s), teachings 223, 317, expelled 244, persecutions 321
Manila, capital 210
Mansur, Khan (brother of Sa'id) 290
Maqam 148
Mar Aba I 245
Mar Ammo 320, 321
Mar Augin 240
Mar Dadiso, Synod 241, 245

Mar Maron, monastery 246
Marco Polo 45, 53, 54, 111, 112, 183, 186, 192, 196, 259, 334
Matteo Ricci, Jesuit 86, 144, death 267
Maujdum-i-Azam 294, (see Sayyid Makhdum-i-Azam)
Mauryaian, Empire 74
Mazdaism 49, 69, 327
Mecca 145, 146, 276, 278, 280, 337
Media (Medes) 67
Medina 294
Mediterranean Sea 107, 182, 219, *Mare Nostrum* 203, 331, 334, 335
Meili Zhen Zhu 211
Melik Awat, capital 194, 231
Mencius (Mo Tzu) 87
Merv 81, 82, 107, 203, 321, bishopric 245
Mesopotamia 67, 68, 70, 80, 82, 145, 201, 240, 241, 287, 318, 319, 321, 336
Messiah Buddha 322
Mexico (New Spain) 210
Michele Ruggieri, Jesuit
Middle Kingdom 1, 3, 4, 7, 8, 37, 39, 40, 42, 68, 81, 85, 90, 93, 95-98, 108, 109, 111, 114, 115, 117-119, 148, 160, 212, 215, 220, 226, 234, 271, 321, 322, 324, 331, 334
Miguel López de Logazpi, governor 210
Minfeng 188
Ming Huang 51 (see Xuanzong)
Ming, dynasty 55, 56, 86, 90, 99, 113, 209, 211, 213, 222, 244
Mingdi, Emperor 222
Mingsha Shan (Mingsha Mountains) 116-118
Miran 106, 181, 185, 225, 228, 234, archaeology 182
Mirza Abu-Baker 286, 289, 290
Mirza Muhammad Haidar Dughlat

154, 289
Missionaries 57, 58, 86, 106, 144-146, Arab 110, Sufi 161, Buddhist 219, 234, 235, Nestorian 246, 258, Franciscan & Jesuits 248, 260, 264, 266, in India 263, Dominican 264, English 267, Franciscan envoy 332, 333
Mithradates I 68
Mo Tzu, thinker 87
Modu Shanyu 95
Mogao, caves 109, 117, 118, 120, 193, decline 119
Molucca 207
Mo-mo-ni 325
Mongke, Khan 54, 263, 333, mother 259
Mongol(s)(ic) 3, 43, 53-55, 80, 85, 100, 108, 113, 118, 163, 335, confederation 41, ethnic Tu 90, unification 101, homeland 285
Mongolia(n) 51, 53, 55, 68, 100, 107, Inner 19, 44, 85, 88, 96, 99, 108, 113, 143, 263, 272, Turks 71, Outer 88, 91, 92, 96, 113, 143, Nestorians in 244, 245, Altai region 291, Tatars 321
Monkey King 232
Monophysite 239, Syrian 243
Monotheism 258
Moscow 285
Mosul 70, 241, 259
Mozak (teacher) 322
Mudras 221
Mughals 41, 76, 271, 284, 289, 326, Empire 37
Mughalistan 161, 162, 197, division 286, rule 292, 296, end of Dzungars power 298
Muhammad, Prophet 145-147, 279, 336, grandsons 294, daughter Fatima 294
Muhammad Abdu-Ilah, Khoja 291

Muhammad Amin Khan 297
Muhammad ibn Ahmad al-Biruni, scholar 319
Muhammad ibn Is'haq al-Nadim, scholar 319
Muhammad Khan, Sultan 290, 291
Muhammad Mu'min 297
Muhammad Sadiq, historian 294
Muhammad Yusuf, Khoja 161, 297, 292, death 296, son 197
Mummies 187
Muo Yu, Khan 323
Muqam (Maqam) 148, Twelve Muqams 197
Muslim(s) 70, 86, 90, 101, 110, Middle East 276
Mutou Valley 150
Muzat (Muzart), river 155, 156, pass 158
Myanmar 91

N
Najashi, King 146
Nanjing 43, 55, Treaty of 57, 213
Nanking (Nanjing) 57
Nanyang 223
Nanyue, kingdom 207
Napal 234
Naqshbandiyah 274, 277, 294, 295, Yemeni 279, Silent Ones 279, Bai Shan vs. Hei Shan 291
Narmada, river 203
Near East 54, 187, 203-205, 260
Nepal 91, 217
Nestorian(s)(ism) 49, 53, 54, 69, 92, 223, 317, 325, bishopric 81, dyophsitism 238, Central Asia 244, Mongolia 244, 246, Merv 246, monument 247, parts 248, monastery 259, decline 318
Nestorius 49, patriarch 238, condemned 239, death 240
New Territories 58
Nicaea, Council 237, 240

Nicholas IV, Pope 263, 334, 363
Nicholas of Pistoia, friar 264
Niccolo Polo 334
Nihavand, battle of 81
Nile, river 201, valley 206
Ningbo 57, 324
Ningxia, province 19, 44, 85, Hui population in 272, capital 272, products 273
Nirvana 50, 154, 193, 216, 218, posture (Shayana) 112, 322
Nisibis, 240, 243, 260, theological school and monastery 240, bishop of 241
Niuhuru, Empress Dowager 162
Niya 106, 150, 181, 189, 188, Darya (river) 188, archaeology 190
Nong Hui (see Yongtai)
North Africa 182
Northern Chinese 7, 8
Northern Jin, dynasty 4
Northern, route 3, 97, 98, branch 234
Northern Song, dynasty 4
Nuwa (Nu-gua) 89, Goddess 151

O

Oghul Chaq, Satuq's uncle 274, 283
Oghuz, tribe 109, 281, 287
Ogotai, Khan 76, 284, 285, death 332
Oirats 291, 297 (see Dzunghars) 296
Okinawa 213
Olopun 246, 248, 258
Opium Wars 2, 40, 58, 208, First 57, 213, Second 57
Oracular script 17, records 18
Ordunbaliq, capital 100, 282
Orkhon, river 323
Orkhun Uyghur Empire 100, 282, capital 100
Osh (Ush) 161, 162, 294
Osman (Othman) 287

Ottoman(s), Empire 204, 208-210, 287, 337
Oxus, river (see Amu Darya) 68, 72, 92, 94, 95, 245, 284, 287, 321

P

Pahlavi 336
Pakistan 41, 70, 74, 92, 159, 226, 275, 284, Wakhan region 195
Palestine 80, 287, 334
Pamir, mountains 72, 76, 96, 98, 107, 118, 179, 187, 193, 195, 219, 230, 231, 235, 286, 291
Pamiris 92
Pan Ch'ao, General 193
Panyu, 207
Paris 325
Parni, tribe 68, 77
Parsa 162
Parthia(n) 49, Empire 68, 336, monk 215, texts 326
Pataliputra 74 (see Patna)
Patna 74
Patriarchal 16
Patriarchate of the East 241
Patrilineage 16
Patrilineal, descent 16
Paul of Tarsus, Saint 237
Paul III, Pope, Bull 266, 364
Paul Pelliot 119, 233, 258, 325
Paulicians 317
Pax Mongolica 334
Pax Sinica 246
Peacock, river 153
Pearl S. Buck, American missionary 268
Pearl, river 201, 205, 207-209
Pei Ju 111, 144
Peking 40, 58, 59 (see Beijing), Treaty of 57
Perfection of Wisdom Doctrine 119
Peroz 81, 319
Persia(n), Empire 49, 67, 71, 85, 86, 205, 209, 219, 223, 333,

381

Church 240, 245, language 322, 336, Texts 326, Book of Kings 327
Periplus of the Erythraean Sea 201
Peshawar 74
Peter of Lucalongo, merchant 264
Peter Parker, American missionary 267
Philip I, King 54
Philip II, King 210
Philippine Islands, colonization 210
Phrataphernes, governor 73
Ping, King 20
Pingdi, Emperor 42, 347
Pisan 203, 331
Pitaka (Tri-) Sutras 113, 120
Pliny the Elder, historian 93
Po Chu, poet 46
Portugal 336
Portuguese 55, 337, navigators 208, state in India 209, in Xiamen 213,
Prester John 259
Priapatios 68
Protectorate of Western Regions 96, 98
Ptolemy I 201
Ptolemy II (Philadelphos) 201
Punjab 284
Purushapura 74, 226 (see Peshawar)
Pushkalavati, capital 74, 226
Pushtuns 92

Q
Qaidam, plateau Qinghai 185
Qais ibn Sa'ad Ansari, Arab missionary 146-148, 275
Qazilbash 284
Qi Daozu 278
Qi, dynasty, Northern 185, 220, 327, Southern 186
Qi, tribe 18, Warring State 23
Qiang, tribe 18, 19, 44, 108, 184

Qianling, mountains 50
Qianlong, Emperor 8, 161, 163, 298, mother 162, 356
Qijia, culture 88, 90
Qijiaping, village 88
Qilian, mountains 90, 111, 114, 115, 143
Qin, dynasty 7, 20, 85, 87, 207, Western 44, state 23, 24, 37-39, legal code 38, 39, First Empire 89, Early (Former) 118
Qin'an 88
Qing, dynasty 38, 40, 56-58, 113, 120, 162, 247, 286, annexes Xinjiang 93,
Qingdao 58
Qinghai, province 19, 88, 108, 143, 184, 186, lake 183, 228, 234
Qingming, festival 7
Qingquan 89
Qingshui, river 88
Qingzhou 226
Qinling, mountains 85
Quanrong, tribe 20
Quanzhou 4, 147, 206, 260, (Chinchu/Zaytun) 212, Manichaens in 324, Muslim traders 212, 275, population 213
Qum 278
Quraysh, tribe 146

R
Rabban Bar Sauma 260
Rabban Markos 260
Rafael Perestrello 209
Rama, deity 74, brother 74
Red, river 202
Red Sea 201, 202
Religion of Light 324
Robert S. Maclay, American missionary 268
Robert Morrison, English missionary 267

Roman Empire 1, 192, 203, 219,
    Eastern 182, Papal 337
Rome 1, 201, See of 237, 241, 319
Rouran, tribe 96, 280, (Tujue) 97,
    149, khanate 149, defeated 150
Rui de Brito Patalim, captain 209
Ruizong, Emperor 50, 351
Russia(ns) 56, 58, 91, 107, 263,
    285, 287, 298
Rustam, commander 80
Ruzi, Emperor 42, 347
Ryukyu Islands (Okinawa)
    annexation 213

S

Sa'ad ibn abi Waqqas 80, 145,
    210, cousin 146
Safavid Empire 337
Sa'id Ali, Sultan 160
Sa'id ibn Zaid, Arab missionary
    146-148
Sa'id Khan, Sultan 196, 287, 289,
    son 197, cousins 289, 290,
    birth/death 290, brother
    Mansur 290
Sakya, lineage 217
Sakyamuni Gautama 50, 112, 115,
    216, 217
Salar 90, 108, 109, 280
salat (prayer)337
Salyr, tribe 109
Samanids 101, 273, 283, ousted
    274
Samarkand 2, 82, 107, 161, 196,
    197, 203, 230, 245, 283, 284,
    286, 295, capital 100, Aq
    Taghliqs 292, Kara Taghliq
    296
Samuel Dyer, English missionary
    267
Sandracottus 74
Sanskrit 78, 193, 226, 229-231,
    234, 337
Saracens 86
Sargodha, Punjab 294
Sartaq, Khan 263, son of 263, wife
    263, father 333
Sasanian 80, 92, 101, 205, 206,
    dynasty 71, 318, Empire 243,
    320
Satsuma, Lord 213
Satuq Bughra Khan, Sultan 273,
    283, 289, 294
saum (fasting) 337
Sayyids 294
Sayyid Burhan-ud-Din Kilic 294
Sayyid Jalali, Khoja 292
Sayyid Jalalu-ud-Din, 294
Sayyid Kamal-ud-Din Majnum
    294
Sayyid Makhdum-i-Azam 162
Scythians 69, 79
Sea of Marmara 287
Second Opium War 57
Second Uyghur Empire 152, 283
Second World War 325
Sehi 225 (see Faxian)
Seleucia 241
Seleucid 68, Empire 77
Seleucus I Nicator 71
Seljuk, Turks 109, 206, 287, 331,
    mosques 160
Seneca the Younger, statesman 1
Seres 93
Sri Lanka (see Ceylon)
Seven Overloards 37
Sha Jio Shan (see Mingshan) 116
Sha Wu Jing, characters 232
Shaanxi, province 19, 39, 44,
    population 85
shahada (witness) 337
Shahi Beg, Khan 290
Shandong, peninsula 7, 212,
    province 17, 19, 21, 40, 42,
    58, 89, 186, 226
Shang, dynasty 8, 17-20, 39, king
    18, matriarchal 18,19, rulers
    38
Shang Jia Wei 18
Shang Yang, thinker 87
Shangchuan, island 209, 267
Shanghai 44, 57

Shanshan, kingdom 95, 96, 180, 226, 228

Shanxi, province 7, 19, 41, 85, 186, 327
Shapur I, King 319, son 320
Shazhou 98
Shen Sha Shan (see Mingshan) 116
Shengshen, title 50
Shen Tsung, Emperor, 267, 355
Shi, Sogdian lord 327
Shi Anchang 327
Shihuangdi 38, 87, 95 death 39
Shiji 18
Shimonoseki, Treaty of 58
Shiva 326
Shiwei, tribe 97, 263
Shravakayana 154, 193
Shu Han, kingdom 43, tribe 44
Shuja-ud-Din Ahmad 290
Shule, settlement 97
Shunzhi, Emperor 162, 356
Siberia 92, 105, 107, 291
Sichuan 19, 37, 39, 44, 51, 98, 99, 184-186, 202
Siddhartha Gautama 50, 112, 115, 216, 217
Silk 71, 88, 105, 202, 321, 331
Silk Road 1, 2, 42, 52, 71, 72, 76, 86, 87, 89-91, 93, 96, 111, 115, 116, 221, 318, 321, 331, *si chóu zhi lu* 41, origin 3, 4, 73, nadir 3, 109, first era 3, second era 3, population densities 3, decline 3, 4, Southern branch, 94,106, 114, 118, 144, 151, 179, 192, 228, 233, alternative 185, Northern branch 97,98, 106, 107, 114, 144, 149-151, 164, 179, 224, 229, *Seidenstrasse* 105, Middle 107, infancy 224
Silla, kingdom 211, 233
Sima Qian, historian 18, 92, 94, S*hiji* 18

Singing Sand , mountain (see Mingsha) 116
Sino-images 220
Sino-Japanese War 58
Siraf 206
Sivas, 160
Slavic 78
Sleeping Tiger 38
So Man, General 180
Sogdian(s) 92, 106, 245, 321, merchants 150, monks 221, conversions 246, Balasaghun 273, language 322, texts 326, tombs 327
Sogdiana 51, 67, 68, 76, 181, 221, 234, 235, 245, 318
Sokaktani beki 54, sons 259
Somalia 202
Song Yun, monk 185, 225, 227
Song, dynasty 54, 119, 213, 275, 324, Northern 52, 53, 86, 90, 112, 201, 207, Southern 52, 53, 113, 201, 207
Song of Everlasting Sorrow 46
Sources of Happiness 163
South China Sea 4, 58, 185, 201, 202, 205, 207, 219, 226, 335
Southern, route 3, branch 234
Southern Song, dynasty 4
Spain, 336, New (Mexico) 210
Spanish American War 210
Spanish East Indies 210
Spice Islands 207
Spring and Autumn, period 21, 44, *Annals* 21
Strabo, historian 79
Straits of Malacca 202, 232
Stupa 218, 222
Subashi, city 154, zenith 155, community 225, 230
Sufi(sm) 161, Khojas 197, 272, Naqshbandiyah 274, Kadariyah 275, Guangdong, Guangxi,Yunnan, Gansu, Guizhou 278, Qinghai, Gansu, Henan 278

Sui, dynasty 3, 44, 45, 85, 108, 111, 118, 120,144, 229, 281, tomb 327
Suishu 281
Sulayman al-Tajer al-Sirafi 206
Sumatra, island 202
Sumerian 201
Sun Wu Kung 225, 232
Suoyang (see Anxi) 115
Sutras 113, 119, 215
Suyab 71
Suzhou 98
Suzong, Emperor 51, 247, 351
Sven Anders Hedin 181
Swastika 221
Swedish East India Company 210
Syncretic 247, 322
Syr Darya, river 68 (see Jaxartes), 286
Syria(n) 49, 70, 71, 74, 80, 203, 206, 249, 287, 336, Church 239, Chalcedonian 240, orthodox monophysite Church 243, priest 247, 248, 259
Syriac 247, 268, 337
Syzygos (kindred spirit) 319

T
Tabriz 264
Taghliq, Aq vs. Kara 291, 296, 297
Taiping Uprising 40
Taiwan 58
Taiyuan, Sogdian tomb 327
Taizong, Emperor 15, 42, 49, 50, 97, 147, 228, 231, 247, 258, 281, imperial edict 248, 351
Tajik 85
Tajikistan (Tajik) 41, 67, 72, 91, 92, 159, 285
Taklamakan Desert 41, 91, 94, 95, 98, 106, 107, 143, 148, 159, 180, 183, 188, 234, 280
Takshashila 74 (seeTaxila)
Talas 71, battle of 99, 282
Talas, river 99, 273

Tamerlane (see Temur)
Tang, dynasty 3, 15, 20, 42, 45, 52, 53, 81, 85, 90, 96, 109, 114, 118, 201, life 46, 51, legal code 49, population 87, defeated 99, fashions 120
Tang, King 18
Tangiers 54
Tangut, Xianbei tribe 19, 43, chief 273
Tanhung, founder 229
Tanzania 202
Taoism (see Daoism) 317, 324, Book of 89, temples 325
Taprobane (Ceylon) 93
Tarikh-i- Rashidi 289
Tarim Basin 41, 52, 71, 73, 79, 80, 91, 93, 94, 100, 150, 160, 179, 184, 187, 188, 193, 220, 225, 283, 284, 296, 318, 321, 322
Tarim, river 95, 107, 179, 180, 286
Tashkent 2, 82, 107, 230, 290, Stone City 70
Tatars, tribe 263, 264, 321, 322
Taxila 74, 75, 107, 226
Tehran 107
Temur(ids) 196, 197, 284, 286, 289, 334
Tengger Desert 272
Termez 220
Terracotta Army 39
Thailand 219
Theodore of Mopsuestia 238, 241
Theodosius II, Emperor 238
Thirty Six Kingdoms 152, 154, 188, 357
Three Baskets Doctrine 113
Three Jewels 234
Three Kingdoms 43, 90
Tianjin, Treaty of 57
tianxia 7, 8
Tian Shan, mountains 71, 75, 76, 93, 95, 100, 106, 144, 149, 187, 234, 282, 285, 291, 323
Tianshui 88, 89, 229

Tiberius Claudius, Emperor 93
Tibet(an) 19, 52, 92, 93, 110,118, 182, 233, 234, plateau 44, 91, 184, 233, 234, conquests 98, hegemony ends 99, Empire 108, 114, 182, 184, Autonomous Region 110, 183, Yarlung culture 182, Lamaism 219, Nestorian evangelism 243
Tiele, tribe 149, 280, 281
Tigris, river 70
Timothy Richard, Welsh missionary 268
Tocharian 41, 69, 78, 79, 92, 154, 188 East (Turfanian) 80, West (Kuqaian) 80, proto 187, texts 326
Toghril, Khan 53
Toghun Temur 264
Tokuz Khatun 54, 259
Tokuz-Oghuz, tibes 281
Tomb Sweeping, festival 7
Tonkin, Gulf of 202, 212
Tongzhi, Emperor 162, 356
Torgut, tribe 152
Tortoise shells 17, use in divining 17
Torugart, pass 107, 159, 274
Trabizond 107
Trajan, Emperor 1
Transoxania 82
Transoxiana 82, 161, 273, 274, 283, 286, 295, 321
Treaty ports 57
Tripoli 333
Tsu-Hsi 59 (see Cixi)
Tu, ethnic Mongols 90
Tu Fang, tribe 19
Tughluk Temur, Khan 289
Tughrul 287
Tujue (see Rouran) 97, 149
Tumsul 225
Tungut, Manchurian tribe 4
Tunis 334
Tuoba, Xianbei tribe 43, 96, 326, part of Tibetan Empire 184
Turdi 162, 163
Turfan 97, 100, 106, 107, 149, 151, 189, 196, 229, 282, 283, 286, 289, 290, 296, 325, population 150, Dzungars in 297
Turgesh, tribe 100
Turkish 268
Turkistan 91, West 100, 188, Mani 321
Turkmenistan 51, 70, 72, 73, 81, 92, 100, 245, 284, 286
Tuva, tribe 281
Tuyu valley (Tuyugou) 151, 229
Tuyuhun, Xianbei tribe 184, embassy 185

U

Udun Uyghur Buddhist Kingdom 194
Uighur, tribe 51
Ulrich Theobald 222
umma 336
Umar ibn al-Khattab, Caliph 80, 145-147
Umayyad, caliphate 82
United States 56
Upanishads 120
Ur-people 78
Ural, river 164, 332
Urumqi 106, 107, 187
Ush (Osh) 161, 294
Ushnisha 220
Uthman ibn Affan, Caliph 294
Uways al-Qarani, sage 148
Uyghur(s), tribe 51, 52, 71, 80, 85, 90, 92, 97, 280, power growth 99, First Empire 86, 100, 152, 323, 324 (see Orkhun), four Il-khanates 100, beliefs 151, Autonomous Region 101, Second Empire 152, 283, Karakhanid khanate 194, sub-groups 280, ethnonym *Gaoche*, Wheel-

Wagon 281, three kingdoms 282, Yellow 282 (see Yugur), texts 326
Uyghuristan 286
Uzbekistan (Uzbek) 51, 67, 70, 73, 92, 100,196, 220, 245, 284, 286, 336

V

Vahram I, King 320
Vatican 260
Venice (Venetian) 45, 54, 203, 210, 331, merchants 334
Vietnam (Vietnamese) 42, 55, 58, 202, governance 21, archaeology 212
Vinaya, monastic rules 227
Vishnu 326
Vladimir 285
Volga, river 78, 79, 152, 263, 285, 291, 332, 333

W

Wakhan, region Pakistan 195
Walter Henry Medhurst, English missionary 267
Wang, Empress 50
Wang Anshi, minister 53
Wang Gui, eunuch 113
Wang Meng 42, 96
Wang Wei, poet 46
Wang Yuanlu, monk 119
Warring States, period 8, 21-24, 37, 44, *Record of the* 22
Wei Mie, tutor 112
Wei, dynasty 43, 154, 217, 225, state 23, clan 43, rule 90, Northern 43, 44, 114, 118, 150,151, 222, 263, 327, tribe (see Tuoba) 217, 227
Wei, kingdom 184
Wei, river 7, 20, 45, 87, 88, 108, 185, 229
Weihai, naval base 58
Weiyuan, county 20
Wendi (Wen Ti), Emperor 41, 114, 347, 351
West Turkistan 286
Western Han, dynasty 18
Western Regions 68, 93, 94, 97, 99, 100, 101, 108, 111, 116, 118, 143-145, 148, 152, 181, 188, 193, 195, 222, 225, 228, 229, 234, 281, 331, Protectorate 96
White Horse, temple 222
White Pagoda, mountains 108
William Milne, English missionary 267
William of Rubruck, friar 263, 333
Wooden Pagoda Temple 113
Wu Ding, ruler 17, 18, capital 18, father 18, alliance 18, wife 18, son 18
Wu Han, kingdom 43
Wu, state 22, tribe 44
Wu Zetian, Empress 15, 42, 50, 51, 322
Wudi, Emperor 41, 94, 105, 114, 115, 222
Wuhan 38
Wulei (Luntai) 96
Wusun 75, 179
Wuwei (Guzang) 144, 150
Wuzong, Emperor 247, 324, imperial edict 247, 324, 328

X

Xia, dynasty 7, 8, Western 108, 112, 113, 118, 273
Xiahe, 110
Xiamen 4, 57, Amoy 86, port 205, Portuguese in 213, Catholic bishop 264
Xian Feng, Emperor 162, 356
Xi'an (see Chang'an) 41, 49, 50, 71, 85, 87, 98, 99, 105, 106, 108, 151, 182, 185, 259, 271, mosque 147, stelae 247
Xianbei, tribe 43, 44, 91, 92, 227, Tuoba 43, 96,184, Rouran 96, Khitan 96, Shiwei 97,

Tuyuhun 184
Xiangfei (Iparhan) 161-163
Xianjiao (Zoroastrianism) 327
Xianyang 87
Xiao Wendi, Emperor 43
Xiao Yi 18
Xiaonan, village 275
Xiaotun, village 17
Xicheng, district beijing 267
Xin Shi (district), cemetery 211
Xingxing, gorge 147
Xining 183, 184, population 185
Xinjiang, province 39, 41, 51, 52, 58, 88, 100, 289, international boundaries 91, population 91, 'New Frontier' 93, Uyghur Autonomous Region 101
Xiongnu, tribe 41, 75, 91, 92, 94-97, 105, 117, 144, 179, 180, 280, 281
Xiyang, village 39
Xiyu (western territory) 93, 286, (see Xinjiang)
Xuangao 229
Xuantu, administrative district 211, 212
Xuanzang, monk 69, 151, 153, 154, 157, 158,194, 225, 228, in Hami and Turfan 229, in Aksu 230
Xuanzong, Emperor 46, 51, 99, 147, 273, 322, 351, edict 323, 328
Xue Rengui, General 115
Xue, tribe 281
Xunhua 108

Y
Yaghshahir 153 (see Karashahir)
Yahya Khoja 297, son Ahmad 297
Yakut, tribe 281
Yan, Emperor 7, state 23, dynasty 44
Yang Guifei 51, 99
Yang Jian, General 44, 45
Yang Xuanzhi, chronicler 222

Yangdi, Emperor 45, 144, 351
Yangguan, fort 90, 114, 117
Yangi Hisar 161, citadel 287
Yangshao, culture 89
Yangtze, river 19, 20, 43-45, 55, basin 324
Yangzhou 86, 147, 206, Muslims 275
Yanqi, kingdom (Karashahir) 97, 153, 357, Hui Autonomous County 153
Yantuo, tribe 281
Yarkand 106, 118, 161, 162, 180, 225, other names 195, 196, river 195, population 195, mosques 196, kingdom founder 196, 197, state of 287, 289, 290, Kara Taghliq in 292, Dzungars in 296, 297
Yarlung, Tibetan culture, valley 182
Yazdegird III 80, 81
Yazedbouzid (Issu), General 247, son of Milis 247
Yellow, as a term 40
Yellow Emperor 7, 40
Yellow, river 7, 17, 39, 40, 45, 52, 85, 88, 186, 272, (Huang He) 108
Yellow Sea 157, 212
Yemen 54
Yenisei, river 280, 282
Yenisei Kyrgyz 246, 282, 324
Yi Jing, monk 225, 232
Yi, tribe 18, 19
Yide, Prince 50, 51
Yijing, monk 69
Yin, capital 18
Yinchuan 272
Ying Zheng, King 37, 38
Yining (see Almaliq) 286
Yinxu, capital 18
Yizhou 98
Yolbars, Khan 291, governor 292, 296
Yongjing 109

Yongtai, Princess 50, 51
Yongzheng, Emperor 57
Yu the Great 7
Yu Hong, chief 327
Yuan, dynasty 53, 54, 86, 108, 118, 211, 213, 244, 275
Yue, tribe 44
Yuezhi 41, 71, 76, 79, 91-95, 179, envoy 222
Yuezhi/Kushan, Empire 41, 76, 95, 192, 219, people 73, defeated 160
Yugur 280, 282
Yumen 89, 115, Huiji 114, Tang recovers 114, gate 226, 229
Yumenguan, fort (gate) (see Jade Gate) 90, 114, 117
Yumi 75
Yunnan, province 19, 58, 98, 99, 184, 202, 207, 268
Yunus Khan, Sultan 196, 290
Yurungkash, river 187, 192, 194
Yussef Has Hajib (Yussuf Hajif), poet 163, 164, 283
Yutian 75, settlement 97
Yuwesi, Arab missionary 146, 148
Yuzhi, mountains 95

Z

Zaghunluq, village 187, mummies 187, 188
zakat (alms) 337
Zarathustra (see Zoroaster) 49, 327
Zaytun 265 (see Xiamen)
Zeno, Emperor 241
Zhalan, cemetery 267
Zhangdi, Emperor 42, 348
Zhanghuai, Emperor 50, 351
Zhang Qian 41, 42, 73, 76, 94, 95, 105, 204
Zhang Taiyan, writer 39
Zhangye 91, 111, 113, 144, 282, population 112
Zhao, state 23
Zhao Kuangyin 52
Zhaoqing, 267
Zhe Zong, Emperor 112, 353
Zhejiang, province 19, 44, 52, 86, 324
Zheng Fouze, monk 225, 227
Zheng He, Admiral 55, 207
Zhi 19
Zhong-gua 1, 8
Zhong-hua 1, 8
Zhongzong, Emperor 50, 51, 351
Zhou, dynasty 8, 21-23, 37, 50, 85, Eastern 20, 22, Western 21, 87, Northern 114, 118, 185, 327, Book of Zhou 185, 186
Zhu Ba Jie, character 232
Zhu Yuanzhang, peasant leader 55
Zither 121
Zoroaster, prophet 49, 319, 327
Zoroastrian(ism) 49, 69, 223, 240, 245, 317, 325, 326, sacred book 70, 71, 77, expelled 244, motifs 327
Zu Ji 18
Zuo Zongtang, General 277

www.ingramcontent.com/pod-product-compliance
Lightning Source LLC
Chambersburg PA
CBHW060549230426
43670CB00011B/1749